D0122519

Catholic Schools in a Declining Church

Andrew M. Greeley

William C. McCready

Kathleen McCourt

Catholic Schools in a Declining Church

SHEED & WARD, INC.
SUBSIDIARY OF UNIVERSAL PRESS SYNDICATE
KANSAS CITY

Library of Congress Cataloging in Publication Data

Greeley, Andrew M   1928-
    Catholic schools in a declining church.

    Report on a project of the National Opinion
Research Center, following up an earlier study, The
education of Catholic Americans, by Greeley and P. H.
Rossi.
    Bibliography: p.
    1. Catholic Church in the United States—Educa-
tion. I. McCready, William C., 1941- joint
author.   II. McCourt, Kathleen, joint author.
III. National Opinion Research Center. IV. Title.
LC501.G67 1976   377'.82'73   75-32237
ISBN 0-8362-0648-7

Contents

PART I. THE CONTEXT

PART II. THE IMPACT OF CATHOLIC EDUCATION

APPENDICES

Acknowledgments

It is impossible in this sort of team research to delineate who made which intellectual contribution to the common enterprise. Indeed, even the researchers themselves are frequently incapable of remembering where each suggestion came from. Andrew M. Greeley was the principal investigator and William C. McCready, Kathleen McCourt, and Shirley Saldanha were co-principal investigators on the research project reported in this volume. The day-to-day operational direction of the questionnaire design and the data collection was carried out by Kathleen McCourt and Shirley Saldanha. The design of the questionnaire and the analysis itself was carried on by all four above-mentioned researchers. Andrew Greeley wrote the first draft of chapters 1, 2, 5, 6, 9, and 11. William McCready drafted chapters 8 and 11. Kathleen McCourt prepared the first draft of chapter 7.

The text for each chapter was reviewed by all three other authors and modified in most instances according to their suggestions. Joan Fee was principally responsible for the chapter on the changing (or nonchanging) political attitudes of American Catholics (chap. 4). The ordering of authors of this volume was chosen by random chance. However, the principal researcher must bear the major burden of the blame for whatever deficiencies the report may exhibit.

All NORC research projects bear a considerable debt

to the "group mind," that collection of skills, wisdom, and insight which make the National Opinion Research Center (NORC) such a superb place to do social research. This project is more in debt to the collective NORC ability than most. We acknowledge our gratitude to James Murray and the Current National Survey group for making the Catholics in their sample frame available to us. To Martin Frankel, NORC's technical director, we are grateful for his reassurance about the validity of our sample. Eve Weinberg, special assistant to the associate director of NORC, and Shirley Knight directed the field work and helped solve the agonizing problem of whether or not to tell respondents that it was a survey of Catholics. The field supervisors were Sandra Coleman, Katie Strong, and Jean Williams, each of whom contributed to the excellent response rate.

Our debt to the method of social change analysis developed by NORC's director, James Davis, is obvious throughout. Without his techniques, his patience in explaining them to us, and his encouragement of our work, we would never have begun to comprehend the rich possibilities in this mode of analysis. Garth Taylor and John Fry of NORC's Social Change Project provided immense help and support in the development of our social change model and in explaining to us the marvels of the "Catfit 3" computer program. Edmund Meyers, NORC's director of data processing services, assisted us in the use of the Catfit 3 on the Dartmouth time sharing computer system.

Shirley Saldanha, in addition to her labors as a co-principal investigator, supervised the preparation of the data file. Larraine Granger and Daryl Burrows served as research assistants, and Karen Newman found data for us from previous surveys for measuring apostasy.

Our senior colleagues at NORC, Norman Nie, James Coleman, and Zdzislawa Walaszek, made periodic indispensable suggestions. Professor Nie, in particular, challenged our flabby assumptions every inch of the way. (Of course we challenged him back.) Peter H. Rossi, from the vast distance of the University of Massachusetts at Amherst, provided wise kibbitzing.

Virginia Reich, Julie Antelman, and Eileen Petrohelos typed and retyped various drafts of the manuscript.

Data collection and processing were funded by a grant from the National Institute of Education, #4172.

We do not propose to let any of the above take an undue share of the credit for the project; therefore we absolve them from undue share of the blame for its deficiencies.

PART I
THE CONTEXT

1

Catholic Schools and Social Change

This book reports on a replication of the 1963 National Opinion Research Center (NORC) study of the effectiveness of the value-oriented education carried out in the Roman Catholic schools in the United States (Greeley and Rossi 1966). It is therefore an exercise in the sociological study of both value-oriented education and social change. We propose not merely to analyze the impact of Catholic schools on adult religious behavior but also to see whether that impact has changed in the decade since the first NORC study was conducted, a decade marked by great turbulence in the Roman Catholic church in the United States.

Our study is part of the growing body of social change research being done by American sociologists.[1] In recent years scientists have become increasingly persuaded that social research must involve more than a description of social statistics and must include analysis of social dynamics. Much of the social change research has involved replication of previous studies, using exactly the same questions as the prior research, or the analysis of change in responses to measures which have been asked in past surveys and continue to be asked at periodic intervals in other ones.

When the idea for the replication of the 1963 NORC study emerged, we felt fortunate indeed that James Davis, then director of NORC, and his colleagues were developing both a logic and a methodology for social change analysis concurrently with our collecting and analyzing the data about the effectiveness of Catholic education. Our debt to Professor Davis and his team will be obvious throughout this report.

Introduction

There are five general reasons for studying Catholic schools and one specific one for the replication of the 1963 study:

1. Catholic schools are a superb laboratory for the study of the conditions under which value-oriented education is effective.

2. With the emphasis on alternative educational systems increasing, the Catholic school system remains the largest single alternative to public education in the country. (Despite the decline in attendance in recent years, Roman Catholic parochial schools enroll slightly under one-tenth of the primary school children in the country.)

3. Recent research has raised serious questions about how "successful" schools are in achieving the results expected of them, under what circumstances they are effective, and what might be done to make them so.[2] The Catholic school system provides a readily available laboratory for studying the circumstances under which very specific goals are or are not achieved by the educational enterprise.

4. Considerable questioning has been taking place recently about the transmission of values in American society. The relative importance of home, peer group, schools, and the mass media remains to be determined. A parochial school system is explicitly concerned with the transmission of a fundamental world-view, a world-view which may or may not be shared by the family, the peer group, or the media to which the child is exposed.

5. Finally, Catholic schools continue to be a major matter of public policy debate. They were a matter of controversy in the 1972 elections, and at the present moment, an extremely controversial tax credit bill is before Congress. Under such circumstances there could be no question that the Catholic

schools are a subject of some importance for the future of American education.

Why specifically did we replicate the 1963 NORC study? The 1963 data provide a base line of information about the effectiveness of Catholic schools before the impact of the Second Vatican Council. A replication of this study in 1973 provides information about the cataclysmic events which have affected the Roman Catholic church since the Council. It enables us to measure the effectiveness of value-oriented education, indeed the survival of a system dedicated to that kind of education, under the stress of immense pressure, perhaps the strongest pressure the institution which sponsors the schools has experienced in half a millenium.

The 1963 Study

In the fall of 1963, NORC administered questionnaires to 2,071 Catholic American adults (about 40 percent of whom had attended Catholic schools), 990 teenage Catholic children then in high school (a little less than half of whom were in Catholic schools), and 700 parents of such children who were not in the original sample (but whose spouses were).

The following were the principal findings of the 1963 research:

1. Graduates of parochial schools were as likely to interact with non-Catholics in their adult lives as were Catholics who went to public schools. There was no evidence that parochial schools had an isolating effect.

2. Parochial school graduates had lower scores on measures of racism and anti-Semitism than did Catholics who did not attend parochial schools. These differences were particularly striking when those who had attended Catholic colleges were compared with those who had not.

3. There was no economic disadvantage in having attended parochial schools. On the contrary, those who did attend Catholic schools were moderately more successful both eco-

nomically and educationally than those who did not.

4. There was no evidence either among adults or among teenagers that the religious education programs operated for Catholics attending public schools had any effect on either religious behavior or social attitudes.

5. The Catholic teenagers attending Catholic schools were substantially more religious in all measures of religious attitudes and behavior used in the survey than Catholic teenagers attending public schools. These differences showed no relationship with the religiousness of the parents. However, no such large differences were observable between the Catholic-school Catholics and public-school Catholics in the young adult years of life. Whether the phenomenon was one of rapid erosion, of differences in religious behavior after high school, or of marked increase in effectiveness of Catholic education in the years immediately before the study was impossible to determine.

6. Holding constant the availability of school and the religiousness of parents, there were moderate differences of occupational and educational achievement between Catholics who attended parochial school and those who did not.

7. Parochial school attendance was about as powerful a predictor of adult religious behavior as were sex and social class. The impact of Catholic education on the religious behavior of adults was especially powerful under two circumstances: (a) when the respondent came from a devout Catholic family or (b) when the respondent received a Catholic education in grammar school, high school, and college. Under the latter circumstance, not only was the impact of Catholic schooling on adult religious behavior striking, it was also quite independent of the religiousness of the parents of the respondent.[3]

8. There was a high level of political, economic, and emotional support for the parochial school system among Catholics. This support in both sympathy and propensity to send one's children to such schools *increased* with social class and educational level.

Subsequent Findings

The data collected in 1963, which was analyzed and reported in *The Education of Catholic Americans,* was subjected to considerable secondary analysis. Andrew M. Greeley reported in *Why Can't They Be Like Us?* that parochial schools seemed to be particularly effective among German and Irish Catholics and particularly ineffective among Polish and Italian Catholics. Donald Light (1966) found that Catholic high schools were substantially more successful at integrating the educationally, economically, and personally disadvantaged into the life of the school than were other high schools. William McCready (1966) reported the very considerable effectiveness of Catholic schools on the elite population represented by the *Commonweal* readership, and in a subsequent study, McCready (1972) delineated the transmission of religious values across three generations.[4] Edward Cleary and Hans Mohl, in studies yet to be published, replicated the NORC study in Peru and Australia, with substantially the same findings reported above.

The Last Ten Years

Since the end of the Second Vatican Council, profound changes have affected the Roman Catholic church. Liturgical and disciplinary regulations which had stood for a millenium and a half have been swept away. Authoritarian structures which had stood since the Counter-Reformation have been rapidly replaced by democratic or quasi-democratic structures, reaching from the parish council to the senate of bishops which meets biennially in Rome. Very considerable numbers of priests and nuns have resigned their ecclesiastical roles. Church attendance has declined, Catholic attitudes toward such critical issues as birth control, abortion, and premarital sex have undergone much more rapid change than has the official teaching (McCready-Greeley 1972). Westhoff and Bumpass (1973), in a recent study on attitudes toward birth control, raise the question as to whether the official Roman church enjoys any credibility at all as a teacher of sexual morality. The NORC study of the American Catholic priesthood (NORC 1971) shows a dramatic move to the left on the subject of clerical acceptance of birth control among the laity, despite the papal encyclical which banned the pill. From top to bottom, then, the Roman church has been shaken by ideological, cultural, and structural changes. In many respects, it is hardly recognizable as the organization it was at the time of the 1963 study.

Simultaneously, the Catholic population has gone through dramatic social change. In 1961, at the time of the beginning of the NORC study of college students, 25 percent of those enrolled in American colleges were Catholic (about the same proportion as in the general population). The most recent American Council of Education survey of college students indicates that 35 percent are Catholic. Andrew Greeley (1973) has shown that Catholics are now represented in the junior faculties (professors under thirty-five) at elite universities in approximately their proportion in the general population. Greeley (1972) also has shown that Irish Catholics are second only to Jews in economic, occupational, and educational success in American society, and that younger Italian and Polish Catholics have higher educational and economic scores than the mean for their age group among northern whites in large cities.

In the years since the 1963 study, then, the American Catholic population has decisively crossed the line separating the lower middle class from the upper middle class. At the same time, a small but influential Catholic radical movement has emerged, and according to as yet unpublished data (Nie, Petrocik, Verba 1975), the general Catholic population has moved decisively to the left politically.

In the meantime, however, there has been a serious crisis in Catholic schools. The shortage of nuns has led to a dramatic increase in the number of lay teachers. Priests and sisters are no longer as confident as they were that the apostolate of Catholic education is a valid vocation. Attendance in such schools has declined, in substantial part at least, because Catholic school construction has almost ceased since the Second Vatican Council. There was controversy within the Roman church before 1963 about the existence of a separate Catholic school system, but in the past decade this controversy has risen to a crescendo. It seems safe to say that only a handful of Catholic theoreticians are prepared to defend the continuation of Catholic schools.

The data published in the annual *Official Catholic Directory*—while generally of the quality which would give professional statisticians nightmares (it underestimates Catholics by between two and three percentage points of the American population, or between four and five million people)—gives some idea of the rise and fall of Catholic schools since the end of World War II. In 1945, there were 10,912 Catholic schools with 2,590,660 students. In 1965, the schools had increased by 31 percent (to 14,296) and the students by 35 percent (to 3,505,186). But in the most recent (1975) *Directory*, the schools had decreased by 24 percent since 1965 and enrollment had fallen by 35 percent (to 2,959,788).

Enrollment in elementary schools continues to fall. Between 1974 and 1975 it dropped by slightly under 120,000—a 3 percent decline from the previous year and a 7 percent decline since 1973. On the other hand, enrollment in Catholic high schools in 1975 almost reached the 1 million mark it had attained in 1965—an increase of 13,638 since the previous year. Enrollment in Catholic colleges also increased by more than 15,000; it is now 422,243—almost 40,000 higher than it was ten years ago. In 1965, 14 percent of the grammar school children in the country were in Catholic schools; in 1975, this fell to 8 percent. The secondary drop was from 9 percent to 7 percent.

If one speaks of a decline in Catholic school attendance, one must be careful to specify that most of this decline has taken place at the elementary school level. At the secondary level enrollment also fell but has begun to inch back up toward its 1965 high. And college enrollment is actually higher than it was ten years ago and seems to be continuing to climb despite all the problems that private higher education is experiencing.[5]

Some of the decline in elementary school enrollment may be due to changing patterns of family size and child spacing. Some of it is also the result of the disinclination of bishops and school adminstrators to replace the inner-city parochial schools from which Catholic families have moved to new sub-urban schools. Finally, some of the decline may result from a conscious repudiation by Catholics of the idea of parochial school or a decision that in one's own community the public schools simply offer better educational opportunities. It might also be that the costs of Catholic schools are too high. American Catholicism has traditionally refused to engage in systematic research on itself, so while theories as to the reason for the decline abound, there is no evidence to support any of them.

Nevertheless, in the central sections of many large cities in the northeast and north central regions, parochial schools have become alternative educational facilities for a considerable number of black students, most of whom are not Catholic. Indeed many such schools have enrollments at approximately the same levels they had when the students were white and Catholic. As Catholic administrators have striven to keep up with the increasing costs, particularly those of running alternative educational facilities in the inner city without large Sunday collections to subsidize them, bitter battles have been waged in the state legislatures and the courts around the nation to obtain some sort of governmental aid for these schools.

In summary, then, during the past decade, the Roman Catholic church has undergone an extraordinarily profound and pervasive change. The Catholic population has changed its economic and social status, and parochial schools are hard-pressed financially, intellectually, and administratively.

Issues Involved in the Replication of the 1963 Study

There are, as we have said in the introduction to this chapter, several reasons for studying Catholic education in the United States quite apart from the fact that the system happens to be religiously oriented. It is an educational enterprise concerned with value formation, and it is the principal alternative educational system presently available in the United States. One could easily ignore the substantive nature of the religious commitment of these schools and still find their impact a fascinating subject for social science and educational research.

The 1963 study adddressed itself to the question of value-oriented education and to an alternative educational enterprise operating under what might have been termed "ordinary" circumstances. At the time of the 1963 study there was little doubt in the minds of most of the clients of the Catholic schools that it was worth the money involved or that the schools would continue to exist. Catholic schools were under no particular pressure other than that which any educational enterprise must endure. However, since 1963, changes discussed previously have subjected the system to very considerable pressure. Thus the questions which arise are not merely those which one would expect in an ordinary replication simply seeking to measure changes over time. There are additional questions of how the performance of value-oriented education—indeed its very existence—persisted and how both have been affected by the considerable changes of the past decade. Tables 1.1 and 1.2 attempt to present schematically the criteria for success of the Catholic schools in the 1963 study and the criteria for success that seemed to us to be appropriate for replication.

TABLE 1.1

Criteria for Success of Value Oriented Education

Area	Under Ordinary Circumstances		After Decade of Pressure		
	Success	Finding	Maintenance	Development	Failure
Organizational involvement	Frequent activity	Successful for those from pre-disposed families or college	Continued activity	Nuanced involvement	Decline
Ethical values	Official values of organization	Successful for those from pre-disposed families or college	Unchanged values	More sophisticated values	Erosion of values
Organizational knowledge	Indoctrination	Successful for those from pre-disposed families or college	Continued indoctrination	More elaborate knowledge	Decline of knowledge
Basic world-view	Official world-view accepted	No finding	Repetition of world-view	Adaptation	Collapse of world-view
Racial and social attitudes	Official attitudes (non-racist)	Successful in proportion to duration of value education	No change in decade	More "progressive"	More "racist"
Organizational loyalty	Intense loyalty	No finding	No change in decade	More discriminating loyalty	Less loyalty

Table 1.2

Criteria for Survival of Alternative Education

Under Ordinary Circumstances	Under Pressure
1. Positive relation to social class if population is up-wardly mobile.	1. Positive relation to elite groups who seem to be di-recting movement of popula-tion group.
2. Positive relation to youth if population is young.	2. Continued support of non-elites.
3. Persistence of motivations:	3. Willingness to continue fi-nancial sacrifice in absence of old motivations.
1. Value education	4. Emergence of new motivations:
2. Loyalty-oriented education	1. Education for leadership
3. Transmission of knowledge	2. Social action and com-munity responsibility edu-cation
	3. Educational innovation
	4. Need to maintain alterna-tives

We assume that value-oriented education is concerned with maintaining and promoting organizational involvement, trans-mitting the ethical values and the doctrinal knowledge of the institution that maintains it, sustaining the basic world-view, explicit or implicit, of that organization, and developing those social attitudes and that sort of organizational loyalty which the institution deems appropriate. Under these circumstances, the successful value-oriented educational enterprise is one which produces frequent organizational activity, acceptance of the official ethical values, capacity to repeat the official views the organization endorses, acceptance of the underlying world-view of the organization, commitment to its social atti-tudes and values, and a high level of organizational loyalty.

In the 1963 study, it was discovered that organizational activity, ethical values, and the transmission of official organi-zational knowledge were successfully generated by the Catholic schools, especially for those students who came from devout homes and for those who received all of their education within the Catholic system, up to and including college. It was also found that there was a direct relationship between the number of years one spent at Catholic school and one's propensity to accept the appropriate social and racial attitudes and values. There was, however, no evidence that organizational loyalty was affected one way or the other by attendance at Catholic schools.

The second three columns of table 1.1 present three sets of criteria for the success of a value-oriented educational enterprise under pressure severe enough to force the institution which sponsors the schools to modify notably their structure and style. The set of criteria in the fourth column would indicate that graduates of parochial schools in the 1970s were substantially unchanged from those studied in the 1960s. Their organizational activities, their values, their religious knowledge, their world-views, their racial and social attitudes, and their organizational loyalties would be approximately the same as those of their predecessors a decade ago. In the fifth column, the set of criteria would indicate that under the pressure of notable change in the institution, the graduates of the value-oriented schools have been more likely than those who did not go to such schools to adapt to the new circumstances in which they find themselves. Their organizational involvement would be more nuanced, their values more sophisticated and subtle, their knowledge more elaborate and less rigid, their world-view restated in terms deemed more appropriate, their social and racial attitudes more enlightened, and their organizational loyalty more discriminating. To the extent that the criteria in the fifth column are sustained by our research, it can be said that value-oriented education is quite successful in preparing students for dramatic, indeed traumatic, changes in the sponsoring institution.

Finally, the last column represents a set of criteria which would indicate the exact opposite of the outcome described in the fifth column. Organizational involvement would decline, values would erode, knowledge would decline, the world-view would be abandoned, and the respondents would be both more racist and less loyal than they were a decade ago. Under such circumstances, one could legitimately conclude that value-oriented education, far from facilitating adjustment to change, growth, and trauma, actually impeded adjustment and achievement.

It need not be pointed out that these questions are of very considerable import for value-oriented education. No institution attempting to inculcate values in young people can afford to take the risk that what it is doing may be counterproductive. If, on the other hand, there are certain kinds of value-oriented education that equip students to respond maturely and intelligently to unexpected social change, particularly change in the values propounded by the institution itself, then these educational methods and techniques are of the highest importance.

Table 1.2 turns to the second principal question of our research: criteria for the survival of alternative education. Under ordinary circumstances, we contend, an alternative educational system's future is relatively assured if the young and upwardly mobile parents in the population are sending their children into the system's classrooms. Such a situation will exist when value education, which inculcates loyalty and which transmits its basic values, is considered important to the population whose children are likely to attend the schools. Parenthetically, it is worth noting that in 1963 Catholic education met all the criteria in the first column of table 1.2. There was a positive relationship with both youthfulness and social class, and a strong endorsement of the three motivations for a separate school system.

But a separate school system under pressure must maintain the support both of the elites which appear to direct the movement of the population group and of the non-elites. If the schools are pleasing only the elites, they may well go out of business for lack of attendance and support. If they are pleasing only the non-elites, their situation will deteriorate as more and more of the rank and file follow the elites in another direction.

Furthermore, the target population, those who constitute the pool from which potential students will be drawn, must display a willingness to continue the financial sacrifice required in American society to support a separate school system. This report will investigate whether the motivations for this sacrifice are deteriorating or not and whether new motives are appearing to sustain the financial sacrifice. We list at the end of the second column in table 1.2 four possible new motivations for a separate school system: education for community leadership, education for social action and responsibility, education according to the most innovative and creative new techniques, and the conviction that it is necessary to maintain educational alternatives. If such goals are beginning to develop in the target population, then it is safe to assume that the alternative educational enterprise does have a reasonably bright future.

Questions to be Answered

Effectiveness of Education

1. Does a strong, value-oriented education predispose one to accept dramatic transformation in the basic value system in which one was educated? Are Catholic school educated Catholics more likely or less likely than others to accept the dramatic changes which have occurred in their church in the last decade? By comparing convictions about the church in the 1963 and 1973 samples, we can ascertain if disillusionment has set in and among which groups it might be greatest in the last decade. The basic analytic structure will be to compare the respondents from the 1963 study with those from the 1973 project. Available data show that church attendance has been declining in recent years. By comparing these groups, we

can see if the decline has been more dramatic for the Catholic school educated respondents than for the public school educated Catholics. The high investment in their church—both financial and emotional—displayed by the former group in 1963 may have prepared them for great disillusionment, resulting in their abandoning the institution.

2. In the midst of the pervasive changes that have occurred, will the effectiveness of the parochial schools on adult religious behavior increase or decrease or remain the same since the time of the first study in 1963? There has been a major shift in emphasis on what are critical religious symbols. The traditional symbols of church attendance and other ritual behavior appear to have declined in importance in favor of more experimental and personal symbols. Will parochial school Catholics be as highly committed to the new symbols in 1973 as they were to the old ones in 1963, or will they be indistinguishable from public-school Catholics on both sets of symbols?

3. Will the very considerable differences reported in *The Education of Catholic Americans* between Catholic school adolescents and Catholic adolescents in public schools persist into adult life, or will it turn out that such a phenomenon was purely a result of a transient situation that existed only so long as the young people were in fact in a Catholic high school? If erosion of the very high levels of religious practice among parochial school Catholics does occur after high school, when does it happen?

4. Will those younger Catholics who have come out of the Catholic school system since the Second Vatican Council display any signs in their adult religious behavior of the striking shift of emphasis which has occurred within the Catholic school system since the Council began?

5. What will be the impact on the attitudes and behavior of parochial school Catholics of the increasingly greater separation between popular Catholic practice and official Catholic church teaching? Have their attitudes changed more or less

rapidly than those of their fellow Catholics who were educated in public schools, or have they changed at the same
rate? These data could reveal important facts about the
process by which strongly held values change over a period of
time.

Attitudes toward Catholic Schools

1. What is the nature of the change in Catholics' commitment to and understanding of their schools in the last decade?
Despite postconciliar upheaval, the proportion of Catholics
who support parochial schools, as measured by periodic
diocesan surveys, does not seem to have changed much in the
last decade. However, national data about the extent and the
nature of this support are of considerable importance for all
American educational planners.

2. What sort of financial expenditures are American Catholics
willing to make to sustain their commitment to their schools?
The actual costs of Catholic schools have increased dramatically, but the apparent costs have increased even more because the hidden subsidies from parish to school in the form
of plant maintenance and free teaching by nuns are no longer
so effectively hidden now that the Catholic schools operate
on a much more realistic bookkeeping and accounting basis.

3. How important a political issue to Catholics is the question of aid to parochial schools? We know from both the
1963 research and other research that the majority of Catholics do support such aid. We do not know if such aid is
politically salient to them; that is, whether it would be of
decisive importance in affecting their choice of a candidate
for whom to vote. The issue of aid to parochial schools had
some importance in the 1972 presidential election because
both candidates seemed to believe that it might be salient to
Catholic voters, but there is no evidence either way on the
subject.

4. Which social classes are most likely to support Catholic
schools? In 1963 it was clear that support for the schools in-

creased with rising social class. It may well be that since then the curve has taken a U-shape, with the lower middle classes being more supportive and the upper middle classes being less so.

Procedures and Methods

Our sample of 1,128 American adult Catholics was drawn from an existing NORC sample frame. These respondents were interviewed by NORC's trained field staff. The response rate in the 1974 study (82 percent) was above the 80 percent rate which is normally taken to be satisfactory in American survey research and was also 5 percentage points above the response rate in the 1963 study. A description of the sample design, of the response rate, and of the indices compiled from the responses to individual items is presented in the technical appendices. In addition, a copy of the 1974 questionnaire is appended with the distribution of responses to both the 1974 and the 1963 surveys included. (1963 responses are in parentheses for those questions that were asked in both years.)[6]

Analytic models are used in many of the chapters in this book. The use of such models is still infrequent in the sociology of religion, but it is our conviction that sociology is little more than a descriptive discipline unless causal or explanatory models are specified at the beginning of the research process. Such models are something less than precise descriptions of reality but something more than just analytic tools. They are, from the viewpoint of the social scientist, approximations of reality; but they are tentative and subject to modification and change. They are, as one scholar observed, "isomorphic with reality" (Barber 1974).

Since this report is concerned with both religious behavior and social change, there are two analytic models which shape it, a religious behavior model and a social change model. The first model (Fig. 1.1) assumes that adult religious behavior will be influenced by the religiousness of one's spouse, the number of years one has attended Catholic schools, the number of years of education one has had (which is also an indicator of social class), and one's age, sex, and the religiousness of one's parents. Spouse's religiousness is influenced in its turn by the five prior variables that are on its left in the model. The number of years one has spent in Catholic schools is by definition a function of the number of years of education one has had; it is also influenced by age, sex, and especially by the religiousness of one's parents. The critical question in the 1963 study was whether there was any direct relationship between years of Catholic education and religious attitudes or behavior once parental religiousness was taken into account.

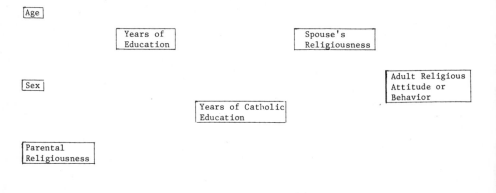

Figure 1.1--Religious Behavior Model

We are not interested in using the social change model to predict or to explain the responses to items concerning attitudes or behavior. We are interested in showing the change in the proportion of our sample giving a specific response over time. There are fundamentally two ways a population can change: (1) those in a population cohort who were interviewed in a previous sample may have changed in their attitudes or behavior, or (2) the older cohort may not have changed at all but the new cohort, that youthful generation which has come into the survey sample since the previous research, may be different in its attitudes and behavior from its predecessor. This difference may explain the change in the proportion having a specific attitude or engaging in a specific behavior. For example, most of the growth of political "independency" in the last ten years has not been the result of changing political affiliation among the old cohorts. It has resulted from a new cohort's coming into political adulthood and having not yet chosen (it may never choose) a party affiliation. Obviously, both the influx of a new cohort and changes in an older cohort may contribute to the social change between two surveys taken over a considerable time span.

Figure 1.2--Social Change Model

When we attempt to explain such change, we try to find an intervening variable that will explain why the new cohort has different attitudes or behaviors and why the older cohort (or cohorts) may have modified its attitudes or behaviors. James Davis, in his reanalysis (1974) of the Stouffer Civil Liberties Study, uses educational attainment as an intervening variable. The new cohort is better educated than the older, and this explains in part the change in the attitudes of Americans toward civil liberties—but only in part. The older cohort has also changed; and, furthermore, all educational categories have become more tolerant. Davis and his colleagues have developed a special coefficient to measure the linkages (or "transmittances," as they call them) between the variables in a social change model. We shall discuss that coefficient later when it relates appropriately to our research.

For the present, however, we turn to the religious behavior model, which is quite different from the Davis social model. The religious behavior model utilizes the techniques of multiple regression and path analysis to depict the relationships within a set of dependent variables and between dependent and independent variables. There are four types of relationship portrayed in the model: (1) the "simple" relationship, (2) the "standardized" relationship, (3) the "direct" relationship, and (4) the "indirect" relationship.

A "simple" relationship is one which exists between two variables without taking into account any third variable. A "standardized" relationship is one which takes into account any other variable (or variables) that may relate to the two variables about which the relationship is stated. The other variables may be either "prior" or "subsequent" in the model. Thus in Fig. 1.1, a standardized coefficient between the years of Catholic education and adult religious attitudes or behavior is one that takes into account age, sex, parental religiousness, years of education, and spouse's religiousness. It is a "pure" relationship or a "net" relationship. The linkage expressed in the "standardized" coefficient is not explained away by any of the other variables in the model.

A "direct" relationship is one which links two variables without passing through any intervening variable. It differs from a "simple" relationship in that the latter ignores any intervening variables while the "direct" relationship states that there are no intervening variables. It will be reported in this book that there are stronger relationships in 1974 than there were in 1963 between age and adult religious behavior. To the extent that this relationship is purely a function of the fact that some people are older than others, it will be expressed by a direct path from age to adult religious behavior. To the extent that some of this influence is mediate through the fact that older people's spouses are more religious, there will be an "indirect" relationship also.

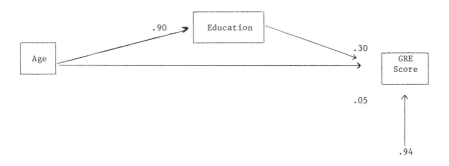

Figure 1.3--Path Diagram Relating GRE Score to Age and Education

Fig. 1.3 illustrates the kind of analysis that we propose. Let us assume a population of students that is ordered on three different scales—their age, the number of years of education they have had, and their scores on the Graduate Record Examination (GRE). Let us assume further that on their ages they may score anywhere from 1 to 25; on their education, anywhere from 1 to 16 years; and on their GRE score, anywhere from 0 to 100. The correlation coefficient is the measure of the extent to which there is a relationship between one's position on one of these scales and one's position on another scale. Thus the relationship (r) of .32 between age and GRE score (table 1.3) is a description of the extent of the relationship of where one is on the age scale and where one is on the GRE score scale. This is a "simple" relationship, and it totally ignores the possibility of any intervening variables.

Table 1.3

CORRELATIONS OF GRADUATE RECORD EXAMINATION
SCORE WITH AGE AND EDUCATION

Variable	r	r^2	R	R^2	R^2 Change
Age	.32	.10	.32	.10	.10
Education	.30	.09	.35	.12	.02

Since age is obviously something that is prior to taking the exam, it can be assumed that one's position on the age scale is causally connected to one's exam score. In other words, the older you are, the more likely you are to get a good score. Moving to the next column, r^2 (which is simply r multiplied by itself) is the amount of "variance" on one scale that can be explained by "variance" on another scale. The r^2 between age and GRE score is .10, which means that about 10 percent of the "variance" on the GRE score scale can be explained by age. Age "causes" 10 percent of the differences among the young people in their GRE scores. But we also note from table 1.3 that education relates to GRE score with a correlation of .30, so one's position on the education scale bears some relationship to one's performance in the exam. If age and education were completely independent of one another, their combined influence (R) would be .43 (the square root of the combined coefficients of age and education). They would explain about 19 percent of the variance on the exam score; but a moment's consideration makes it clear that there is a strong relationship between age and education and that, therefore, a substantial part of their causal influence on exam scores would overlap.

The statistic R is a measure of their joint influence on GRE score, and the statistic R^2 is the measure of the explanatory power of the two variables combined. We see from table 1.3 that the R of age and education together (presented in the education row of the table) is .35, and that the R^2 is .12. The overlap between age and education is therefore quite considerable because when one adds education to the model, the R goes up by only 3 points and the R^2 by only 2 points. The final column of the table, R^2 Change, shows the increase in the explanatory power of the model produced by adding education to the causal system containing age and GRE score.

One might assume from looking at table 1.3, then, that age was the principal "cause" of a high score on the GRE, since our addition of education to the model only improves its explanatory power by 2 percentage points. However, another moment's consideration will reveal that this would be a false conclusion. In all likelihood we would realize that what happens is that age is correlated with education and education is correlated in its turn with position on the GRE score scale. Age, then, "causes" the number of years that the young person has attended school, and this "causes" his position on the GRE measure. The relationship between the number of years a person attends school and his score on the GRE may be said to have been "standardized" for the effect of age.

The flow chart in fig. 1.3 illustrates this relationship.[7] There is a .90 correlation between age and education, a .30 correlation between education and GRE score, and a .05 relationship between age and GRE score with education taken into account. In other words, most of the influence of age flows through education to the GRE score, which is an "indirect" relationship. A smaller proportion of the influence flows "directly" from age to GRE score, a "direct" relationship. Older students get better scores mostly because they have had more schooling. The line linking age and GRE score is called the "direct path" between age and exam score, and the lines between age and education and between education and GRE score can be multiplied to produce the "indirect path" of age's influence on exam score. The measure of the indirect path is the product of the two path coefficients, or .9 X .3 = .27. Thus, of the r of .32 between age and GRE score, .27 is indirect and .05 is direct.[8]

The advantage of the diagram in fig. 1.3 is that it enables us to consider simultaneously the direct and indirect paths by which a prior variable influences a subsequent variable. In this particular instance, for example, we note that even though the addition of education to our model only improves our explanatory power by 2 percentage points, education is, nevertheless, the principal channel by which age exercises its influence on GRE score. A small R^2 change, therefore, does not indicate that the variable which causes this rather small addition to the explanatory power of the model is unimportant.

It will be noted that there is a third arrow pointing into GRE score with a .94 at its base. This third arrow is called the "residual path." The square of the residual path coefficient indicates the amount of variance in GRE score not explained by the model. Thus a .94 squared is .88. Twelve percent of the variance in GRE score is explained by age and education, and 88 percent of the variance remains unexplained by the model. It can be said, therefore, that age and education do in fact play some causal role in a young person's performance on the GRE, but that even when their full causal impact is taken into account, 88 percent of the variance in the position of students on the score scale remains to be explained.

Social science does not expect to be able to explain 100 percent of the variance. Such determinism of human attitudes and behavior can scarcely be expected to exist in reality. The amount of explained variance that satisfies the researcher depends upon the nature of the analysis in which he is engaged.

Plan of the Report

The next four chapters will set the context for our analysis of the changing impact of Catholic education on adult religiousness. We will first outline the changes that have occurred in Catholics' attitudes and behavior since 1963. In the next two chapters we turn to demographic and political changes (or lack thereof) among American Catholics in recent years. Finally we will attempt to discover the underlying cause of the dramatic decline in Catholic religious belief and practice since 1963.

In Part II we turn explicitly to the question of Catholic schools. We address ourselves to the principal focus of the report, the relationship between value-oriented education and social change, including attitudes toward race, in chapter 6. Chapter 7 contains a discussion of Catholic attitudes toward Catholic schools. More specific areas of Catholic schools and finances, religious leadership, and basic beliefs are discussed in chapters 8, 9, and 10. Finally, we conclude with a summary and conclusion, followed by a personal statement by Andrew M. Greeley in the Afterword.

2

A Declining Church:
A Descriptive Overview

Our principal concerns in this book will be to analyze the
components of social change and to reexamine the impact of
value-oriented education on adult religious behavior. But before we can turn to those subjects, it is first necessary to set
the context. In this chapter we will offer a descriptive overview of the religious changes in the Catholic population that
occurred between our 1963 survey and the 1974 survey.
These changes will provide the raw material for the analysis to
be conducted in later chapters of the book. In the next two
chapters we will describe the demographic and political context in which American Catholics find themselves. Such con-
texts are the backdrop against which the drama of religious
change has been acted out.

New Church

Catholics like the "new church," are still somewhat sympathetic to the priesthood, are much less inclined than in the
past to accept the traditional teachings on sexuality and authority, still strongly support Catholic education, have modified their devotions both upward and downward, and are still
strongly loyal to the church.

More than four-fifths of the Catholic population approve of
the English liturgy; approximately two-thirds approve of the
guitar mass, lay clothes for nuns, and progressive religious
education; and four-fifths approve of sex education in Catho-

lic schools. The proportion of Catholics going to weekly communion has doubled in the last ten years. A little less than a third of American Catholics would support the ordination of women as priests.

More than four-fifths of the sample would vote for a qualified woman for president. More than one-third of them live in integrated neighborhoods, and almost three-quarters have their children in integrated schools. The principal reason for not sending children to Catholic schools is exactly the same as it was a decade ago: just over a third of the respondents who have school-age children not attending parochial schools say simply that there are no Catholic schools available.

We could find little evidence that any more than a minority are opposed to the post-Vatican II or "new church." Sixty-seven percent thought the changes were for the better, only 19 percent thought they were for the worse. (The rest thought the changes made no difference.) Only 23 percent disapprove of the "handshake of peace." The only change that falls slightly under majority approval is the distribution of communion by lay people (45 percent). A slight majority (54 percent) do think, however, that there have been enough changes in the church. The changes that receive first mention most often among those who want more changes are that the clergy be allowed to marry (16 percent) and that there be a modification of the birth control teachings (10 percent). Eleven percent of those who would like to see changes want to return to the old ways.

Religious Devotion

There has been a/decline in most measures of religious devotion. Seventy-one percent reported weekly mass attendance in *The Education of Catholic Americans* (Greeley, Rossi 1966); that proportion has now fallen to 50 percent. Monthly confession has declined from 38 to 17 percent. (Those going to church "practically never" or "not at all" have increased from 6 to 12 percent, and those "practically never" or "never" going to confession have increased from 18 to 30 percent.) Visits to the church to pray at least once a week have declined from 23 to 15 percent, and daily private prayer has fallen from 72 to 60 percent. The proportion who "never pray," however, remains low at 4 percent, and the proportion who pray at least once a week continues to be a quite high 82 percent.

Many of the traditional forms of religious behavior have also declined. The percentage of Catholics attending a retreat within the last two years has fallen from 7 percent to 4 percent; making a Day of Recollection, from 22 percent to 9 percent; making a mission, from 34 percent to 6 percent; reading a Catholic magazine or newspaper, from 61 to 56 percent; and having a religious conversation with a priest, from 24 to 20 percent.

However, some of the newer forms of religious life that were practiced infrequently a decade ago (and were not included in our study) have now attained a surprising popularity. Sixty percent have attended a charismatic or pentecostal prayer meeting during the last two years; 8 percent, an informal liturgy at home; 3 percent, a marriage encounter; and 20 percent report having attended a religious discussion group.

The most notable positive change is an increase in the proportion receiving weekly communion—from 13 to 26 percent. Another way of putting this is that less than one-fifth of the weekly mass attenders received communion a decade ago, while more than half do so now.

Only 53 percent of the Catholic population think that it is "certainly true" that it is a sin for a Catholic to miss weekly mass if he or she could easily attend. The principal reasons for not going to church, however, seem to have little bearing on dissatisfaction directed at the new liturgy. Those who attend mass less than once a week were asked why they did not go to church more frequently, and only 4 percent said they "do not get anything out of mass," while only 7 percent professed not to like the changes in the mass. (Respondents were able to give as many reasons as they wished for nonattendance; for clarity, in this analysis we discuss only the first-mentioned reasons.) The principal reasons for not going to church today seem the same as a decade ago: 10 percent of those who do not go cannot get there because they are too old, too sick, or the church is too far away; 19 percent cite laziness or a lack of energy; 14 percent say they have to work on Sundays; and 14 percent say they simply do not want to go.

Morale

Despite the political turbulence and the religious change of the past decade, the morale of American Catholics has not deteriorated. Thirty-eight percent of the Catholic population describe themselves as "very happy" in 1974, as opposed to 36 percent in the 1963 survey. Eighty percent say they are very satisfied with their marriage. (Twenty-nine percent reported their childhood as "happier than average" in 1974, as opposed to 25 percent in 1963.) Thirty-one percent remembered their parents' marriage as "extremely happy" in the more recent survey, while only 22 percent had the same recollections a decade ago. Sixty-one percent of the respondents thought that their parents' marriage had been "extremely happy" or "happier than average" in 1974, while only 45 percent made the same judgement in 1963.

A majority of Catholics (53 percent) thought they lived in a good neighborhood, while 38 percent thought their neighborhood was about average. Thirty-five percent reported that they lived in integrated neighborhoods, and only 9 percent said that their neighborhood was "not so good."

On the subject of neighborhoods, about three-fifths of the Catholic population said they lived in a neighborhood in which at least half the population was Catholic (no change in the last decade). Thirty-three percent said that they lived in a neighborhood where at least half of the population was of the

same ethnic group as their own. (We could find no relationship at all between any of these neighborhood variables and
any religious attitudes or behavior.)

Authority and Faith

There has been a substantial decline in acceptance of the
legitimacy of ecclesiastical authority. In 1963, 70 percent
thought that it was "certainly true" that Jesus handed over
the leadership of his church to Peter and the popes; ten years
later that proportion has fallen to 42 percent. Only 32 percent think that it is "certainly true" that the pope is infallible
when he speaks on matters of faith and morals.

In terms of personal faith, only 38 percent say that they
feel "very sure" when they speak to their children about religious beliefs and values. In 1973, 27 percent of the Catholics
thought that it was "certainly true" that God would punish
the evil for all eternity, a decline of 25 percentage points in
the last decade. Thirty-eight percent thought that it was "certainly true" that the Devil existed, while 26 percent thought
it was "probably true." Still, 86 percent have never thought
of leaving the church; 83 percent are married to other Catholics; and 82 percent were married by a priest (down 5 percent
since 1963). Despite their own endogamy, the proportion who
think it "very important" for young people to marry someone
within their own religion has fallen from 56 percent to 27
percent in the last ten years, and the proportion who think it
is "not important at all" has tripled to 40 percent.

Loyalty to the church remains, but it is being transformed.
A lot of things appear to be not nearly as certain or important as they used to be.

But it would be a mistake to think that there is an overt
revolt against religious leadership, or that dissatisfaction with
political leadership carries over to the church. We asked our
respondents whether or not they approved of the way the
pope, the bishops, and their parish priest were handling their

jobs (using the exact wording that Gallup uses periodically to measure support for the American president). Table 2.1 shows that the local parish priest has a much higher rating than any American president has enjoyed for the last forty years on the average. The pope is one percentage point more popular than John Kennedy was on the average, and is slightly ahead of Franklin Roosevelt (3 percentage points) and Dwight Eisenhower (5 percentage points). The bishops are the least popular of the church leaders, with only a little better than three-fifths of the respondents approving of the way they handle their jobs. Thus the hierarchy ranks beneath Kennedy, Roosevelt, and Eisenhower in popularity, but ahead of Johnson, Nixon, and Truman.

TABLE 2.1

POPULARITY OF CHURCH LEADERS AS
COMPARED WITH AVERAGE POPULARITY
RATING OF AMERICAN PRESIDENTS
(PERCENT APPROVE)

Parish priests	82
Pope	71
Kennedy	70
Roosevelt	68
Eisenhower	66
Bishops	62
Johnson	54
Nixon	48
Truman	46

It is clear that religious leadership is much less important than political leadership for most people, and that they are much less likely to have strong feelings on the subject. Still, whatever antipathy there may be for certain church policies and whatever decline in confidence there may be in certain church doctrines, we do not see in our data much evidence of a strong disaffection for ecclesiastical leadership.

The Priesthood

The general approval American Catholics feel for the work of their clergy does not extend to the quality of their sermons. In 1952, in the Ben Gaffin *Catholic Digest Study* (1952), 43 percent described the Sunday sermon as "excellent." In a replication of this study done by Gallup in 1965, the percentage had fallen to 30, and in our project of 1974, the percentage has fallen still further, to 23. Thus, in a little over two decades, satisfaction with the professional quality of sermons has diminished by half. One consolation for the Sunday preacher is that the satisfaction level can't go down much more.

Similarly, in 1952 those who described their clergy as "very understanding" with respect to parishioners' problems were 72 percent of the population; in 1965 the percentage had fallen to 62, and in 1974 it was down to 48 percent. There may be a general sympathy for the way the clergy are doing their jobs, but there has been a drastically diminishing level of approval in specific judgments of clerical competence. (To add another dimension, we found only 47 percent who believed the clergy to be "very understanding" in their dealings with teenagers.)

In 1963, 66 percent of the respondents said they would be very pleased if their son decided to become a priest; ten years later the proportion has fallen to 50 percent, which is 2 percentage points more than would be pleased if their son decided to become an author or a stockbroker, 16 points less than would be very pleased if a son became a business executive, and 23 points less than if a son became a college professor.

The religious sisterhoods have suffered a comparable loss of favor. Sixty percent would have strongly supported a religious vocation for their daughter a decade ago; only 50 percent would do so today.

There does not seem to be very much antagonism toward those who have left the priesthood. Thirty-two percent would have a great deal of sympathy for those who have left, and another 40 percent would have some sympathy for them. Despite the argument frequently heard in high ecclesiastical circles that the laity would not accept a married clergy, 80 percent of our respondents say they would be able to accept such a change, and 63 percent say they are in favor of it.

There is no way to escape the conclusion that the image of the priesthood has slipped dramatically in the last ten years. Catholics still like their priests, but they don't seem to respect them nearly so much as they once did.

Sexuality

Other researchers have documented changes in birth control practices and attitudes among American Catholics. This change is merely one indicator of a comprehensive shift in Catholic sexual values. Ten years ago only 29 percent agreed strongly with the notion that husband and wife may have sexual intercourse for pleasure alone. That proportion has now risen to 50 percent. Remarriage after divorce was approved by 52 percent a decade ago; it is now approved by 73 percent. Artificial contraception was approved by 45 percent a decade ago; it is now approved by 83 percent (so much for the impact of *Humanae Vitae*). Sexual relations between an engaged couple was approved by only 12 percent in 1963; it is now approved by 43 percent. In 1963, 41 percent thought that "a family should have as many children as possible and God will provide for them." Today, only 18 percent would agree with that statement. Eighty percent approve of sex education in Catholic schools. Seventy-two percent think that abortion should be legal if there is any danger of a handicapped child.

It does not necessarily follow, however, that approval of the positions described above indicates a willingness to engage in them. When asked "whether or not you think it should be possible for a pregnant woman to obtain a *legal* abortion," 36 percent said "Yes, if the woman is married and doesn't want any more children." When asked what they would do themselves in such a situation, only 8 percent of the women said they would definitely have an abortion, and another 19 percent said they would consider it. (The questionnaire item was "Now imagine that you are married and you become pregnant, but you and your husband have serious reasons for not wanting to have another child.")

In theory, and to some extent in practice, a substantial proportion of the Catholic population has turned away from what is still the official sexual teaching of the church. This is dramatically pointed out in the decline of the numbers who believe the church has the right to teach what views Catholics should take on birth control. In 1964, 54 percent saw the church as having this right; in 1974 that figure has dropped to 32 percent.

The proportion supporting the church's right to teach on racial integration has declined from 49 to 37 percent, despite the fact that Catholics have become substantially more pro-integration in the past ten years. The proportion supporting the church's right to teach on immoral books and movies has fallen from 86 to 60 percent. On the other hand, there has been an increase from 43 to 51 percent for those who think the church has the right to teach on the matter of federal aid to education.

Parochial Schools

One thing that seems unchanged is the support for parochial schools. About 28 percent of the parents of school-age children have children in parochial schools. The principal reason for nonattendance is, as it was a decade ago, the unavailability of schools—the first-mentioned reason of 38 percent of those whose children are not in Catholic schools. The second most frequent first-mentioned reason is that Catholic schools are too expensive, and this answer was given by 24 percent (up 6 points in the last decade). Only 13 percent suggest that the public schools are better, a reason given by 12 percent in 1963. Thus, the main reason for the decline in parochial school attendance seems to be the unavailability of the schools, with a secondary reason being the increase in costs.

But support for the idea of parochial schools is overwhelming. Eighty-nine percent reject the idea that the Catholic school system is no longer needed in modern life. Seventy-six percent support federal aid for parochial schools (up 3 percentage points in the last decade). Sixty-six percent reject the notion that lay teachers cannot do as good a job as nuns (thus deservingly putting to rest a pertinacious bit of clerical folk wisdom). Eighty percent are willing to put their money where their mouth is in support of Catholic education: they say they would contribute more to their Sunday collections if the pastor requested them to do so in order to solve financial problems that threatened the closing of the parish school. Of those who say they would be willing to contribute more, 59 percent would be willing to contribute more than fifty dollars, and 31 percent would be willing to contribute more than one hundred dollars a year to keep the parish school open. This suggests that there are hundreds of millions of dollars of untapped resources, should the leadership choose to utilize them.

Whether or not there ought to be parochial schools is a subject that has been widely debated in Catholic books and journals for the last twenty years. There is no evidence that this debate has affected in the slightest the commitment to parochial schools of the overwhelming majority of American Catholics. On the contrary, it would appear that there are more resources available to support the continuation of parochial schools than the church is currently using.

Social and Political Attitudes

Four-fifths of the Catholic population say they would vote for a qualified Jew or a qualified black or a qualified woman for president. This finding is especially interesting when one considers that fifteen years ago less than one-half of the Protestants in the country would say they would vote for a qualified Catholic. Ninety-four percent of white Catholics say they would accept school integration for their children where a few of the other children are black, 70 percent would accept it where half the children are black, and 34 percent would accept it where more than half the children were black. It is fashionable to dismiss such findings on the assumption that the respondent is simply saying what he or she is expected to say. However, the fact that 74 percent of those with school-age children have them in schools where there are black students gives some credence to this high support for integrated education. (There has been a dramatic shift to the left in Catholic political and social attitudes over the last two decades. Evidence of change in racial attitudes has been reported in two articles by Andrew Greeley and Paul Sheatsley [1971, 1974]. Changes in other attitudes will be reported shortly in an NORC study by Norman Nie, Sidney Verba, John Petrocik, and Andrew Greeley [1975]. The findings reported in the text of this book are consonant with those of the other two projects.)

Conclusions

In this overview we have limited ourselves, for the most part, to description, postponing analysis, commentary, and speculation for later chapters. Nevertheless, some comments can be made.

One national news magazine claimed that *The Education of Catholic Americans* was mired in "qualifications." Unfortunately, the real world is unlike that of the national news magazine; it is gray and complicated. Any attempt to describe reality that does not take into account conflicting tendencies ought to be viewed with serious skepticism. No single descriptive conclusion of the present state of American Catholicism is possible.

On the one hand, the changes in the church have proved popular (and the notion that the new liturgy has driven people away can safely be described as complete fiction). Fundamental loyalty to the church continues, parochial schools are vigorously endorsed, and there are more financial resources available to support the schools than the church has yet been willing to use. There are no signs of anticlericalism or of any vigorous antipathy to church leadership. Church attendance is down among adults (though it remains high among teenagers), and communion reception is up. Some traditional forms of piety have declined, but other, newer forms seem to have attracted surprisingly large numbers of people.

Catholics have accepted integration, and while the majority do not yet support the ordination of women (though some might think that the size of the minority supporting it is fairly large), they would vote for a qualified woman (or black or Jew) for the presidency.

On the other hand, the image of the priesthood has slipped badly with both adults and young people. On two important measures of professional performance, sermons and sympathy in dealing with people, the decline of the priestly image in the last twenty years has been very great.

Finally, the acceptance of the Catholic sexual ethic has declined dramatically, despite *Humanae Vitae*. Catholics seem uncertain about some of the tenets of faith that were once considered to be of critical importance, and they lack confidence in their capacity to hand on religious values to their children.

3

The Demography
of American Catholicism

Introduction

A massive and frequently overlooked fact about American
Catholicism is that it is the product of relatively recent immigration.[1] At the time of the first NORC Parochial School
Study, half the American Catholic population were either immigrants or the children of immigrants. A decade later, 15
percent of American Catholics had been born outside the
country, 39 percent reported that their father had been born
outside the United States, and 36 percent reported their
mother was not native born. Fifty-five percent said that all
their grandparents had been born abroad, while only 20 percent said that all four grandparents had been born in this
country. If one needs four American-born grandparents to be
thoroughly fourth generation, then four-fifths of the American Catholic population are still third generation or less;
which is to say that, at the most, they are only two generations away from the immigration trauma.

Not only are Catholics recent immigrants, they were frequently unwelcome immigrants. The report of the infamous
Dillingham Commission in 1911 suggested strongly that eastern and southern European immigrants were genetically inferior and socially undesirable; and the immigration laws after
the First World War were in great part written to keep Slavic
and Italian Catholics out of the country. A Catholic presidential candidate was overwhelmingly rejected in 1928, and when
a Catholic was finally elected in 1960, it was by a very narrow margin.

Most discussion of the alleged economic and intellectual inferiority of American Catholics, whether advanced by non-Catholics like Gerhard Lenski and, more recently (and more irresponsibly), Kenneth Hardy, or by Catholic self-critics like Msgr. John Tracy Ellis, Prof. John Donovan, and the late Gustave Weigel and Thomas O'Dea, have tended to ignore or to minimize the importance of immigration. O'Dea says quite explicitly that the "anti-intellectualism" of American Catholics cannot be attributed to their recent immigration or their peasant status before emigration. Professor O'Dea was an admirable sociologist, but he never troubled to provide empirical verification for such an assertion.

Before we attempt any serious discussion of the changes in the American Catholic church in the last decade and of the impact of those changes on parochial schools, it is necessary to summarize briefly the data available on the demography of American Catholics, in order to reconstruct some of the socio-economic history of Catholics in the United States since the high point of immigration at the turn of the century.

Since there is no religious question asked in the federal census, the only way we can obtain information about American denominations (or ethnic groups) is through the sample survey. The typical sample survey of the sort that NORC and other national private data-gathering agencies collect has 1500 respondents. Since we have reason to believe that Catholics are 25 percent of the country and the largest of American religious groups, a typical national sample will have 425 Roman Catholics and a smaller number of each of the other denominations within Protestantism (Bogue 1959). It is therefore necessary to follow the example set by Donald Bogue in his chapter on religion and combine a number of sample surveys into one large composite sample. Some analysis, based on eight NORC samples taken between 1963 and 1970, has already been reported.[2] This composite sample was dubbed "NORC$_1$." More recently, another composite sample ("NORC$_2$") was used to analyze the intergenerational mobility of American religio-ethnic groups (Greeley 1975). For the purposes of this chapter, the two composites have been combined and the 1963 and 1974 parochial school studies added to create a composite of twelve surveys.[3]

Description

After a preliminary description, we shall attempt two analytic enterprises in this chapter. First, we shall endeavor to ascertain whether the economic and educational position of American Catholics is the result to any appreciable extent of a "purely" Catholic factor, or whether it could be attributed to the lower educational attainment of parents, which would have been inevitable with a population still close to the immigrant experience. Second, by using a technique of cohort reconstruction, we shall attempt to outline the socioeconomic history of Catholics in the present century.[4]

Only Baptists report lower parental educational levels than Catholics, although Catholics are only slightly lower than Lutherans in the educational attainment of fathers. On the other hand, when we come to the generation of the respondents, Catholics are ahead of Baptists and Lutherans in their educational achievement and a half-year behind Methodists. They are still substantially below Presbyterians, Episcopalians, and Jews in educational achievement. But between the parents' generation and the respondents' generation, Catholics have reached the white national average in educational achievement.

Catholics are slightly below the national average in occupational prestige score.[5] In their occupational attainment, Catholics are ahead of Baptists and Lutherans, only slightly behind Methodists, but substantially behind Episcopalians, Presbyterians, and Jews. If Catholics are very close to the national average in terms of education and occupational prestige, they are, however, much higher than the national average in income.

TABLE 3.1

EDUCATION, OCCUPATIONAL PRESTIGE, AND INCOME FOR DENOMINATIONS (BLACKS AND SPANISH-SPEAKING EXCLUDED)

(SuperNORC Composite Sample)

Denominations	Number of Years of Father's Education	Number of Years of Own Education	Occupational Prestige Score	Income	N =
Protestant Denominations					
Baptist	8.17	10.70	37.21	$ 8,693	1833
Methodist	9.50	11.86	41.13	10,103	1539
Lutheran	8.84	11.24	38.90	9,702	1105
Presbyterian	10.69	12.66	46.39	10,976	652
Episcopalian	12.18	13.47	48.19	11,032	322
Other Protestant Denominations	8.62	11.19	38.33		1651
Protestant, no denomination	9.81	11.29	40.62		255
Catholic	8.58	11.50	40.40	11,374	5733
Jew	10.24	13.98	48.89	13,340	357
All white Americans	9.13		40.58	11,382	

While 32 percent of all Americans in the country have been to college, 29 percent of American Catholics have attended (table 3.2). This is a higher proportion than for the Baptists and Lutherans but less than for the other denominations. Seventy-one percent of the Catholics in metropolitan regions have gone to college, about the same proportion as Episcopalians, though considerably less than the 95 percent of the Jews who are metropolitan dwellers.

TABLE 3.2

COLLEGE EDUCATION AND METROPOLITAN DWELLING FOR DENOMINATIONS
(BLACKS AND SPANISH-SPEAKING EXCLUDED)

(SuperNORC Composite Sample)

Denominations	Percent College	Percent Metropolitan
Baptist	23	46
Methodist	32	51
Lutheran	22	53
Presbyterian	51	65
Episcopalian	59	72
Catholic	29	71
Jew	60	95
All Americans	32	

Jews and Episcopalians are less likely to be married than Catholics, but the 74 percent married figure for Catholics makes their proportion smaller than those of the other Protestant denominations (table 3.3). Furthermore, despite Catholic injunctions against divorce, the 6 percent of Catholics who are divorced or separated represents a higher proportion than is to be found among the Baptists, Methodists, Presbyterians, or Jews; although it is substantially less than the 11 percent of Episcopalians who are separated or divorced.

TABLE 3.3

MARITAL STATUS OF DENOMINATION MEMBERS (BLACKS AND SPANISH-SPEAKING EXCLUDED)

(SuperNORC Composite Sample)

Denominations	% Married	% Widowed	% Divorced	% Separated	% Not Married	% Total
Baptist	79	8	3	1	8	99
Methodist	76	11	3	1	9	100
Lutheran	77	7	3	3	10	100
Presbyterian	78	8	3	1	10	100
Episcopalian	66	11	9	2	12	100
Catholic	74	7	4	2	14	101
Jew	72	10	2	1	15	100

TABLE 3.4

REGIONAL DISTRIBUTION OF AMERICAN DENOMINATIONS (BLACKS AND SPANISH-SPEAKING EXCLUDED)

(SuperNORC Composite Sample)

Denominations	New England %	Mid Atlantic %	East North Central %	West North Central %	Southeast %	East South Central %	West South Central %	Mountain %	Pacific %	Total %
Baptist	3	3	11	4	37	15	16	2	9	100
Methodist	1	9	26	9	26	7	10	4	11	103
Lutheran	3	20	37	19	7	1	2	3	8	100
Presbyterian	2	18	24	12	15	5	5	6	14	101
Episcopalian	9	29	12	1	19	2	5	7	17	101
Catholic	11	29	22	7	7	1	8	2	13	100
Jew	7	54	15	4	10	0	1	2	8	101
All Americans	5	18	21	7	15	5	9	4	14	98

Finally, Catholics are disproportionately concentrated in the northeast and east north-central regions of the country, with 62 percent of the Catholic population there as opposed to 44 percent of the total white American population. Catholics are underrepresented in the southeast, east south-central, and mountain regions. They are approximately evenly distributed in the west north-central, west south-central, and Pacific coast areas.

In summary, during the last decade, American Catholics have approached the national average in education and occupational prestige. They are higher than the national average in family income. They are younger, have larger families, and are disproportionately urban, living primarily in the northeast and north central regions. Only Jews are less likely to be married, and the proportion of Catholics who are divorced or separated seems rather high, given the church's teaching on the subject.

A Catholic Factor?

The first analytic question we must ask is to what extent the "just average" educational, occupational, and economic achievement of Catholics is a function of some kind of "Catholic factor," and to what extent it is the result of an initial disadvantage based on lower levels of parental education. To answer this question we will use a technique of standardization based on multiple regression analysis.[6] A regression equation is computed for each denominational group with respondents' education regressed on fathers' education. Then occupation is regressed on both educations, and, finally, income on both educations and occupation. Part of the result of such an equation is called statistically a b, which can be thought of as an increase of every unit of the y variable for each increase in the x variable. In an equation between height and weight, for example, the b would represent the increase in pounds for every increased inch in height. Thus a b of .5 would mean that each additional inch in height would entail on the average an extra one-half pound in weight. In the present case, the *b* is described as "a conversion rate" or as a "measure of mobility." James Coleman has referred to this rate in the context of mobility analysis as a measure of the "efficacy of resources." It tells us how much one can achieve, for example, in one's own education for each year of one's parents' education.

Once one has computed the "mobility rates" for all the denominations, one asks what would happen if all the denominations had the same distribution on a prior variable. What would the educational attainment of our respondents, for example, have been like if the average parental education of all the denominations had been the same? For the purposes of this analysis, we will assume that the national average for whites represents the middle ground to which all others are compared (table 3.5).

TABLE 3.5

DIFFERENCES FROM NATIONAL AVERAGE IN EDUCATIONAL ACHIEVEMENT
OF AMERICAN DENOMINATIONAL GROUPS--
NON SPANISH-SPEAKING WHITES ONLY

(Years of Education)

Denominational Group	Gross Difference from Mean	Net Difference from Mean[*]
Jews	2.5	2.2
Episcopalians	2.0	-0.3
Presbyterians	1.2	0.4
Methodists	0.4	0.1
Catholics	0.0	0.8
Lutherans	-0.3	-0.1
Baptists	-0.8	-0.2
National Average = 11.5		

[*]Taking into account mother's and father's education.

TABLE 3.6

DIFFERENCES FROM AVERAGE IN EDUCATIONAL ACHIEVEMENT OF AMERICAN
DENOMINATIONAL GROUPS IN METROPOLITAN REGIONS OUTSIDE
THE SOUTH--NON SPANISH-SPEAKING WHITES ONLY

(Years of Education)

Denominational Group	Gross Difference from Mean*	Net Difference from Mean*
Jews (315)	2.0	1.8
Episcopalians (185)	1.7	0.2
Presbyterians (325)	0.9	-0.1
Methodists (513)	0.4	0.1
Catholics (3898)	-0.4	0.3
Lutherans (522)	-0.5	-0.2
Baptists (353)	-0.9	-0.8

National average for metropolitan regions outside the South = 12.0

*Taking into account mother's and father's education.

To narrow it slightly, in table 3.5 we focus on educational achievement of Catholics outside the South in metropolitan regions and compare them to their counterpart Protestant and Jewish denominational groups. We multiplied the Catholics' conversion rate for own education by the Catholic deviation from the mean father's educational achievement of the average. Then we added or subtracted, depending on the sign of the conversion rate, from the difference between Catholic respondents' own educational achievement and the average. A -1.3, which represents the Catholics' disadvantage in northern cities compared to the average in father's education, was multiplied by the Catholic educational conversion rate, and the product subtracted from the -.4, which is the difference in own educational achievement between Catholics and the average in northern cities. Table 3.6 shows the result of such a procedure performed for each denominational group. It is a table of "standardized" or "net" educational differences among the American religious denominations in metropolitan regions outside the South.

When father's education is taken into account, the Catholic educational attainment is higher than that of all Protestants compared to the national average as well as the average for metropolitan regions outside the South. Catholic educational mobility is diminished somewhat in northern cities, but still remains higher than Protestant mobility.

TABLE 3.7

DIFFERENCES FROM NATIONAL AVERAGE IN OCCUPATIONAL PRESTIGE
OF AMERICAN DENOMINATIONAL GROUPS--
NON SPANISH-SPEAKING WHITES

(0-99)

Denominational Group	Gross Differences	Net Differences[*]
Jews	8.50	7.00
Episcopalians	7.90	4.10
Presbyterians	6.00	3.30
Methodists	0.80	0.10
Catholics	0.10	0.10
Lutherans	-1.40	-1.20
Baptists	-3.10	-2.00

National average = 40.3

[*]Taking into account parental education and own education.

The next question is "What is the 'efficacy of resources' for Catholics in the world of occupation?" What use do they make of their father's education and their own education in achieving occupational success? Despite their superior educational mobility, Catholics do not have much advantage in occupational mobility in the nation. In the cities they show a slight deficit (tables 3.7 and 3.8). The reasons for this could be external (discrimination) or internal (lack of ambition or industry).

TABLE 3.8

DIFFERENCES FROM AVERAGE IN OCCUPATIONAL PRESTIGE OF AMERICAN DENOMINATIONAL GROUPS IN METROPOLITAN REGIONS OUTSIDE THE SOUTH--NON SPANISH-SPEAKING WHITES ONLY

Denominational Group	Gross Differences	Net Differences*
Jews	6.6	5.5
Episcopalians	7.7	6.2
Presbyterians	5.5	3.6
Methodists	1.3	0.7
Catholics	-1.3	-0.6
Lutherans	-2.1	-1.7
Baptists	-5.1	-3.8

Average in metropolitan regions outside the South = 41.8

*Taking into account parental and respondent's education.

Once they have obtained a given level of occupational achievement, how do Catholics do in income? Is there a "Catholic ethic," as Gerhard Lenski has suggested, that impedes economic achievement? The standardization process we used before suggests that this is not the case (tables 3.9 and 3.10). Only Jews earn more money than Catholics. Even when we do not take into account background variables, Catholics still show higher family incomes than Protestant denominational groups. The lower occupational mobility of Catholics, then, does not seem to be the result of any lack of ambition or industry. We must seriously ask, therefore, whether there may be discrimination against Catholics at the upper levels of the professional, business, and academic worlds.

TABLE 3.9

DIFFERENCES FROM NATIONAL FAMILY INCOME AVERAGE OF
AMERICAN DENOMINATIONAL GROUPS (1974) DOLLARS
--NON SPANISH-SPEAKING WHITES ONLY

Denominational Group	Gross Differences	Net Differences[*]
Jews	$ 3,387	$ 1,460
Catholics	1,421	1,656
Episcopalians	1,079	- 199
Presbyterians	1,023	- 988
Methodists	210	- 42
Lutherans	- 555	- 123
Baptists	-1,260	- 473

National average = $9,953

[*]Taking into account parental education, respondent's education, and respondent's occupational prestige.

TABLE 3.10

DIFFERENCES FROM AVERAGE FAMILY INCOME OF AMERICAN DENOMINATIONAL
GROUPS IN METROPOLITAN REGIONS OUTSIDE THE SOUTH (1974
DOLLARS)--NON SPANISH-SPEAKING WHITES ONLY

Denominational Group	Gross Differences	Net Differences
Jews	$ 2,295	$ 1,059
Catholics	1,211	1,782
Methodists	549	121
Presbyterians	277	-1,026
Episcopalians	- 145	-1,927
Lutherans	- 655	- 287
Baptists	-1,110	- 64

Average in metropolitan regions outside the South = $10,623

We can summarize this phase of our analysis with the observation that most of the differences that remain between Catholics and other American denominations in the twelve years covered by the SuperNORC composite were attributable to deficiencies in paternal education, which this generation of respondents seems to have eliminated.

Indeed, when we remove the influence of father's education (table 3.10), Catholics move into a position where their income is inferior only to the highly successful Jews. Given their beginnings, then, the Catholic adults in the composite have done very well educationally, occupationally, and financially.

As one might imagine, those Catholic groups that were here earlier have done much better (tables 3.11 and 3.12). The Irish, for example, are nine-tenths of a year above the nation-

TABLE 3.11

DIFFERENCES FROM NATIONAL AVERAGE IN EDUCATIONAL ACHIEVEMENT
OF GENTILE WHITE ETHNIC GROUPS

Ethnic Group	Gross Difference	Net Difference
Irish Catholic	1.0	0.6
British Protestant	0.9	0.1
German Catholic	0.1	0.2
Scandinavian Protestant	-0.1	0.0
German Protestant	-0.2	-0.2
Polish Catholic	-0.3	1.2
Italian Catholic	-0.4	0.8
Irish Protestant	-0.6	-0.3
"American" Protestant	-0.6	0.0
Slavic Catholic	-0.7	0.0
French Catholic	-0.7	-0.4

National Average = 11.5

al average in educational achievement.[7] When father's education is taken into account, Slavic, Italian, and Polish Catholics are also above the national mean; and the French are only slightly below it.[8]

TABLE 3.12

DIFFERENCES FROM AVERAGE IN EDUCATIONAL ACHIEVEMENT
OF WHITE GENTILE ETHNIC GROUPS--METROPOLITAN
REGIONS OUTSIDE THE SOUTH

Ethnic Group	Gross Difference	Net Difference
British Protestant (736)	0.8	0.0
Irish Catholic (653)	0.4	0.4
German Protestant (577)	0.0	-0.1
German Catholic (754)	0.3	0.0
Irish Protestant (236)	-0.4	0.1
"American" Protestant (881)	-0.4	-0.3
Polish Catholic (410)	-0.5	1.2
Scandinavian Protestant (236)	-0.7	-0.8
Italian Catholic (820)	-0.9	0.5
Slavic Catholic (352)	-0.9	-0.1
French Catholic (257)	-0.9	-0.5

National Average = 12.0

By the early 1970s, Polish, Slavic, and Italian Catholics were very close to the national mean in occupational prestige; the Irish were 3 units above it, surpassing the most successful gentile group in American society, the British-American Protestants. When the standardization model was applied, Polish, Slavic, and Italian Catholics moved substantially above the mean, and in the case of the Poles, "caught up" with the Irish.

TABLE 3.13

DIFFERENCES FROM NATIONAL AVERAGE IN OCCUPATIONAL PRESTIGE
OF AMERICAN GENTILE WHITE ETHNIC GROUPS

Ethnic Group	Gross Differences	Net Differences
British Protestants	3.6	0.2
Irish Catholics	3.4	0.8
German Catholics	0.6	0.7
German Protestants	-0.3	-0.1
Italian Catholics	-0.8	0.4
Polish Catholics	-0.3	1.2
French Catholics	-1.0	0.3
"American" Protestants	-1.7	-1.5
Scandinavian Protestants	-2.0	-1.6
Slavic Catholics	-2.7	-1.2
Irish Protestants	-3.6	-2.6

National Average = 40.3

Taking into account educational backgrounds, in other words, the turn-of-the-century immigrants had begun to do very well indeed by the early 1970s. Their success is reflected in their gross income levels (table 3.15). All the Catholic ethnic groups were above the 1970 national mean in income, and when all the background variables are taken into account in the standardization model, the Polish and Slavic Catholics have even passed their Irish confreres (table 3.16).

We conclude this first phase of the analysis by observing that both Thomas O'Dea in the 1950s and Kenneth Hardy in the 1970s were fundamentally wrong. Whatever residue of occupational, educational, and economic inferiority remains in the Catholic adult population is almost entirely the result of the immigrant experience at the turn of the century and not of any pure "Catholic factor." On the contrary, we shall see shortly that the Irish Catholic group, which was here before

TABLE 3.14

DIFFERENCES FROM AVERAGE IN OCCUPATIONAL PRESTIGE OF
AMERICAN GENTILE WHITE ETHNIC GROUPS--
METROPOLITAN REGIONS OUTSIDE SOUTH

Ethnic Group	Gross Difference	Net Difference
British Protestants	3.1	2.2
Irish Catholics	2.4	1.0
German Catholics	1.5	2.6
German Protestants	0.9	0.8
Scandinavian Protestants	-0.6	0.2
"American" Protestants	-1.9	-1.2
Polish Catholics	-2.2	0.0
French Catholics	-3.0	-2.5
Italian Catholics	-3.1	-2.5
Irish Protestants	-3.3	-3.0
Slavic Catholics	-3.9	-0.5

National Average = 41.8

the turn of the century and still dominates American Catholicism organizationally (much to the discomfiture of other groups), has been immensely successful in America. They only look unsuccessful when they are compared with the Jews.

The Route Upward

We have established the fact that American Catholics have been achieving relative mobility in American society. Now we must endeavor to trace the historical outline of their struggle for mobility. In the process we shall discover that the Vatican Council occurred just at the time when the youngest generation of Catholics marked the definitive end of the immigrant era.

TABLE 3.15

DIFFERENCES FROM NATIONAL AVERAGE IN FAMILY INCOME
FOR GENTILE WHITE ETHNIC GROUPS (1974 DOLLARS)

Ethnic Group	Gross Differences	Net Differences
Irish Catholics	$ 2,473	$ 1,438
Italian Catholics	1,795	3,701
German Catholics	1,679	1,921
Polish Catholics	1,345	2,104
Slavic Catholics	873	2,802
British Protestants	401	- 494
French Catholics	235	991
German Protestants	- 195	- 110
Scandinavian Protestants	- 356	86
"American" Protestants	- 679	271
Irish Protestants	- 806	- 129

National Average = $9,953

There are, of course, even fewer data about the Catholic past than about the Catholic present. The federal census cannot ask a religious question, and until very recently, most Catholic history books were institutional histories of dioceses or religious orders or biographies of prominent ecclesiastics. However, there is a technique of demographic analysis that may be used to recreate the past of a given subpopulation. If one divides the population into cohorts based on year of birth, one can observe the historical events that were occurring in the various phases in the life cycle of a given cohort. All one needs to do is to obtain information from the members of a given cohort as to decisions made at specific times in the life cycle. This technique is used rarely in survey research because it requires a very large sample or repeated samples across time. With a large composite, it is possible to build

TABLE 3.16

DIFFERENCES FROM AVERAGE FAMILY INCOME OF GENTILE WHITE
ETHNIC GROUPS (1974 DOLLARS)--METROPOLITAN REGIONS
OUTSIDE THE SOUTH

Ethnic Groups	Gross Differences	Net Differences
Irish Catholics	$ 2,170	$ 1,654
German Catholics	1,999	2,716
Italian Catholics	1,254	3,684
Slavic Catholics	900	2,476
Polish Catholics	813	1,427
French Catholics	465	1,712
British Protestants	259	- 538
"American" Protestants	- 233	17
Irish Protestants	- 347	873
German Protestants	- 425	- 413
Scandinavian Protestants	- 913	- 756

National Average = $10,623

substantial cohorts based on year of birth (we chose a cohort
of ten-year span, although any number of years would do).
We were able to build cohorts not only for the whole population, but for the denominations and ethnic groups within the
population (table 3.17). With such information available we
can ask, for example, when it was that a given denomination
(or ethnic group) was able to send as many of its young
people to college as did the rest of the country and when it
was able to launch its young on career paths which were not
dissimilar to those of the rest of the country's young. Most
people (though by no means all) attend college in their late
teens and early twenties and embark on career paths at that
time. Thus if we know the proportion of college attendance
of those Roman Catholics who came to their college years in
the Roaring Twenties, for example, we can get some feel for

TABLE 3.17

COHORTS OF AMERICAN RELIGIOUS DENOMINATIONS--NON SPANISH-SPEAKING WHITES ONLY

(SuperNORC Composite Sample)

Years of Birth	Year of Col-lege entry	Era Name	Baptist	Methodist	Lutheran	Episcopalian	Presbyterian	Catholic	Jew
1880-1889	1900-1909	Edwardian	71	92	47	23	54	100	18
1890-1899	1910-1919	World War I	178	184	107	36	176	235	24
1900-1909	1920-1929	Roaring '20s	256	249	164	49	112	452	53
1910-1919	1930-1939	Depression	312	294	203	69	131	610	76
1920-1929	1940-1949	World War II	346	284	206	47	108	715	67
1930-1939	1950-1959	Cold War	374	244	220	59	92	670	63
1940-1955	1960-now	Vietnam	258	170	150	34	74	532	49

what the social and economic state of the Catholic population was at that time. Similarly, if we know what that cohort's mean occupational level is presently, we can at least get a feel for the career path decisions made by the young people coming into young adulthood between the First World War and the Great Depression.

To simplify our discussion we have given each cohort a name that identifies the era in which its members came into young adulthood. Alas, in all too many cases our names identify a war. Admittedly, such a way of interpreting history is both speculative and tentative, but it does have the advantage of dealing with ordinary people rather than with organizations and institutions, great ecclesiastical and political leaders.

Table 3.18 contains the proportion attending college for denominations in each of the cohort groups. (It is interesting to note, incidentally, that the proportion of the total population attending college has almost tripled from the Edwardian era to the Vietnam era.)

Table 3.19, which is based on the chances of attending college in a given denomination, is easy to read. Perhaps the most striking fact to be learned about American Catholics from table 3.19 is that there was a sharp increase in the ratio of college attendance to non-college attendance between the Edwardian era and World War I, then a leveling off in the Roaring Twenties, and a slow rise to the Cold War era, with an increase in the Vietnam generation which surpasses the national ratio.

How can we explain this phenomenon? The most plausible explanation is that two things happened between World War I and the Roaring Twenties. First, the children of the last great wave of immigrants began to come of college age; second, German Catholics suffered a severe shock and consequent devastation of morale because of the wave of anti-German feeling that swept the country during the First World War. The nativism of the Dillingham Commission and the immigration laws, the anti-German reaction to the war, and the surge of anti-

TABLE 3.18

PROPORTION DENOMINATIONAL GROUPS ATTENDING COLLEGE BY COHORT--NON SPANISH-SPEAKING WHITES ONLY

(Percent)

Denominational Group	Edwardian	World War I	Roaring '20s	Depression	World War II	Cold War	Vietnam
Baptists	10	8	11	20	22	23	28
Methodists	22	25	26	29	35	36	45
Lutherans	13	8	15	17	27	30	43
Episcopalians	32	32	45	44	45	54	65
Presbyterians	48	56	53	57	47	71	65
Catholics	7	15	14	19	29	31	45
Jews	17	29	42	47	69	64	88
All	17	18	18	23	29	32	43

TABLE 3.19

ODDS RATIOS ON COLLEGE ATTENDANCE FOR AMERICAN DENOMINATIONAL GROUPS--NON SPANISH SPEAKING WHITES ONLY

(Proportion Attending to Proportion Not Attending)

Denominational Group	Edwardian	World War I	Roaring '20s	Depression	World War II	Cold War	Vietnam
Baptists	.11	.05	.12	.25	.28	.30	.45
Methodists	.28	.33	.35	.41	.54	.56	.82
Lutherans	.15	.09	.18	.20	.37	.43	.75
Episcopalians	.55	.47	.82	.79	.82	1.17	1.86
Presbyterians	.92	1.27	1.13	1.33	.89	2.45	1.86
Catholics	.08	.18	.16	.23	.39	.45	.82
Jews	.20	.41	.72	.89	2.23	1.78	7.33
National	.20	.20	.22	.30	.41	.47	.75

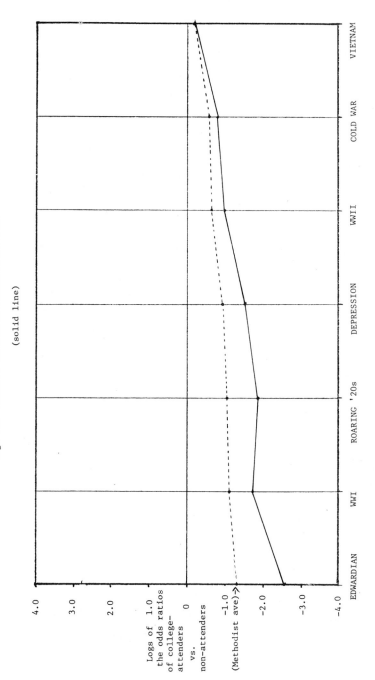

Fig. 3.1--CATHOLIC COLLEGE ATTENDANCE OVER TIME

(solid line)

Fig. 3.2--JEWISH COLLEGE ATTENDANCE OVER TIME

(solid line)

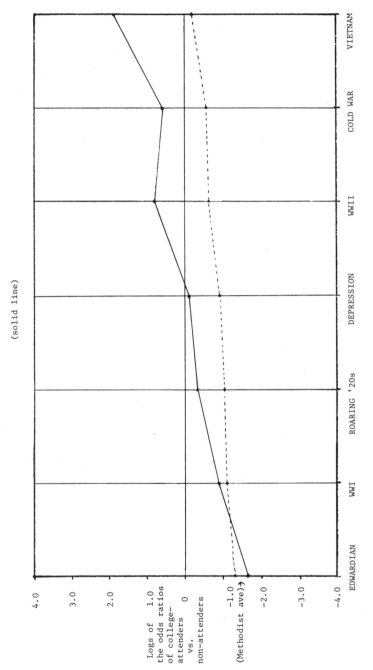

Catholic prejudices in the 1920s, as well as the sheer problem of acculturating masses of new immigrants and their children, doubtless constituted a severe blow to the American Catholic population.

The educational progress of Catholics took a sudden leap forward in the years between the end of World War II and the Vietnam era. In the Vietnam generation Catholics are more likely to go to college than Baptists and Lutherans. They still lag behind Jews, Presbyterians, and Episcopalians, but are ahead of the national average.

The relative progress of Catholics and Jews can be visualized from Figs. 3.1 and 3.2. The "slope" of increasing college attendance for both Jews and Catholics is sharper (and statistically more significant) than the national average. But the Jews begin close to the national average, through the years going much higher, while Catholics begin much lower and through the years slowly "catch up," intersecting the national slope only during the Vietnam generation.

If we turn to the individual Catholic ethnic groups, we can find a fascinating, more detailed narrative of the history of the first three-quarters of the twentieth century (table 3.20). The Irish and the Germans were ahead of all Protestant groups except the British in college attendance. The superior college achievement of the Irish Catholics has remained relatively constant from World War I until the present. German Catholics, however, seem to have suffered a severe decline in the ratio of college attendance during the Roaring Twenties (table 3.21).

The Polish, Slavic, and Italian Catholic groups, beginning during the First World War with a ratio of college attendance of about half the national average, did not improve their relative standing much until the World War II decade (table 3.22). The children and grandchildren of the southern and eastern European immigrants drew even with the rest of the society in the years after 1945. It would appear that they profited most from the G.I. Bill and the prosperity of the World War II era and after.

TABLE 3.20

NUMBER OF RESPONDENTS BY GENTILE WHITE ETHNIC GROUPS FOR EACH AGE COHORT

Ethnic Group	World War I	Roaring '20s	Depression	World War II	Cold War	Vietnam
Protestant						
British	221	310	366	334	306	183
German	198	156	310	329	324	224
Scandinavian	64	85	86	89	98	65
Irish	90	136	138	132	131	85
"American"	286	378	481	521	521	349
Catholic						
Irish	56	147	200	167	167	101
German	40	165	218	186	186	97
Polish	15	78	160	82	82	61
Slavic	22	96	176	74	74	55
Italian	55	139	261	171	171	125
French	18	63	85	108	183	41

TOTAL = 17,222

TABLE 3.21

PERCENT ATTENDED COLLEGE BY COHORT BY ETHNIC GROUP

Ethnic Group	World War I	Roaring '20s	Depression	World War II	Cold War	Vietnam
Protestant						
British	29	34	38	42	43	54
German	16	20	23	28	33	38
Scandinavian	16	21	20	40	32	59
Irish	16	18	26	25	28	34
"American"	13	17	24	25	29	34
Catholic						
Irish	24	26	32	43	38	59
German	24	12	19	29	32	45
Polish	7	4	9	20	34	49
Slavic	9	11	12	21	36	42
Italian	7	9	14	21	29	45
French	11	13	19	21	22	19
ALL	17	18	23	29	32	43

TABLE 3.22

ODDS RATIOS ON COLLEGE ATTENDANCE FOR AMERICAN GENTILE WHITE ETHNIC GROUPS

(Proportion Attending College to Proportion Not Attending)

Ethnic Group	World War I	Roaring '20's	Depression	World War II	Cold War	Vietnam
British Protestant	.41	.52	.61	.72	.75	1.17
German Protestant	.19	.25	.30	.45	.49	.61
Scandinavain Protestant	.19	.27	.25	.67	.47	1.44
Irish Protestant	.19	.22	.35	.33	.39	.52
"American" Protestant	.15	.20	.32	.33	.41	.52
Irish Catholic	.32	.35	.47	.75	.61	1.44
German Catholic	.32	.14	.23	.36	.47	.82
Polish Catholic	.08	.04	.10	.25	.52	.96
Slavic Catholic	.10	.12	.14	.27	.51	.72
Italian Catholic	.08	.10	.16	.27	.41	.82
French Catholic	.12	.15	.23	.27	.28	.23
National Odds	.20	.22	.30	.41	.47	.75

We compare the slopes of the three Catholic ethnic groups which differ significantly from the national slope in Figs. 3.3, 3.4, and 3.5. They all start much lower than the national average and move sharply upward during the years after World War II, so that by the Cold War era they have intersected the national slope. Thus the upward movement of the Catholic ethnics is not just part of the general increase in college attendance but represents a special relative improvement vis-a-vis the rest of the society.

Another way to look at it is to point out that if sending one's children to college at the national average level is a sign of "acculturation," German and Irish Catholics had already achieved it by the beginning of the First World War. The Catholic slope was pulled down by the great influx of eastern and southern European immigrants between 1880 and 1920. However, within less than a quarter of a century after the passage of restrictive immigration laws, these groups were already close to acculturation as measured by sending children to college at the national average. This is an impressive performance for those who, according to the Dillingham Commission, were supposed to prove difficult to absorb into American society.

Conclusion

The reconstructions we have attempted through the analysis of the composite file are at best tentative, speculative, and uncertain—at least in their specific detail. Still, granting all the uncertainties, a number of general observations may be made with some confidence about American Catholics:

1. There is no such thing as a "Catholic factor" that impedes educational, economic, and occupational success. The lower scores on these measures for American Catholics were almost entirely the result of the immigration experience.

2. The American Catholic population has absorbed a number of severe shocks during the present century: massive waves of generally unwelcome immigrants, the anti-German re-

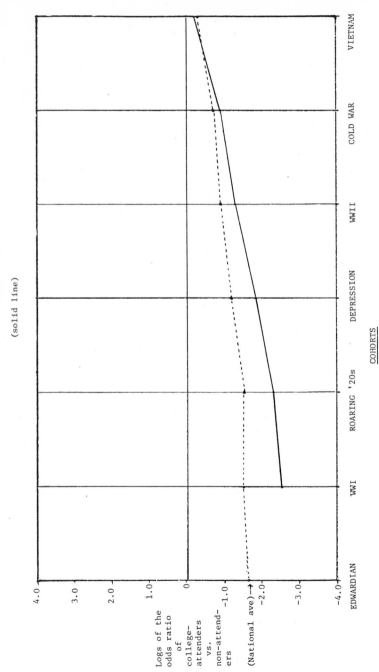

Fig. 3.3--ITALIAN COLLEGE ATTENDANCE OVER TIME

(solid line)

Fig. 3.4--POLISH COLLEGE ATTENDANCE OVER TIME

(solid line)

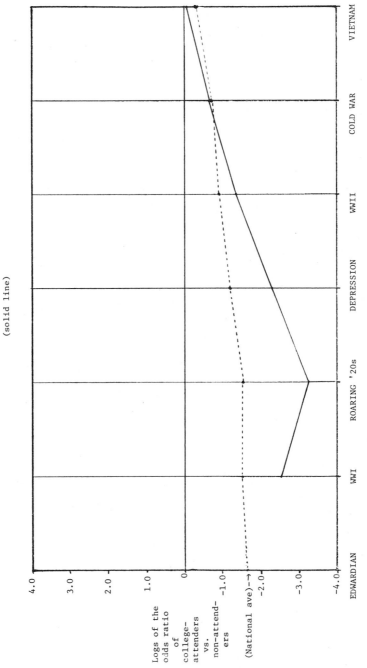

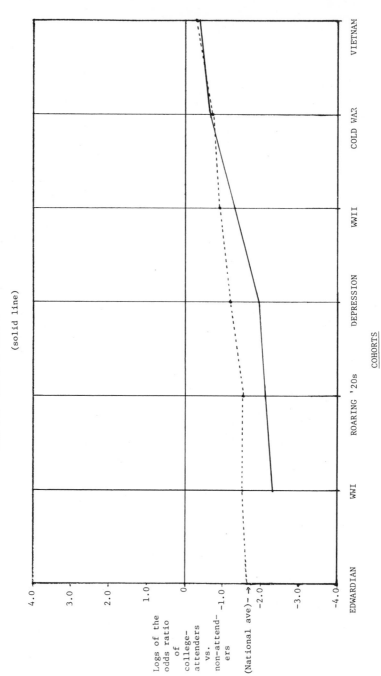

Fig. 3.5--SLAVIC COLLEGE ATTENDANCE OVER TIME

(solid line)

action to the First World War, the Great Depression, and, more recently, the immigration of the Spanish-speaking. By the time of the Vietnam years, the population had managed to absorb all but the last of these shocks.

3. The Irish Catholics began the present century ahead of the national average in education, occupation, and income. Despite a dip during the Great Depression, the Irish have been able to maintain this advantage. They are now the most successful gentile group in American society, and, for the generation under thirty, seem to be threatening the Jews in income. The surprising phenomenon about the Irish is not the fact of their success but that it can be traced back to the beginning of the century. It would seem that the reason no one noticed it (including the Irish) is that the standard of comparison for ethnic success has always been the Jews—a standard that derives from one of the most outstanding success stories in all human history.

4. The First World War seems to have been a blow from which German Catholics took a long, long time to recover.

5. The southern and eastern European groups of turn-of-the-century immigrants have slowly and persistently made their way into the American mainstream, so that by the time we arrive at the Cold War and Vietnam generations, the descendants of these ethnic groups have become part of the mainstream of American society by anyone's standards. The stereotype of the "blue-collar ethnic" simply does not apply to the southern and eastern Europeans under forty.

6. While the French Catholic group has not shown the progress of the southern and eastern European immigrants, the low scores of these Catholics on many educational, occupational, and income measures are almost entirely a function of the problems and obstacles these groups are still experiencing. Given the amazing success of the Italians, the Poles, and the Slavs, we cannot reject the possibility of equally dramatic success in the years ahead for the French (and the Spanish-speaking).

7. In fine, the result of the last three-quarters of a century is that Catholics under forty have elbowed themselves into a position in American society in which they are behind only the Presbyterians, the Episcopalians, and the Jews in their achievement. In the Vietnam generation, the Irish Catholics are second only to the Jews in education and second to no one in income. The Italian Catholics are second only to the Irish in income.

It is a remarkable success story. The American Catholic population has absorbed immigration, war, and depression. It has seized for itself not only parity, but for some groups, in some matters, superiority in American society. The Irish in particular have been, despite their own frequently agonized lamentations, extraordinarily successful. Unfortunately for American Catholics they have become successful only when success is no longer considered important. When the rest of the society valued educational, occupational, and economic success, Catholics didn't have it. Now that they have achieved it, it seems that the intellectual elites are disposed to write off achievement as the result of selfishness and greed.

In conclusion, it is interesting and perhaps ironic that the ferment of the Vatican Council should have occurred in the Catholic church at the same time that the eastern and southern European ethnic groups were moving into a position of parity in the American economic struggle and the Irish were pulling ahead. Whether this accidental concatenation of two powerful social forces will be a benefit or a hindrance to the Catholic church in American society remains to be seen.

It might be argued that the religious changes in American Catholicism, which we described briefly in the last chapter and to which we will turn in later chapters, are the result of the social and economic changes which we have traced in the present chapter. One may argue that the religious behavior of American Catholics would have changed even if there had not been a Second Vatican Council or an encyclical letter on birth control. It is surely the case that when a substantial proportion of your population has attended college, you must approach religion in a somewhat different fashion than you did when most of your membership was not so well educated. But it does not necessarily follow that social and economic change will generate religious, attitudinal, and behavioral change. The first, second, and even third-generation American Catholics were to an overwhelming extent committed to being both American and Catholic. But they were also to a very substantial extent committed to being Democrats. While there is obviously not a perfect parallel between politics and religion, it could be argued with equal plausibility that the educational, occupational, and economic success of American Catholics would wean them from their loyalties both to the Catholic church and to the Democratic party. That there has been an erosion in Catholic religious behavior we have demonstrated in chapter 2 (and we will return to this theme later). If there has been a similar erosion in Democratic party support, then one would have a plausible argument that the social and economic changes of the past three-quarters of a century have made inevitable both political and religious attitudinal and behavioral change among American Catholics. If, on the other hand, there has been relatively little in the way of political change for American Catholics, we must admit the possibility that religious change, however it may have been prepared for by economic change, was something special and unique.

In the following chapter, Joan Fee will investigate the question of whether there has been a departure from the Democratic party and from moderate liberal political positions by American Catholics as a result of their economic success and their movement to the suburbs—a disaffiliation which in some quarters is almost taken for granted. To anticipate Ms. Fee's findings somewhat, there is very little evidence of change either in political attitudes or political affiliations among American Catholics, despite the social and economic changes and the political unrest of the last two decades.

4

Political Continuity and Change

Joan L. Fee

Although American separation of church and state has prevented a direct connection between religious denominations and political parties, throughout U.S. history the parties have offered a differential appeal to voters of various religious convictions.[1] With the advent of survey analysis, the tendency of Catholics and Jews to consider themselves Democrats and of white Protestants to think of themselves as Republicans has been well documented.[2] However, party identification appears to be in a state of flux. Also documented are the growing number of voters who abandon party identification in favor of an independent stance and the shifting allegiances of the once solidly Democratic South.[3] Perhaps receiving less attention are the changing economic fortunes of religious groups in America. In the years since World War II, Catholic Americans have surpassed white Protestants in median education and income while Jewish Americans have maintained their position at the top of the socioeconomic scale.[4] This chapter will study the patterns of party identification among American religious groups over the past twenty years, paying particular attention to the partisanship of Catholics.

Before beginning the analysis, it seems appropriate to consider why religious groups would subscribe to different brands of politics. Theoretical justifications assume two main forms:

1) the historical explanations, which describe how the religious-political connection begins; and 2) the maintaining theories, which show how the relationship survives over time. In the case of American Catholics, for example, the historical theories take three main directions:

1. *a*) Catholics historically have been an outgroup, low on the social and economic ladder and discriminated against. Thus, they turned to the Democratic party (dramatized by Roosevelt's egalitarian New Deal).[5]

   b) Catholics were pushed into the Democratic party by the belligerent anti-Catholic and pro-nativist stands of the Whig Republicans, who bequeathed strands of these traditions to the Republican party.[6]

2. *a*) The salient candidacy of Al Smith, occurring at a time of emerging political involvement among immigrants, married Catholics to Smith's party, the Democratic party.[7]

3. *a*) At the time of the great immigrant arrivals, the party out of power in the North, where most immigrants settled, was the Democratic party. In order to gain strength, it appealed to the immigrants through political machines.[8]

   b) Immigrant leaders, excluded from other avenues of advancement, forced their way into the Democratic party, bringing their followers with them.[9]

Once Catholics have been attracted to the Democratic party, some mechanism must insure their over-time allegiance. There are several theories as to how this might be accomplished:

1. Historicist causes: People cling to familiar patterns out of tradition.[10]

2. Parental socialization: Catholics adopt the Democratic identification of their parents.[11]

3. Differential association and group pressures: Catholics tend to associate with Catholics; their political conversations reinforce the group trend.[12]

4. Demographic characteristics: Religion, in fact, may be a spurious correlate of party identification, passed on because other factors like socioeconomic status remain constant over generations.[13]

5. Rational choice: Catholics may continue to consider themselves Democrats because the party seems more sympathetic to the group, including them in leadership positions.[14]

While we cannot test all of the historical and maintaining theories offered, we hope that our over-time analysis will tend to support or to refute some of these explanations of religious-political association, and the Catholic-Democratic relationship in particular. The first section will study in detail political party identification and nonidentification among American social and religious groups over the past twenty years. It will use an innovative technique perfected by Kim and Schmidt in their study of party identification-canonical regression.[15] The technique allows a view of two dimensions of party identification—1) Democratic vs. Republican party support, and 2) party identification vs. independency—to be studied at the same time.

The second section will focus on an offshoot of the "differential association and group pressure" maintaining theory. The offshoot stresses the difference between acculturation and assimilation among ethnic-religious groups, noting that groups may adapt to American ways, acculturating, while maintaining a separate ethnic identity, resisting assimilation. This separate ethnic identity may reinforce a group political trend. Parenti says, "From birth in the sectarian hospital to childhood play groups to cliques and fraternities in high school and college to the selection of a spouse, a church affiliation, social and service clubs, a vacation resort, and, as life nears completion, an

old age home and sectarian cemetary—the ethnic, if he so de-
sires, may live within the confines of his sub-societal-matrix—
and many do."[16] However, as individuals suburbanize, assimilation may set in through exposure to a more heterogeneous
population than the individual encountered in the old neighborhood. This assimilation, in turn, may weaken ties to the
group political trend.

Indeed, Greer found in a Saint Louis study that Catholic
suburbanites voted more Republican than did their inner-city
counterparts, although they continued to identify as Democrats.[17] We will note the degree of suburbanization among
the various religious groups over the twenty-year period under
study and will observe the political identification of the
groups according to place of residence. Although this forms a
rather crude test of assimilation since it does not take into
account homogeneity of neighborhood, it will provide some
indication of the political impact of suburbanization. Finally,
we will compare the party identification patterns of the
groups to their scores on a left-right opinion scale.

The data are taken from the Michigan Survey Research
Center election studies. In order to provide a maximum number of cases for analysis at each point in time, the studies
have been grouped into three periods: early (1952, 1956,
1958), middle (1960, 1962, 1964), and late (1968, 1970,
1972)—each period containing two presidential elections and
one congressional election study.

Section 1

To begin the analysis, two sets of dummy variables are constructed, one representing the categories of party identification, and the other representing the demographic characteristics of religion, education, region, race, and place of residence (inner-city vs. suburb vs. other). A canonical correlation
is run in order to determine the degree to which social background characteristics predict party identification. Then, a sec-

ond canonical correlation is computed to determine to what extent religion alone could predict party identification. The results appear in table 4.1.

TABLE 4.1

CANONICAL CORRELATION OF PARTY IDENTIFICATION

	Dimension I	Dimension II
A. With Religion, Race, Residence Place, Region, and Education		
Time 1	.3317	.1198
Time 2	.3220	.1178
Time 3	.3336	.1504
B. With Religion		
Time 1	.1572	.0421
Time 2	.1743	.0813
Time 3	.1574	.0833

Canonical correlation, a simple correlation between the sets of variates, first selects a factor accounting for a maximum amount of variance in the sets of variables, and then selects a second factor accounting for a maximum amount of the residual variance not accounted for by the first factor, and so on. As noted in table 4.1, party identification and the demographic variables correlate on two statistically significant dimensions (one of which turns out to be the Democratic vs. Republican factor; the other, the independent vs. party identifier factor), which will be discussed in more detail below. Here we note that there is a moderate relationship between party identification and the social characteristics studied, and that the relationship seems quite stable over the years.[18] Furthermore, given the moderate nature of the social characteristics-party identification relationship, religion is not a bad predictor of party identification. The correlation of religion

TABLE 4.2

UNADJUSTED AND ADJUSTED PARTISANSHIP (DIMENSION I) AND INDEPENDENCY (DIMENSION II)
SCORES BY DEMOGRAPHIC CATEGORIES, TIMES 1, 2 AND 3

Category	Unadjusted, Simple Scores						Adjusted, Partial Scores					
	Time 1(52-58)		Time 2(60-64)		Time 3(68-72)		Time 1(52-58)		Time 2(60-64)		Time 3(68-72)	
	Dimension I	II	Dimension I	II	Dimension I	II	Dimension I	II	Dimension I	II	Dimension I	II
Religion:												
Protestant	-7.6	6.1	-9.1	4.4	-8.3	6.0	-11.4	6.3	-12.8	3.9	-12.4	6.5
Catholic	18.4	-12.6	25.0	-4.9	21.5	-5.6	30.6	-13.3	35.1	-3.2	30.5	-7.4
Jew	40.7	-19.9	37.2	-30.7	34.3	-25.0	48.7	-26.9	51.1	-29.7	55.9	-25.7
Other	3.7	-25.0	-23.5	.1	-3.6	-43.8	10.2	-30.3	-21.2	1.3	-7.7	-38.3
None	-4.9	-31.5	10.0	-60.0	4.0	-37.8	-4.7	-33.2	14.9	-58.3	9.7	-38.2
Race:												
White	-2.8	-.1	-3.7	-.3	-7.5	-1.8	-1.6	.5	-2.7	.2	-6.5	-1.4
Black/other	28.5	4.0	36.2	.5	61.4	14.6	18.6	-5.4	28.7	-2.5	54.4	11.3
Residence Area:												
City	16.2	3.6	20.0	-5.5	21.7	9.3	12.9	14.2	14.3	3.1	4.6	1.2
Suburb	-21.8	-1.9	-8.4	-6.2	-9.9	-7.0	-6.8	1.7	-3.7	-1.5	-5.6	3.4
Other	.1	-.1	-1.7	2.1	.9	-3.2	-1.5	-3.3	-1.6	-.2	.6	-.9
Education:												
Not high school graduate	8.5	1.7	14.0	2.6	19.0	-.6	6.2	1.6	13.3	2.6	15.7	8.4
High school graduate	-4.3	-3.3	-9.3	-2.5	-6.9	-1.0	-1.8	-3.0	-7.7	-2.1	-5.3	-6.6
College graduate	-34.5	4.3	-23.0	-3.7	-31.6	.2	-30.8	4.2	-24.5	-2.4	-28.4	-.4
Region:												
North/other	-14.5	-3.2	-11.3	-3.9	-9.3	1.6	-17.4	-2.9	-15.1	-2.4	-9.6	3.7
South	36.6	9.0	23.4	7.7	18.8	-3.5	44.8	7.6	32.1	5.1	19.6	-7.5
Ethno-Religious:												
White Protestants	-7.9	5.4	-10.1	2.2	-13.6	2.8	-10.0	6.1	-13.7	2.0	-16.0	1.5
Irish, Polish Catholics	20.7	-19.1	45.8	-14.6	29.7	-2.4	32.8	-19.6	53.7	-13.5	37.7	-.2
Other Catholics	14.2	-13.9	20.3	-1.3	15.1	-11.7	25.0	-14.1	29.1	-.3	21.5	-2.1
Jews	40.3	-20.4	37.9	-32.1	32.5	-27.2	44.5	-27.3	46.8	-29.8	46.1	-.7
Blacks, Spanish	31.0	5.4	41.7	0	64.7	11.2	14.0	-.2	25.5	-.7	52.8	1.3
Others	-23.7	3.1	-21.2	2.4	-26.3	-.5	-18.1	3.5	-18.3	3.3	-21.8	.1

81

with party identification is about half that of party identification with all of the social characteristics taken together. The predictive power of religion in relation to the other social characteristics is rather surprising, since it does not take race into account. Its power is somewhat diluted by the fact that black and white Protestants hold such different party allegiances.

Table 4.2 reveals a number of interesting things. First, when the scores have been adjusted, religion (and in the early periods, region) becomes more important, while the other social characteristics decline in value, indicating the consistent importance of religion as a distinct contributor to political views. In contrast, the other social characteristics tend to reinforce each other. Second, the religious scores and racial scores—and the combined religio-ethnic scores—are noticeably higher than the scores of other categories with greater distance between groups, indicating greater political differences along religious and ethnic lines than among other educational or residence groupings.

DIFFERENCES IN DIRECTION OF PARTY IDENTIFICATION AND IN
PARTISANSHIP VS. INDEPENDENCY AMONG WHITE PROTESTANTS
AND CATHOLICS, TIMES 1 THROUGH 3

	Time 1	Time 2	Time 3
Direction of Party Indentification			
Total Difference	−26	−34	−30
Expected on the Basis of Other Social Characteristics. .	+16	+14	+13
Religious Difference	−42	−48	−43
Partisanship vs. Independency			
Total Difference	19	9	12
Expected on the Basis of Other Social Characteristics. .	−1	2	−2
Religious Difference	20	7	14

As far as individual religous groups are concerned, the Protestant commitment to Republicanism remains fairly steady
over the period studied, as does the Catholic commitment to
the Democratic party. The Catholic Democratic score jumps
slightly in time 2, a result of a sharp jump in the 1960 Kennedy election, and the Catholic independency rate falls slightly during that time period. The figures above, taken from
table 4.3, more clearly demonstrate the stability of the Protes-
tant-Catholic differences, with some fluctuation during time 2.
The stability remains more true of Republican-Democratic differences than of differences in independency.

Among Jews, interestingly, the actual Democratic commitment seems to have dropped slightly over the years, but the
adjusted scores have risen. In other words, the proportion of
Democratic Jews in relation to the rest of the population is
declining slightly—but with rising Jewish educational levels
and suburbanization, the importance of religion as a Demo-
cratizing factor is rising.

The "other" religious category forms such a small proportion of the population that the trends here are probably not
too reliable, although there seems somewhat of an affinity
toward Republicanism and independency among this group.
More interesting are the growing number of Americans who
express no religious affiliation. These voters show a consistent
tendency to choose independency in political affiliation as
well as independency in religious affiliation. Indeed, they represent the most consistently independent group of voters in
the United States.

The ethno-religious categories at the bottom of table 4.2
provide additional information, particularly on the Catholics.
The inclination of Irish and Polish Catholics to consider
themselves Democrats approaches the Jewish inclination; in
fact, their Democratic leanings exceed those of the Jews in
the middle period containing the Kennedy election. On the
other hand, the blacks from time 1 to time 3 evolve from one
of the weaker Democratic ethnic supporters to the most Dem-

ocratic ethnic grouping. The Catholic groups and the Jews at time 1 show the greatest tendency toward independency; by time 3 the differences between the religious-ethnic groups seem to have diminished in the area of independency vs. partisanship.

Figure 4.1 summarizes the information contained in the tables on religion and partisanship. The two triangles represent the changing *social* distance between the different party identifications in time 1 (the unbroken line) and time 2 (the broken line). Kim and Schmidt (1974) explain the rationale behind this social distance technique.[19] Suffice it to say here that scores are the mean partisan scores on each dimension of social background characteristics. The figure shows us that in time 1 and time 3, the greatest difference in social characteristics occurs between Republicans and Democrats. In contrast, the Republicans and Independents are closest in social characteristics during the Eisenhower years of time 1, but by time 3 the Democrats and the Independents represent closer social backgrounds.

The quadrangle and pentagon in Fig. 4.1 show the *partisan* differences between the various religious groups (obtained directly from the adjusted scores of table 4.2). We see that during the Eisenhower years, those of "other" religions and of no religion, on the average, are close in party identification; and that by time 3, they maintain the proximity, but do a flip-flop on the Democrat-Republican scale. The Jews and Protestants experience the greatest distance in partisan identification—with the distance growing from time 1 to time 3. As a matter of fact, political distance between religious groups seems to be intensifying slightly over time—as shown by the increase in area of the time 3 quadrangle over that of time 1 caused by the greater distances between the partisan scores of most religious groups. Between Protestants and Catholics, however, differences in partisanship actually decreased slightly from a difference of 46.4 points in time 1 to a difference of 45.1 points in time 3. This decrease in partisanship probably

Figure 4.1:   Social Distance between Partisan Groups and Partisan
              Differences between Religious Groups, Times 1 and 3

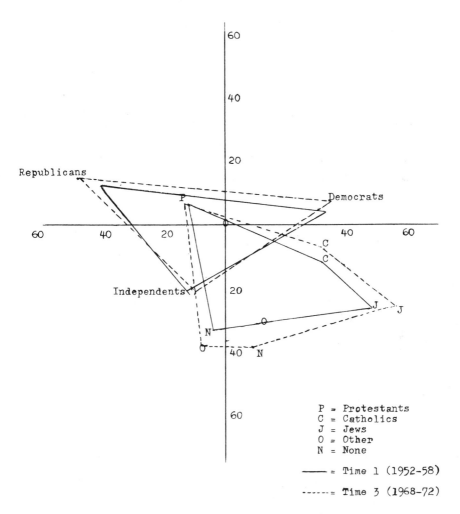

results from the increasingly Democratic identification of
black Protestants. Table 4.3 summarizes the differences in
partisanship noted in Fig. 4.1. The left-hand score in each

column is the difference between the groups at time 1; the right-hand score represents the time 3 difference.

It should be recalled from table 4.1 that the middle time period produced the largest correlation between religion and party identification on both dimensions. These partisan distances, therefore, would be larger during time 2 than during times 1 and 3. It seems, however, that the short-term force of a religiously salient election produced the increase in the political-party religion relationship during time 2. For this reason, we have graphed times 1 and 3, which should reflect a more accurate picture of the over-time, long-term trend. From table 4.1 we also remember that the relationship between religion and party identification increased along dimension II between times 1 and 3, with dimension I remaining the same. Thus, most of the increased distance in partisanship shown over the years results from an increasing relationship between independency and religion rather than from a growing denominational-party relationship. This accords with Fig. 4.1, where, with the exception of the Jews, most of the movement by the religious groups is along the Y rather than the X axis.

To summarize, interesting trends have become evident from the canonical regression of party identification with a variety of social characteristics and from the canonical regression of party identification with religion. First, in relation to other characteristics, religion is a fairly important predictor of party identification—distinct from other social characteristics. Second, as a predictor of Republican or Democratic party identification (dimension I), religion remains fairly stable over time, increasing slightly in time 2, the period containing a religiously salient election.

On the second dimension, independency, religion has become a slightly better predictor of partisanship or lack of partisanship over time. A good part of this predictability seems to stem from the growing number of voters who espouse no religion and no party affiliation. Most probably these people are a young cohort of the Vietnam generation voters. We

TABLE 4.3

DIFFERENCES IN PARTY IDENTIFICATION (DIMENSIONS I AND II COMBINED)
AMONG RELIGIOUS GROUPS, TIMES 1 AND 3*

Religious Group	Protestant		Catholic		Jew		Other		None	
	Time 1	Time 3	Time 1	Time 3	Time 1	Time 3	Time 1	Time 3	Time 1	Time 3
Protestant	---		46.4	45.1	68.7	75.5	42.5	45.0	39.8	49.9
Catholic			---		22.6	31.3	26.5	49.1	40.5	37.2
Jew					---		38.7	64.8	53.8	47.9
Other							---		15.2	17.4
None									---	

*The distance between the groups is quantified according to the following formula:
(Taking Protestants and Catholics in time 1 as an example)

When P_{p1} = adjusted partial partisanship score for Protestants, 1st dimension

P_{p2} = adjusted partial partisanship score for Protestants, 2nd dimension

P_{c1} = adjusted partial partisanship score for Catholics, 1st dimension

P_{c2} = adjusted partial partisanship score for Catholics, 2nd dimension

(from Table 3)

Partisan distance between Protestants and Catholics

$$= \sqrt{(P_{p1} - P_{c1})^2 + (P_{p2} - P_{c2})^2}$$

$$= \sqrt{(-11.4 - 30.6)^2 + (6.3 - -13.3)^2}$$

$$= \sqrt{2148}$$

$$= 46.4$$

should note, however, that those Americans without a religion have in all time periods been independent. (They appear particularly independent in time 2 as compared to members of the major religions, who more steadfastly hold party identifications in this period.) What makes these "no-religionists" more important as time goes on is their increasing numbers.

Concerning the partisanship of the various religious groups: white Protestants and Catholics remain fairly stable in their over-time partisan commitments, the Protestants maintaining a more Republican identification than the rest of the population, the Catholics, a more Democratic one. As mentioned above, those espousing no religion also demonstrate a stable trend, but one of independency rather than partisanship. From time 1 to time 3, the Jews grow slightly less Democratic as compared to the rest of the population; but religion, compared to other social characteristics, becomes a more important predictor of their partisanship. In contrast, black Protestants dramatically increase their allegiance to the Democratic party.

Section 2

Before tackling the relationship between suburbanization and party identification among the religious groups, it is interesting to note the change in residence patterns over the past twenty years. Table 4.4 dramatizes this change. It reflects the proportion of the population in each religious-racial group that lives in the suburbs as a percentage of those located in metropolitan areas. In the case of blacks in time 1, for example, 21 percent of the sample live in the suburbs of large cities (12 Standard Metropolitan Sampling Areas), with the remaining 79 percent inhabiting the inner city.

In each of the time periods under study, the white Protestant group represents the highest proportion of suburbanites. The white Catholics and Jews are suburbanizing at a much more rapid rate than the Protestants. On the other hand, the

TABLE 4.4

SUBURBANIZATION PATTERNS AMONG DIFFERENT RACIAL-RELIGIOUS
GROUPS, TIMES 1, 2, AND 3 (SUBURBANITES AS A PERCENTAGE
OF THOSE LIVING IN METROPOLITAN AREAS)

(Per Cent)

Racial-Religious Group	Time 1 (1952-58)	Time 2 (1960-64)	Time 3 (1968-72)	Difference Time 1 - Time 3
White Protestants . . .	$64_{(969)}$	$71_{(943)}$	$78_{(820)}$	14
White Catholics	$42_{(814)}$	$60_{(740)}$	$68_{(774)}$	26
White Jews	$15_{(209)}$	$32_{(218)}$	$49_{(188)}$	34
White None	$62_{(42)}$	61 (66)	54 (97)	-8
Black Protestants . .	$21_{(224)}$	$23_{(247)}$	$19_{(216)}$	-2

Catholic suburbanization rate has slowed between times 2 and 3 and may be reaching an equilibrium stage. Black Protestants suburbanized little over the years studied and may even have become more urban. The whites expressing no religion do not contain enough respondents to offer a stable trend, but they appear somewhat less suburbanized than white Protestants and, possibly, white Catholics.

We now begin a study of Figs. 4.2 through 4.6. These figures graph the mean party identification scores (when 0 equals strong Democrat, 1 equals weak Democrat, 2 equals a Democratic-leaning independent, 3 equals a "pure" independent, 4 equals a Republican-leaning independent, 5 equals a weak Republican, and 6 equals a strong Republican) of the different racial-religious groups according to their educational and residence patterns. The figures possess the advantage of displaying, perhaps more clearly, the trends discussed in section 1 while presenting evidence on the impact of place of residence on the party identification of religious groups. Unlike the canonical regression scores, however, mean party identification scores do not distinguish between party identifiers and independents. If a group of Catholic *Republican* suburbanites becomes independent and an equivalent group of Catholic suburban *Democrats* also takes on an independent identification, the mean party identification score of the group will remain the same. (This was true of the canonical regression technique concerning Democrat to Republican, or vice versa, group changes; however, such movement occurs less often than a shift toward independency in these times.) With this caveat in mind, we address the figures.

Figures 4.2a through 4.2e note the mean party identification scores of five racial-religious groups—white Protestants, white Catholics, white Jews, those whites who hold no religious affiliation, and black and other nonwhite Protestants—according to their educational backgrounds. The trends shown in Figs. 4.2a and b are most probably more reliable than those of 4.2c, d, and e since the white Protestant and white Catholic groups contain many more people. In these two white groups, Catholic and Protestant, the difference in mean party identification scores among the different educational groups is similar. In both cases, across time, the college educated consistently veer more toward a Republican or independent stance, with the high-school educated slightly more Democratic, and those with less than a high-school education most Democratic of all. A difference exists in degree of Democratic attachment, however, in that the most highly educated Catholics show about the same tendency to call themselves Democrats as the high-school-educated Protestants. Catholics at all levels of education showed the greatest tendency toward the Democratic party in the middle time frame.

In contrast to the white Catholics and Protestants, the Jews and black Protestants seem to be less politically divided along educational lines; within-group party identification is more similar at each educational level. Among the Jews, the most educated show the greatest tendency to call themselves Democrats in two out of three of the time periods. The most Republican-Independent Jewish group in all time frames remains

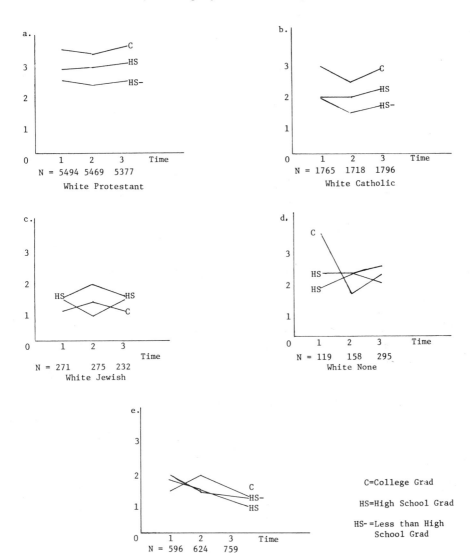

Figure 4.2: Mean Party Identification Scores by Racial-Religious
Group Controlling for Education
(6 = Strong Republican 3 = Independent 0 = Strong Democrat)

C=College Grad

HS=High School Grad

HS-=Less than High
School Grad

the high-school educated. Blacks of all educational levels show a growing Democratic trend over the twenty-year period. The time 2 fluctuation in the college-educated group may result from the small numbers it contains ($N=15$, 28, 41 in times 1, 2, and 3, respectively).

Interestingly, those who hold no religious affiliation seem to be fairly cohesive along partisan lines. Again, the fluctuations among the college educated probably result from the very few cases the category contains in times 1 and 2 ($N=18$, 21, and 62 in times 1, 2, and 3, respectively). By time 3, the three educational groups have come together, as we know from section 1, to a tendency toward independency. In this final time period, the mean party identification score varies less between educational groupings of the nondenominational than it does among white Catholics and Protestants.

Figures 4.3a through e compare party identification scores according to place of residence within the racial-religious groups. Interestingly, among white Catholics, and to a lesser degree, white Protestants, place of residence does not distinguish as well as level of education between the party identification tendencies. Catholics, in particular, show almost identical party identification trends in each of the three residence areas—inner city, suburb, and small city/town/rural. It should be noted that among white Protestants, those living in small cities, towns, and rural areas, unlike their cohorts in most other religious groups, are consistently more Democratic than inner-city dwellers.

Among Jews, however, place of residence distinguishes better than educational level between different party identification patterns, with inner-city residents consistently more Democratic. Those living in small cities, towns, and rural areas— just opposite to the white Protestant trend—remain consistently less Democratic. Perhaps this tendency of Jews to identify less Democratically in smaller areas and for white Protestants to identify more Democratically in the same areas indicates that a pressure toward homogeneous political patterns exists in small towns but not in the suburbs.

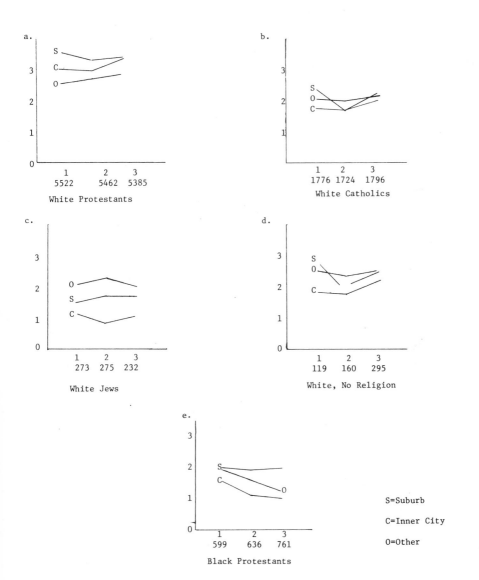

Figure 4.3: Mean Party Identification Scores by Racial-Religious
Group, Controlling for Place of Residence
(6 = Strong Republican, 3 = Independent, 0 = Strong Democrat)

93

Blacks show a pattern of party identification according to place of residence similar to their pattern for levels of education; most blacks are becoming more Democratic. Although the number of suburban blacks is fairly small (an average of 51 cases per time frame), suburban blacks show a stable party identification score—seemingly resisting the group pull toward a more Democratic party identification.

Those whites without a religious affiliation demonstrate similar partisan scores when differentiated by residence size as they did when separated by educational attainment—especially in time 3, which contains the most respondents.

Instead of arraying the various racial-religious groups on a scale of party identification, Figs. 4.4 and 4.5 dramatize the different left-right political opinions the groups hold. Left-right views are measured by a factor-analyzed and weighted scale consisting of five issue areas: black welfare, school integration, economic welfare, size of government, and foreign policy (particularly attitudes toward Communism). The questions under each area are taken from the Michigan Survey Research Center election files, from which the party identification information has also come.[20] The left-right opinions of the different groups fall on a scale ranging from 300 (extremely liberal) to -300 (extremely conservative).

Perhaps the most striking feature in Figs. 4.4a, b, c, d, and e is the swing toward the left by the college educated among all religious groups between times 2 and 3, with the Catholic college educated showing the biggest jump, a rise of 80 points in the two time periods. Yet, this changing political ideology does not seem to have sparked among the well educated a shift in party identification toward the Democrats. This turning toward liberalism among the college educated accompanies a slight swing toward conservatism among the less educated white Protestants, Catholics, and Jews.

Among blacks, education does not seem to affect ideology as much as it does in the other groups. All segments of the black population share quite liberal positions in time 1 and

Figure 4.4: Left-Right Opinion Scores by Racial-Religious
Group, Controlling for Education
(-300 = Very Conservative, 300 = Very Liberal)

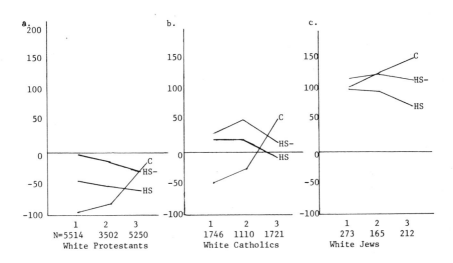

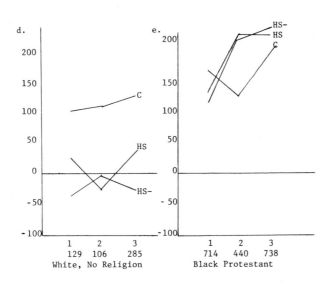

grow more liberal over the years. Again, the downward bump in the pattern of college-educated blacks probably reflects small numbers (only 15 in time 2, 28 in time 1, and 39 in time 3).

Interestingly, those whites holding no religious affiliation show the greatest difference in ideology between the college educated and the less educated. This may result from a division of the "no religion" voters into two groups: the well-educated agnostics, for whom lack of religion is a part of an ongoing ideology; and the not as well educated, who have drifted away from religion but who hold political views closer to those of the rest of the population. The first, more highly educated component expresses ideological views similar to those of highly educated Jews; the other, less educated component offers a political ideology more similar to that of white Protestants and white Catholics. Aside from the no-religion whites, the four groups of white Protestants, white Catholics, Jews, and black Protestants show individually clustered political ideologies which ascend monotonically—spanning the spectrum from the more conservative white Protestants through the middle shades of white Catholics and Jews to the most liberal black Protestants.

Figure 4.5 portrays varying shades of political ideology by residence place. While white Protestants showed the greatest divergence in party identification between suburban respondents and those in small cities, towns, and rural areas, these two groups espouse similar political ideologies. This fact demonstrates that the translation of ideology into party identification is often a garbled one.

Among white Protestants, Catholics, and Jews alike, the leftward movement in political views among the college educated does not produce a liberal swing in the suburbs. In fact, both Catholic and Jewish suburban voters became quite a bit more conservative. This factor indicates a high proportion of suburbanites with less than a college education.

While the number of whites espousing no religion and living

Figure 4.5: Left-Right Scores by Racial-Religious Groups,
Controlling for Residence Size
(-300 = Extremely Conservative   300 = Extremely Liberal)

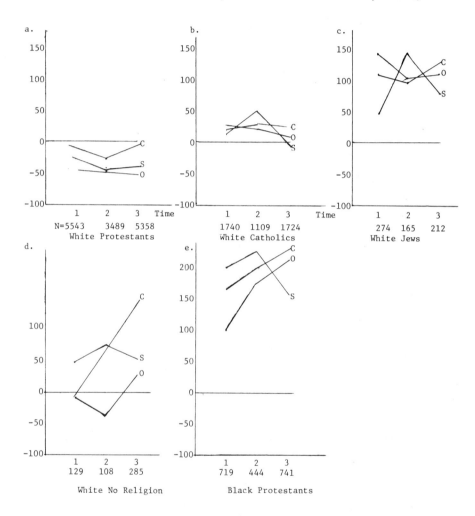

in the city remains quite small ($N=16$, 26, and 45 in times 1, 2, and 3, respectively) the extreme upward direction of this line is interesting. It might reflect a growing tendency among more radical, white, well-educated persons to seek an urban environment. In the 1950s the differences between the inner-city and the suburbs were not so starkly drawn. Today, choosing a suburban residence over an urban one may indicate a more conservative political bent.

If one considers membership in the Democratic party the more liberal partisan identification, the blacks, more than any other group, have evolved throughout the twenty-year period in the most consistent directions. From time 1 to time 3 they became increasingly Democratic and, at the same time, their political ideology evolved to the left.

As a final test of the impact of place of residence on Catholic party identification and political opinions, Fig. 4.6 notes the party identification and left-right scores of white Catholics and Protestants in different residence areas after the effects of education have been removed.[21] The figures show what the scores would be in the different residence areas if educational attainment in the city, suburbs, and other areas were the same. Although removing the effect of education shifts white Protestants and Catholics as a whole into more Democratic and more liberal positions, controlling for education affects relatively little the ordering of scores according to residence place, indicating that, among white Catholics and Protestants, the educational levels are not radically different in the three residence areas.

As far as party identification is concerned, the only period in which the order changes is time 2. Controlling for education shifts Protestant city-dwellers into a more Democratic position than that of Protestant voters in small cities, towns, and rural areas. The educational control in the Catholic population demonstrates that in time 2 suburban Catholics identified more Democratically than did city residents and people

Figure 4.6: Mean Party Identification and Left-Right Scores
by Racial-Religious Group, Controlling for Residence
and Adjusted for Education

Party Identification
(0 = Strong Democrat, 3 = Independent, 6 = Strong Republican)

a.

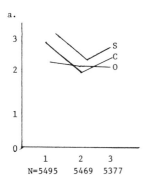

1   2   3
N=5495   5469   5377

White Protestants

b.

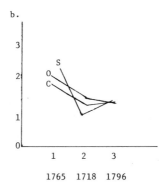

1   2   3

1765   1718   1796

White Catholics

Left-Right Scores
(-300=Very Conservative, 300=Very Liberal)

c.

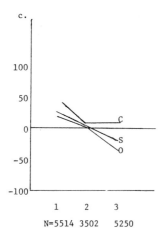

1   2   3
N=5514 3502   5250

White Protestants

S=Suburb
C=Inner City
O=Other

d.

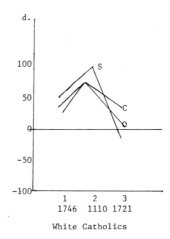

1   2   3
1746   1110 1721

White Catholics

99

living in "other" areas if one takes into consideration the fact that Catholic suburbanites are slightly better educated than their counterparts in other areas. In the area of left-right ideologies, controlling for education brings the Protestant groups into almost identical ideologies in time 2, while Catholic suburbanites draw slightly further away from their coreligionists, becoming slightly more liberal.

Conclusions

At the outset we proposed to study shifts in party identification among religious groups since the 1950s. We hoped to pay particular attention to the impact of suburbanization on the Catholic population and to see if we could corroborate any of the religious-political theories. We have found that religion continues to exert an impact on party identification over the period studied and that, indeed, the impact seems to be increasing slightly as the distance in partisanship between the religious groups grows. This slight increase results not from a greater commitment by religious groups to particular parties, but, rather, from an improving ability to predict independency on the basis of religious affiliation (or nonaffiliation).

Furthermore, the connection between religion and party identification does not seem to diminish greatly with changes in socioeconomic status. While Catholics rose in socioeconomic status from 1952 to 1972, surpassing white Protestants in mean income and education, their attraction for the Democratic party did not diminish. Nor did it diminish when the group suburbanized. Catholic suburbanites hold views nearly as strongly Democratic as those of their coreligionists in other areas. This finding, while not refuting the hypothesis that groups abandon group-held political ties as they assimilate (since we do not know how heterogeneous are the suburban neighborhoods containing Catholics), certainly does not lend weight to the hypothesis.

Within different groups, however, different factors do affect party identification. Among Protestants and Catholics, education seems to determine the direction of party identification. Jews and black Protestants seem to identify differently according to residence pattern. These findings indicate that a general theory on party identification may not always apply to the sub-societal groups within the United States. While parsimony and generalization remain the aims of theory, exceptions to the rule may speak more accurately to the varying experiences of cultural minorities.

Perhaps the most interesting aspect of our study lies in a comparison of party identification with left-right views. While the most highly educated and the least highly educated groups, white Jews and black Protestants, respectively, support the Democratic party, their motives, on the surface, seem quite consistent. Each of these groups concomitantly holds the most liberal ideological views. Yet another highly liberal group, the college-educated "no religionist," chooses to express its political views in independency. And a more conservative group, the American Catholic, also has married itself to the Democratic party.

How does one make sense of these choices by religious groupings? One theory which seems to shed light on these political choices is the "outgroup" or "minority" explanation of attraction to the Democrats. It offers a reason why three such diverse groups as white Catholics, Jews, and blacks might find shelter under the same political umbrella. Each group at certain times in U.S. history has been discriminated against by the establishment and thus might continue to shy away from the more establishment Republican party.

In conclusion, then, our findings seem to support the historical "outgroup" theories of Democratic party identification.[22] The findings tend to refute the spurious correlate theory, that religion is merely a reflection of other demographic characteristics, and to lend no weight to the hypothesis asserting that as the old ethnic groups suburbanize, the

Catholic Democratic ties will diminish. The findings point out the need for more detailed studies of the distinct minority group political patterns within our society—a task made difficult by the small numbers of such people encountered in national surveys.

If one had been asked twenty years ago whether social, educational, and geographic mobility would have a more negative effect on American Catholics' loyalty to their church or on their loyalty to the Democratic party and the moderate liberalism which had marked their Democratic affiliation, one would probably have guessed that the party would be in trouble and the church would not. In fact, the data in the previous chapter suggest that loyalty to many of the church's teachings and practices has been eroded (data in the next chapter will reveal a sharp increase in apostasy rates). However, neither suburbanization nor economic and educational advancement seems to have had much impact on Catholic loyalty to the Democratic party. Such a phenomenon does not prove that the decline in religious loyalty results from other factors besides acculturation and socioeconomic success, but it at least alerts us to the possibility that something shattering happened to one loyalty and not to the other. When one considers the turmoil that has rocked the Democratic party since the 1968 convention, one must face the possibility that whatever happened to the Catholic church during the last decade may have been cataclysmic indeed.

5

Council or Encyclical?

Before we turn to the central analytic question of this book, the impact of drastic social change on value-oriented education, we must first see whether we can explain the religious change that has occurred in the American Catholic population since the analysis reported in *The Education of Catholic Americans*. It would be difficult to understand the meaning of the change in value-oriented education unless we can first of all explain the change in the values which the education was supposed to produce.

But the social scientists who have begun to work in the area of measuring social change in the past few years have discovered that to explain social change is not as easy as it looks. Most historical generalizations about large population groups do not easily admit to falsification. There is no way in which the hypotheses implicit in the generalization can be proven wrong. If a proposition cannot be falsified, neither can it be verified. It may make logical sense, it may be persuasive, it may even be true; but by the canons of evidence normally used in social science research, it must stand as an unproven hypothesis.

Consider three such propositions: (1) American blacks became politically mobilized *because* of the civil-rights movement; (2) The early immigrants to America from England came *because* of religious persecution; (3) Southerners have turned from Democratic to Republican voting in presidential elections *because* of the Democratic party's stand on the race question.

All three propositions seem plausible. One can detail from historical research the growth of each of the pair of variables involved in the proposition. The civil-rights movement did grow and blacks did become more mobilized politically. (Indeed there was almost a revolution of political activism among American blacks in the 1960s [Sewell 1975].) Religious persecution did increase and the Puritans did come to America. The Democratic party did indeed become more black and did attract a larger proportion of blacks as formal affiliates; and southerners do indeed vote for Republican presidential candidates.

But suppose you are asked to specify the links between the variables in each proposition and then prove them. You would be very hard put to do so. We simply do not know what was in the minds of most of the early immigrants to New England, or what amount of the variance of their behavior could be explained by a desire for religious freedom. Furthermore, as our colleague Ellen Sewell has pointed out in her dissertation on black political mobilization (1975), there is no specific "linkage" evidence between the civil-rights movement and heightened black consciousness on the one hand and heightened black political activism on the other. It could easily be that even if there were such links, the civil-rights movement might be an effect rather than a cause. Finally, it is certainly plausible to argue that many economic and social factors were at work in turning the South away from the Democratic party besides the racial crises of the 1950s and 1960s. It is not our intention here to argue for or against the three propositions we cite as examples. We merely intend to emphasize that both popular and scholarly historical generalizations are easily made and argued but very difficult to "prove," in the sense of establishing linking evidence between the variables involved in the proposition.

By the canons of social science research, most historical generalizations must be pronounced interesting but speculative. It does not follow that historical generalizations should never be made, or even that they might not embody insight and truth. But we must realize that they labor under logical deficiencies and may never be scientifically "proven." If we were restricted only to uttering those generalizations which were relatively free of logical deficiencies, we might just as well go off to a Trappist monastery and spend the rest of our lives in silence.

The only way one could establish certainty about the linkage between two variables in a historical proposition would be to monitor at relatively frequent points in time the attitudes of the same individuals in the population. If, for example, one had a panel of Puritans and interviewed them every year, one could specify a link between their increasing resentment of religious persecution and their decision to board the Mayflower and its sister ships. Longitudinal studies of the sort on which this report is based can provide one with the raw material for tentative generalizations about linkage. They are much less expensive than the panel study (though hardly inexpensive), and they are probably sufficient for most investigations of specific linkages in the change over time between two variables. But when one is working with longitudinal data instead of panel data, one gains moderate confidence about specific linkages only through a number of converging probabilities. It is not infallible as a method, but as a form of historical argumentation, it is much superior to the unfalsifiable, and hence unverifiable, proposition.

In this chapter we hope to specify the links between certain historical events, and the changing attitudes associated with those events, and the general decline in Catholic religious devotion described in the second chapter. Our argument will go considerably beyond the unfalsifiable and hence unverifiable propositions which have served as explanations until now. In fact, we will suggest that the converging probabilities of our argument leave little doubt that the evidence available for our argument does specify links, or at least quasi-specify them. No one is likely to come up with better evidence. The alternative argument to the one we propose will appear highly improbable when we are finished with this chapter. Still, we must caution the reader that only the annual or biennial monitoring of a paneled Catholic population since 1963 would have produced an explanation for the decline in Catholic devotion that left no room for argument. Such a panel never existed.

We do not lack for explanations for the decline in devotion within American Catholicism. They can be subsumed under four models:

1. *The "it would have happened anyway" model.* According to this view, the demographic and educational changes that have taken place in American Catholicism since the end of the Second World War have weakened both the intellectual and organizational structures of the immigrant church as well as the loyalty of Catholics to that church. Catholics are no longer immigrants or even the children of immigrants. They have become more or less acculturated into American society and share the values of the rest of the society. The boundaries of the old Catholic subculture have collapsed. Thus, in an almost classic statement of this position, the American bishops reported to the 1974 International Synod of Bishops in Rome that the greatest challenge for American Catholicism was whether there was to be any difference at all between the values of Catholics and the values of the rest of American society. In the perspective of this model, the Second Vatican Council merely accelerated the changes that would have occurred in any case, given the higher levels of educational attainment of American Catholics and the influx of a younger and thoroughly Americanized generation into the American Catholic population.

2. *The "reaction against the Council" model.* This perspective is argued most vigorously by right-wing Catholic journals such as *The Wanderer*, right-wing Catholic organizations such as Catholics United for the Faith, and is echoed to some extent by more liberal Catholic commentators. They contend

that the Catholic population has been "turned off" by the changes in the church in the last ten years. However favorable their initial reaction might have been to the Second Vatican Council, the endless innovations since its conclusion have annoyed and angered the ordinary Catholic, who has reacted to the unwelcome changes by increasingly disaffiliating himself from the church. This "turn to the right" theory would explain, for example, the decline in Catholic church contributions as a revolt against a church which has changed too rapidly and turned away from its traditional teachings.

3. *The "meat on Friday" model.* From this viewpoint the fundamental mistake of Catholic leadership in the last decade was to permit change at all. Once one part of the tightly integrated structure of immigrant Catholicism was called into question, then everything could be questioned. Once it became legitimate to eat meat on Friday, one could doubt the authority of the pope, practice birth control, leave the priesthood and get married, or, indeed, do anything else one wanted to do. The Second Vatican Council was a well-intended exercise in modernization and liberalization, but in fact it opened a Pandora's box; and those who enthusiastically welcomed the changes of the Council could easily consider themselves to be free from all religious and ecclesiastical obligations. If you turn the altar around and put mass into English, anything goes.

4. *The birth control-encyclical model.* The three previous "explanations" are by no means mutually exclusive. One can hear them argued in various versions, often by the same person (for example, the "neoconservative" commentator, James Hitchcock [1971], or the "neoradical" commentator, Garry Wills [1974] [1]). But all three of these explanations have an assumption in common that the Second Vatican Council was primarily responsible for the decline in Catholic devotion in the United States, either as an accelerating factor or as a direct cause. The Council was operative in antagonizing the Catholic population (as in the second model) or in liberating

it (as in the third). Another explanation would exonerate the Vatican Council from responsibility, arguing that the Council was a successful enterprise in reform which was frustrated in its application by the conspiratorial activities of the Roman Curia after its adjournment, by the vacillating administration of Paul VI, and, especially, by the birth control encyclical, *Humanae Vitae*, issued in 1967 and reaffirming the traditional Catholic birth-control teachings despite widespread expectations to the contrary. After the excitement of the Second Vatican Council, it is argued, there was a tremendous euphoria and expectation for change in the church. It was taken for granted by both the Catholic elite and the Catholic masses that many of the more rigid, restrictive Catholic practices would be modified. Pope John had established a commission for reviewing the birth control issue, and Pope Paul, while explicitly forbidding the Council to discuss the subject, had broadened the commission both in membership and scope. As soon as birth control appeared to become a discussable issue, it automatically ceased to enjoy the status of an immutable doctrine. If one could discuss change, change itself was longer an a priori impossibility. The reaffirmation of the birth control teaching in 1968, it is claimed, had a profoundly disillusioning effect on Catholic clergy, lay elite, and Catholic masses. It created a distaste for and alienation from the ecclesiastical institution. The birth control encyclical, paradoxically enough, was issued to restore faith in the institution, but in fact badly weakened it. It did not prevent Catholics from practicing birth control, and it did not stop the erosion of support for the church's birth control teaching either among the clergy or the laity. Catholics were not only more likely to practice birth control, but were also more likely to do it with a clear conscience. A religious institution which could be so patently wrong on such a critical issue was judged to be wrong, or at least questionable, on a wide range of other, related issues.

The first two models can be rejected rather easily. Before

we turn our attention to the two serious and conflicting explanations subsumed under the labels "Council" and "encyclical," we must observe that it is surely the case, as we demonstrated in chapter 3, that the educational and economic
achievement of the Catholic population has changed notably
since the end of the Second World War. It is also very likely
that these changes have produced a large group of American
Catholics who are thoroughly at home in American society
and who share many of the political, social, and familial values of the larger culture. However, the research done at
NORC on ethnicity leaves little doubt about the persistence
of ethnic subcultures despite educational and occupational
achievement (Greeley 1974). Still, one could concede that the
"Americanization" of the Catholic population might have
created a climate in which the change of the last ten years
became possible. However, it could scarcely be contended that
changes in educational levels caused the change in religious
devotion. The mean Catholic educational achievement has
gone up since 1963, but this is almost entirely the result of
the influx of a younger generation into the population. Those
who were adults ten years ago have not appreciably added to
their educational achievement in the ensuing decade. As we
shall see shortly, changes in religious attitudes and behavior
are by no means the result of the influx of a new age cohort.
There has been a substantial decline in devotion among those
who were adults ten years ago even though their educational
attainment has not changed. In addition, we analyzed the data
to determine whether the educational achievement of the
under-thirty generation "explained" *their* lower levels of religious devotion. It was found that quite low levels of religious
practice were not at all related to superior educational
achievement. As we shall see later, there were other factors at
work that affected the younger generation as well as those
who were adults a decade ago.

The right-wing explanation—disillusionment with a church
that was changing its fundamental teachings—simply will not

stand up in the face of the obvious findings of the present research enterprise. As we mentioned in the second chapter, an overwhelming majority of the Catholic population approves of the individual changes that have occurred in the church as the result of the Second Vatican Council. Indeed, the support for the conciliar changes is quite striking. Catholic practices which had remained fixed for fifteen hundred years were swept away, sometimes in the space of a few months, yet large majority support seems to have been won rather early for such changes. In terms of the successful introduction of dramatic modifications, the Vatican Council seems to have been overwhelmingly successful.

In table 5.1 we see that two-thirds of our respondents endorsed the changes in the church as having been for the better, while less than one-fifth thought they were for the worse. Further, majority support for the changes can be found in all demographic groups except for those whose education did not go beyond the grammar school level. While it is true that older people are less likely than younger ones to support the conciliar changes, nonetheless 60 percent of those over fifty endorsed the changes. Support for change is especially high among the college educated; it comes close to nine-tenths for those who attended Catholic colleges. The argument that the Catholic rank and file is opposed to changes in the church, which is heard from both right-wing integralists and left-wing critics, may tell us far more about those who advance the argument than it does about the present state of American Catholics.

So we are left with two competing explanations, the Council and the encyclical. Of course, the two events cannot be separated completely. The Council undoubtedly created an atmosphere in which more was expected from the encyclical than the pope felt he was able to provide. A reaffirmation of the traditional birth control teaching before the Council might have produced a very different effect; but in the dynamic and euphoric situation that existed in the middle and late 1960s, a

TABLE 5.1

APPROVAL OF THE CHANGES SINCE THE VATICAN COUNCIL (QUESTION 92)

"All in all, as far as you personally are concerned, do
you think the changes in the Church have been for the
better, for the worse, or don't they make much difference one way or the other?"

Better	67%
Worse	19%
Don't make any difference	14%

B.   Percent "Better"

Ethnicity	Percent	Age	Percent	Educational Level	Percent
British	64	20	74	Grammar	42
Irish	71	30s	70	High School	69
German	78	40s	65	College	78
Polish	73	50s	60		
Slavic	75	Catholic Education		College Educated	
Italian	54	0 years	63	Catholic	88
Spanish	59	1-10 years	63	Non-Catholic	80
French	75	10+ years	83		
Sex					
Male	66				
Female	67				

papal announcement on the subject could be another matter
altogether.[2]

So while the Council and the encyclical cannot be completely separated, there is still a different logic involved in the
two models. In the Council model it is contended that the
liberalization of the church created by the Council caused the
Catholic population to question the whole range of official
teachings. In the encyclical model, the questioning of ecclesiastical authority is seen as stemming from a refusal to liberal-

ize. Credibility was lost, in other words, not because certain teachings were changed but because one teaching was not changed.

We begin to piece together the clues for the solution of our mystery by asking what connection there is between support for the changes brought about by the Vatican Council and religious devotion. If the liberalization of the Council caused Catholics to question a broad range of religious obligations and practices, then one would expect that it would be precisely among those who supported liberalization that the decline in religious devotion would most likely occur. If the Council were to blame for the decline in Catholic religious practice, one could logically assume that those who were most pleased with the modifications would be those who would feel most easy in their consciences about making their own modifications. If you approve of the destruction of the old traditional form of the mass, you would, according to the Council model, be most likely to feel dispensed from the obligation of going to mass. If you think it is a good thing for guitar music to be played at sacred worship, it is but an easy step to say that it doesn't make much difference whether you go to mass or not. Similarly, if it doesn't make much difference whether you eat meat on Friday or not, then why should you be enthused at the prospect of your son's becoming a priest? It seems to us that such arguments represent the logic of the conciliar explanation for the decline of Catholic devotion and practice.

Support for all the change items in our questionnaire seemed to cluster. Not surprisingly, if you were for one sort of change, you were more likely to be for all the other changes. We performed a factor analysis, and three different "dimensions" of support for religious change emerged (see Appendix V).

The first cluster of responses we call the "Vatican II" factor. It loads most heavily on the changes instituted by the Council and on the general question of support for the changes in the church (the question presented in table 5.1). A second factor we dubbed "priestly change" because it loaded most heavily on items supporting the ordination of women and the freedom of priests to marry. The items most heavily represented by this factor represent not so much changes which have already occurred as those which the respondents would like to see occur. Finally, the third factor, "new ways," loaded heavily on items dealing with new forms of religious education, the wearing of lay garb by women religious, and the decline of such popular devotions as novenas and benediction of the blessed sacrament. The third factor, it should be noted, gets its strongest contribution from items that deal with changes that have occurred since the Council but are not part of the official reform mandated by the Council.

In table 5.2 we present correlations between these three factors and the ten measures of religious devotion, belief, and practice (see Appendix V for details about the construction of these scales). The conciliar-liberalization explanation for the decline in religious practice would lead us to expect negative correlations between the Second Vatican Council factor and the measures of religious behavior. On the contrary, however, in two cases—sexual orthodoxy and doctrinal orthodoxy—there is no significant relation in either direction. On all other measures the Vatican II factor correlates positively with religious devotion—above .2 for mass attendance, communion reception, and Catholic activity; and above .1 with confession, pleasure at son being a priest, and contributions to the church. If anything, support for the Vatican Council changes seems to lead to higher rather than to lower levels of religious practice, belief, and devotion.

There are, however, negative relationships between the priestly change and the new ways factors, which suggest that while approval for present changes does not lead to lower levels of devotion, support for more changes does, a finding not inconsistent with the encyclical explanation. This suggests that

TABLE 5.2

CORRELATIONS BETWEEN ATTITUDES ON CHURCH CHANGES
AND RELIGIOUS ATTITUDES AND BEHAVIOR

	Vatican II	Priestly Change	New Ways
Mass attendance	.20	ns*	−.15
Communion reception	.21	ns*	−.15
Confession	.12	−.12	−.20
Prayer	.09	−.10	−.19
Acceptance of Church's right to teach	.09	−.09	−.10
Catholic Activity	.20	ns*	−.16
Sexual orthodoxy	ns*	−.30	−.27
Doctrinal orthodoxy	ns*	−.18	−.17
Pleasure at son being a priest	.13	ns*	−.14

*ns = correlation not statistically significant

it is not so much change as the frustration of expectations for more change which produces religious alienation. Finally, somewhere between those changes that were officially endorsed by the Council and those which have not yet occurred are the changes represented by the new ways factor. Support for these changes does correlate negatively at moderately high levels with religious belief and practice.

Since both the priestly and the new ways factors correlate with youthfulness and since young people are much less likely than older people to be orthodox in their belief and practice, the correlations in the second two columns of table 5.2 may be spurious, indicating merely that the more youthful respondents support a wide variety of changes indiscriminantly and feel much more relaxed about religious obligations. Holding age constant, we see in table 5.3 that seven of the fourteen correlations of the priestly change and new ways factors in table 5.2 lose their statistical significance. Those who support more changes in the church and who approve nuns' wearing lay garb, lay administration of communion, and new methods of religious instruction are likely to score lower on measures of sexual and doctrinal orthodoxy than are those who are opposed to such changes. Those who are high on the new ways factor are also less likely to attend mass, to go to confession, and to pray daily than those who are opposed to such changes—even when age is held constant.

TABLE 5.3

"SIGNIFICANT" PARTIAL CORRELATIONS WITH "PRIESTLY CHANGE"
AND "NEW WAYS" FACTORS (AGE HELD CONSTANT)

	Priestly change	New Ways
Mass attendance	ns	−.10
Confession	ns	−.17
Prayer	ns	−.15
Sexual orthodoxy	−.24	−.21
Doctrinal orthodoxy	−.16	−.15

There is, then, no evidence that the officially mandated reforms of the Second Vatican Council have produced lower levels of religious devotion. On the contrary, those who favor the conciliar changes are higher on all our measures of belief and practice. Those who want more change, and whose desire for change has been frustrated, are less likely to be orthodox in belief and practice—a finding consistent with the encyclical model. The only ambivalent evidence discovered thus far is a negative relationship between the new ways factor and orthodoxy in belief and devotion. These relationships tell us nothing about a direct relationship between the conciliar change and religious decline, though the very high correlation between these two factors and the sexual orthodoxy scale suggests that the people high on both the priestly change and the new ways factors may be lower on our measures of religious belief and practice precisely because they are committed not only to the changes that have occurred but to more changes and feel frustrated because these changes have not occurred.

In summary, then, while the data do not exonerate the Vatican Council from blame for the decline in religious devotion among American Catholics in the last decade, they at least force us to bring in the old Scotch legal verdict of "not proved" on the Second Vatican Council. The Council may indeed have created an environment wherein certain changes have occurred and others have been expected, which in itself correlates negatively with religious practice. But these relationships suggest that the problems have arisen in the time since the Council and not because of the Council itself. Certainly the positive relationship between support for the Council changes and religious belief and practice would suggest that, whatever has happened since the Council, the Council itself does not seem to have directly caused a religious decline. Whether the decline was indirectly caused by the Council through its impact on subsequent events in the church or whether a subsequent event itself is indeed the primary cause is a question which must remain open at this point in our discussion. Of course, the most important of the postconciliar events was the encyclical letter *Humanae Vitae*. To investigate the impact of this event on Catholic beliefs and practice in the United States, we must now turn to formal social change analysis.

When a change is observed in a population group between 'A and 'A + n, one of two phenomena, or a combination of both, may have occurred. The change may be the result of the influx into the population of a new generation, who entered the age span being studied between the first collection of data and the second. The change in American Catholics, in other words, could be the result of the infusion of a very different young generation into the adult population in the last decade. Furthermore, just as young people become adults, older people die. The devout may have died, the less devout may have become adult—and the entire change phenomenon would then be a matter of what is technically called "cohort replacement."

Or it might be that the new cohort is not much different from its predecessors, and that the decline in church devotion, for example, is evenly distributed throughout the adult population.

Finally, it could be the case that the two phenomena are going on simultaneously. Cohort replacement may be bringing into the population a new age group quite different in its religious behavior from its predecessors, but changes may also be occurring in the religious behavior of those who were adults a decade ago. These changes might be going on at different rates among the different adult cohorts.

Recent social change research provides an example of each of these processes. A study by Norman Nie, John Petrocik, and Sidney Verba (1975) shows that most of the increase in the number of "independents" in the American political affiliation schema results from cohort replacement. The generation that has come of political age in the last decade is far more likely to be independent than its predecessors, but those who were adults before the early 1960s have not abandoned their traditional party affiliations to any great extent. On the other hand, the change in attitudes toward civil liberties documented by James Davis (1972a, 1972b) involved not merely cohort replacement but actual change in adult population groups. It is not merely that the younger generation is more liberal than its predecessors, but also that the predecessor groups are becoming more liberal themselves.

Social change analysis, then, begins with the framework of age cohorts moving through the population and slowly declining through attrition while younger age groups replace them by moving into adult years. Within this paradigm, one attempts to explain the change going on by investigating the change in various subpopulations. Thus Davis asked in his analysis if the growth in tolerance for dissent in the United States over the last twenty years might be attributed to the changing educational composition of the population. If the well educated are more tolerant, and if this correlation does not change between time 1 and time 2, and if there is an increase in the proportion in the population that is well educated, then there will certainly be an increase in toleration. One must then determine to what extent the total increase in population can be explained by the change in the population's educational composition. Davis's finding, incidentally, was that the correlation between education and tolerance had not only held constant but had increased in the two-decade period he was analyzing. Toleration had increased in all educational groups during the time analyzed, so the increase in educational achievement in the American population did not fully explain the increased levels of toleration.

The mathematical manipulations involved in this kind of analysis are complex. Fortunately for us, Davis and his colleagues have devised a logic, a mathematical technique, and a computer program for coping with these complexities. Those who are interested in details should consult the Davis articles (1972a, 1972b).

For the purposes of our analysis we divided the Catholic population into four cohorts and named them according to events which marked their coming to maturity (table 5.4). These were a Depression cohort (those born between 1901 and 1924), a World War II cohort (born between 1925 and 1934), a Cold War cohort (born between 1935 and 1943), and a Vietnam cohort (born between 1944 and 1954). The first three cohorts were interviewed in both the 1963 and 1974 samples, while the Vietnam cohort was interviewed only in 1974. The cutoff age for interviews in the 1963 research was sixty, ·so most of the cohort replacement involved the addition of the Vietnam cohort, since the mortality rate in the Depression cohort has not yet drastically reduced it. Finally, it should be noted once again that we have not interviewed the same people in 1974 that we did in 1963. We assume that those interviewed from the World War II cohort in 1963 were a representative sample of the population between the ages of thirty and thirty-nine at that time; and that those interviewed from the same cohort in 1974 were a representative sample of that age cohort at the time of the second interview. If there is a change in mass attendance among the World War II cohort between 1963 and 1974 (table 5.5), one can say that some members of that population group who were going to church in 1963 are not going in 1974; but one cannot say which specific members account for that change.

TABLE 5.4

COHORTS AMONG AMERICAN CATHOLICS

Title	Born	Age in 1963	Age in 1974
Cold War	1944-54	(not interviewed)	20-30
World War II	1935-43	20-29	30-39
Depression	1925-34	30-39	40-49
World War I	1905-24	40-60	50-70

The trick, then, is to find some intervening variable which has the same relationship in 1963 with mass attendance, for example, as it does in 1974. If the relationship has not changed and if the score of a population group has gone down on the intervening variable, then some of the change in the dependent variable can be accounted for by the change in the prior variable. If the relationship between acceptance of the church's sexual ethic, for example, and attendance at mass is the same in both periods of time and if both sexual orthodoxy and mass attendance have declined, then the change in the sexual ethic explains some proportion of the change in mass attendance. (Or, should one choose to build the model in the opposite direction, some proportion of the decline in sexual orthodoxy can be accounted for by the decline in mass attendance.)

TABLE 5.5

CHANGES IN VARIABLES BETWEEN 1963 AND 1974

(Percent)

	1963	1974	Difference
Mass attendance weekly	71	50	−21
Very pleased with son a priest	66	50	−16
Orthodoxy Scale[a]	45	22	−23
Daily prayer	72	60	−12
Monthly confession	37	17	−20
Active Catholic Scale[b]	45	31	−14
Sexual Orthodoxy[c]	42	18	−24

[a]Two or more items on scale composed of "definite proof of God's existence," "evil punished for all eternity," "God cares about how He is worshipped."

[b]Four or more items on scale composed of conversation with priest, frequent communion, above average contribution to the Church, frequent prayer, Catholic TV, Catholic magazines, Catholic books.

[c]Accepts Church's position on two items (divorce, birth control, pre-marital sex).

In the change analysis we are now attempting, we begin by asking what proportion of the change in our indicators of religious belief and practice can be linked to the decline in the church's sexual ethic? We found little evidence to justify our attributing the decline of Catholic belief and practice to the Second Vatican Council. If it turns out that the "linkage" between the decline in sexual orthodoxy and the decline in the indicators of religious practice and belief was substantial, the encyclical explanation for such decline would gain credence.

In Fig. 5.1 we present a change model based on the linear flow approach to the analysis of social change. The coefficients on the paths of the chart are partialled percentage differences. Those who are high on sexual orthodoxy are 33 percentage points more likely to go to mass every week than those who are not high. The Vietnam cohort is 19 percentage points less likely to go to mass than the Depression cohort. (The comparisons in a "Catfit" model like Fig. 5.1 are always with a base category that is excluded from the figure.) The Cold War cohort is 8 percentage points lower on the sexual ethic scale than the Depression cohort, and the World War II cohort is actually 2 percentage points higher on the sexual ethic score than its predecessor. There has been a 35 percentage point decline in sexual orthodoxy between 1963 and 1974. The World War II cohort is 19 percentage points less in the total population than it was a decade ago, and the Cold War cohort is 1 percentage point less. This decline is explained not so much by an actual decline in the size of those two population groups (since the number of people who have died in the last decade in those two groups is relatively small), as by the movement into adulthood of the Vietnam cohort, which is now 35 percent of the Catholic population under the age of 70. Finally, the "pure" relationship between time and mass attendance is only 1 percent, since mass attendance has in fact declined by 23 percentage points since 1963. We conclude that our social change model can explain 22 percentage points (or 95 percent) of the change in church attendance in the last decade—an almost embarrassingly successful social science venture.

The "Catfit" program will detect "interactions" and tell the analyst whether the relationship between, let us say, the Depression cohort and sexual orthodoxy or sexual orthodoxy and mass attendance has changed "significantly" between 1963 and 1974. Where no statistically significant change has occurred in the relationship, the program pools the relationship at the two points in time and provides a stable coeffi-

122

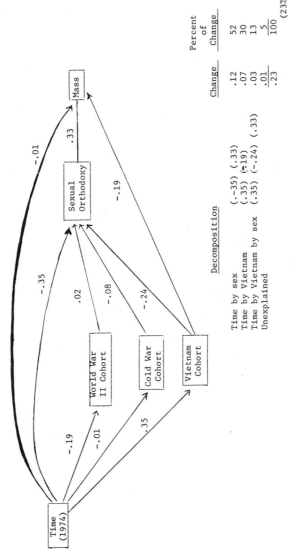

Figure 5.1—Change Model, 1963-1974, for Mass Attendance by Cohort and by Sex Orthodoxy (23 Percent Decline in Mass Attendance)

cient that represents the link between the two variables. Fortunately for our attempts to make this process something less than completely obscure, there has been no significant change between cohorts and sexual orthodoxy or between sexual orthodoxy and mass attendance (or any of our other dependent variables) in the last decade. The internal parameters of our model, in other words, have remained stable.

With the construction of a change model of the sort depicted in Fig. 5.1, it becomes a relatively easy matter to decompose the percentage point differences. One simply estimates the "transmittances," that is to say, multiplies each path by all prior paths in the model. A "transmittance" is the total effect of an earlier variable on a later or dependent variable—i.e., the amount the later variable would increase per unit increase in the earlier variable. (For example, if the transmittance from X to Y is .50, this means that a 1 percent increase in the proportion X would be followed by a .5 percent increase in Y.) To find the transmittance, one traces out all "arrow" paths from X to Y, multiplying the coefficients along each path, and then sums these "path values." There are three important transmittances in Fig. 5.1, time by sex, time by Vietnam cohort (the younger generation), and time by Vietnam cohort by sex. Twelve percentage points of the 23 percentage points of mass attendance change can be linked to the change in sexual orthodoxy in the last decade. Seven percentage points of the change can be attributed purely to the influx of the Vietnam cohort, with lower levels of mass attendance, into the adult population, and 3 percentage points more can be attributed to the lower scores on sexual orthodoxy of the Cold War cohort. In other words, some 65 percent of the change in mass attendance in the last decade is linked to a change in the sexual orthodoxy of the Catholic population.[3]

There is, then, a strong linkage between the decline in church attendance and the decline in sexual orthodoxy among American Catholics. Furthermore, the decline in acceptance of the church's sexual ethic is strongly related to the decline in happiness over the possibility of a son's being a priest (80 percent of that change, including indirect transmittance through cohort replacement, being linked to the change in sexual orthodoxy), daily prayer (70 percent), monthly confession (59 percent), and Catholic activism (59 percent). Furthermore, our social change model involving cohort replacement and change in sexual attitudes is quite successful in accounting for the decline in Catholic religiousness since 1963. In each of the five variables mentioned in table 5.6, the model accounts for at least 70 percent of the change, and in three of the variables—wanting son to be priest, daily prayer, and Catholic activism—it accounts for all the changes.

In theory the causal flow could go in either direction. Because one was attending church less frequently, praying less, going to confession less often, less pleased at the thought of one's son becoming a priest, one might be more likely to think there was nothing wrong with birth control or divorce. However, it is much more likely that the causal flow will be in the opposite direction, that the decline in the acceptance of the sexual ethic and the decline in happiness over a son's becoming a priest are linked together to some more basic alienation from Catholicism. But whatever the structure of that alienation is, it is clear from table 5.6 that it is strongly linked to the decline of sexual orthodoxy.

What might this more general alienation be? The most obvious explanation would be that the church's credibility as a teacher with the right to impose obligations on its members has been called into question. Such deterioration of credibility could be either general or specific, however. It might be linked to a fundamental rejection of the church's right to teach, or it might be more specifically linked to a decline in the credibility of the papacy. If the first possibility turned out to be true, then we would be forced to review the credibility of the Council model. But if the latter is the case, and the deterioration is linked to a lack of credibility of the papacy, we will give still more credence to our encyclical explanation.

TABLE 5.6

EXPLANATION OF CHANGES IN RELIGIOUS ATTITUDES AND BEHAVIOR BY COHORT AND SEX ATTITUDE MODEL

(Percent)

Change Due to Cohort Replacement	Weekly Church	Pleased With Son a Priest	Daily Prayer	Confession	Active Catholic
Direct	30	23	30	14	41
Indirect (through sex orthodoxy change)	13	17	20	14	11
Change Due to Change in Sex Orthodoxy	52	60	50	45	48
Unaccounted by Model	5	0	0	27	0
Total	100	100	100	100	100

To test these alternate possibilities, we used two items that were asked of our respondents in both 1963 and 1974. The first deals with the church's right to teach on matters of racial integration (table 5.7), and the other, with whether "Jesus directly handed over the leadership of his Church to Peter and the popes." Racial integration is a controversial subject on which the church has spoken very explicitly in the last decade. As we noted earlier, even though Catholics have become more racially tolerant, they have also declined in their willingness to concede the church's right to dictate their attitude on racial matters. Such decline would seem to be a reasonable indicator of deterioration of the church's general credibility as a teacher. On the other hand, acceptance of the pope as successor to Peter as the Christ-appointed leader of the church would seem to be a reasonable indicator of papal credibility.[4]

While there has been a decline in the willingness of Catholics to accept the church as teacher, this decline does not account for much of the deterioration on other measures of religious behavior and practice (table 5.8). Indeed, only about 5 percent of the changes in the six variables we are analyzing can be explained by the decline in general teaching credibility, as measured by the church's right to teach on racial matters.

However, when acceptance of the pope as successor to Peter and head of the church is introduced into the change model, a substantial difference occurs (table 5.9). The percentage of change in dependent variables accounted for by a change in belief in papal leadership is 32 percent for mass (including the indirect transmittance of cohort replacement), 43 percent for happiness with a son's becoming a priest, 32 percent for daily prayer, 22 percent for confession, and 29 percent for the active Catholic scale. When we look at sexual orthodoxy with the addition of the papal leadership variable, we see that the "explanatory power" of sexual orthodoxy shown on table 5.6 decreases on table 5.9—20 percentage points for mass attendance, 13 percentage points for happiness at son being a priest, 17 percentage points on daily prayer, 4 per-

TABLE 5.7

CHANGES IN ATTITUDE TOWARD CHURCH AUTHORITY

(Percent)

	1963	1974	Change
Church has a right to teach on racial integration (% "yes")	49	37	12
Jesus directly handed over the leadership of his Church to Peter and the popes (% "certainly true")	70	42	28

TABLE 5.8

EXPLANATION OF CHANGES IN RELIGIOUS ATTITUDES AND BEHAVIOR BY MODEL OF COHORT, SEX ORTHODOXY CHANGE AND DECLINE IN TEACHING AUTHORITY AS MEASURED BY RACIAL TEACHING

(Percent)

	Mass	Pleased with Son a Priest	Daily Prayer	Confession	Active Catholic	Contribution
Cohort Replacement						
Direct	29	23	25	14	41	23
Indirect (through sex orthodoxy change)	14	14	20	14	9	6
Sex orthodoxy change	47	57	50	40	46	23
Race teaching decline	5	6	5	5	4	5
Unaccounted by model	5	0	0	27	0	43
Total	100	100	100	100	100	100

TABLE 5.9

EXPLANATION OF CHANGE IN RELIGIOUS ATTITUDES AND BEHAVIOR BY MODEL OF COHORT, SEXUAL ORTHODOXY CHANGE AND PAPAL BELIEF CHANGE

(Percent)

	Mass	Pleased with Son a Priest	Daily Prayer	Confession	Active Catholic
Cohort Replacement					
Direct	20	7	30	9	24
Indirect (through sex orthodoxy change)	12	3	5	14	5
Indirect through pope change	5	3	7	4	5
Sex orthodoxy change	34	47	33	41	42
Pope change	29	40	25	18	24
Unaccounted by model	0	0	0	14	0
Total	100	100	100	100	100

centage points on the confession scale, and 6 percentage points on the active Catholic scale. In other words, change in sexual attitudes and change in attitudes toward the pope are closely linked in accounting for the decline of Catholic religiousness.

We can therefore make the following conclusions:

1. The decline in Catholic behavior and practice is linked to the decline in acceptance of papal leadership.

2. The decline in the acceptance of papal leadership is linked to the decline of the acceptance of the church's sexual ethic. For the purposes of the present phase of our argument, it does not matter which way the causality flows—whether the decline in the acceptance of the sexual ethic has led to a decline in papal credibility or vice versa; nor is it necessary to assert that all the change in the acceptance of papal leadership is explained by the change in acceptance of sexual teaching or vice versa. (In fact, the correlation between the two in the Catfit model is about .25 in both directions.) All that matters here is that there is a link between the two variables and that the two, both independently and jointly, are linked to the decline in Catholic belief and practice since 1963.

3. When the papal variable is introduced into the change model, it replaces some of the "explanatory power" of the sexual orthodoxy variable. The decline in Catholic religiousness, in other words, is in part the result of a joint decline in acceptance of the pope as leader in the church and acceptance of the church's sexual ethic.

We have obviously tilted quite far toward the encyclical explanation as opposed to the Council explanation. We could find no evidence to link the Council to the decline in Catholic belief and practice; we found substantial evidence linking that decline to a rejection of the church's sexual ethic and to erosion of the credibility of papal leadership. In the absence of panel data, we cannot say with absolute certainty that people first begin to be less happy about the possibility of their son's becoming a priest and to pray less frequently and then turn against the Catholic sexual ethic and papal credibility. But the probabilities seem high that the causality flows in the opposite direction: one disagrees with the church's sexual teaching, rejects the authority of the leader who attempts to reassert that teaching, and then becomes alienated from other dimensions of religious belief and practice.

Whatever the causal flow may be, there is nothing in our evidence to suggest that the Council caused a change in Catholic religious practice and a great deal to suggest that the birth control encyclical caused the decline. Indeed, the evidence in favor of this latter explanation is very strong.

There is another test that we can make. No questions were asked in 1963 about conciliar changes, because none of them had yet been implemented. However, our respondents were asked whether they would support the reform in which the mass would be said in English. We thus had measures in both points in time of attitudes toward the English liturgy, although the wording is necessarily different, since one question was asked before the fact and the other after. We can also separate two of the three components of the sexual orthodoxy scale—attitudes toward divorce and attitudes toward birth control. If these three variables are put into a social change model (leaving out cohorts for the sake of simplicity), we can compare the impact on religious practice and behavior at both points in time of conciliar change for those sexual attitudes not linked explicitly with *Humanae Vitae* and for those sexual attitudes about which *Humanae Vitae* was written.

Figure 5.2 shows this second model, Social Change Model II, as applied to the decline in mass attendance. There is virtually no change between 1963 and 1974 in support for the English liturgy (85 percent at one time point and 87 percent at the other), and only a small positive relationship between support for the English liturgy and mass attendance. Furthermore, there is no statistically significant relationship between support for the English liturgy and the other three variables in

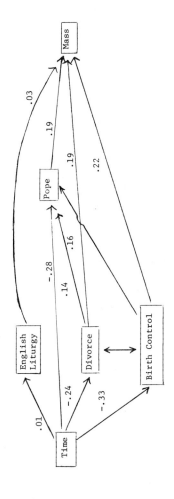

Decomposition of Mass Change

Birth Control	48%
Divorce	26
Pope	26
English Liturgy	0
Unaccounted for	0

Decomposition of Change in
Attitude toward Pope

Divorce	11%
Birth Control	25
English Liturgy	0
Unaccounted for	64

Figure 5.2--Social Change Model II, 1963-1974, Religious Behavior by Attitude toward the Papacy by Mass in English, Divorce, and Birth Control

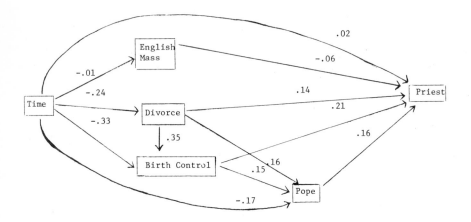

Figure 5.3--Social Change Model II with Support for Son's Vocation to Priesthood as Dependent Variable (Sexual Attitudes Influence Attitudes toward Pope)

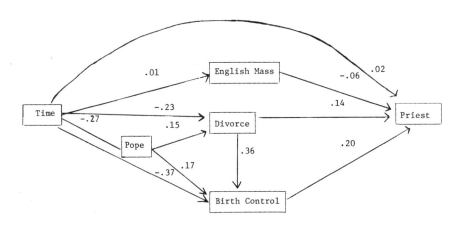

Figure 5.4--Social Change Model II with Support for Son's Vocation to Priesthood as Dependent Variable (Attitudes toward Pope Influence Sexual Attitudes)

the model. Hence none of the decline in church attendance can be attributed either directly or indirectly to the English liturgy. If one assumes that divorce and birth control changes have influenced the decline in willingness to accept the leadership of the pope, then 36 percent of this latter decline can be accounted for by the two prior variables. (One can make the opposite assumption with no change in the ultimate conclusions of the model.) Finally, *all* of the decline in mass attendance can be accounted for by Social Change Model II—48 percent attributable to birth control change, 26 percent to change in divorce attitudes, and 26 percent to change in attitudes about papal leadership.

There is also a small positive change in support for a priestly vocation for one's son (Fig. 5.3) once the divorce-birth control-pope system is held constant. Instead of a decline of 16 percentage points in the proportion "very pleased" with a son's vocation, there would have been an increase of two percentage points had it not been for the changes associated with birth control and divorce. One can assume further that the papal attitude change caused the change in the other two variables in the subsystem (Fig. 5.4) without affecting the outcome of the model. Sixteen percent of the decline in divorce opposition would be explained by decreased willingness to accept the papal leadership, and 14 percent of the decline in birth control opposition would also be explained. However, it seems far more probable that the model in Fig. 5.3 represents the major direction of the causal flow.

Applying Social Change Model II to prayer, confession, and Catholic activism (table 5.10), we find that change in birth control attitudes accounts for 30 percent of the decline in daily prayer, 38 percent of the decline in monthly confession, and 42 percent of the decline in Catholic activism, while divorce change accounts for a third of the decline in prayer, 16 percent of the decline in confession, and 29 percent of the decline in activism. It should be noted that the nature of the model is such that these relationships are *net*; that is, they represent the influence of a change in birth control attitudes, taking into account any related or overlapping change in divorce attitudes.

The change in birth control thinking, then, is clearly the most important factor at work in the decline of Catholic devotion and practice during the last decade, with related declines in divorce attitudes and respect for the papacy combining with birth control to account for *all* of the deterioration in mass attendance, support for a priestly vocation in one's family, and Catholic activism. In the remaining two cases (prayer and confession), the model accounts for most of the change; only 12 percent of the change in daily prayer and 30 percent of the change in monthly confession cannot be attributed to the factors at work in the model.

None of the change is attributable to the English liturgy— the only available measure of attitude toward the Second Vatican Council at both points in time.

It is worth noting that the model accounts for *all* of the change in four of the five variables. Indeed, positive paths appear between time and weekly mass attendance (4/10 of 1 percent), support for a vocation for one's son (2 percent), daily prayer (3 percent), and Catholic activism (8 percent). The presence of such a positive path means that if it had not been for changes in sexual attitudes and attitudes toward the papacy, the proportion of those "very pleased" at the prospect of a son's becoming a priest would have gone up from 65 percent to 67 percent instead of down to 50 percent. The proportion praying every day would have risen from 72 to 75 percent instead of falling to 60 percent, and the proportion high on the Catholic activism scale would have risen from 45 percent to 53 percent instead of falling to 31 percent.

There was, in other words, a dynamic built into the events of the last decade which would have led to an increase in Catholic religiousness had there not been a deterioration in the sexual ethic and in support for the papacy. Given the positive response to the changes instituted by the Second Vatican

TABLE 5.10

CHANGE IN RELIGIOUS ATTITUDES AND BEHAVIOR 1963–1974 AS ACCOUNTED FOR BY SOCIAL CHANGE MODEL II

(Percent)

	Mass	Support for Son a Priest	Daily Prayer	Monthly Confession	Catholic Activism
Percent accounted for by English liturgy	0	0	0	0	0
Percent accounted for by change in divorce attitudes	26	19	33	16	29
Percent accounted for by change in birth control attitudes	48	56	30	38	42
Percent accounted for by change in attitudes toward pope	26	25	25	16	29
Percent unaccounted for by the model	0	0	12	30	0
Total change	100	100	100	100	100

Council, it is not unreasonable to assume that the Council is at least in part connected with such a dynamic. Or to put the matter more bluntly, it is very likely that if it had not been for the positive dynamic introduced by the Council, the deterioration analyzed in this chapter would have been even worse.

In order to separate the positive dynamic, which is associated with the frequency of communion reception and is linked to the Council, from the negative dynamic, which is associated with the decline in sexual orthodoxy and support for the pope, we developed Social Change Model III. The three "internal" variables—the advent of the cohort under thirty, the decline in acceptance of papal leadership, and the decline in sexual orthodoxy—represent the negative dynamic. The direct path from time represents the positive dynamic, if it is positive. When the increased weekly reception of communion is put into the model, it should lead to a decline in both the direct path from time and the indirect path through the three internal variables if increased reception of communion represents a positive dynamic at work. The net change must be whatever the actual decline in the variable being measured has been over time.

If we apply this test to the active Catholic scale (table 5.11), we see that without the influence of communion reception, the changes "internal" to the model would have led to a decline of 21 percentage points between 1963 and 1974 (from 45 to 24 percent). (This is 1½ times greater than the actual decline, which is why the "total" decline in table 5.11 equals 150 percent.) In fact, however, the positive force attributed to the change over time attenuates the decline so that instead of a 21 percentage point drop, there is only a 14 percent decline in the active Catholic scale, a decline that is linked to the encyclical *Humanae Vitae* and that was cancelled out by a positive force also at work during this time period (Fig. 5.5). The extent to which this positive force is linked with the increased reception of communion and thus to the effects of the Council can be judged by what happens to the positive path from time when communion is introduced into the model. If the positive path declines, it means that the increase in communion reception accounts for proportionately more of the positive force mentioned above.

In fact, the positive path does decline; it vanishes at zero when communion reception is brought into the model (table 5.11). In other words, the increase in communion reception accounts for all of the positive dynamic at work in Social Change Model III. Therefore, if the Second Vatican Council

TABLE 5.11

ACTIVE CATHOLIC SCALE AND SOCIAL CHANGE MODEL III

(Total Decline = 14%)

i. With Increase in Communion Reception Left Out

Explained by change in attitude toward pope	-.028	- 20%
Explained by change in sexual attitudes	.144	-102%*
Explained by new cohort	.038	- 27%
Total decline attributed to changes in sex and pope attitudes and cohort change	-21.0	-150%*
Explained by change over time	.700	50%
Actual total change	- .140	100%

ii. With Increase in Communion Reception Put In

Total Total explained by sex, pope, and generation	- .140	100%
Direct path from time	.000	000%
Total Change	- .140	100%

*The "internal" percentages of Table 5.11 - i add to more than 100 because the decline would have been greater if it had not been for the increase in activism over time.

138

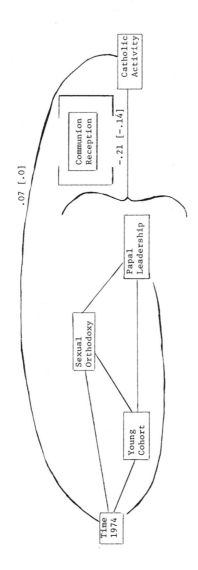

*The statistic in brackets indicates relationship when weekly reception of Holy Communion is placed in the model.

Figure 5.5--Social Change Model III with the Impact of Frequent Reception of Communion*

had been the sole force at work from 1963 to 1974, the proportion above the mean on Catholic activism would have risen 7 points (from 45 to 52 percent). If, on the other hand, the encyclical *Humanae Vitae* had been the sole force, that same proportion would have declined 21 points (from 45 to 24 percent). What actually happened was that the two forces operated simultaneously. The larger, negative force of the encyclical masked the smaller, positive force of the Council; but the Council had the effect of attentuating the larger, negative influence of the encyclical by about one-third.[5]

Left to itself the Council would have led to an increase of about one-sixth in Catholic religious practice. Left to itself the encyclical would have led to a decline of almost one-half. The net result is a decline of almost one-third as far as the active Catholic scale is concerned. Far from causing the problems of the contemporary American Catholic church, the Council prevented them from becoming worse.[6]

But did not the Council prepare for a hostile reception of the encyclical? If there had been no Second Vatican Council, would not the Catholic population have been much more likely to accept the papal decision made by *Humanae Vitae*? At first this seems a reasonable and plausible assumption. However, it may misjudge how well aware the typical American Catholic was of the "new spirit" generated in the church by the Council. For most Catholics, it seems safe to assume, the Council was not a matter of central concern in their daily lives. It was an interesting and colorful event, no doubt, but they were not listening very closely to the arguments that went on about the nature of authority in the church. It may be that their expectations on the subject of birth control, an issue that was of central concern to many, were raised somewhat by the conciliar atmosphere only to be more decisively shattered by the encyclical. Yet it seems very likely that, regardless of the Council, the opening up and then the closing down of the birth control question would have produced much the same impact that it did. Furthermore, research done by Westoff and his colleagues at Princeton (Westoff and Bumpass 1973) has shown that changes in birth control practice were going on among Catholics long before the Council and would most likely have continued no matter what happened at any meeting of bishops in Rome. Quite simply, the invention of the birth control pill called for a formal decision. That decision was made, and the Council was irrelevant to the issue, save, perhaps, for generating more publicity about decision-making in the church.

In 1965, 77 percent of Catholic women under forty-five were practicing some form of conception control, 28 percent of whom were using the church-approved rhythm method. Five years later, after the encyclical, there was only a 4 percentage point increase in those using conception control (up to 81 percent), but a decline of half in those using the rhythm method (down to 14 percent). The proportion using the pill went up from 12 percent to 28 percent; and the proportion using other methods besides the pill and rhythm remained unchanged at 37 percent for the five-year period. All of the increased nonconformity involved the use of the pill, and much of it resulted from the replacement of rhythm by the pill. It would appear that a large number of Catholic women made up their minds in the late 1960s that the pill was more effective than the rhythm method and no less immoral. Indeed, the women who were using the pill in the late 1960s were *more* likely to receive communion at least once a month than those who practiced rhythm or no method of birth control. Twenty-six percent of the former group received communion once a month as opposed to 23 percent of the latter group, and among those under thirty, 37 percent of the pill users were receiving monthly communion, as opposed to 18 percent of the rhythm users and 15 percent of the no birth control group.

An additional piece of evidence of a change in attitude in the late 1960s can be found in the dramatic increase in monthly reception of communion by pill users. While only 11

percent received monthly communion in 1965, 25 percent did
so five years later. For those under thirty the proportion of
monthly communicants among pill users increased from 20
percent to 37 percent (Westoff and Bumpass 1973:179-80).

At just about the time *Humanae Vitae* was being drafted
(desperate last-minute efforts were being made to stop it,
according to Vatican rumors current at the time), a substantial segment of American Catholic women were making decisions contrary to the pope's: the pill was not sinful, and its
use was not an obstacle to reception of the sacraments. As
Westoff and Bumpass note (1973:41), "It seems clear that the
papal encyclical has not retarded the increasing defection of
Catholic women from this teaching." Presumably they would
have made such a decision with or without *Humanae Vitae*.
The encyclical apparently did not impede their decision or reverse it. One can only speculate on whether it may have been
counterproductive of its explicit intent and may actually have
led to an increase in the use of the pill by women who were
angry and disappointed by it.

In any case the development of the pill created a new moral situation which the church would have had to deal with
whether or not there had been a Vatican Council. Between
1960 and 1965 (before the end of the Vatican Council), the
use of unapproved forms of birth control had increased
among American Catholics from 38 percent to 51 percent,
with almost all of the change during those years being
accounted for by the invention of the pill. The change in the
second half of the decade was, as we have noted, almost entirely the result of a switch from rhythm to the pill. Until
1968 this change had rather little impact on religious practice,
as we shall see shortly. It was only after the encyclical that
weekly church attendance began to drop precipitously. The
Second Vatican Council did not produce the birth control
pill; it did not lead Catholic women to use it before 1965;
and it can hardly be said to have caused more to use it after
1965. Perhaps all the Council did was to give women more

confidence about receiving communion even when they were using the pill. Thus the Council did not lead to a decline in religious practice but allowed women to continue to accept the sacraments who otherwise would not.

The Council and the pill, then, are relatively unrelated phenomena save for the fact that the Council may have mitigated the negative effect that the birth control decision apparently has had on religious practice.

In our initial proposal for this research, it did not even occur to us to mention the encyclical as an important factor. We proposed a study of the impact of the Second Vatican Council on Catholic education. That the impact was not of the Council but of the birth control encyclical was a thought forced on us by the data. Indeed, we are willing to admit considerable surprise at the power of the "tilt" of the data in the direction of the encyclical. Rarely in social research does one find results as clean and decisive as those presented in table 5.11.

We attempted one final test. We asked the 1974 respondents how close they thought they were to the church on a five-point scale. Then we asked them how close they thought they had been ten years ago. Thirty-five percent put themselves in the two highest categories today, while 61 percent placed themselves in those categories a decade ago—a decline of 26 percentage points. If one creates a scale by subtracting the present location from the one a decade ago, one gets a measure of perceived decline in church relatedness among the 1974 respondents. One can then correlate that decline with the variables in the social change model. The relationships will be much smaller because we are only measuring present attitudes on the model variables, but we will at least be able to see the relationship between present attitudes and perceived change (table 5.12).

The correlations in table 5.12 are "net," that is, they represent the "pure relationship" between the given variable and decline in closeness to the church, with the intercorrelations among the four filtered out. Support for the conciliar changes

TABLE 5.12

NET CORRELATIONS ("BETA") BETWEEN DECLINE IN
"CLOSENESS" TO THE CHURCH AND VARIABLES
IN THE SOCIAL CHANGE MODEL II

Support for Vatican II	-.20
Divorce attitude	.01
Birth control attitude	.14
Attitude toward pope as head of the Church	.05

correlates *negatively* with decline in closeness to the church at a reasonably high level (-.20). This means that those who support the Council are less likely to see their church relatedness as declining, and suggests that if it had not been for the Council the decline in Catholic church practice might have been greater than in fact it actually is. The other three variables all relate positively to the decline, with approval for birth control being by far the strongest predictor (.14). Thus the explanation presented in the Social Change Model II is confirmed by our 1974 respondents' self-perception: The Council brought you closer to the church, birth control takes you farther away from it. (The correlation between the sexual orthodoxy index and present position is -.26, and between support for the Council and present position is .25.)

The argument we have presented has been complex. The reality of the human condition is rarely simple, and while longitudinal data does provide us with a very powerful tool for coping with the complexity of social change, it does not simplify the task so much as it reveals the difficulty of specifying the linkages implicit in historical generalization. We have not made a completely unchallengeable case in favor of the encyclical explanation for the decline in Catholic religiousness. However, it must be said that in any choice between the encyclical explanation and the conciliar one, the data available to us offers no evidence to support the latter and a great deal to support the former.

There are a number of other data sets which enable us to test further the two explanations. Information on religious apostasy taken from four NORC data files and one Survey Research Center, University of Michigan, data file enables us to ask whether there has been an increase in apostasy in the Catholic church in recent years and, if so, when this increase began.

We were able to make measurements at three points in time: 1955, well before the Vatican Council; 1967, after the implementation of many of the conciliar changes and the year before the birth control encyclical; and 1973-74, the year of the second parochial school study.

TABLE 5.13

"GROSS" AND "NET" APOSTASY RATES FOR AMERICAN CATHOLICS
AND PROTESTANTS--1955[a], 1967[b], 1973-74[c]

Year	Catholics		Protestants	
	Gross %	Net* %	Gross %	Net %
1955	$-8_{(375)}$	-2	$-3_{(1067)}$	-1
1967	$-8_{(390)}$	-2	$-6_{(980)}$	-1
1973-74	$-14_{(819)}$	-7	$-9_{(1978)}$	-5

[a]From a 1955 American Institute of Public Opinion survey:
   "What is your religious denomination?"
   "What was your religious preference previously?"

[b]From a 1967 American Institute of Public Opinion survey:
   "What is your religious preference?"
   "What was your religious preference previously?"

[c]From the NORC 1973 and 1974 General Social Surveys:
   "What is your present religion?"
   "What was your religion when you were 16?"
(There is some indication that slightly more people will give their religious preference as Catholic than will say Catholicism is their "religion." Hence, the 1967
figures may underestimate the actual apostasy rates at that time, and the differences
between 1967 and 1973-74 may be overestimated. Analysis done by our colleagues
Kathleen McCourt and Garth Taylor would lead us to believe that the differences
would affect the rates by no more than 2 percentage points in the overall sample.
Thus one could assume as possible a 1967 gross rate of 10 per cent for Catholics
and a net rate of 4 per cent. We have no way of knowing how this variation in
response may be distributed through the age and educational groups in the population.)

*Apostates minus converts.

Eight percent of those who had been raised Catholic were no longer Catholic in 1955, and the proportion did not change until 1967. Neither did the net loss to the church change in those years—a partial balancing of apostasy by an influx of converts. But six years later the net apostasy rate had more than doubled, and the gross apostasy rate had almost doubled. While there was an increase in apostasy for Protestants in the same six-year period, it was not nearly as great as the rise of apostasy rates among Catholics.

Nor is this increase in apostasy limited to those in the Cold War cohort. There was little change in apostasy rates between 1955 and 1967 at all age levels. Those rates doubled for those under 30 and over 50 between 1967 and 1973 (table 5.14). Nor was there much change in the gross apostasy rates between 1955 and 1967 for those who had attended high school, though there was a notable increase in that period (from 3 percent to 13 percent) in apostasy rates for those who had attended college. But between 1967 and 1973, the apostasy rate of those who had not graduated from high school doubled; the rate of those who had graduated from high school but had not attended college almost doubled; and the rate of those who had attended college went from 13 to 22 percent. In other words, in the year before the birth control encyclical, the Catholic church had lost a little more than one-tenth of its members who had attended college. Six years later, it had lost almost one-quarter of those members. The

TABLE 5.14

APOSTASY RATES FOR CATHOLICS BY AGE

Age	Gross %			Net %		
	1955	1967	1973-74	1955	1967	1973-74
Under 30	$-13_{(81)}$	$-11_{(100)}$	$-22_{(265)}$	+2*	-4	-15
31-49	$-8_{(208)}$	$-8_{(161)}$	$-13_{(304)}$	-2	+4*	-7
Over 50	$-6_{(189)}$	$-5_{(132)}$	$-11_{(249)}$	-4	-2	-4

*Net gain for Catholics

TABLE 5.15

APOSTASY RATES FOR CATHOLICS BY EDUCATION

Education	Gross %			Net %		
	1955	1967	1973–74	1955	1967	1973–74
Not graduate from high school	-9(211)	-6(131)	-12(264)	-3	+2*	-7
High school graduate	-7(121)	-8(161)	-14(293)	0	-5	-2
Attended college	-3(87)	-13(71)	-22(260)	+1*	-0	-15

*Net gain for Catholics

magnitude of the problem can be seen from the fact that in 1973-74, the Catholic church had lost 30 percent of its college-educated people under 30 and 18 percent of its college-educated people between 31 and 49 (table 5.16). That this is not a problem which affects all religions should be clear from the fact that only 21 percent of Protestants under 30 who attended college have left their religion.

But we should not think that the increase in apostasy is merely a youthful phenomenon of the well educated. Consider the group over 50 who did not attend college. In 1967, 5 percent of those who had not graduated from high school had left the church and 3 percent of those who had graduated had left. By 1973-74, these percentages had gone up, respectively, to 11 percent and 12 percent, a doubling in the former case and a quadrupling in the latter. While the effect of the new apostasy among Catholics is most obvious among the younger and the better educated, this dramatic departure from the church is increasing remarkably in all populations and at all age levels.

The college-educated under 30 are the ones most likely to have been affected by the turbulence of the Vietnam era, and they are also the ones most likely to be politically unaffiliated. Is there any chance that, with time, they will begin to

TABLE 5.16

APOSTASY RATES FOR CATHOLICS BY EDUCATION AND AGE

Age and Education	Gross % 1955	1967	1973-74	Net % 1955	1967	1973-74
Under 30						
Did not graduate from high school	-10(32)	-6(17)	-16(49)	-6	0	-14
High school graduate	-9(34)	-8(48)	-14(96)	-3	0	-2
Attended college	-27(15)	-16(37)	-30(119)	-7	-16	-25
31-49						
Did not graduate from high school	-11(109)	-5(62)	-12(88)	+4*	+8*	-6
High school graduate	-6(78)	-8(84)	-10(122)	+3	-6	-9
Attended college	-5(21)	-8(26)	-18(92)	+10*	+20*	-10
Over 50						
Did not graduate from high school	-7(69)	-5(71)	-11(127)	-6	-3	-5
High school graduate	0(80)	-3(44)	-12(74)	0	-4	-4
Attended college	0(11)	-6(17)	-10(48)	0	-1	-2

*Net gain for Catholics

drift back into the church just as they drifted away? The 1973-74 data are based on the pooling of two NORC General Social Surveys. If one separates the two surveys and looks at the apostasy rates for the college-educated under 30 in 1973-74, one notes (table 5.17) that the 1974 rates are considerably lower than the 1973 rates, a phenomenon which might be explained either by a return to the church or by a sampling variation inherent in such small case bases. However, even if the 1974 figures turn out to be more accurate, there has still been a dramatic increase in the number of departures from the church among this age group in the last seven years.

A final source of information on religious apostasy is a data file made available to us by Prof. M. Kent Jennings of the University of Michigan. Professor Jennings and his colleagues interviewed a group of high school students in 1965. They asked them what their religion was at that time and then, in 1973, reinterviewed the same students, asking them the same question (table 5.18). The 23 percent gross apostasy rate for Catholics in the Jennings sample is roughly the same as the 22

TABLE 5.17

APOSTASY RATES AMONG CATHOLICS UNDER 30 WHO
ATTENDED COLLEGE--1973 AND 1974

	Gross %	Net %
1973 (55)	-35	-33
1974 (64)	-22	-16

TABLE 5.18

APOSTASY RATES AMONG CATHOLICS FOR 1965 HIGH SCHOOL STUDENTS
REINTERVIEWED IN 1973[a]

Religious Affiliation	Gross %	Net %
Protestant (1406)	-16	-10
Catholic (484)	-23	-10
Jew (79)	-16	-16

	Education			
	Non-College		College	
	Gross	Net	Gross	Net
Protestant (551)	-9	-3	-19 (855)	-15
Catholic (167)	-18	+ 4*	-25 (317)	-18
Jew (9)	-23	-23	-15 (70)	-15

[a]Data supplied by M. Kent Jennings, Institute for Social Research, University of Michigan.

percentage point gross apostasy rate for Catholics under 30 in the 1973-74 General Social Survey of NORC. The 25 percent gross apostasy rate in this sample for Catholics who had attended college is virtually the same as that reported in table 5.17 for the 1974 General Social Survey. In other words, one can be reasonably confident that approximately one-quarter of those Catholics under 30 who attended college have left the church since 1967.[7]

But whatever may be said about the return of the disaffiliated or the acquisition of converts, the fact remains that since the year of the birth control encyclical there has been a massive increase in apostasy among American Catholics. This is obviously a *post hoc, ergo propter hoc* argument, as are most historical arguments. If it is offered merely as confirming evidence to be viewed in conjunction with the other evidence already presented in this chapter, it emphasizes that the increase in apostasy did not begin after the Council and its changes; it only began after the birth control encyclical.

So, too, did the decline in weekly church attendance, as measured by the Gallup organization (table 5.19). Between 1965 and 1967, church attendance had only declined 1 percentage point. But after the encyclical, weekly church attendance dropped from 66 percent to 55 percent. The reform of the liturgy by its translation into English apparently did not drive many people away from the church, a fact which should not be surprising since we know the people like the new liturgy. But in the wake of the birth control encyclical, there has been a massive decline in weekly church attendance.[8] While this deterioration in church attendance has occurred among American Catholics, the proportion of Protestants going to church has not changed at all.

Also, in the *post hoc, ergo propter hoc* variety of argumentation, the proportion of Catholics seeing the church as losing its influence in American society increased 5 percentage points between 1962 and 1965 (table 5.20). But between 1965 and 1968 (the year of the publication of the birth con-

TABLE 5.19

WEEKLY* CHURCH ATTENDANCE (GALLUP DATA)
FOR CATHOLICS AND PROTESTANTS 1965-1974

	Catholics	Protestants
1965	67%	38%
1966	68	38
1967	66	38
1968	65	39
1969	63	38
1970	60	37
1971	57	38
1972	56	37
1973	55	37
1974	55	37

*"Did you attend church last week?"

(Between the end of the Council and the publication of
Humanae Vitae the weekly church attendance declined only
1 percentage point. Between the encyclical and 1973, it
declined 11 percentage points.)

TABLE 5.20

CHURCH LOSING INFLUENCE IN AMERICAN SOCIETY

	Catholics	Protestants
1962	23%	34%
1965	28	50
1967	48	60
1968	62	69
1970	75	75
1974	59	52

150

trol encyclical), the percentage of Catholics who saw the church as losing its influence increased by 48 percentage points. While in the last four years there has been evidence that people see the church as regaining some of its influence, Protestants are now less likely than Catholics to see their church as losing influence.

Finally, in 1966 the resignation rate for American priests was approximately one-half of 1 percent. In 1967 it had moved close to 1 percent. In the years immediately after the encyclical, however, it jumped dramatically. Two percent of the diocesan priests and more than 3 percent of the religious priests in the country resigned in 1969 (table 5.21). Another way of putting it is that in the two years immediately after the birth control encyclical, 3.6 percent of the diocesan priests and 5.2 percent of the religious priests in the country left the priesthood.

There were doubtless many factors at work in the decisions of individual lay Catholics to stop going to church, or to leave the church, or to see the church as losing influence in American society, as well as in the decisions of priests to leave the priesthood. We are not suggesting that the birth control encyclical was the only factor at work, but that when viewed

TABLE 5.21

AVERAGE RESIGNATION RATES IN AMERICAN DIOCESES AND
RELIGIOUS INSTITUTES, BY YEAR

(Number of Resignations per 100 priests)

Year	Dioceses	Religious Institutes
1966	0.4	0.6
1967	0.9	0.9
1968	1.6	2.0
1969	2.0	3.2
N . .	(85)	(87)

with the other evidence presented in this chapter, the data in tables 5.13-5.21 seem to suggest strongly that the publication of the encyclical letter *Humanae Vitae* marked a turning point in the attitudes of many Catholics, clergy and laity, toward their church. It seems to have served as a catalyst for decision-making, or perhaps, to switch the metaphor, the straw that broke the camel's back.

We did not begin this analysis with any intention to "make a case" for the encyclical explanation for the deterioration of American Catholic belief and practice. Indeed, the principal investigator has a number of times in public print expounded the "it would have happened anyhow" and the "meat on Friday" explanations. (Indeed, the latter phrase is his.) But our exploration of the data forced us to conclude first of all that there was no evidence to be found linking the Council to religious decline among American Catholics. Then we were forced to admit strong and converging evidence that the decline is linked mostly to the encyclical letter *Humanae Vitae* and to a connected loss of respect for papal authority, and that far from causing the decline, the positive dynamics released by the Council prevented the loss from being worse. We doubt very much that anyone could analyze our data and arrive at a different conclusion.

There may be some debate about whether or not converging probabilities ever produce certainty, and even if one grants that proposition, it is still open to question whether we have amassed enough evidence in favor of the encyclical explanation for religious decline among American Catholics. To settle the matter completely, we will be content with the observation that the overwhelming burden of evidence available to us points to the encyclical rather than the Council model.

For the ecclesiastical policymakers, the nature of the certainty generated by the data may not be a pertinent issue. To fulfill their responsibility, it would seem, they must view the encyclical explanation as practically certain and make policies accordingly. Indeed, we suggest as a hypothesis for further discussion that the response of the American clergy and the hierarchy to *Humanae Vitae* contributed substantially in its own right to the decline in Catholic religiousness. The members of the clergy generally remain silent in public, though approximately three-quarters of them will not insist on the sinfulness of birth control in the confessional. The hierarchy publicly and personally support the encyclical (70 percent of the bishops in the NORC priesthood study believe that all artificial contraception is morally wrong, as opposed to 29 percent of the priests; and 59 percent would deny absolution to those who practice birth control, as opposed to 26 percent of the priests); but they have not tried to invoke canonical penalties against those of their priests who "permit" birth control. Nor have they vigorously tried to enforce acceptance of the encyclical among the laity. It would be small wonder if many among the laity have the impression that the religious leaders are talking out of both sides of their mouths.

It is not the function of social scientists to make theological judgments. Ethical values cannot be arrived at by counting noses. Still we must note that the encyclical letter has been both a failure and an organizational and religious disaster. It was a failure because it did not succeed in turning around the erosion of support for the Catholic church's traditional birth control teaching. On the contrary, in the years since the encyclical, opposition to that teaching in the United States among both clergy and laity has increased rather than decreased. Furthermore, it would appear that the encyclical has been counterproductive. Far from reasserting the teaching authority of the church and the credibility of the pope, it has led to a deterioration among American Catholics of respect for both. Finally, it seems to have been the occasion for massive apostasy and for a notable decline in religious devotion and belief. It does not follow, therefore, that religiously the encyclical was a mistake. Defenders of the pope might argue that even if he had known that the encyclical would fail, that it would be counterproductive, and that it would lead to a considerable loss in the church, it would still have been necessary for him to reaffirm both the church's teaching and its teaching authority. No one claims, however, that the encyclical is infallible or that the teaching of *Humanae Vitae* cannot be changed at a later time. Social scientists must leave to the theologians the question of whether or not the pope had no choice but to issue the encyclical. We must also leave to the theologians the question of whether four-fifths of the laity and the clergy in the church can be wrong in this matter (assuming that the American response is not untypical of the response of the rest of the Catholic world). "The learning Church," Catholics were told in their schools in years gone by, was also "infallible." And the *sensus fidelium* ("the sense of the faithful") is one of the signs of authentic Christian teaching. The sociologist must observe that a very heavy price indeed has been paid for a document whose principal teaching is, by all accounts, still subject to change.

PART II
THE IMPACT OF CATHOLIC EDUCATION

6

Value-Oriented Education and Social Change

The central focus of this report is the relationship between value-oriented education and social change. The task in this chapter, which is the core of our analytic effort, is to provide answers to seven questions about value-oriented education and social change:

1. Are those who receive value-oriented education more likely or less likely to support change in the institution whose values they were taught in their educational experience?

2. Do relationships between value-oriented education and adult behavior persist even in a time of dramatic and confusing transition in the institution which sponsored the value-oriented education?

3. In times of transition, does value-oriented education become more important or less important to the institution experiencing a transitional crisis?

4. Since in our previous research we established that there was a particularly strong relationship between value-oriented education and adult behavior for those whose families predisposed them for such education, it must be asked whether this particularly strong link persists in a time of major social change in the value-generating institution.

5. Is a new generation coming of age in a time of transition likely to be influenced at all by the value-oriented education it received just before or just after the change?

6. A relationship between value-oriented education and economic achievement was documented in our previous research.

Does that relationship persist even in a time of notable social change in the value institution?

7. Does value instruction apart from the school context offer an adequate substitute for value-oriented education in the school milieu? Our previous research indicates that it does not. However, in a time of transition, when strong emphasis is placed on value instruction outside of the school, is there any increase in the impact of such instruction?

The questions are difficult even to ask because they deal not with static situations but with the dynamics involved in social change. Yet they are even more complicated to answer because there is no simple answer for most of them. However, to provide a brief overview for this chapter, the following preliminary responses may be given:

1. There is a small positive relationship between value-oriented education and the acceptance of change in the value-teaching institution.

2. Some of the relationships between value-oriented education and adult behavior have changed in the last decade; others have not.

3. Among those that have changed, some relationships have become stronger and some weaker.

4. Among those from highly religious backgrounds, some relationships between value-oriented education and adult behavior are now no different from the relationships for those from less religious backgrounds. On the other hand, some differences remain in the strength of the relationships, and some new differences have emerged.

5. If anything, value-oriented education seems more important rather than less important for the generation under thirty.

6. The apparent economic advantages of value-oriented education persist despite the social change.

7. Value instruction outside the school context, as a substitute for value-oriented education, seems no more adequate now than it did a decade ago.

As we observed in the introduction, we will have to reanalyze the data on which *The Education of Catholic Americans* was based. There is now available to us a repertory of technical, analytic, and data-processing skills much more elaborate than those that were available in the middle 1960s. The reader who wishes to compare this analysis with the one of a decade ago will find footnote references in this chapter to the appropriate passages in *The Education of Catholic Americans.*

Catholic Education and Adult Behavior, 1963 to 1974

The first question we want to ask is whether there is a relationship between Catholic education and adult behavior, and whether this relationship has changed between 1963 and 1974. We will use six scales—Catholic activism, support for vocation, sexual orthodoxy, doctrinal orthodoxy, acceptance of the church's right to teach, and sacramental reception—for which we have comparable items in both surveys. We will also consider six individual responses—the proportion attending mass weekly, receiving communion weekly, going to confession monthly, saying prayers every day, judging birth control to be wrong, and the proportion contributing more than 2.3 percent of their income to the church. We will also consider a number of scales that are to be found only in the 1974 study (for descriptions of the scales, see Appendix V).[1]

In this chapter we will make substantial use of the "z" or "standardized" score. A standardized score is created by constructing a scale so that its mean becomes zero and the standard deviation becomes 100. The score itself represents the percentage of a standard deviation above or below the mean, where the average member of a given subgroup is to be located. Thus in table 6.1, Catholics with more than ten years of Catholic education in 1963 were 49 percent of a standard deviation above the mean on the Catholic activism scale.

The standardized scores used in this chapter are calculated using the mean of the respective year, so that comparisons can be made between the variations of the groups under con-

TABLE 6.1

STANDARDIZED SCORES ON RELIGIOUS SCALES BY PAROCHIAL
SCHOOL ATTENDANCE, 1963 AND 1974*

Religious Scales	1963			1974		
	More than 10 Years	1-10 Years	0 Years	More than 10 Years	1-10 Years	0 Years
Catholic activism	49	6	6	48	6	-25
Support for vocation	30	9	-16	13	9	-13
Sexual orthodoxy	48	2	-18	4	0	- 4
Doctrinal orthodoxy	49	1	-14	20	3	- 5
Church's right to teach	38	4	-17	19	3	- 3
Sacramental reception	61	6	-25	31	7	-13

*The standardized scores (or "z" scores) are average position of a scale whose mean is zero and whose standard deviation is 100. A score of 38 means that a group has an average score of 38 per cent of a standard deviation above the mean. The absolute values of the means have declined from 1963 to 1974, so the above table shows only the difference among groups within the same point in time but not the differences at the two time periods.

sideration at two different points in time—they may not be made between the absolute scores of a given year. Thus in table 6.1, there is more distance in 1974 between the two extreme education groups in their scores on the Catholic activism scale than there was in 1963. In 1974, they are 73 percent of a standard deviation apart, whereas in 1963, they were 43 percent of a standard deviation apart. Catholic education seems to have had more of an effect in 1974 than it had in 1963. We must remember that we established in the previous chapter that the Catholic activism scale, like all our other scales, experienced an absolute decline in the last decade. Thus the finding in the first two rows of table 6.1 does not indicate that those with more than ten years of Catholic education have a higher activism score in 1974 than did their predecessors in 1963. It merely indicates that there was a greater difference between the two extremes in 1974 than there was in 1963. No comparisons can be made in table 6.1 between 1963 and 1974 scores.

The two extreme groups have grown somewhat closer together in their scores on the support for religious vocation scale. Forty-six standardized points separated them in 1963, 26 points separate them in 1974.[2]

The most striking finding in table 6.1 is the virtual collapse of the relationship between Catholic education and sexual orthodoxy. Only 8 standardized points separate the two groups in 1974, whereas 66 points separated them in 1963. The decline in the church's sexual ethic, which we discussed in the previous chapter, seems to have been especially strong among those who were once most orthodox—those Catholics who had more than ten years of Catholic education.

In each of the three remaining scales, doctrinal orthodoxy, the church's right to teach, and sacramental reception, there has been an apparent contraction of the differences between those who had more than ten years of Catholic school and those who did not attend Catholic school at all. Differences persist in adult life as they are correlated by Catholic school attendance; but they are not as sharp as they used to be; and in both the doctrinal orthodoxy and the right to teach scales, there is little difference between those who had between one and ten years of Catholic education and those who did not attend Catholic school at all.

One can therefore conclude tentatively that while all differences based on religious education have vanished in the sexual orthodoxy scale, and while religious education apparently is more strongly related to Catholic activism now than it was ten years ago, the most typical result of the social change of the last decade is a narrowing of the differences between those who had more than ten years of Catholic education and those who did not attend Catholic school at all.

Similarly, when we look at individual items (table 6.2), the decline in the past decade seems to be fairly evenly distributed among the three groups in religious behavior (one cate-

gory shows a positive score rather than a decline: those who
receive weekly communion). The single exception in the even
distribution of decline is in the proportion who see contraception to be morally wrong. There has been a decline of 57 percentage points among those who have had more than ten
years of Catholic education, 39 percentage points among
those who have had one to ten years of Catholic education,
and 31 percentage points among those who did not attend

TABLE 6.2

PERCENT HIGH ON RELIGIOUS BEHAVIOR BY PAROCHIAL
SCHOOL ATTENDANCE, 1963-1974

Religious Behavior		More than 10 Years	1-10 Years	0 Years
Weekly mass	1963	91	74	62
	1974	65	44	36
	Difference =	-26	-30	-26
Weekly communion	1963	27	14	7
	1974	41	27	19
	Difference =	+14	+13	+12
Monthly Confession	1963	54	40	31
	1974	20	21	16
	Difference =	-34	-19	-15
Daily prayer	1963	81	75	65
	1974	62	43	40
	Difference =	-19	-32	-25
Contraception wrong	1963	71	54	46
	1974	14	15	15
	Difference =	-57	-39	-31
Contribution (more than 2.3 per cent of income	1963	47	43	38
	1974	26	19	13
	Difference =	-21	-24	-25

Catholic school at all. The extraordinarily large decline from 71 percentage points to 14 percentage points among those who have had more than ten years of Catholic education has had the practical effect of bringing that group even with the other two groups in the population. Differences between those who went to Catholic schools and those who did not persist in the other five variables in table 6.2, and show approximately the same percentage point difference as a decade ago. Indeed, on each of the variables the decline seems to be somewhere between 20 and 30 percentage points for each of the educational groups. Catholic education, in other words, does not *seem* to have had any impact at all in inhibiting the deterioration of religious practice in the last ten years. This conclusion is in fact spurious, as we shall see by the chapter's end. In fact, the biggest change in table 6.2 is in the decline of acceptance of the church's birth control teaching among those who have had more than ten years of Catholic education.

Catholic education also has an effect on those forms of

TABLE 6.3

STANDARDIZED SCORES ON "NEW SCALES" BY
CATHOLIC EDUCATION (1974 ONLY)

"New" Scales	More than 10 Years	1-10 Years	0 Years
Anticlerical	-47	-5	25
Priest competence	-10	5	5
Vatican II	40	-6	-6
Change priest	25	-3	-10
"New ways"	16	5	-9
Catholic media activism	26	6	-10
New style activism	43	3	-16
Old style activism	56	12	-24

adult religious behavior measured by scales developed especially for the 1974 study. Those who have attended Catholic
schools are less likely to be anticlerical and less likely to rate
their clergy as competent, but are more likely to support the
changes of Vatican II, to approve of some of the new ways
that have emerged since the Council, and to support changes
in the priesthood such as the ordination of women and a married clergy. They are also more likely to listen to or read the
products of the Catholic media and to be both "new style"
and "old style" activists (table 6.3).[3]

In answer to the first of the questions with which we began
the chapter, there seems to be in table 6.3 strong evidence
that value-oriented education does correlate with a willingness

TABLE 6.4

CORRELATIONS BETWEEN NUMBER OF YEARS OF CATHOLIC EDUCATION
AND RELIGIOUS ATTITUDES AND BEHAVIOR

Attitudes and Behavior	1963	1974
Catholic activism	.24	.28
Sexual orthodoxy	.18	.00
Doctrinal orthodoxy	.18	.10
Church's right to teach	.17	.08
Contribution	.03	.13
Mass attendance	.14	.11
Communion	.17	.14
Confession	.12	.03
Prayer	.08	.08
Vatican II		.16
"New ways"		.14
New style activism		.21
Catholic media activism		.16
Old style activism		.29

to accept changes in the value-teaching institution.

The preliminary findings which we have documented in this section are summarized in table 6.4. The simple correlations between years in Catholic school and adult religious attitudes and behavior have increased for contribution to the church and decreased for sexual orthodoxy, doctrinal orthodoxy, the church's right to teach, and going to confession. They have remained virtually the same for Catholic activism, mass attendance, communion reception, and prayer. There are also moderate to substantial correlations between Catholic education and the acceptance of change in the church and involvement in various kinds of Catholic activism. Our preliminary response to the second question of the set with which we began this chapter is that some relationships have grown stronger, some have grown weaker, and some have remained the same since 1963.

Models of Religious Behavior

The authors of *The Education of Catholic Americans* developed a four-variable model (although they didn't know enough then to call it that) to explain adult religious behavior.[4] The four variables that went into the model were sex, religiousness of parents, level of educational achievement, and attendance at Catholic schools. They found that when they held the first three variables constant, there was still an association between Catholic education and adult behavior. They also discovered that instead of the relationship's being a spurious effect of parents' religiousness, it indeed became strongest precisely among those respondents who came from a very religious background (in which both parents had gone to mass every Sunday and at least one had received communion every week).[5]

The difficulty with the technique used in *The Education of Catholic Americans* was that there was no way the two authors could add up their net partial gammas to obtain a multiple gamma that would enable them to say how much adult religious behavior was explained (or predicted) by their model.[6] In the present analysis we will use the multiple regression techniques and the path analysis flow model for which the computer hardware and software, as well as the analytic techniques, were still in an early stage of development in 1964 and 1965. Furthermore, two variables that were not used in 1963 will be added to the model—age and spouse's church attendance. We use the former because it is a much more important predictor of Catholic religious behavior now than it was a decade ago (as is clear from the cohort replacement effect discussed in the previous chapter). We use spouse's church attendance because, while it does not relate to years of Catholic school education, it is nonetheless a very important predictor of adult religious behavior.[7]

In Fig. 6.1 we present the path model which we will use throughout this chapter. We assume that sex, age, and religiousness of parents all represent the first step in the model. Educational achievement comes before years of Catholic education because years of Catholic education are necessarily a function of the number of years one has been in school. (If you have only gone to school for four years, that puts an absolute limit of four on the number of years of Catholic education you might have.) We also assume that these five prior variables might influence spouse's church attendance. Finally, we eliminate from the model all relationships that are under .1 (unless, as is the case in the relationship between educational achievement and spouse's church attendance, the path coefficient [beta] is above .1 in one year and under .1 in the other year).

Most of the internal relationships in the model have not changed since 1963. The internal path coefficients which represent the 1963 relationships are quite similar to those that represent the 1974 relationships. Educational attainment correlates more highly with spouse's church attendance now than it did in 1963 (.17 as opposed to .07), and there has been a

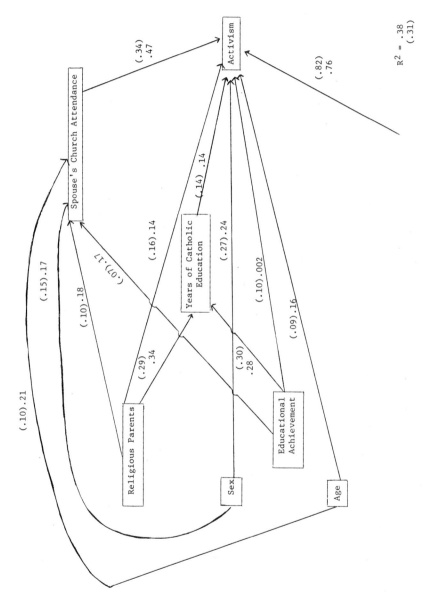

Figure 6.1--Path Model to Explain Catholic Activism (1963 Paths in Parenthesis)

167

doubling of the relationship between age and spouse's church attendance (from .1 to .2) during the last ten years—a function of the higher correlation between age and church attendance, which we will discuss shortly.

Since the internal relationships have undergone little change, we are free to concentrate on the direct paths between the predictor variables and activism in the model, though it is easier to do that by simply looking across the top row in table 6.5. There has been an increase in the relationship between age and activism in the past decade (.09 to .16) and a decrease in the standardized coefficient between education and activism (from .10 to .002). The strength of the relationship between spouse's church attendance and Catholic activism (from .34 to .47) has increased considerably. However, there has been virtually no change in the relationship between Catholic education and Catholic activism in adult life since 1963. The explanatory power of the model, though, has increased. In 1963, 31 percent of the variance in activism could be explained by our religious behavior model, while in 1974, 38 percent of it can be explained by our model. Religiousness of spouse (as measured by church attendance) has become a much more important factor in the Roman church in transition.

The persistence of a statistically significant relationship between Catholic education and activism in adult life is in direct contradiction to the comment on page 106 of *The Education of Catholic Americans* (*ECA*). However, the activism scale used in the present analysis is much more comprehensive than the organizational membership indicator used in the prior analysis.

The figures in the column under spouse's church attendance show that in seven of the ten cases, spouse's church attendance has become a more important predictor of adult religious behavior now than it was ten years ago. Perhaps in a time of religious transition, the family of procreation exercises a much stronger internal religious influence than it would in a

TABLE 6.5

PATH COEFFICIENTS (BETA) BETWEEN RELIGIOUS BEHAVIOR MODEL VARIABLES AND RELIGIOUS ATTITUDES AND BEHAVIOR, 1963 AND 1974

Dependent Variables	Age		Sex		Parental Religiousness		Educational Achievement		Spouse's Church Attendance		Catholic Education (years)		R		R^2	
	1963	1974	1963	1974	1963	1974	1963	1974	1963	1974	1963	1974	1963	1974	1963	1974
Catholic activism	.09	.16	.27	.24	.16	.14	.10	.002	.34	.47	.14	.14	.55	.62	.31	.38
Church's right to teach	-.01	.19	.08	.01	.04	.10	.09	.09	.21	.22	.10	.05	.30	.36	.09	.13
Sexual orthodoxy	.02	.29	.20	.07	.15	.12	.12	-.13	.28	.17	.07	.02	.43	.46	.19	.20
Doctrinal orthodoxy	-.03	.03	.05	.11	.11	.08	.11	.07	.12	.13	.09	.09	.27	.24	.08	.06
Contribution	.17	.32	.07	.01	.12	.00	.09	.00	.20	.32	.04	.15	.31	.52	.09	.27
Sacramental reception	.03	.13	.21	.20	.21	.00	.14	.00	.41	.55	.10	.06	.59	.66	.35	.44
Mass attendance	.05	.05	.13	.13	.26	.13	.11	-.11	.23	.66	.03	.05	.43	.70	.18	.50
Communion	.07	.15	.17	.19	.28	.10	.14	.02	.23	.56	.13	.07	.46	.65	.18	.42
Confession	.05	.05	.14	.06	.25	.13	.09	-.12	.20	.41	.05	.00	.43	.47	.12	.22
Private prayer	.07	.11	.24	.27	.14	.09	.00	-.03	.06	.17	.04	.02	.34	.34	.09	.12

time when the external religious system was stable. Similarly, in the age column, the figures indicate that in seven out of ten cases age has become a stronger predictor than it was a decade ago. There was relatively little difference, save in activism and in contributions, between the young and the old ten years ago. Now the differences tend to be very large. While religious devotion is declining at all age levels, the decline has been most precipitous among the generation which has entered adult life in the last ten years. Sex, on the other hand, plays a less important role in the model. On the teacher, sexual orthodoxy, contribution, and confession scales, it does not appreciably increase in importance on any variable. Women are more devout than men, but surely no more devout than they were a decade ago, and in some instances, less so. Parental religiousness has declined in half the cases and increased in only one, the church's right to teach, as a predictor of adult religiousness. It may well be that just as in a time of transition the influence of the family of procreation grows stronger, the influence of the family of origin grows weaker. The impact of the number of years of education also has declined on nine of the ten variables; it has held its own only on the church's right to teach. However, in three cases—sexual orthodoxy, mass attendance, and confession—the decline has produced a negative relationship. A decade ago the better educated were more sexually orthodox, more likely to go to mass, and more likely to go to confession. Now they are less likely to do so. Education thus continues to play a role in the model, but it now functions erratically, sometimes relating positively with adult religiousness and sometimes negatively.

Having looked at these other changes in the model, we can now turn to the impact of Catholic education. It has held its own in the decade in the categories of activism and doctrinal orthodoxy. Its influence on sexual orthodoxy has diminished to virtual insignificance. It has declined on the church's right to teach and the sacramental scales and on the reception of communion scale. Its influence on confession and private prayer was insignificant a decade ago and continues to be so. The relationship has increased only on the church contribution variable. If one looks down the column represented by Catholic education (years) 1974, one notices only two relationships above .1, Catholic activism and contribution to the church (with the latter showing a considerable increase). A decade ago there were four relationships over .1—Catholic activism, the right to teach, sacramental reception, and the reception of communion (which we shall detail in a later chapter[8]).

However, there are promising coefficients between Catholic education and the "new scales" used only in the 1974 survey (table 6.6). Three of the five standardized coefficients are higher than .1—new style activist (.10), Catholic media activist (.13), and old style activist (.19). In addition, there are .08 correlations between years of Catholic education and acceptance of the changes of Vatican II and of "new ways" in the church. The decade has not been a complete disaster for value-oriented education. But the principal conclusion to be drawn from tables 6.5 and 6.6 is that age and the family of procreation are now much more important in predicting adult religiousness for Catholics than they were ten years ago. Hence, interestingly enough, we are in all cases but one able to explain on table 6.5 more variance in 1974 than we were in 1963.

One is faced with the question (to be discussed in greater detail later in this chapter): "How big is 'big,' how small is 'small'?" In nine of the fifteen variables in our 1974 analysis, number of years in Catholic schools is a stronger predictor of religiousness of respondent than is the religiousness of the respondent's parents. On the other hand, a decade ago Catholic schooling was a stronger predictor than parents' religiousness only once. Furthermore, in ten of the fifteen cases, the number of years of Catholic education has a stronger positive relationship with religiousness than does the number of years of education (each variable having been standardized for the

TABLE 6.6

PATH COEFFICIENTS FOR RELIGIOUS BEHAVIOR MODEL AND "NEW SCALES"

Dependent Variable	Age	Sex	Parents' Religious-ness	Education Achievement	Spouse's Church At-tendance	Catholic Education (years)	R	R^2
Vatican II	-.08	.05	-.02	.13	.15	.08	.28	.08
"New Ways"	-.10	-.06	-.08	.12	-.14	.08	.28	.07
New style activist	.01	.09	.09	.22	.09	.10	.32	.11
Catholic media	.16	.17	.05	.01	.20	.13	.38	.14
Old style activist	.24	.13	.16	.13	.38	.19	.62	.38

other). All of this was true of only two of the ten comparisons that could be made in 1963. On balance, then, Catholic education now appears to be a stronger predictor of adult religiousness than either parental religiousness or level of educational achievement. It seems to have resisted the traumas of religious transition better than either pure educational achievement or the family of origin.

Religiousness of Parent and the "New Generation"

In the early phases of the design of the 1963 project, one of the principal concerns of the two investigators was to determine whether the apparent relationship between Catholic education and adult religious behavior, which one of the investigators had already reported in an earlier article (Rossi and Rossi 1961), was a spurious relationship based on the fact that those who went to Catholic schools came from families where there was a higher level of religious practice. In fact, then, it might have been that the parochial school Catholics were more religious in adult life not because they had gone to parochial schools but because they had come from religious families. The research reported in *The Education of Catholic Americans* established that initial relationships between parochial school education and adult religious behavior diminished when parental religiousness was taken into account. The authors commented about this phenomenon:

Two processes might be at work behind the decline in the coefficients of association when parental religiousness is taken into account. ... It could be that the apparent effect of Catholic schooling is in reality the result of the family environment in which the child grew up: devout Catholic families send their children to Catholic schools, and the children are devout not because of the schools but because of the family. If this were what was happening, the decline in the gamma coefficient should take place in each of the subgroups based on parental religiousness. A second possibility is that the religiousness of the family reinforces the impact of the school and that it is only among those from highly religious families that one can expect the school to have much influence. In these circumstances, the gamma would rise for the respondents from very religious backgrounds and decline for those with less religious backgrounds.

It is the latter process which seems to be at work in Table 4.3. Not only are the relationships not diminished among those respondents one of whose parents went to communion every week; they are, in fact, substantially strengthened. We can go so far as to say that, for all practical purposes, the religious impact of Catholic education is limited to those who come from highly religious families. With the exception of the relationship between Catholic education and religious knowledge, only one gamma coefficient in the lower three parental-religiousness groups is above .11. But among those from highly religious backgrounds, all gamma coefficients are

Table 4.3 Zero-Order, Partial, and Net Partial Gamma Associations between Catholic Education and Adult Religious Behavior, with Parental Religiousness Controlled

Religious Behavior	Zero-Order	Partial (Parental Religiousness)				Net Partial
		High	Higher Middle	Lower Middle	Low	
Sacramental index	.26	.34	.11	.09	.10	.14
Church-as-teacher index	.15	.22	.03	.15	.12	.12
Religious knowledge index	.30	.40	.26	.20	.22	.26
Doctrinal orthodoxy index	.19	.34	.11	.09	.10	.14
Ethical orthodoxy index	.12	.20	.05	.07	.01	.07
Sexual mores index	.19	.21	.08	.09	.11	.12
Organizational membership*	.15	.34	.11	−.08	−.10	.04

* Membership in at least one Church-related organization.

above .2, four of them are above .3, and one (religious knowledge) is .4.

Thus the impact of Catholic education on the religious behavior of adults coming from families who were not highly religious is limited to their religious knowledge, and even on this index the relationship is virtually twice as strong among those from highly religious backgrounds. In all other instances the strength of the relationship between Catholic education and adult religious behavior among those from highly religious families is close to, or in excess of, three times as great as it is among the next most religious group.

The magnitude of these differences in gamma coefficients is even more surprising when one remembers that the only difference between the highest group and the second highest in family religious background is that the former had at least one parent who went to communion every week; in both groups both parents were Catholic and both went to church every Sunday. (Greeley and Rossi 1966:85-87)

The authors concluded:

A combination of Catholic education and parental devotion produces a remarkably high level of religious behavior in adult life. . . . Catholic schools had an impact only on those who came from families in which one parent received Communion every week. Their "success" is almost limited to these families, but among such families it is quite impressive. (Greeley and Rossi 1966:87)

The first step in our reanalysis of this phenomenon of the combination of parochial school education and high religious background was to transform the gammas of the 1963 research into the betas that we used in our present analysis. The first two columns in table 6.7 report essentially the same phenomenon as that recorded by the different statistical measure used in *The Education of Catholic Americans*. The standardized relationship between parochial schooling and adult religiousness (with the two exceptions of daily prayer and activism) is anywhere from two to seven times as strong among those from high religious backgrounds as it is among those from low religious backgrounds. Indeed, only on the right to teach variable, the activism variable, and the reception of communion variable is the correlation among low religious

TABLE 6.7

STANDARDIZED COEFFICIENTS BETWEEN YEARS OF CATHOLIC EDUCATION AND
MEASURES OF ATTITUDE AND BEHAVIOR FOR CATHOLICS FROM
HIGHLY RELIGIOUS BACKGROUNDS

	1963 Religious Background		1974 Religious Background	
	Low	High	Low	High
Right to teach	.10	.21	.03	.09
Doctrinal orthodoxy	.03	.10	.07	.12
Sacramental reception	.03	.19	.09	.02
Sexual orthodoxy	.03	.08	.04	-.12
Contribution	.04	.28	.03	.25
Mass	.03	.11	.05	.05
Communion	.13	.28	.08	.07
Confession	.03	.13	.04	.07
Prayer	.04	.01	.01	.15
Activism	.13	.17	.08	.27
Vatican II	--	--	.05	.15
New Ways	--	--	.03	.08
New style activist	--	--	.03	.19
Catholic media	--	--	.13	.26
Old style activist	--	--	.10	.26

more than trivial. On the other hand, only two of the betas between Catholic education and adult religiousness for those from very religious families are under .1 (sexual orthodoxy and prayer), and four of them are higher than .2. Whether one uses the gamma probability coefficient or the beta variance-explaining coefficient, the result is the same: parochial schools have their strongest effect, indeed, in most cases, their only nontrivial effect, on those who come from families where at least one parent was a weekly communicant.

The situation has changed somewhat in the last decade. There is a negative relationship now between parochial schooling and sexual orthodoxy for those from highly religious families. For those whose parents were very religious, the degree of sexual orthodoxy declined as the years of Catholic schooling increased. Furthermore, the gammas for both the teacher index and the sacramental index from highly religious families have declined substantially from 1963 to 1974 (from .21 to .09 on right to teach and from .19 to .02 on the sacramental index). So too has the relationship between parochial education, mass attendance, communion reception, and monthly confession. For all practical purposes it makes no difference on these variables whether one's family was highly religious or not.

But the strong relationships between parochial education and contribution to the church and Catholic activism persist in 1974 for those from very religious family backgrounds. A new relationship emerges for this group (a .15 beta) between high religious background and daily prayer. Furthermore, on the new scale, there are stronger relationships for those from very religious backgrounds between parochial schooling and acceptance of Vatican II, approval of "new ways," and the various styles of Catholic activism—old style, new style, and media activist. Indeed, the relationship in this group between both media and old style activism and number of years of Catholic education is .26. One concludes, therefore, that in those areas where there is still some relationship between Cath-

olic education and adult religiousness—principally, financial support of the church and Catholic activism—that relationship is
particularly strong for those who come from very religious
backgrounds. In acceptance both of the changes in the church
and of the various modalities of active Catholic commitment—in
which there is some relationship between attendance at Catholic
schools and adult attitudes—the relationship is especially strong
among those from the highly religious families. Family background is simply not as important as it was a decade ago in
predicting religious behavior (as we noted in a previous section).
Nor is it as important as it used to be in conditioning the impact
of Catholic schools; but it is not therefore unimportant. In such
dimensions of ecclesiastical structure as activism and financial
support of the church, as well as in acceptance of conciliar
change, parental religiousness still strongly specifies the relationship between number of years in Catholic school and adult
religiousness. But the effect is not merely structural, for unlike
the finding of 1963, there is now a presentable correlation for
those from very religious family backgrounds between Catholic
education and daily prayer. Family background may not specify
the relationship between Catholic education and adult religiousness for such public activities as mass, communion, and confession, as it did ten years ago, but it does specify the relationship for private prayer, which it did not do ten years ago.

The authors of *The Education of Catholic Americans* reported that those who were still in Catholic schools at that
time (the adolescent subsample, drawn from the children of
adult respondents) were considerably more religious than their
confreres in public schools (Greeley and Rossi 1966:chap. 8).
They raised the question of whether this was a short-range
effect of Catholic education that would diminish when the
adolescents left the Catholic schools behind and moved into
adulthood or whether it represented a notable increase in the
effectiveness of parochial schools. Since the "Vietnam cohort"
is much less likely to be orthodox or devout than its predecessor cohort group and since those who attended Catholic

schools in this cohort are less devout and less orthodox than older people who attended Catholic schools, the question can easily be answered. The high level of religiousness observed among the Catholic school adolescents of a decade ago has eroded. But a more subtle question remains. Granted the considerable decline of religiousness in the Cold War cohort, it may still be possible that there is a stronger relationship for this group between Catholic education and adult religiousness than there is in the entire population. Paradoxically, such seems to be the case. Those under thirty are less religious than the preceding generation, but Catholic education has had a greater impact on their adult religious behavior on a number of variables than it had for those over thirty.

Table 6.8, for example, shows that the beta between Catholic education and Catholic activism for those under thirty is .24. For mass attendance it is .16, three times that for the

TABLE 6.8

STANDARDIZED COEFFICIENTS BETWEEN YEARS OF CATHOLIC
EDUCATION AND ADULT RELIGIOUSNESS FOR THOSE
UNDER 30 ONLY (VIETNAM COHORT)

	Under 30	All Respondents
Activism	.24	.20
Support	.15	.12
Mass	.16	.05
Communion	.07	.07
Confession	.00	.00
Private prayer	.16	.02
Media activism	.31	.13
Old style activism	.23	.19
New style activism	.04	.13
Vatican II	.18	.08
New ways	.09	.08

whole population. The correlation between years of Catholic school and daily private prayer is .16 for those under thirty and .02 for the rest of the sample. Furthermore, the beta is also higher for those under thirty for Catholic media activism and, as we shall see in subsequent chapters, it is also higher for support for religious vocation and for rejection of anti-clericalism. Finally, there is a much stronger relationship for those under thirty with support for the Vatican Council changes (.18) than there is in the whole population (.08).

In some respects those under thirty are like those from highly religious families. They manifest a much stronger impact from Catholic education for such structural variables as activism and such devotional variables as private prayer than do other age and religiousness groups among American Catholics. There are three possible explanations for the stronger correlations among those under thirty: it may simply be that

TABLE 6.9

INFLUENCE OF CATHOLIC EDUCATION AND SEX, 1963 AND 1974

(Standardized Coefficients--Betas)

Religious Scales	1963		1974	
	Men	Women	Men	Women
Catholic Activism	.14	.09	·25	.11
Church's right to teach	.14	.10	.13	.01
Doctrinal orthodoxy	.16	.07	.06	.11
Sexual orthodoxy	.15	.07	.09	.00
Sacramental reception	.17	.10	.19	.00
Vocation support	.01	.10	.14	.01
Church contribution	.01	-.07	.18	.02
Catholic media activism			.16	.10
New style activism			.15	.05
Old style activism			.29	.07

TABLE 6.10

SOME VARIABLES OF RELIGIOUS BEHAVIOR MODEL
FOR MEN AND WOMEN, 1963 AND 1974
(Standardized Coefficients--Betas)

| | 1963 | | 1974 | |
	Men	Women	Men	Women
Spouse's Church attendance	.10	.17	.28	.23
Parents' Religiousness	.15	.13	.17	.09
Catholic Education	.10	.06	.16	.05

these relationships are typical of any age group under thirty (though they were not true of those in their twenties a decade ago); it may be that the improvement in the quality and sophistication of Catholic education in recent years has made that education more effective; or it may be that in a time of transition and tremendous external pressures (such as the Vietnam war), those who have had more Catholic education are the ones who are most likely to maintain their loyalties to the church despite the religious and social turmoil which surrounds them. We are inclined to the third explanation. One interesting conclusion that might be drawn from it is that as far as both structural continuity (and, as we shall see, that includes both activism and support for vocations) and private piety are concerned, parochial schools may well be more important for the church in the years ahead than they have been in the past.

Sex, Ethnicity, and Catholic Education

In 1974 Catholic education appears to have its strongest impact on those under thirty and those from highly religious families. Are there any other subpopulations where its impact is especially pronounced? Women are more religious than men and some ethnic groups are known to be more devout than others. What does Catholic education accomplish within these subpopulations?

In 1963 Catholic education had slightly more influence on men than on women, an average net correlation of .10 for men and .06 for women (tables 6.9 and 6.10). Only in the matter of support for religious vocations was the effect of Catholic schools stronger on women than men. The picture for women changes only slightly in the decade between 1963 and 1974, declining from .06 to .05. However, the net impact of number of years of Catholic school attendance on men goes up sharply to .16, with an especially notable increase in the two structural variables of Catholic activism (increasing for men from .14 to .25) and contribution to the church (from .01 to .14). If male leadership is harder to come by in a religious organization, then Catholic schools may be more important for the church now than they were ten years ago.

The influence of parents' religiousness on women has declined in the last ten years; it has gone up for men. Furthermore, the influence of spouse's religiousness has almost trebled for men (from .10 to .28) while going up much less for women (.17 to .23). All three factors in the religious behavior model in table 6.10—Catholic education, parents' religiousness, and spouse's religiousness—are more important in 1974 for men than they are for women. In times of religious change, all three factors seem to be more important for the sex that was less religious to begin with and whose religiousness has declined more in the last decade. (The average net correlation between female and religiousness has gone up from .07 to .11 since 1963.)

The same finding seems to hold true for ethnic groups. On all the variables under study (table 6.11), American Catholic ethnic groups can be ranked in neat hierarchical order across the page: the Irish and the Germans are the most religious, the Poles fall on the mean, and the Italians and the Spanish-speaking are substantially beneath the mean. Nor has there

TABLE 6.11

ETHNICITY AND RELIGIOUSNESS, 1963 AND 1974

(Standardized Deviations from Mean of the Given Year)

Religious Scales	1963					1974				
	Irish	German	Polish	Italian	Spanish-Speaking	Irish	German	Polish	Italian	Spanish-Speaking
Church's right to teach	21	07	01	-21	-14	10	24	-04	-25	-09
Doctrinal orthodoxy	19	09	-06	-15	-23	00	08	-14	-13	-23
Sexual orthodoxy	26	16	02	-30	-43	12	-01	00	00	-08
Sacramental reception	24	18	00	-22	-56	28	43	-07	-20	-31
Activism	23	10	-03	-14	-49	39	29	-22	-31	-31
Church contribution	13	13	01	-02	-36	31	09	31	-17	-28
Media activism						24	14	-14	-26	-07
New style activism						29	14	03	-09	-23
Old style activism						39	36	10	-15	-45

TABLE 6.12

INFLUENCE OF CATHOLIC EDUCATION AND ETHNICITY

(Standardized Coefficients)

Religious Scales	1963					1974				
	Irish	German	Polish	Italian	Spanish-Speaking	Irish	German	Polish	Italian	Spanish-speaking
Church's right to teach	.13	.03	.03	.14	.09	.11	.05	-.14	.15	.12
Doctrinal orthodoxy	.15	.03	.11	.09	.09	.15	.13	-.05	.22	.16
Sexual orthodoxy	.00	.07	.06	.15	-.15	.00	.04	.22	.15	.19
Sacrament reception	.07	.11	.09	.13	.03	.06	.06	.45	.21	.10
Activism	.06	.09	.09	.21	.01	.09	.07	.45	.21	.28
Church contribution	-.08	.02	.11	.02	.16	-.07	.17	.19	.13	.03
Media activism						.19	.04	.32	.22	.38
New style activism						.00	.09	.02	.01	.17
Old style activism						.07	.13	.43	.16	.07

TABLE 6.13

SOME VARIABLES OF RELIGIOUS BEHAVIOR MODEL FOR ETHNIC GROUPS, 1963 AND 1974

(Standardized Coefficients)

Religious Scales	1963					1974				
	Irish	German	Polish	Italian	Spanish-Speaking	Irish	German	Polish	Italian	Spanish-Speaking
Catholic education	.07	.07	.08	.12	.05	.04	.08	.22	.18	.17
Spouse's church attendance	.04	.09	.15	.12	.21	.18	.32	.49	.22	.22
Parents' religiousness	.14	.19	.14	.11	.16	.10	.13	.07	.06	.05

been much change in this picture between the two time points save on the issue of sexual orthodoxy. With the exception of the Spanish-speaking, the impact of Catholic education generally grows stronger at both points in time as you look from left to right on table 6.12. To put it simply, the Irish are more religious to begin with; they perhaps have less need for or will benefit less from Catholic schooling. The Italians are less religious to begin with, and hence they either have more need for or benefit more from such schooling. Finally, while the average beta (table 6.13) slips slightly for the Irish from 1963 to 1974 and remains virtually unchanged for the Germans, it goes up sharply for the other three groups—from .08 to .22 for the Poles, from .12 to .18 for the Italians, and from .05 to .17 for the Spanish-speaking.

Under the impact of the dramatic changes of the past ten years, then, Catholic schools have become more important precisely for those groups that were less religious to begin with, that is, men, young people under thirty, and Polish, Italian, and Spanish-speaking Catholics. In the case of the first two, they are also the groups for whom the religious decline has been the sharpest. Catholic schools appear to be effective at keeping in the church the members of those groups most likely to drift out.

There is something of a paradox at work here. Catholic schools continue to have a stronger impact on those from more religious families, but they also have a stronger impact on those population groups which were less religious to begin with and which in some cases have become even less so during the last decade.

The "Catholicity" factor which was used as a measure in the last chapter to summarize the use of the social change models can also be used to summarize our analysis of the religious behavior model (tables 6.14 and 6.15). The model explains 9 percent more of the variance in 1974 than it did in 1963. The predictive power of age has gone up from .05 to .20, and the predictive power of sex has gone down from .28

to .19. Education, once a moderately strong predictor of "Catholicity" (.15), now has a negative relationship with that variable (-.07). Parental religiousness has declined, while spouse's church attendance has moved from .42 to .50. Catholic education was .15 ten years ago and is .23 now. It is now a stronger net predictor of one's position on this scale than age, sex, educational attainment, or parental religiousness. Dramatic change in the church, in other words, has affected the importance of other variables in determining adult religiousness and it has increased the impact of Catholic education.

The number of years one has attended Catholic schools has declined somewhat as a predictor of Catholicity for women. But the relationship between Catholic education and Catholicity has risen sharply for men (.18 to .23). It has gone up slightly for those from very religious families. The result is that the differences between men and women and between more religious and less religious family backgrounds have increased over the last decade. The difference is now .08 between men and women, as opposed to .0 a decade ago; and it is now .20 between those from less religious and those from more religious families, as opposed to .16 a decade ago.

The sharpest differences, however, have occurred among the age groups (table 6.15). There was only a .08 beta between years of Catholic education and Catholicity for those under thirty a decade ago (the Cold War cohort). For their successors (the Vietnam generation), however, the relationship has jumped to .21. In the meantime, for those over thirty, the beta has declined from .16 to .12. Hence there has been a change of .17 in the differences in impact of Catholic education on adult religiousness in the two age groups. There also has been a decline in the relationship for the Germans and Irish. Large increases have occurred for the Italians, Poles, and Spanish-speaking.

The use of the Catholicity factor as a summary measure highlights the paradox of this chapter: Catholic religiousness

TABLE 6.14

AVERAGE STANDARDIZED COEFFICIENTS WITH "CATHOLICITY FACTOR" IN
RELIGIOUS BEHAVIOR MODEL, 1963 AND 1974

	1963	1974
Parental religiousness	.28	.22
Age	.05	.20
Sex	.28	.19
Educational achievement	.15	-.07
Years of Catholic education	.15	.23
Spouse's church attendance	.42	.50
Total variance explained	.38	.47

TABLE 6.15

STANDARDIZED COEFFICIENTS (BETAS) BETWEEN YEARS OF CATHOLIC
EDUCATION AND "CATHOLICITY" FACTOR FOR CERTAIN SUBGROUPS

	1963	1974
Male	.18	.23
Female	.17	.15
Religious parents	.19	.23
Less religious parents	.03	.03
Under 30	.08	.21
Over 30	.16	.12
Irish	.06	.05
German	.12	.10
Polish	.08	.27
Italian	.13	.25
Spanish-speaking	.07	.24

has gone down, but the importance of Catholic education has gone up because of its heightened impact on certain ethnic groups, young people, and men—the last two groups being those among whom religiousness has most sharply declined. In other words, Catholic education has slowed the decline more effectively for those groups wherein the decline has been the most serious. Catholic education seems much less effective for those showing a less serious decline. Furthermore, its relative impact is now even greater on those who will build the future—respondents from more religious families, young people, and men (who are the decisive religious socializers [McCready 1972]). Thus, in terms of both cutting losses and restructuring for the future, Catholic schools seem substantially more important today than they were a decade ago.

How Big is "Big"?

The standardized coefficients (betas) between number of years in Catholic school and adult religiousness are generally not large. Can one conclude that Catholic schools are not effective? To a considerable extent the answer depends upon how much one believes that adult behavior can be shaped by background influences. A model of adult behavior with a very high R^2 would be one in which most behavior of human beings could easily be predicted if we knew the pertinent background variables. Obviously humans remain very unpredictable, and the complexity of a personality is such that one scarcely can expect any background influence to produce an overwhelming correlation, for such an influence would take randomness and variety out of human action. The religious behavior models presented in this chapter are generally about as successful in predicting adult religiousness as are the social stratification models of Sewell, Duncan, and their associates in predicting income levels.

Catholic education in 1974 is as strong a predictor, on the average, of adult religious behavior as the religiousness of parents. It is stronger than level of educational attainment or sex. Furthermore, the average influence of Catholic schools has remained constant between 1963 and 1974, while parents' religiousness, educational attainment, and sex have declined (and age and spouse's religiousness have increased) in predictive effectiveness. The .16 beta for parental religiousness may seem rather small until one stops to consider how difficult it is even to achieve a standardized correlation coefficient that high.

At the time *The Education of Catholic Americans* was written there was little material available from other educational impact research from which comparisons could be made.[9] Tables 6.16 and 6.17 originated in the reanalysis of the Equality of Educational Opportunity Study (EEOS) (done by

TABLE 6.16

RAW AND STANDARDIZED CORRELATIONS BETWEEN PER PUPIL
EXPENDITURE, PROPORTION SCHOOL WHITE, AND
VERBAL ACHIEVEMENT SCORES*

	Per Pupil Expenditure			Proportion White		
	Raw	Beta 1[a]	Beta 2[b]	Raw	Beta 1[a]	Beta 2[b]
Sixth Grade						
Northern blacks	.07	.01	.02	.15	-.01	-.03
Northern whites	.04	.01	.02	.16	.06	.04
Ninth Grade						
Northern blacks	.00	.01	.04	.14	.22	.20
Northern whites	.07	.06	.08	.12	.06	.05
Twelfth Grade						
Northern blacks	.00	.00	.01	.15	.09	.06
Northern whites	.08	.03	.04	.06	.06	.03

*Adapted from Marshal S. Smith, "The Basic Findings Reconsidered," in D. P. Moynihan and F. Mosteller (eds.), Equality of Educational Opportunity.

[a]Net of family background factor, facilities and curriculum factor, student body factor.

[b]Net of all but family background factor.

TABLE 6.17

REGRESSION COEFFICIENTS FOR SCHOOL ACHIEVEMENT

Standardized regression coefficients for six background variables[1] at grades 6,9, and 12 for Northern whites and blacks. Each coefficient is estimated in an equation containing all other background variables, Proportion Whites in the School, and three sets of schoolwide variables measuring Curriculum and Facilities, Teacher Characteristics, and Student Body characteristics. Individual Verbal Achievement is the dependent variable.

	Northern Blacks			Northern Whites		
	6th Grade	9th Grade	12th Grade	6th Grade	9th Grade	12th Grade
Reading Material in Home	.11*	.08*	.04	.12*	.11*	.17*
Items in Home	.13*	.05	.02	.08*	.04	-.00
Siblings	.08*	.13*	.09*	.10*	.14*	.09*
Structural Integrity of Family	.06	.07*	.04	.06*	.08*	.03
Parents' Education	.10*	.09*	.14*	.19*	.23*	.19*
Urbanism of Background	.01	.04	.05	-.09*	.07	.01

[1]The background variables are described in detail in Appendix A.
*An asterisk next to a value signifies that this coefficient is significant at the .05 level (t>1.96, N = 1000).

James Coleman and his colleagues) that was prepared by Marshal S. Smith for a collection of essays (Mosteller and Moynihan 1972). The standardized coefficients between per-pupil expenditure in a school system and verbal achievement scores are virtually nonexistent for both blacks and whites, and the standardized coefficients between the proportion white in a school and the academic achievement of blacks is notable (approximately .2) only for ninth-grade northern blacks. Generally speaking, the only substantial beta for family background variables with individual verbal achievement is parental education.

Of course, any comparison between the standardized coefficients in tables 6.16 and 6.17 and those produced in the early tables of this chapter is at best only illustrative. The dependent variable in the EEOS study is present performance in school; the dependent variable in our research is adult performance after one has left school (in some instances, many years after school). What a comparison between the EEOS coefficients and those reported in this study does suggest is that in both social research and social policy, one must be content with relatively modest results. As our colleague Sidney Verba once remarked, "Reality is a .3 correlation."

Sometimes it seems to be a lot less than that.

Whether the massive modern resources poured into Catholic schools are worth the effort is an issue that is beyond the scope of this chapter. Schools do have as much impact on adult religiousness, apparently, as does the religiousness of one's parents, which might be considered a not unimportant accomplishment. Furthermore, in lieu of a proven method of matching parental influence through some other method besides parochial education, it might be argued that a .08 standardized coefficient is better than nothing. But whether the schools are worth the cost is a decision that should be made not by social scientists but by the administrators of the schools and their clientele. The administrators seem to have made the decision: they are closing down many of the existing schools and not building new ones. As we shall see in the next chapter, however, the clientele appears to have made a different judgment.

Catholic Education and Racial Attitudes

There has been substantial change in racial attitudes among Americans since 1963 (Greeley and Sheatsley 1971; Greeley and Sheatsley 1974). Catholics were more sympathetic to racial integration than were Protestants even in the North in 1963; they have lengthened this lead in the last ten years. Unfortunately, the items chosen for use in the first study of the impact of Catholic schools were from the "bottom end" of the Guttman scale that NORC uses to measure racial integration; that is, those items which have been least likely to change in the last decade (see appendices II and III for those items). Hence there is no change in the mean score on the scale used in this project since 1963 (table 6.18), and we are unable to analyze the components of change.

However, those two groups which had either 8-12 years of

TABLE 6.18

CATHOLIC EDUCATION AND RACIAL ATTITUDES--1963-1974

i. Mean Score on Racism Scale

Years of Catholic Schooling	1963	1974
0	1.60	1.73
1-8	1.63	1.68
8-12	1.45	1.27
13 or more	1.31	0.94
All	1.57	1.60

ii. Mean Score on Support for Integrated Education (Proportion of Blacks Acceptable in School)

0	1.98
1-8	1.55
8-12	2.02
13 or more	2.30

iii. Net Correlations (Religious Behavior Model) between Years of Catholic Education and Racial Attitudes

	1963	1974	
	Racism	Racism	Support for Integration
All respondents	.00	-.07	.00
College educated	-.04	-.20	.11

Catholic education or more than 12 years had lower racism scores than other Catholics ten years ago. They have even lower scores in 1974. Indeed, the only change measurable by the scale used in this project occurred precisely among those with more than 8 years of Catholic education. Furthermore, those with more than 12 years of Catholic education score the highest on a scale devised to measure an acceptable level of integration (proportion of black students in school—see Appendix V for scale construction) (table 6.18-ii).

It is possible, however, that such correlations are merely the result of the fact that those who had high levels of Catholic education also had high levels of education. Therefore, we must apply our religious behavior model and take out the effects of age, sex, educational attainment, parents' religiousness, and spouse's religiousness. When that is done, the only positive relationship between Catholic school attendance and racial attitudes is on the 1974 racism scale. The net correlation is modest (.07), but the net correlation for number of years of any education is only -.17. Thus it can be said that compared to number of years of education, the number of years of *Catholic* education makes a not unimportant addition to improving racial attitudes. Furthermore, it makes this improvement in 1974 when it did not make it in 1963 (table 6.18-iii).

It was reported in *The Education of Catholic Americans* that the major effect of Catholic education on racial attitudes came among those who went to college. Using our present methods of analysis, we can see that among the college educated the net correlation between years of Catholic education and the racism scale in 1963 was -.04, and that in 1974 it had become -.20. Among the college educated the beta between Catholic schooling and support for integrated schools was .11.

In 1963, then, the only impact of Catholic education on racial attitudes was among the college educated (although this was not merely the result of their education but represented a distinctively *Catholic* input). This impact, very small in 1963, has increased greatly during the past ten years, and now a modest net correlation can also be found among the general public.

It would be a mistake to exaggerate the importance of both the impact of Catholic education on racial attitudes and the increasing size of that impact. Even among the college educated in 1974, only 4 percent of the variance in racial attitudes can be explained by their having attended Catholic schools. But it would also be a mistake to underestimate the importance of the relationship between racial attitudes and Catholic school attendance. Total years of education also explains only about 4 percent of the variance in racial attitudes. Among the college educated, in other words, having had a Catholic education seems to double the educational impact on racial attitudes. It is not a trivial accomplishment. Educational impact research has taught us to have modest expectations. However, our greater sophistication about the difficulties involved in value change has taught us to be grateful for modest success.

Catholic Education and Economic Achievement

At the time the research which resulted in *The Education of Catholic Americans* was being prepared, there was considerable controversy about whether Catholicism was a barrier to economic achievement. A number of authors, both Catholic and non-Catholic, suggested that the Protestant ethic was alive and well, and that Protestants were more strongly motivated to achieve than Catholics. Others argued that the rigidity of the authoritarian controls of the Catholic church inhibited the growth of independence and ambition, which were necessary for economic and intellectual success.[10] Since that time the controversy has settled down, mostly because the overwhelming weight of evidence is that whatever may be said about the Protestant ethic, Catholics are more successful economically and educationally in the United States today than are white Protestants.[11]

But in the perspective of those who thought that Catholicism would inhibit economic achievement, it was logical to assume that Catholic schools, representing, as they purported to, the quintessence of the "Catholic ethic," would inhibit economic achievement even more. In other words, it was one strike against you to be Catholic and another to go to Catholic schools. The research reported in *The Education of Catholic Americans* showed, however, that parochial school attendance correlated *positively* with economic achievement. There was a profit to be made by going to Catholic schools.

The same finding is presented in clearer perspective in our reanalysis of the 1963 data (tables 6.19 and 6.20). Those who spent at least ten years in Catholic schools had 13.6 years of education in 1963 and 14 years in 1974, more than a one-

TABLE 6.19

ACHIEVEMENT OF CATHOLICS BY PAROCHIAL SCHOOL ATTENDANCE 1963 AND 1974
(FOR ONLY THOSE RESPONDENTS WITH MORE THAN TEN YEARS EDUCATION)

1963	Father's Education (In Years)	Own Education (In Years)	Occupational Prestige Score	Income (In Dollars)
0 years in Catholic school (365)	7.6	12.8	38.4	7,977
1-10 years in Catholic school (491)	8.6	13.0	42.9	8,526
More than 10 years in Catholic school (211)	9.3	13.6	51.0	9,300
1974				
0 years in Catholic school (201)	8.7	12.8	40.1	14,865
1-10 years in Catholic school (241)	9.7	12.8	40.2	14,701
More than 10 years in Catholic school (132)	9.9	14.0	47.9	16,628

TABLE 6.20

NET EDUCATIONAL, OCCUPATIONAL, AND INCOME DIFFERENCE FROM THOSE
WITH MORE THAN 10 YEARS CATHOLIC EDUCATION 1963 AND 1974
(FOR ONLY THOSE WITH MORE THAN TEN YEARS EDUCATION)

	Own Education		Occupational Prestige		Income (in Dollars)	
1963	Gross	Net[a]	Gross	Net[b]	Gross	Net[c]
0 years in Catholic schools	-0.8	-0.7	-12.6	-2.2	-1,323	-476
1-10 years in Catholic schools	-0.6	-0.6	-8.1	0.0	-874	-355
1974						
0 years in Catholic schools	-1.2	-1.0	-11.5	-4.3	-1,763	-537
1-10 years in Catholic schools	-1.2	-1.0	-7.9	0.0	-1,927	-1,091

[a]With father's education taken into account

[b]With father's education and own education taken into account

[c]With father's education, own education, and occupation taken into account

year advantage over those who did not go to Catholic schools
at all. Even when we apply the standardization technique described in chapter 3, those who attended Catholic schools still
hold on to their educational advantage, an advantage which is
not purely a function of the superior education of their fathers.

Those who had more than ten years in parochial schools in
both 1963 and 1974 also have a lead of more than ten units
in occupational prestige over those who had no Catholic education. They are approximately more than eight units over
those who had 1 to 10 years of Catholic schooling. In 1963
their income advantage over the former is more than $1,300;
over the latter, it is almost $900. In 1974, this advantage in-
creases to $1,700 over those who had no Catholic education
and almost $2,000 over those who had 1 to 10 years. What
seems to provide the economic payoff in 1974 is a lot of

Catholic education. However, the differences in occupational prestige diminish considerably when we remove the effects of both the respondent's and the respondent's father's educational level through standardization. At both points in time those who went to Catholic schools maintain their advantage over those who did not (though it becomes rather small); but there is no difference between the two Catholic school groups. However, the income differences remain at both points in time, and indeed there is still more than a thousand dollars advantage in having more than ten years of education in Catholic schools.

There are a number of possible explanations for this economic advantage of Catholic education—an advantage which ran against the 1963 expectations:

1. Catholic schools are academically better than public schools, and provide their students with better intellectual skills, which in turn enable them to be more successful in the occupational world.

2. Those who attend Catholic schools learn habits of self-restraint and diligence (which is to say that they acquire the Protestant ethic?) that enable them to do better in the world of economic achievement.

3. Even if one holds constant the educational achievement of parents, it may still be the case that Catholic school attenders come from families where there is a higher motivation for economic achievement. The financial sacrifice made to provide Catholic education, for example, may be one evidence of such familial motivation.

4. Writers from the National Bureau of Economic Research (NBER) have recently raised the possibility of family influence within religious groups as an explanation of economic achievement (Juster 1974:19-20):

Economists and other social scientists have recently begun to pay close attention to the possible role of pre-school investments in children by parents, as it affects subsequent educational attainment. . . . Parental influences of this sort may also have effects on market productivity and earnings over and above any impact on school performance, and if so, returns on education can be affected.

To show the potential importance of these kinds of factors [possible influence on earnings of different amounts of parental time spent with preschool or school-age children], it is worth pointing out that cultural background as reflected by religious preference has a very powerful influence on observed earnings in both the Taubman-Wales and the Hause chapters. In the data sets used for both chapters, respondents were asked to report their religious preference as among Protestant, Catholic, Jewish, and other (including none). Taking account of family background factors like father's and mother's education and occupation, variables for both Jewish and Catholic religious preference have a significant (positive) impact on observed earnings relative to respondents reporting a Protestant preference. The Jewish religious preference variable also shows a significant impact on earnings in the Rogers sample.

Although the precise factors reflected in these religious preference variables are unknowns, plausible hypotheses are that they reflect differences in the cultural background to which respondents were exposed during their formative years, or differences in the quantity or quality of parental time inputs, rather than differences in specific religious values or practices. The appropriate research stance seems clear. The existence of strong statistical differences in behavior patterns associated with religious preference variables—or, as in other studies, with variables reflecting race or sex—points toward the existence of forces whose influence needs to be better understood and more fully interpreted, rather than toward an inference of causal relationships from observed statistical associations.

If such family background factors do correlate with religion, then it would not be surprising to find such background dynamics especially vigorous in those families who were sufficiently Catholic to pay for ten or more years of Catholic education for their children.

Another possibility is that those who have considerable amounts of parochial schooling are in some fashion better integrated into the Catholic community, and that, for psychological or financial reasons, this integration has a certain profitability. There are moderate correlations between income, education, and occupation and growing up in a Catholic neighborhood, living in a Catholic neighborhood now, and having a high proportion of your three closest friends Catholic (in excess of .1). However, there are almost no differences among the three educational groups (table 6.21) in their mean scores on these measures, so we cannot use the standardization model of holding constant those differences. Still there remains the possibility that even though the groups have on the average, for example, the same proportion of their three closest friends Catholic, they make different economic use of these friendships. They may be able to convert them differentially into income.

TABLE 6.21

DEVIATIONS FROM MEAN FOR CATHOLIC EDUCATIONAL GROUPS IN
CATHOLIC COMMUNITY MEASURES--1974

	Growing up in Catholic Neighborhood	Living in Catholic Neighborhood Now	Three Best Friends Catholic
0 years in Catholic schools	.03	-.02	-.05
1-10 years in Catholic schools	-.01	.10	-.10
More than 10 years in Catholic schools	-.02	-.05	.27
Mean	(3.26)	(3.00)	(2.02)

It must be remembered that the "conversion rate" in a regression equation (the "*b*") represents the change in the metric of the dependent variable which is accounted for by a change in the metric of the independent variable. Thus a "*b*" between income and proportion of friends Catholic would represent how much income one adds for each new unit of Catholic friend, holding constant all the other variables in the equation. One can see in table 6.22 that there is a surprising difference in the ability of the three Catholic educational groups to convert "friendship" into income. Each extra Catholic friend is worth $3,681 for those with ten years of Catholic education and $859 for those with no Catholic education. There is a net loss of $310 of income for each Catholic friend among those who had between 1 and 10 years of Catholic education. There is a similar though smaller phenomenon at work for living in a Catholic neighborhood now and growing up in a Catholic neighborhood. The impact of Catholic friendship on income is illustrated with another statistic in table 6.23. The beta for those with all Catholic education is .41; for those with no Catholic education it is .07; and for those who were in between it declines to -.05. For those living in a Catholic neighborhood the figures are .26, .13, and -.15, respectively.

TABLE 6.22

CONVERSION RATES ("B") FOR LIVING IN CATHOLIC COMMUNITIES
BY CATHOLIC EDUCATIONAL GROUPS - 1974
FOR THOSE WITH 10 OR MORE YEARS OF EDUCATION

	Growing Up in Catholic Neighborhood	Living in Catholic Neighborhood Now	Three Best Friends Catholic
0 years in Catholic schools	$ 467	$ 731	$ 859
1-10 years in Catholic schools	219	- 868	- 310
More than 10 years in Catholic schools	660	1727	3681

TABLE 6.23

SIMPLE AND STANDARDIZED CORRELATIONS WITH INCOME FOR LIVING IN
CATHOLIC COMMUNITY MEASURES BY EDUCATIONAL GROUPS--1974
(FOR ONLY THOSE WITH MORE THAN 10 YEARS EDUCATION)

	Growing Up in Catholic Neighborhood		Living in Catholic Neighborhood Now		Three Best Friends Catholic	
	r	Beta	r	Beta	r	Beta
0 years in Catholic schools	.10	.06	.10	.13	.00	.17
1-10 years in Catholic schools	.01	-.03	.12	-.15	.02	-.05
More than 10 years in Catholic schools	.09	.07	.08	.26	.13	.41

There are clearly a number of baffling mysteries at work. Why should there be any relationship at all between where you live and the religiousness of your friends, on the one hand, and economic success, on the other? And why should this relationship be positive for those who had a lot of Catholic education? Morris Rosenberg (1964) suggested some time ago that growing up in a neighborhood where one was a member of a minority group had some effect on self-esteem and that this, in its turn, weakened to some extent one's economic achievement. But our data indicate that the neighborhood you grew up in is less important than the one you live in now and your present friendship patterns. Could it be that those who are in Catholic relational situations have better morale than Catholics who do not, and that therefore a Catholic education produces "better-adjusted" adults?

On Bradburn's psychological well-being scale ("How happy are you now? Very happy, pretty happy, not too happy"), we could find no difference among the three Catholic educational groups in psychological well-being (table 6.24).

But there were different relationships between proportion of three closest friends Catholic and psychological well-being for the Catholic educational groups (table 6.24-i), with those

TABLE 6.24

PSYCHOLOGICAL WELL-BEING, CATHOLIC EDUCATION, CATHOLIC FRIENDS, AND INCOME--1974

(i)   Correlations between Proportion of Catholic Friends and Psychological Well-Being
      for Three Catholic Educational Groups

0 Years in Catholic Schools	0-10 Years in Catholic Schools	More than 10 Years in Catholic Schools
.10	-.18	.11

(ii) Net Correlation between Psychological Well-Being and Income with Father's Educa-
      tion, Own Education, Occupation, Proportion of Catholic Friends Held Constant--
      for Three Catholic Educational Groups (beta)

.28	-.08	.08

(iii) Income Conversion Rates for Proportion of Three Best Friends Catholic with
      Psychological Well-Being Taken into Account and Not Taken into Account

Well-Being not Taken into Account	$859	$-310	$3681
Well-Being Taken into Account	509	220	1481

who had some Catholic education displaying a negative relationship between Catholic friends and psychological well-being
(-.18), and the other two groups showing a positive relationship. For those who had some Catholic education, a Catholic
friendship network seemed to produce less happiness than for
those who had either no Catholic education or a lot of it.
Furthermore, with all the other variables in the model held
constant (including number of close friends Catholic), there
were positive relationships between income and psychological
well-being for Catholics with no Catholic school education
and those with a lot, and a negative relationship between
psychological well-being and income for those with some
Catholic education (table 6.24-ii). In this group Catholic
friends produce less happiness, and less happiness produces
more income.

Finally, if one compares the conversion rates for Catholic friendship with psychological well-being in two ways—with psychological well-being not included in the equation—one can see (table 6.24-iii) that while the differences are not eliminated, they are diminished; and the negative relationship for those who had some Catholic education becomes positive. Thus, psychological well-being is involved in the differences among the three Catholic educational groups in the ability to convert friendship into income. Being integrated into the Catholic community does produce a higher level of psychological well-being, which, in turn, explains in part the higher economic convertibility of friendship. But why this should be true only for those who have more than ten years of Catholic education and not for those who have less remains a mystery. Furthermore, why it should be true also for those who have no Catholic education at all (though less dramatically than for those with more than ten years of Catholic schooling) is equally mysterious. Also, some of the differential convertibility of friendship seems to be related to social-psychological factors, but much of it does not. It could certainly be the case that those who have had many years of Catholic education are part of a Catholic business and commercial network that gives them an economic advantage; but then why would those who had no Catholic education also be able to profit from such a network? And why would the network be counterproductive for those who have had some Catholic education? There could easily be ethnic group differences at work, but our sample is not large enough to explore that possibility.

In retrospect, we must confess to a sense of a lost opportunity that we did not provide materials in our questionnaire to explore this issue more fully, especially since we had similar findings with our much cruder tools of a decade ago—there are, however, just so many items one can cram onto a questionnaire. There is an economic profit in having more than ten years of Catholic education, and it seems to be the result of a greater ability to convert Catholic community ties into income. The dynamics of this conversion process, however, must await more detailed investigation.

In summary, the advantage of parochial school attendance in educational attainment is not simply a function of the superior education of the respondents' fathers. The advantage in occupational prestige over those who had some Catholic school education vanishes between 1963 and 1974, but it continues over those who had no Catholic education. So, too, does the financial advantage, although in part that is the result of some aspects of Catholic community life we do not fully understand. The last ten years do not seem to have diminished these particular advantages of Catholic education in the slightest.

Religious Instruction

The Catholic church endeavors to provide religious education for the children of Catholic families who do not attend Catholic schools. This is done generally through the religious instruction classes of the Confraternity of Christian Doctrine (CCD) taught during release time or in afternoons, evenings, or Sunday mornings. Many Catholics argued in the early 1960s that such instruction classes were a preferable alternative to Catholic schools in the new era that began with the Second Vatican Council (Ryan 1964). While there was little evidence available at the time to indicate that such instruction classes had much impact on the adult behavior of those who attended them, those who advocated a strong emphasis in this direction contended that rather little in the way of resources had been put into the Confraternity of Christian Doctrine, and that an apparent test of the effectiveness of this alternative form of Catholic education could only be made when substantial efforts were expended. It is doubtful that anyone would now question that substantial efforts have been put into the CCD in the last ten years. In many Catholic parishes

TABLE 6.25

EFFECT OF CATHOLIC RELIGIOUS INSTRUCTION ON THOSE WHO DID NOT GO TO CATHOLIC SCHOOLS, 1963 AND 1974

(Standardized Scores)

Religious Scales	10 or More Years in Catholic Schools	1-10 Years in Catholic Schools	Religious Instruction in Grammar and High School	Religious Instruction in either Grammar or High School	No Religious Instruction in School
1963					
Catholic activism	49	6	1	-17	-56
Support for vocation	30	9	4	-11	-36
Sexual orthodoxy	48	2	- 5	-20	-29
Doctrinal orthodoxy	49	1	00	- 7	-36
Church's right to teach	38	4	- 2	-14	-32
Sacramental reception	61	6	- 9	-18	-47
1974					
Catholic activism	48	5	-13	-32	-32
Support for vocation	13	9	- 3	-19	-13
Sexual orthodoxy	4	0	- 6	- 0	-13
Doctrinal orthodoxy	20	3	- 9	- 7	- 6
Church's right to teach	19	3	2	0	-24
Sacramental reception	31	7	- 9	-15	-20

TABLE 6.26

PERCENT HIGH ON RELIGIOUS BEHAVIOR BY RELIGIOUS INSTRUCTION FOR THOSE WHO DID NOT GO TO CATHOLIC SCHOOLS

	10 or More Years in Catholic Schools			1-10 Years in Catholic Schools			Religious Instruction in both Grammar and High School			Religious Instruction either in Grammar or High School			No Religious Instruction in School		
	1963	1974	Change	1963	1974	Change	1963	1974	Change	1963	1974	Change	1963	1974	Change
Weekly mass	91	65	-26	74	44	-30	74	37	-37	64	39	-25	50	29	-21
Weekly communion	27	41	14	14	27	13	7	21	14	8	20	12	6	15	9
Monthly confession	54	20	-34	40	21	-19	37	19	-18	31	14	-17	25	12	-13
Daily prayer	81	62	-19	75	43	-32	75	44	-31	67	44	-23	56	33	-23
Contraception wrong	71	14	-57	54	15	-39	56	18	-38	44	13	-31	41	12	-29

such instruction has replaced Catholic education. New suburban parishes have constructed not Catholic schools but Catholic "learning centers." Some of the most enthusiastic and dedicated priests and religious in the country have moved into such work.

There does not seem to be much evidence in the adult population that instruction classes are an adequate substitute for parochial schools (tables 6.25 and 6.26). It is generally the case, in both 1963 and 1974, that some religious instruction is preferable to no religious instruction. However, the differences between those who had some religious instruction and those who had none seem to have diminished rather than increased in the last decade. It would appear, therefore, that religious instruction classes were less effective than parochial schools in impeding the religious decline in the Catholic population during the last ten years.

Nor has the emphasis on CCD instruction in the last decade proved to be an effective substitute for Catholic education for the Vietnam generation, some of whom surely benefited from the increased emphasis on CCD (table 6.27). Indeed, on a number of items—reception of communion, going to confession, praying daily, acceptance of the Vatican Council reforms—there is little difference between those who had no religious instruction at all and those who had religious instruction during both high school and college years (table 6.28). On a number of other measures—vocation support, Catholic activism, the church's right to teach, sexual orthodoxy, support for "new ways," and Catholic media activism—there was not much to choose from between those who had religious instruction at one level or the other but not both and those who had no religious instruction at all.

However, the differences in tables 6.25, 6.26, 6.27, and 6.28 are raw differences, with none of the background variables in our model taken into account. If one standardizes for educational achievement and religiousness of parents, perhaps one can find an effect of CCD instruction that may be more

TABLE 6.27

RELIGIOUS ATTITUDES AND BEHAVIOR BY CATHOLIC EDUCATIONAL BACKGROUND FOR
THOSE UNDER 30 (VIETNAM GENERATION)

(Percent)

	10 or More Yrs. in Catholic Schools	1-10 Yrs. in Catholic Schools	Religious Instruction in both Grammar and High School	Religious Instruction in either Grammar or High School	No Religious Instruction in School
Weekly mass	47	41	35	22	9
Weekly communion	22	14	9	3	8
Monthly confession	6	13	16	2	14
Daily private prayer	52	50	57	47	14
Contraception is wrong	8	9	12	0	8

TABLE 6.28

STANDARDIZED SCORES BY CATHOLIC EDUCATIONAL BACKGROUND FOR THOSE UNDER 30 (VIETNAM GENERATION)

	10 or More Yrs. in Catholic Schools	1-10 Yrs. in Catholic Schools	Religious Instruction in both Grammar and High School	Religious Instruction in either Grammar or High School	No Religious Instruction in School
Support for vocation	16	0	-20	-77	-54
Doctrinal orthodoxy	7	-14	-15	-33	-42
Catholic activism	5	-18	-37	-69	-77
Church's right to teach	-8	-2	-23	-28	-16
Sex mores	-23	-40	-37	-47	-53
Sacramental reception	-5	-16	-29	-65	-79
Contribution	46	-9	-34	-49	-41
Vatican II	58	2	-15	-14	3
New ways	52	24	2	-16	-13
Priestly change	46	8	6	-7	-44
Catholic media activism	23	7	-4	-23	8
New style activism	22	4	-5	-17	-34
Old style activism	7	-7	-10	-26	-43

favorable to that approach to religious instruction.

When we use a multiple regression technique that "takes out" the effect of parental religiousness and educational achievement, we still find little evidence that religious instruction outside the Catholic schools is an adequate substitute for the schools. Such instruction (table 6.29) is indeed better than nothing in most cases, although in 1974 there is no difference between those who have no instruction and those who have some instruction in the doctrinal orthodoxy, vocation support, sexual orthodoxy, and new style activism measures. Nor have the CCD exertions of the past decade produced any remarkable impact on those in the Vietnam generation. Those who have had some instruction have higher scores than those who have none, in most cases, but there is generally very little difference between those who have had religious instruction only in grammar school or high school and those who have had it at both times. The extra work seems to have been wasted.

The CCD program may be useful to the church as a symbol of its interest in and concern for those who do not go to Catholic schools. It also seems to be better in some cases than no religious instruction at all, but it does not even begin to substitute for Catholic schools. Nor is there much evidence to suggest that the CCD has improved its performance through the intensive efforts of the last decade. Note, for example, the differences between the members of the Vietnam generation who had ten or more years of Catholic education and those who had religious instruction in both grammar and high schools on the support of Vatican II and media activism measures (table 6.30). In the former case the difference is almost half of a standard deviation, and in the latter, almost three-fourths of a standard deviation—and this is when we hold constant both educational attainment and parental religiousness. In winning support for the Council from young Catholics and in persuading them to read religious books and periodicals, the CCD was a dismal failure.

TABLE 6.29

SCORES ON RELIGIOUS VARIABLES BY CATHOLIC INSTRUCTION WITH EDUCATIONAL LEVEL AND PARENTS' RELIGIOUSNESS HELD CONSTANT

("Z" Scores)

	10 or More Yrs. in Catholic Schools	1-10 Yrs. in Catholic Schools	Religious Instruction in both Grammar and High School	Religious Instruction in either Grammar or High School	No Religious Instruction in School
1963					
Vocation support	10	06	06	-06	-24
Doctrinal orthodoxy	30	01	-03	-04	-24
Sacramental reception	27	03	-09	-05	-18
Sexual orthodoxy	25	00	08	-09	-08
1974					
Vocation support	08	08	-09	-15	-14
Doctrinal orthodoxy	08	-07	-09	-08	-07
Sacramental reception	24	04	-07	-02	-22
Sexual orthodoxy	07	-06	12	00	00
Old style activism	27	19	-17	-09	-23
New style activism	16	00	-12	-03	-05
Catholic media activism	21	01	-04	-16	-03

TABLE 6.30

SCORES ON RELIGIOUS VARIABLES BY CATHOLIC INSTRUCTION WITH PARENTAL RELIGIOUSNESS
AND EDUCATIONAL LEVEL HELD CONSTANT FOR THOSE UNDER 30 IN 1974

("Z" Scores)

	10 or More Yrs. in Catholic Schools	1-10 Yrs. in Catholic School	Religious Instruction in both Grammar and High School	Religious Instruction in either Grammar or High School	No Religious Instruction in School
Sexual orthodoxy	-18	-29	-56	-51	-.62
Doctrinal orthodoxy	02	-20	-12	-17	-40
Sacramental reception	-19	-19	-40	-47	-72
Vocation support	13	02	-24	-85	-54
Vatican II	42	-07	00	00	-47
Media activism	29	12	-47	-47	-58

Catholic Education and Religious Change

Our final task in this chapter is to link our analysis of the impact of Catholic schools with the social change models developed to account for the decline of Catholic practice in the previous chapter. Are the dynamics of decline different for the three different levels of Catholic schooling with which we have been concerned?

First of all, the proportionate decline is less among those who went to Catholic schools for more than ten years (table 6.31-A). In 1963, two-thirds of them were above the median score on the Catholic activities factor. A decade later the proportion of those above the same median score had fallen to 43 percent—approximately the same proportion that was above the factor median a decade ago among those who had no Catholic education. The impact of the last decade, in other words, was to reduce the religiousness of those who had gone to Catholic schools for more than ten years to about the level attained a decade ago by those who had not gone to Catholic schools at all.

But the proportionate decline among the other two groups was even greater. When we divide the percentage above the 1963 median now by the proportion above the same median a decade ago, we observe that the decline for those with more than ten years of Catholic schooling is .37, while for the other two groups it is about .44. The decline in "Catholicity" was sharp for all three groups but less sharp for those with more than ten years of Catholic education.

The dynamics of the change, however, are similar for all three groups. Our Social Change Model III accounts for three-fourths of the change in "Catholicity" among those who had no Catholic education. It accounts for all the change among the other two groups. The positive paths that emerge for those two groups show the operation of the dynamic we have linked with the Council. In each case more than half of the change can be accounted for by the changing sexual ethic of

TABLE 6.31

CATHOLIC SCHOOLS AND SOCIAL CHANGE MODEL III

A. Percent above Median on Catholicity Factor

Years of Catholic Schooling	1963	1974	Percentage Point Decline	Proportionate Decline
0	42%	24%	-18	43%
1-10	54	30	-24	44
More than 10	68	43	-25	37

B. Variables Contributing to Decline with Positive Paths from Time

Variables	Years of Catholic Schooling		
	0	1-10	More than 10
Papal authority change	-6%	-12%	-2%
Sexual orthodoxy change	-53	-63	-63
Cohort--Direct	-8	-16	-26
Indirect	-9	-9	-9
Unaccounted for by model	-24	0	0
Total	-100	-100	-100
Positive path from time	0	.004	.024

C. Change in Weekly Reception of Holy Communion

Direct path from time*	15	25	41
Indirect path from time**	-06	-13	-21
Total	09	12	20

D. Increase in Catholicity if Effect of Increased Weekly Reception of Communion Were not Depressed by Changes in Sexual Orthodoxy and Acceptance of Papal Authority

Percent increase	0	6	6
Total above 1963 mean if increase had occurred	42	60	74

*Increase net of depressant variables (sex orthodoxy, attitude toward pope, and cohort)
**Impact of depressant variables

215

American Catholics. Indeed, if one combines the indirect effect of cohort (which is almost entirely through the change in sexual attitudes) with sexual orthodoxy change, we account for 62 percent of the deterioration in "Catholicity" among those who did not go to Catholic school and 72 percent among the other two groups.

Catholic education, then, impeded somewhat the religious deterioration of the last decade among those who had more than ten years of Catholic education. But the restraining effect of Catholic education did not change the fundamental dynamics of deterioration; it only softened the effect somewhat. Most of the change in Catholic practice is the result of changing sexual attitudes no matter what the method of education. Indeed, the strongest decline (direct path from time) in the sexual ethic is among those who had more than ten years of Catholic schools (.47, as opposed to .41 for those who had some years of Catholic schooling and .28 for those who had none). Catholic education by no means immunized those who had it from the effect of the changing sexual ethic.

However, Catholic schools seem to have produced adults who are more open to the positive influences of the Vatican Council (a development which we have suggested can be monitored by the increase in the weekly reception of communion). The net increase in weekly communion reception is 20 percentage points for those who went to Catholic schools for more than ten years, and 12 percent and 9 percent, respectively, for the other two groups (table 6.31-C). How strong the positive force at work among those with considerable Catholic education actually is can be judged from the fact that were it not for the depressant effect of the negative variables in the model, weekly reception of communion would have gone up 40 percentage points among this group. The net effect of the changes linked to *Humanae Vitae* on the increase in frequent reception of communion by those who had more than ten years of Catholic education, in other words, was to cut the potential of this increase in half.

The encyclical both diminished the direct impact of the Council and masked the impact that survived. It would appear that had it not been for the encyclical (table 6.31-D), the positive forces at work in the church during the last decade would have produced a situation wherein 74 percent of those with more than ten years of Catholic education would be above the median, rather than 43 percent. Sixty percent of those with some Catholic education would be above the median, rather than 30 percent. And these increases would have occurred despite the propensity of the Vietnam generation to be less religious than its predecessors. (The indirect paths from time to cohort to Eucharist to "Catholicity" have been taken into account in table 6.31-D.)

Obviously, "what might have been" speculations based on mathematical models cannot serve to refute history. We cannot say what might have been with absolute certainty. Still, speculations based on the relationships produced by our models are much better grounded than almost any other type of historical speculation we might engage in. There were strong positive forces at work in American Catholicism during the past decade, especially among those who went to Catholic schools. There were stronger negative forces at work from which those who attended Catholic schools were not immune. Catholic education impeded the decline that did occur; it likely would have facilitated the growth that might have been.

Conclusion

In response to the questions posed at the beginning of the chapter, we can now say that those who have experienced value-oriented education are somewhat more likely to accept changes in the value-teaching institution when these changes occur. Under the impact of value transition, some of the relationships between value education and adult behavior increase in magnitude, particularly in such institutional matters as active involvement in and financial contribution to the institution, and, as we shall see in a subsequent chapter, favorable attitudes toward the institutional leaders. There is also an increase in the relationship between value-oriented education and private ritual behavior, as represented by daily prayer, in the new generation. On the other hand, public ritual behavior—such as mass attendance and reception of the sacraments—is less influenced by value-oriented education than it was a decade ago, and the relationship between sexual orthodoxy and value-oriented education has completely disappeared.

Spouse's religious behavior and sex have become much more important in predicting adult religious behavior, while both educational attainment and parental religiousness have declined in importance. There has been little change in the average contribution of Catholic school education to adult behavior during the last decade. Catholic education is now a more important predictor of adult religiousness than parental religiousness; it is as important a predictor as educational attainment.

There continues to be an educational and economic advantage in parochial school attendance, and the economic advantage seems to be the result of some not-fully-understood ability among those who had more than ten years of Catholic education to convert integration into the Catholic community into economic success—to the tune of more than a thousand dollars a year in 1974.

There is no evidence that the Confraternity of Christian Doctrine discussion classes can function as an adequate substitute for Catholic schools. Some religious instruction is better than none, but not much better.

Catholic schools are more important in shaping the religious behavior of men than they were a decade ago, and, both for men and for those under thirty, the schools serve to slow down the rate of decline in religiousness. The schools are more critical to the church now than they were a decade ago for two reasons: they prevent losses where losses are most likely to be the worst, among men and among the young; and they build for the future by influencing men, who are more effective religious socializers, and the young, who have more years ahead of them. Both of these school influences bear on the maintenance of religious traditions within families, which is also a pivotal point for the future stability of the church.

Furthermore, this heightened importance seems to be especially present in the most central kinds of religious behavior—structural support, shown in such measures as activism, vocational support, and contributions, and internalized religion, as manifested in private prayer, for example.

And to heap the last paradox onto the pile, when Catholic schools were less important to the church, more resources were poured into them. Now that the schools are more important, fewer resources are allowed them. *Humanae Vitae,* it would seem, is not the only mistake made by Catholic religious leadership during the past ten years.

7

Parochial Schools 1974: Their Use and Support by Catholics

The recurring debate on the separation of church and state in the United States gained fresh momentum in 1960 with the election of John F. Kennedy to the presidency. Those who feared a Catholic takeover of governmental institutions pushed for legislation to prohibit any government funds from going to Catholic schools. Others, seeing a Catholic in the White House, felt the time was ripe to get aid for Catholic educational institutions. President Kennedy himself took a stand against Catholic schools' receiving federal funds.

What has happened in the intervening years? In terms of legislation, some compromises have been reached: federal funds have been granted to Catholic institutions for direct services such as supplementing lunch programs, buildings, and special facilities. The controversy for a while receded from the public domain. Now it appears to be again gaining momentum.

In the meantime, the costs of both public and Catholic education have skyrocketed. Catholic elementary and high schools, without the massive government subsidies necessary to keep them in operation, have been forced to close their doors. Since 1965, there has been a 32 percent decline in the number of Catholic high schools and a 13 percent decline in the number of Catholic elementary schools.[1] This fact alone could bring about a sizeable decline in the use of Catholic schools over the past decade, even if attitudes toward those schools were to remain constant. As well as the fact of fewer schools being available, higher tuition rates, necessitated by higher operating costs, have forced many Catholic parents to send their children to public rather than Catholic schools.

In part, the higher operating costs for Catholic schools can be attributed to the decline in religious vocations. As a result of the dramatic decrease in the number of women becoming and remaining nuns, in 1974 lay teachers constituted 61 percent of the faculty of Catholic schools. In contrast, thirty years ago, when these figures were first recorded, lay teachers were only 8 percent of the faculty of Catholic schools.[2] (Lay teachers, by the way, are considered to be at least as good as nuns by over two-thirds of the Catholic sample.)

The first question, then, is how does use of Catholic schools today compare with use ten years ago, given the problems that have besieged the system? In brief, there has been a sharp decline in use. In 1964 Greeley and Rossi looked at all school-attending children in families where both parents were Catholic. They found that 44 percent of these children were attending Catholic schools.[3] In 1974, again just looking at those 83 percent of the families where both parents are Catholic, we find only 29 percent of Catholic children in parochial schools. A school system originally intended to provide for the spiritual and secular education of all Catholic children is today living up to that promise for only little more than one-quarter of its children.

From what kinds of families do these children who are attending Catholic schools come? Do those parents who send their children to Catholic schools differ from those who use the public schools? One might expect, for example, that those using the Catholic schools would be financially better off; or, perhaps, more sure of their religion. We will see if these traits do, in fact, characterize the parents as well as ascertain whether or not there are other background or attitudinal differences between Catholics who use the parochial schools and those who do not.

We will then look at the reasons parents give for sending their children to either Catholic or non-Catholic schools. And we will see what the Catholic population as a whole thinks of Catholic schools today and how much financial support it is willing to extend to that system. We will also look at where Catholics stand today on the question of federal aid to Catholic schools. We will answer these questions using 1974 data and, then, wherever possible, we will compare the Catholic population of today with that of a decade ago with respect to these issues.

First of all, let us examine the question of who uses the Catholic schools today. Seventy-five percent of the Catholics in this sample of adults between 18 and 65 have children. Thirty-nine percent have children who were in either elementary or high school at the time of the interview. Yet only a little over one-quarter (28 percent) of parents with school age children have those children in Catholic schools.

In what ways are these parents different from Catholic parents who send their children to the public schools? Do those from certain ethnic groups disproportionately make use of Catholic schools; or do those who have had more Catholic education themselves continue the tradition of Catholic education for their children? Table 7.1 compares the Catholic parents who are using the public schools for their children with Catholic parents who are using parochial schools on a number of demographic variables—income, age, ethnicity, total education, and amount of Catholic education.

The only criteria, as it turns out, which account for significant differences between the groups are age and total years of Catholic education. Parents in their forties are more likely than parents in any other age group to send their children to parochial schools. Parents with little or no Catholic education are also less likely than those who have had a Catholic high school education to send their children to parochial schools.

TABLE 7.1

Characteristics of Parents of School Age Children,

By Use of Catholic Schools

	One or more Children in Catholic School(s)	No Children in Catholic School	N
Income:			
Less than $6,000	4%	96%	28
$6,000 - 9,999	26	72	50
$10,000-12,499	34	66	61
$12,500-14,999	26	74	58
$15,000-19,999	31	69	80
$20,000 or over	24	76	68
*Age:			
20-29	2%	98%	20
30-39	27	73	136
40-49	34	66	133
50 and over	23	77	71
Ethnicity:			
British	14%	86%	19
Irish	29	71	50
German	30	70	43
Polish	45	55	30
Spanish-Speaking	19	81	43
Slavs	38	62	30
Italians	33	67	60
French	9	91	10
Black	27	73	7
Other	17	83	35
Education:			
0-8 years	19%	81%	47
9-11 years	20	80	49
12 years	26	74	162
13 + years	36	62	101
**Catholic Education			
None	23%	77%	179
1-8 years	24	76	98
9-12 years	42	59	59
13 + years	27	73	11

*Significant at .05 level
**Significant at .10 level

(Although respondents educated in Catholic colleges reverse the linear trend—they are less likely to make use of the Catholic schools than those with nine to twelve years of Catholic education.)

There is a linear relationship between education and the use of Catholic schools, that is, as respondents' education goes up, the likelihood that they will use the Catholic schools for their children also increases. This tendency, however, is not strong enough to be statistically significant.

Use of Catholic schools by income groups is somewhat complicated: as income increases, up to $12,500, the use of Catholic schools also increases; such use then dips for those families making between $15,000 and $20,000, and down once more for those families making over $20,000. With the exception of those families making under $6,000 annually, the differences in usage are not very great among income groups.

The demographic variables outlined in table 7.1, while providing some overview, do not go very far in helping to explain who is using the Catholic schools today. To uncover more about the differences between families who make use of the Catholic schools and families who do not, we decided to compare these families along a number of additional dimensions. Do they, we asked, differ in their certainty about their religious beliefs? Do they have different attitudes toward racial integration? Are Catholic schools being used as a mechanism for white parents to avoid sending their children to the public schools with black children?

First, with respect to certainty of religious beliefs in the two groups—there turns out to be virtually no difference. Forty-four percent of the parents in both kinds of families feel "very sure" of their religious beliefs. Only a few of either group claim they are not very sure or not at all sure (see table 7.2). It is not, then, serious doubts about their religion that keep families from sending their children to Catholic schools.

We compared the two groups of parents on three measures

TABLE 7.2

Certainty of Religious Beliefs,
By Use of Catholic Schools

	Respondent Has Child in Catholic School	Respondent Has No Child in Catholic School
Very Sure	44%	44%
Pretty Sure	49	45
Not too Sure	6	10
Not at all Sure	1	2
	N = 98	N = 254

of racial attitudes: (1) there is an obligation to work for the end of racial segregation; (2) blacks should not push themselves where they are not wanted; and (3) whites have a right to live in an all white neighborhood if they want to and blacks should respect that right. There is no significant difference between the users of Catholic schools and the users of public schools on any of these attitude measures (table 7.3). Those with children in public schools are slightly more likely to take the most pro-black position on the question of whether or not there is an obligation to work for the end of racial segregation (37 percent to 31 percent). While there is little difference between the groups on this, more striking is the fact that so few from either group come out for this moral position. This may reflect an unwillingness on the part of Catholics to deal with the realities of racism and integration. It may also reflect (given the way in which the item is worded) a general resistance to authority, rules, and obligations which has become evident among, indeed characteristic of, Catholics in 1974. In any case, this same item was agreed with strongly by 46 percent of the respondents in the 1964 study.

Due to rounding out of fractions, totals in some tables do not add up to exactly 100 percent.

TABLE 7.3

Attitudes and Behavior Toward Blacks,

By Use of Catholic Schools for Children

	Respondent Has Child in Catholic School	Respondent Has No Child in Catholic School
There is an obligation to work for the end of racial segregation (Agree Strongly)	31%	37%
Blacks should not push themselves where they're not wanted (Disagree)	50	41
Whites have a right to live in an all-white neighborhood if they want to and blacks should respect that right (Disagree)	40	37
Blacks are living in R's neighborhood now	41	34
Blacks are attending school with R's children	62*	78*

*Significant at .01 level

On the question of whether whites have a right to live in an all-white neighborhood and whether blacks should push themselves where they're not wanted, those with children in Catholic schools are slightly more integrationist (50 and 40 percent pro-black responses on these items compared to 41 and 37 percent among users of the public schools). It is important to emphasize again that none of these attitudinal differences are statistically significant.

When we look at actual behavior, however, the picture is somewhat different. Those parents who send their children to Catholic schools are slightly more likely to live in integrated neighborhoods (41 percent to 34 percent). Nonetheless, what might appear to follow logically from this—that their children would more likely be in integrated classrooms—does not. In fact, parents using the Catholic schools are significantly *less* likely to have their children in integrated classrooms (62 percent to 78 percent). While this is hardly grounds for claiming that Catholic schools are used to avoid integrated classroom situations, it does show that the experience of integrated schooling is less likely for those in the parochial schools. What is probably most striking, however, is the high percentage of children in both groups who attend school with black classmates.

More helpful than either demographic, attitudinal, or religious correlates of Catholic school use for understanding the parental choice of schools are the reasons the parents themselves give for selecting either a parochial or a public school for their children's education.

Those respondents who had one or more children in a Catholic school—either elementary or high school—were asked why they had chosen a Catholic school for their child or children. Respondents were free to give as many reasons as they wished. We have chosen the first reason mentioned for analysis here.

TABLE 7.4

Main Reason for Sending Own Children to Catholic School

Better Education in Catholic Schools	34%
Religious Instruction	19
More discipline	18
Other reasons	29
	N = 98

As table 7.4 shows, the most frequently mentioned reason for selecting a Catholic school is better education; about one-third of the respondents make this choice. The religious instruction and the better discipline available in Catholic schools each are named by about one-fifth of the respondents.

Twenty-nine percent give some other reason for their choice of a Catholic school, for example, all the child's friends attend the school or the parents just never thought of anything else. It is worth noting that the historical reason for the establishment of parochial schools has resoundingly passed; they no longer are supported by Catholic parents as a "way of arming (Catholic children) against forces regarded as inimical to their faith."[4] Only a minority see religious instruction as their primary reason for choosing a Catholic school.

Table 7.5 shows a breakdown of these responses, dichotomized on certain key characteristics of this sample. Better education proves to be a more popular choice for those parents with at least some college education (62 percent of this group cite this reason compared with the overall 34 percent), and for those living in cities of more than 50,000 population (56 percent). Religious instruction is a more important reason for people who are over fifty years of age (70 percent of this group, compared to 19 percent of the total sample), those who have less education (45 percent), and those who live in smaller cities and towns (47 percent). Interestingly, more discipline is cited as a reason for choosing Catholic schools by 35 percent of the college educated; this is twice the selection rate of this reason by the entire group.

The reasons for selecting a parochial school apparently vary depending on what is most valued by the parents and, of course, on what is available. Younger and better educated parents select Catholic schools when they can thereby provide their children with a superior education and, in some cases at least, a more disciplined environment. Older and less educated parents select Catholic schools because they are concerned that their children receive sound religious instruction.

Parents who have their children in non-Catholic schools were also asked the reasons for their choice. Again, the first mentioned reason has been chosen for analysis. The criterion of better education, most frequently mentioned by parents with children in parochial schools as the basis of their choice,

TABLE 7.5

Main Reason for Sending Own Children To Catholic Schools by Age, Income,

Education, Catholic Education, and City Size (1974)

Reason	Age		Income		Education		Catholic Education		City Size	
	18-49	50-70	Under 15,000	15,000+	12 years or less	Some college or more	0-10 years	11-20 years	50,000 or less	More than 50,000
	%	%	%	%	%	%	%	%	%	%
Better education	52	20	46	50	37	62	47	52	29	56
Religious instruction	20	70	31	22	45	3	28	26	47	18
More discipline	28	10	24	28	18	35	26	21	24	26

is named by only 9 percent of this group. Why, then, do they choose public schools? Most often because Catholic schools are unavailable (38 percent say this) or too expensive (24 percent) (table 7.6). It would appear that non-Catholic schools are chosen by default more often than on the basis of any positive attraction which counters the Catholic schools.

TABLE 7.6

Main Reason for Sending Child(ren) to Non-Catholic School

No Catholic School Available; Catholic School too Far Away	38%	
Catholic Schools Too Expensive	24	
Better Education in Non-Catholic Schools	9	
Other Reason	29	N = 291

Looking at table 7.7, however, we again see variability in choices by certain respondent characteristics. While only a few of the total sample choose a non-Catholic school because it offers better education, approximately one-quarter of those with higher income and higher education make this the basis of their choice. It is likely, of course, that those with more income and more education live in communities where, in fact, there are alternatives finer than the Catholic school system. The cost of Catholic schools is the most compelling deterrent for urban dwellers. Cost as a deterrent is also above the mean for those without college education and, not surprisingly, those who are financially less well off. For these last two groups, however, the non-availability of a Catholic school is a stronger deterrent than cost. The lack of a proximate parochial school is felt most strongly by those living in large cities and those with more education and more Catholic education.

We took a special look at those Catholic families who were making $20,000 or more in 1974. If the Catholic population in the United States continues to be upwardly mobile, this

TABLE 7.7

Main Reason for Sending Own Children to Non-Catholic Schools by Age, Income, Education, Catholic Education, and City Size (1974)

Reason	Age 18-49 %	Age 50-70 %	Income Under 15,000 %	Income 15,000+ %	Education 12 years or less %	Education Some college or more %	Catholic Education 0-10 years %	Catholic Education 11-20 years %	City Size 50,000 or less %	City Size More than 50,000 %
No Catholic school available	52	58	52	55	51	60	50	64	69	38
Catholic schools too expensive	35	32	42	23	42	14	38	19	23	45
Better education in non-Catholic schools	13	10	6	22.	7	27	13	17	8	16

group may well be viewed as a prototype for the future attitudes and behaviors of a large segment of the Catholic population. In our sample, only 24 percent of families in this income bracket with school age children use the Catholic schools.

The investigators had two competing hypotheses about why these wealthier families were choosing non-Catholic schools for their children: (1) they have good alternatives available in either the public school system of their more affluent communities or in private schools; (2) since parochial schools are concentrated in urban areas, there are no Catholic schools available in the neighborhoods where wealthier families live. As it turns out, both these hypotheses are shown to have some validity: 47 percent of all families making over $20,000 claim that no Catholic school is available to them; this is 9 percentage points greater than for the Catholic group as a whole (table 7.8). If the 8 percent who say their children were not accepted due to overcrowding at the local Catholic school are included in this number and, indeed, such a situation is the equivalent of unavailability—the percentage giving

TABLE 7.8

Reason Given for Sending Children to Non-Catholic School,

For Those With Income Over $20,000

		Deviation From Total Sample
No Catholic School Available	47%	+ 9
Too Expensive	8	-16
Better Education	20	+11
Child Not Accepted Due to Overcrowding	8	+ 3
Child Wanted to Go To Public School	2	- 2
Other Reasons	15	

N = 59

this reason rises to 55. While only 20 percent cite the better education available in schools other than Catholic, this is more than double the percentage of the total sample giving such a reason. The cost of Catholic education is a relatively insignificant deterrent for this group.

We also looked at the various ethnic groups to see what, if any, variation by ethnicity there was in reasons for choosing non-Catholic schools (table 7.9). The most frequently mentioned reason for every group, except the Spanish-speaking, was that there was no Catholic school available. The Slavs, Poles, British, and Spanish-speaking are above the mean of 38 percent on this reason. The Spanish-speaking are most likely to cite the high cost of parochial schools as a reason for not using them; almost half (45 percent) of the Spanish-speaking Catholics give this reason while the range for the other groups is 6 to 28 percent. With this exception, there is little variation by ethnicity in the reasons that are given for not sending children to Catholic schools.

More than any selected background characteristic or particular attitude or value, the availability and cost of Catholic ed-

TABLE 7.9

Why Do You Send Your Children to Non-Catholic Schools? (1974)

		British	Irish	German	Polish	Slavs	Italians	Spanish-Speaking
(1)	Better Education	5%	11%	14%	--	6%	19%	--
(2)	Too Expensive in Parochials	28	19	9	27	6	19	45
(3)	No Catholic School Available	40	23	38	41	48	36	40
(4)	Child not Accepted in Catholic Due to Overcrowding	9	4	10	--	--	-5	5
(5)	Child wanted to go to Public School	--	13	--	14	6	2	--
(6)	Other Reasons	18	30	29	18	33	19	10
N		(19)	(40)	(35)	(20)	(22)	(44)	(38)

ucation seem determinative of who uses the schools. As well, the distribution of Catholic school attendance by ecological area turns out to be revealing, not only of where parochial school attendance is greatest now but also of how the distribution has shifted over the last decade. As table 7.10 shows, Catholic children living in the city are more than twice as likely to be going to Catholic schools as Catholic children living in the suburbs—the availability factor in operation. This was true in 1964 as well, but the cities at that time were ahead of the suburbs by only 11 percentage points; now cities are 26 percentage points more likely than suburbs to send their children to Catholic schools.

TABLE 7.10

Percentage of Children Attending Catholic Schools

By Ecological Area, In Families Where Both Parents Are Catholic

	1964	1974	Difference
City	52% (850)	46% (164)	– 6
Suburbs	41 (867)	20 (318)	–21
Outside SMSA	38 (564)	27 (140)	–11
Total	44 (2281)	29 (622)	–15

While the overall drop in Catholic school attendance has been sharp, the most dramatic drop has been in the suburbs. It is of note that in 1964 the actual number of Catholic school children living in the suburbs was almost precisely equal to the number of Catholic school children living in the cities. By 1974, however, there were twice as many children living in the suburbs as in the city. Catholics, like other Americans, have been a part of the great urban exodus. These families have increasingly settled in the suburbs, and the suburbs do not have parochial schools to educate their children. Our data enable us to measure the impact on Catholic school attendance of the combination of suburban movement of

Catholics and the changing pattern of reasons given for not sending children to Catholic schools.

In 1963, 44 percent of the children in families in which both parents were Catholic attended parochial schools. In 1974, this proportion had declined to 29 percent. (This one-third decline in attendance is roughly the same as the decline of two million reported in the Catholic directories during the last ten years.) Hence the proportion not attending increased from 56 percent to 71 percent (table 7.11). Partialing out the various reasons for nonattendance by region at the two points in time, we can see that 11 of the 15 percentage points are explained by suburban movement, and 10 percentage points, by the increase in parents giving nonavailability as the answer. Nine percentage points—or 60 percent of the increase in non-attendance—can be accounted for by an increase in suburban nonavailability. The failure to build new schools accounts for two-thirds of the decline in Catholic school attendance—almost all of this in the suburbs.

It has generally been assumed that the higher costs of Catholic schools and the availability of better public schools would explain most of the decline in Catholic school attendance. In fact there has been a decrease of 3 percentage points in the proportion of Catholic children not attending Catholic schools because of the better quality of public schools. This decrease partially cancels out the increase of 8 percentage points which is attributable to high costs of Catholic education. Thus in terms of net loss of Catholic enrollment, one-third seems to be the result of higher costs and two-thirds the result of the failure to build new schools to keep pace with the moving Catholic population.

It does not necessarily follow that parents would have sent their children to Catholic schools had they been available. Our data merely establish that most of the decline in attendance can be accounted for by parents giving nonavailability as the main reason for not sending their children to Catholic schools. However, there is no reason to think that the proportion

TABLE 7.11

REASONS FOR CHILDREN NOT GOING TO CATHOLIC SCHOOLS BY TIME

| Reasons | 1963 and 1974 Proportions Not Attending[a] | | | | | | | | Difference[b] | | | |
| | City | | Suburb | | Rural | | Total | | City | Suburb | Rural | Total |
	1963	1974	1963	1974	1963	1974	1963	1974				
Public Schools Better	.03	.02	.04	.03	.03	.02	.10	.07	-.01	-.01	-.01	-.03
Costs	.04	.07	.04	.07	.02	.04	.10	.18	.03	.03	.02	.08
Unavailability of school	.03	.03	.11	.20	.08	.09	.22	.32	.00	.09	.01	.10
Other	.02	.02	.10	.10	.02	.02	.14	.14	.00	.00	.00	.00
Total	.12	.14	.29	.40	.15	.17	.56	.71	.02	.11	.02	.15

[a]1963 proportion not attending = .56; 1974 proportion not attending = .71

[b]Total differences = .15

which would have made use of the schools had they been available would have changed in the past ten years.

The data in table 7.11 go a long way toward explaining the paradox of Catholic schools, their continued popularity with the laity combined with a drastic decline in attendance. Children are not going to Catholic schools in great part because their families have moved to places where there are no Catholic schools. And there are no Catholic schools because new ones have not been built.

We made one final comparison between the parents who are using the parochial schools and the parents who are not: do users of Catholic schools have, as we would expect, a greater willingness to give financial support to those schools than Catholic parents with school age children who are not using the parochial schools? In a word, yes. Those who have children attending Catholic schools are significantly more willing, given a hypothetical situation, to give additional money to the financing of a parochial school which would otherwise close. Only 10 percent of those with children in Catholic schools say they would give nothing more, while 24 percent of those with children in non-Catholic schools say they would give nothing additional. Sixty-nine percent of the parents with children in the Catholic schools would make an additional sacrifice of over fifty dollars, while only 46 percent of the other group would give this much (table 7.12). While it is not surprising that those who feel they are getting more are willing to give more, only 15 percent of all these parents would give nothing more. To provide a context for comparison, we point out that a distinct majority of the total Catholic sample (54 percent) claimed they would be against a tax increase for purposes of raising additional funds for public schools.

One characteristic of the parochial school system, like the public school system, is that those who do not have children in the schools are still asked to contribute to support of the system. Given this, it is important to know how the Catholic population as a whole feels about Catholic schools. All re-

TABLE 7.12

Willingness to Give More To

Parochial Schools, By Use of Parochial Schools*

	Child(ren) Attending Catholic School	No Child Attending Catholic School
Amount Willing to Give:		
Nothing	10%	24%
Up to $50	22	30
$50-200	57	36
$200 or more	12	10
(N)	(69)	(46)

*Difference is significant at .01 level

spondents were asked what they saw as the advantages of Catholic schools. Over half (52 percent) name religious instruction as one of their two choices; almost two-fifths (37 percent) mention greater discipline; and only about one-fifth (22 percent) argue that the quality of the education or teaching is superior. Eleven percent claim there is no advantage at all to a Catholic education.

As table 7.13 shows, the ordering and even the magnitude of the perceived advantages have changed little over the past

TABLE 7.13

ADVANTAGES OF SENDING CHILDREN TO CATHOLIC SCHOOLS

Advantages	1963	1974
Religious instruction	49%	52%
Better discipline	31	37
Better education, better teaching	25	22
Moral education	8	10
More personal attention to child	6	8
No advantage	6	11

decade. In 1963, religious instruction was named by half; discipline, by one-third; and better education, by one-quarter. At that time, only 6 percent claimed no advantage. The attitudes of the Catholic population as a whole toward the Catholic school system appear to have undergone little change in the decade.

What is of interest, however, is that, while the Catholic population as a whole supports Catholic education because of the religious instruction it provides, this is not the reason, as we saw, given by the parents who have children in the Catholic schools. The parents who are using the schools argue that their children are there because the education is better; the availability of religious instruction ranks as a purely secondary reason. This suggests that the Catholic adult population, perhaps giving little regular thought to this question, presents a "correct" answer that is somewhat abstracted from reality. Catholic adults who are actually confronting the educational needs of their children reorder priorities.

TABLE 7.14

Percentage of Catholics Holding

Certain Attitudes Toward Catholic Schools

	Percent Agree
Schools Should Get Federal Aid	76%
Parents Should Get Tax Refund	62
Government Should Give Voucher	30
There are Anti-Catholic Feelings in the Government	39
Catholic Schools are No Longer Needed	10
Lay Teachers are as Good as Nuns	66
Sex Education Should be Taught in the Catholic Schools	80
New and Progressive Ways of Teaching are Good	65

We also looked at the attitudes of the total sample toward a range of issues having to do with Catholic education (table 7.14). The position that the federal government should give religious schools money to help pay teachers' salaries and build new buildings is held by over three-quarters of the respondents (76 percent). There has been little change since 1964, when 73 percent took this position.

Support for Catholic schools receiving federal aid in general is expressed more strongly than support for other specific plans that have been proposed to ease the financial burden on

TABLE 7.15

Influence of Education, Catholic Education, and "Cath"*

on Attitudes Toward Parochial Schools

(Standardized Coefficients--Betas)

	R's Education	R's Catholic Education	"Cath"*
Schools Should Get Federal Aid	.17	.10	.22
Parents Should Get Tax Refund	-.04	.14	.23
Government Should Give Voucher	-.04	.00	.26
There are Anti-Catholic Feelings in Government	-.18	-.04	.18
Catholic Schools are no Longer Needed	.07	-.08	-.25
Lay Teachers are as Good as Nuns	.22	.02	.03
Sex Education Should Be Taught in Catholic Schools	.28	.09	-.11
New and Progressive Ways of Teaching are Good	.06	.05	.04

*"Cath" = a composite variable made up of a respondent's score on the following: participation in the activities of the Catholic Church, acceptance of the Church teachings on sex and Catholic doctrine, acceptance of the Church's right to teach moral positions, reception of sacraments, frequency of prayer and financial support of the Catholic Church.

Catholic parents. Still, a majority (62 percent) agree that parents who send their children to Catholic schools should get a refund on their local taxes. Only 30 percent, however, feel that the government should give tuition money directly to parents and let them decide for themselves which school they want their children to attend. It may be that this last plan, a voucher system, is less familiar to the general public.

While most Catholics would like to see some form of federal aid forthcoming to parochial schools, only 39 percent attribute the lack of such funding to the existence of anti-Catholic feelings in the government.

There is strong support for lay teachers, with two-thirds of the Catholic population believing they are as good at teaching as nuns. And there is overwhelming support (80 percent) for the teaching of sex education in Catholic schools as well as for new and progressive ways of teaching in general (65 percent). Finally, only a handful of Catholics (10 percent) believe that the Catholic school system has outlived its usefulness and is no longer needed. Despite the fact that use of Catholic schools is down, support for the institution remains high.

Table 7.15 presents a further breakdown of the attitudes toward Catholic schools, attempting to see specifically if the amount of education or the amount of Catholic education or the level of integration into Catholic activities and teachings ("Cath") a respondent has correlates with any particular attitude or set of attitudes toward the parochial schools.

We see that "Cath" is far more strongly correlated with attitudes that support the Catholic schools than either total education or Catholic education. Support of federal aid to Catholic schools, a tax refund to users of Catholic schools, a government voucher plan to cover Catholic school tuition, and the belief that Catholic schools are still needed—all have standardized correlations with "Cath" of over .22. This means that an individual's current involvement in the activities of the

Catholic church, combined with acceptance of the teachings of the church, is more likely to influence his or her support for Catholic schools than either the amount of Catholic education or the total amount of education he or she has had.

On the other hand, support for sex education in the Catholic schools is negatively correlated with "Cath" (-.11)—those who are more "Catholic" are less likely to be progressive in this area. Finally, "Cath" has a slight positive correlation (.18) with a belief that there are anti-Catholic feelings in the government.

The total amount of a respondent's education is most important in explaining attitudes toward sex education in the Catholic schools (.28) and attitudes toward lay teachers (.22). Both lay teachers and sex education are more likely to be supported by those Catholics who are better educated. There is a slight negative correlation (-.18) between amount of education and the belief that there are anti-Catholic sentiments in the government.

The amount of Catholic education a respondent has is not very important in determining any of these attitudes toward the parochial schools. No standardized coefficient here reaches anything stronger than .14.

It turns out, then, that present levels of involvement with and integration into the Catholic church are a stronger influence on the attitudes one holds toward parochial schools than is the amount of time one actually spent in that school system in the past.

Conclusion

Paradoxically, the Catholic schools in 1974 are in a state of declining use and sustained high regard. In 1964, 44 percent of all school age children from Catholic families were attending Catholic schools; in 1974, that figure has dropped to 29 percent. This is a dramatic decline, but a decline neither caused nor accompanied by a belief that the Catholic schools no longer offer a good education—quite the contrary. Those who are using Catholic schools most often claim it is precisely because they offer an education better than that offered by available alternatives; those who are using public schools do *not* say it is because they are better educationally but rather because Catholic schools are inaccessible—either geographically or financially. Thus, we see Catholic school attendance in the cities dropping because urban residents cannot afford the increasing tuition and we see Catholic school attendance in the suburbs dropping because parochial schools have not been built to keep up with the shift of the Catholic population from city to suburbs.

Even as use of the parochial schools declines, we find that only 10 percent of the Catholic population believes the Catholic school system has had its day and should be allowed to sink into nonexistence. Rather, the great majority of the Catholic population believes the Catholic school system should be getting financial assistance from the federal government in order to assure its continued existence. As well, the majority of Catholics appear to wish the parochial school system to move in increasingly progressive directions: 80 percent favor sex education; 66 percent support lay teachers; and 65 percent favor generally new and progressive ways of teaching.

Support of the Catholic school system, then, seems heavily based on the fact that such a school system offers a good education, a viable alternative to public schools. There appears much less emphasis in 1974 on the religious instruction the schools provide, the traditional need for arming children with the fundamentals of Catholicism that they might do combat in the secular world without losing their faith. It is likely that the integration of Catholics into the American middle class, which has been documented in earlier chapters, is largely accountable for this shift in emphasis.

8

Financial Support for Church and Schools

The Catholic church in America is financially dependent upon the good will and continuing contributions of its members. The church receives no subsidies from the government and levies no taxes. If Catholics stop giving money to the church, it suffers a decline. In this chapter we tell the story of just such a financial decline.

The financial dependence of the church upon its members is a direct parallel to the dependence of the parochial schools upon the church. Most parish elementary schools receive a large proportion of their income from the parish collections, and many high schools are also very dependent upon voluntary contributions from parents and alumni. Therefore, the mechanism of giving, which is so crucial for the church, is also critical for the continuation of the parochial schools in this country.

Estimates of the finances of the Catholic church must be crude approximations. It is doubtful that any one person or office knows the actual financial figures of the church. There is no central accounting agency or any standardized accounting method for all dioceses. We have estimated the contributions to the church and its schools by asking people how much money they have given during a single year. We also asked how much money they would give under certain "emergency" conditions. From these data and from rough estimates of the Catholic population that have been extrapolated from the United States census, we have formulated a profile of the financial situation of the Catholic church in America.

Three factors must be taken into account when we estimate the changing finances of the church during the past decade. First, there has been the impact of inflation on the value of the dollar. Today it takes about $1.60 to purchase the goods and services that cost $1.00 ten years ago. In order to compensate for inflation, we adjusted some of our figures, using the Consumer Price Index devised by the Department of Labor. The second complicating factor is that there are more Catholics in the country today than there were in 1963. We will take this into account by estimating the population increase from the census figures. Finally, the standard of living among Catholics has risen during the past decade, which means that a given quantity of money has a different meaning to a family today than it did ten years ago. In order to account for this change we will refer to the proportion of one's income which has been given to the church as our measure of support.

In this chapter we will discuss financial contributions to the church and schools and make some ten-year comparisons. Then we will review demographic and attitudinal correlates of giving to the church and examine the giving patterns of different social groups, concentrating on the linkage between contributing to the church and attitudes about various religious and social issues. Next we will try to discover what the causes of the decline in financial support might be, using the social change model developed in previous chapters for this purpose. Finally we will discuss the as yet untapped potential support for the parochial schools among American Catholics.

Contributions to Church and School

There is more money being given to the Catholic church today than there was ten years ago; but due to inflation, increasing Catholic population, and rising incomes, the church's real financial condition has worsened appreciably. As can be seen in table 8.1, there has been an apparent increase in income of 44 percent, but when we account for the inflated condition of the dollar, the increase is only 12 percent. So while there has been a 10 percent increase in per capita con-

TABLE 8.1

INCOME, CHURCH CONTRIBUTIONS AND SCHOOL EXPENDITURES
FOR CATHOLICS IN 1963 AND IN 1974

	1963	1974	Percentage Difference
Mean Income (Current dollars)*	$7,645	$13,701	+44%
(Inflation-free)**	$12,232	-------	+12%
Mean Contribution to the Church (Current dollars)*	$164	$180	+10%
(Inflation-free)**	$262	---	-31%
Mean Expenditures on Catholic schools (Current dollars)*	NA	$343	
Proportion of Income Donated to the Church	2.28%	1.58%	-31%
Proportion of Income spent on Catholic Schools	NA	3.32	
Total Contribution to the Church (Current dollars)*	$2,620,000,000	$3,841,000,000	
(Inflation-free)**	$4,218,000.000	-------------	
Total Spent on Catholic Schools		$805,177,000	
Grand Total		$4,646,177,000	

tributions, inflation has so damaged the purchasing power of the dollar that there has been an actual 31 percent decline in per capita contributions over the past decade.

It is impossible to say just how large the increase in expenditures on tuition for Catholic schools has been because the questions were different in the two NORC surveys.[1] We can be sure that there has been an increase, since costs have risen. We do know that the average tuition cost was $343 in 1974.

A revealing figure in table 8.1 is the proportion of income which was contributed to the church in each of the two time periods. This statistic is invariant to the rise in the Catholic standard of living and shows that there has been a 31 percent decrease in the proportion of income contributed during the decade. This means that even though Catholics are able to afford a more generous contribution to their church, they have reduced the portion of their assets they give for church support.

In order to get some idea of the total number of dollars actually contributed to the church, we have multiplied the mean contributions by the estimated population of Catholic families and unrelated individuals from the appropriate census counts.[2] In 1963 there were about 4.8 billion inflation-free dollars contributed to the church, not including expenditures on schools. In 1974 this figure had decreased to 3.8 billion. Adding the 1974 school expenditures to the contributions, we arrive at a total of 4.6 billion dollars, which represents all of the revenue that has accrued to the church from voluntary sources.

Contributions have not kept pace with either inflation or the growth of the Catholic population. Is this phenomenon the same for all groups within the Catholic population, or do some subgroups show a different pattern? Is the decline among those who disagree with the church on key issues, or is it evenly spread across the spectrum of attitudes? We will discuss these questions in the following section.

Correlates of Contributing

Since most church contributions are made in the form of donations to the Sunday collection, we can hypothesize that there is a relationship between going to mass and giving to the church. In table 8.2 we can see that the greatest decline in contribution, as measured by the proportion of income given, is among those who attend mass most regularly. Those who seldom attend mass have changed their pattern of contribution least of all. They were the least likely to give money to the church and they still are. The most committed church members are those most likely to have decreased the proportion of their income which they give to the church.

TABLE 8.2

PROPORTION OF INCOME GIVEN TO THE CHURCH

	1963	1974	Per Cent Difference
Frequency of Mass Attendance			
Seldom	.87	.74	−15
Monthly	1.72	1.42	−17
Weekly	2.69	2.15	−21
Educational Level			
Elementary	1.97	1.58	−20
High School	2.21	1.42	−36
College	2.43	1.92	−21
Ethnic Heritage			
British	2.34	1.41	−40
Irish	2.42	2.18	−10
German	2.61	1.73	−34
Italian	2.30	1.13	−58
Polish	2.02	2.66	32

Educational level does not appear to be consistently related to the decline in contribution, as measured by proportion. Those with a high-school education suffered the greatest decline, but each of the three groups decreased the proportion of their income given to the church by a substantial percentage.

Lastly, there are only two ethnic groups which did not reduce their contributions by more than one-third. The Irish decrease was 10 percent, while the Poles actually increased theirs by about one-third. It may be that the Poles, many of them first-generation Americans, are at a point in their social history where "church" is still very important to them. They may still be a part of that immigrant brand of Catholicism that took contributions to the church for granted. The groups that have been here for a longer period of time may not be involved in the church in the same way.

The phenomenon of "contributions" can be seen from a slightly different perspective in table 8.3. Here, instead of proportion of income, we use the average number of "inflation-free" dollars contributed to the church during the year in question.[3] The conclusions drawn from this table are quite

TABLE 8.3

CONTRIBUTION TO THE CHURCH
(Inflation-Free Dollars*)

	1963	1974	Per Cent Difference	Dollar Difference
Frequency of Mass Attendance				
Seldom	$ 64.23	$ 63.39	-01	$ - .84
Monthly	121.24	86.23	-29	-35.01
Weekly	214.03	192.35	-10	-21.68
Educational Level				
Elementary	108.41	72.97	-33	-35.44
High School	169.23	129.79	-23	-39.44
College	207.57	180.76	-13	-26.81
Ethnic Heritage				
British	330.32	174.23	-47	-156.09
Irish	166.71	176.57	06	9.86
German	251.56	160.14	-36	-91.41
Italian	189.31	101.52	-46	-87.79
Polish	123.29	218.97	78	95.68

*Inflation-free dollars are the actual figures reported adjusted by the consumer price index for the appropriate year.

similar to those drawn from table 8.2. With regard to the relationship between mass attendance and the decrease in contributions, for example, the respondents who go to mass more often are most likely to have decreased their contributions by the greatest amount. With regard to the relationship between educational level and contributions, all levels have reduced their contributions, but the college educated have done so the least. When we look at the ethnic groups, only two have increased their contributions, taking inflation into account, and one, the Irish, has done so only slightly. The Poles are giving nearly one hundred dollars per year more to the church today than they did in 1963. It may be that groups with different cultural heritages have different ways of showing their support for the church (just about half of all the bishops in the American Catholic church are of Irish extraction, for example). The Poles seem to show their support with money.

One way to peer into the future is to find out the nature of the relationships between contributions and other attitudes. If we discover strong relationships between contributions and attitudes inimical to the support of the church, then contributions may well continue their steady decline.

In table 8.4 we compare the correlations between contributions and various attitudes and behaviors for the two time periods of our studies, 1963 and 1974. The coefficients are remarkably steady for most of the variables, but there have been two important changes. First, the correlation between giving to the church and having a Catholic education has gone up from .12 to .20. Second, the correlation between holding a rigid set of sexual values and giving to the church has gone down from .20 to .15 during the past decade. A Catholic education is more important now in terms of its financial yield to the church than it was ten years ago; while the association between rigid sexual mores and contribution to the church has weakened over the same period of time.

Agreement that the church has the right to teach on matters of faith and morals is more strongly correlated with con-

TABLE 8.4

1963 AND 1974 CORRELATION COEFFICIENTS BETWEEN
CONTRIBUTION TO THE CHURCH AND ASSORTED INDEPENDENT
VARIABLES

	Contributions to the Church	
	1963	1974
Mass Attendance	.31	.36
Age	.10	.11
Education	.23	.25
Number of Years of Catholic Education	.12	.20
Parental Religiosity	.11	.15
Sacramental Index	.34	.36
Spouse's Mass Attendance	.28	.36
Income	.34	.37
Rigid Sexual Morality	.20	.15
Church's Right to Teach	.14	.19
Anticlericalism	*	-.26
Satisfaction with the Values Taught in Catholic Schools	*	.02
Satisfaction with the Quality of Education in Catholic Schools	*	.08
Number of Children	.03	.01
Tolerance toward Black People	.04	.06

* Not asked in 1963.

tributing to the church now than in the past. Other variables, such as age, education, and number of children, are associated with giving to the church at the same levels they were ten years ago. Interestingly, the respondents' satisfaction, or lack thereof, with the values being taught and the quality of the education in Catholic schools has little or nothing to do with whether or not they give money to the church. Contributing, so far, seems quite separate from the evaluation of the efficacy of the school system.

We can see from table 8.4 that there have been changes in the relationships between two important variables and contribution practices. Now we will develop two models, one for

Figure 8.1

PATH MODEL FOR CONTRIBUTIONS TO CHURCH IN 1963

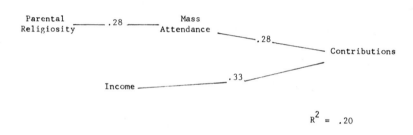

Figure 8.2

PATH MODEL FOR CONTRIBUTIONS TO CHURCH IN 1974

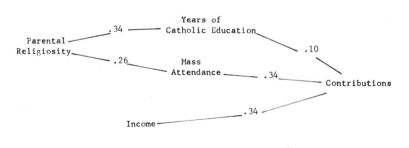

1963 and one for 1974, in order to compare the total effects of a set of factors on the level of contribution. In Fig. 8.1 we explain about 20 percent of the variance in contributions with three factors: mass attendance, parental religiosity, and income. Of these, income is the most important predictor.

In Fig. 8.2, we explain more than one-quarter of the variance in contributions with four variables: mass attendance, parental religiosity, income, and the number of years of Catholic education the respondent had. This last variable does not appear in the 1963 model figure because at that time it did not generate a coefficient to contributions. In 1974, however, Catholic education, all other variables notwithstanding, is a predictor of contributions to the church.

The implication of the difference between these two models is that Catholic education is more important now for the financial well-being of the church than it was ten years ago. Those Catholics who have been exposed to more parochial education have resisted the downward trend in contributions better than those who received less Catholic education.

Loss of Contributions: 1963 to 1974

In order for us to discuss the aggregate loss of revenue from voluntary sources during the past decade, we shall estimate the way the financial picture would look today had several factors been different. What if people were giving today at the same rate they were in 1963? What if there had been no inflation? What if certain church policies had not been promulgated?

In table 8.5 we present the data pertaining to the potential income available to the church through contributions and the magnitude of the failure to meet that expected level. In the first row of table 8.5, we can see that the Catholic population has increased by 34 percent during the past decade. This means that there would have to be a concomitant increase in contributions just to keep pace with the increased number of potential contributors. In the second row of the table, we can see that there has been an apparent increase in the total amount of money being given to the church of 32 percent. However, when inflation is taken into account, there is actually a 9 percent decrease.

TABLE 8.5

AGGREGATE FINANCIAL STATISTICS SHOWING THE
LOSS OF CONTRIBUTIONS DURING THE
DECADE FROM 1963 TO 1974

	1963	1974	Per Cent Change
Number of Catholic Families and Unrelated Individuals	15,972,750	21, 340,500	+34%
Total Contribution (current dollars)	$2,619,531,000	$3,841,290,000	+32%
Total Contribution (inflation-free)	$4,217,444,910	----------	-.09%
Total Contribution if given at the 1963 rate	--------	$5,614,130,697	+114%
Loss in Potential Revenue		$1,772,840,697	

None of the above considers the increased standard of living of the Catholic population as reflected by the increase in its income. What would the total revenue be in 1974 if people had given at the same rate they were giving in 1963? People have more money now than they did then; they ought to be able to give at least at the same rate. The mean inflation-free level of contribution in 1963 was $263. If we multiply that by the 1974 population figures, we arrive at an expected total contribution of over 5.6 billion dollars in 1974. The difference between this expected contribution and the actual contribution is over 1.7 billion dollars. We think this is a realistic estimate of loss. Given the increase in population and con-sumable income, and standardizing for the effects of inflation, the Catholic population could have contributed 1.7 billion dollars more to their church simply by repeating their 1963 level of giving. Why didn't they?

By using the social change model developed earlier in this book, we can assign portions of the total decline in contribu-tions to specific factors. In table 8.6, we attribute portions of the change in the proportion of the population giving more than the inflation-free mean contribution in 1963 and 1974 to four separate factors. There has been a 13 percent decline in the proportion of Catholics who are contributing more

TABLE 8.6

PER CENT OF THE DECREASE IN THOSE GIVING MORE THAN 2.5
PER CENT OF THEIR INCOME TO THE CHURCH ATTRIBUTED
TO FACTORS IN THE SOCIAL CHANGE MODEL

Proportion giving more than 2.5 per cent

1963 = 34%

1974 = 21%

Total Decline = -13.1%

	Per Cent of Total Decline	Raw	Cost in Dollars (Millions)
Mass attendance	14	.005	119
Papal authority	12	.016	136
Sexual orthodoxy	38	.05	901
Cohort - direct	15	.02	187
Cohort - indirect*	—	.02	187
Unaccounted for by model	21	.02	170
Total	100	.131	1.7 billion

*Through mass attendance, sexual orthodoxy, and papal authority.

than the average (from 34 percent in 1963 to 21 percent in 1974). Over one-third of this decline is attributable to changing attitudes about sexual morality; about 30 percent is attributable to direct and indirect cohort changes; 4 percent is accounted for by the decline in mass attendance; and about one-fifth is unaccounted for in this model.

It is not unreasonable to assume that if these factors are responsible for the decline in the proportion giving more than the average, they are also responsible for the loss in *potential* contributions described in table 8.5. Using the 1.7 billion dollar loss as the base for our percentages, we present the relative costs to the church of each of the four factors in the social change model in the last column of table 8.6. The decline in mass attendance cost 119 million dollars in 1974. The changing attitudes toward papal authority and sexual morality cost slightly over 1 billion dollars in potential contributions. The amount of the loss that is directly attributable to the entrance of a new cohort of contributors since 1963 (who perhaps do not give at the same levels as the other cohorts) is 187 million dollars. The amount of loss that is attributable to that same cohort *indirectly,* through their attitudes toward papal authority and sexuality, and their mass attendance, is the same: 187 million dollars. Slightly less than this, 170 million dollars, is unaccounted for by this model.

In other words, almost 70 percent of the loss in potential revenue in 1974 was due to people's attitudes about papal authority and sexual morality, either directly or indirectly. It has been a very expensive decade. The decisions about the church's position on matters of birth control and sexual mores and the way in which the encyclical *Humanae Vitae* was designed and promulgated have been extremely expensive. It would have taken very little on the part of the present Catholic population to have supplied their church with an additional 1.7 billion dollars. All they had to do was to continue giving at their 1963 rate. However, their reaction to decisions which they deemed unconsidered and their mistrust of ecclesiastical authority apparently resulted in their failure to maintain even the status quo.

Support for Parochial Schools

While the contributions have been down from expected levels, the Catholic population seems more than willing to pay for its school system. They gave an estimated total of more than 800 million dollars to their schools in tuition during 1974.[4] This is in the face of the fact that Catholics must sup-

TABLE 8.7

WILLINGNESS TO GIVE ADDITIONAL MONEY TO A CATHOLIC SCHOOL
(Question 65)

Yes, would give more.....80%

No, would not............20%

Per Cent "Yes"

Ethnicity		Age		Educational Level	
British	79	20's	82		
Irish	83	30's	78	Elementary	80
German	88	40's	82	High School	80
Polish	76	50's	80	College	81
Slavic	78				
Italian	77	Catholic Education			
Spanish	88	None	79		
French	79	Some (1-10)	78		
		Lots (10+)	86		
Sex					
Male	83				
Female	78				

port the public schools through their tax contributions whether or not they use these schools. In effect, they are carrying a double burden.

In order to estimate the potential reserves for the parochial school system, we posed for our respondents the hypothetical situation of their local school faced with either receiving increased financial support from the parishioners or closing. Would they be willing to contribute more money? How much? In effect, we were asking, "Will you increase your contribution to defer the higher costs of education, and if so, how much of an increase would you make?"

In table 8.7 we can see that there is broad support for increasing contributions. Four-fifths of the population say they would be willing to give more money to help keep the school open. This figure remains very stable among all segments of the population. About the only difference of interest is that between those with ten years or less of Catholic education

TABLE 8.8

POTENTIAL FUNDS FOR CATHOLIC SCHOOLS GIVEN THE EXPRESSED
LEVEL OF INTENTIONAL CONTRIBUTIONS

Would you contribute more to keep the school open?			
	yes	80%	
	no	20%	

Of those who say "yes," how much more are they willing to give? (Per Year) Mid-Point of Categories	Per Cent	Number of Contributors	Contributions in Dollars
$ 2.50	3	512,172	1,280,430
15.00	20	3,414,480	51,217,200
38.00	18	3,073,032	116,775,216
75.00	28	4,780,272	358,520,400
150.00	19	3,243,756	486,563,400
350.00	10	1,707,240	597,534,000
500.00	2	342,448	170,724,000
	100	17,072,448	1,782,614,646

and those with more than ten. Those who have been more exposed to the parochial school system are the most likely to be willing to contribute more money to keep them open. That is a strong endorsement of the system from its alumni.

In table 8.8 we project the individual responses to the question of how much more one would give onto the entire population, thereby creating an aggregate total of the potential contributions waiting to be tapped by an appeal on behalf of parochial education. Of the four-fifths of the Catholic population who said they would give more to help the schools, one-fifth said they would give about $15 per year more than they are giving at the present time.[5] Multiplying these "intended contributions" by the population estimates for 1974, we arrive at a total intended increase in contributions of 1.8 billion dollars.

Such an increase does not seem unrealistic when we consider that the estimated loss calculated and presented in table 8.6 was 1.7 billion dollars. This money is out there in the pockets of people who might well be persuaded to give it to the church for a good reason, and the possible dismantling of the Catholic school system seems sufficient reason, as far as our respondents are concerned. They have reduced their support for the church in general, but an appeal to their desire to maintain the parochial schools could bring the level of contribution back up to where it would have been had the 1963 levels of giving remained the same through 1974.

One last question is whether or not the willingness to give more money to help the schools is associated with any specific attitude or behavior in the population. In table 8.9 we can see that the correlations between willingness to give and other variables are generally quite low. All are below .20. Mass attendance of both respondent and spouse and agreement with the church's right to teach have moderate positive relationships with increased giving, while anticlericalism and rigid sexual values have moderately strong negative relationships with it.

It is noteworthy that people's opinions of the values being taught in the parochial schools and of the quality of education there have virtually no impact on their willingness to give additional financial support to keep them open. Even those people who are not particularly satisfied with either the values or the quality of education are still willing to increase their yearly contribution to help keep the schools open. It would seem that even when they are not satisfied with what is happening in parochial schools, most Catholics still consider them attractive enough to warrant increased financial support.

Summary and Conclusion

Voluntary contributions to the church have not kept pace with inflation, the population increase, or the rise in income of Catholics during the past decade. This indirectly erodes support for the parochial schools, since much of their financing comes from the local parishes. One-third of this erosion is due to lack of agreement with the church's position on such subjects as divorce and birth control. A relatively small portion of the erosion is due to the fact that people are not attending mass as often as they once did. It is not that the people are unable to give money to the church; they are able to and they do not want to. If people had given to the church in 1974 at the same rate they did in 1963, they would have contributed over 5.6 billion dollars instead of the 3.8 billion actually given. It is certainly a logical possibility that this could have happened, since the income and total population of the Catholic community have gone up. There was no extra sacrifice needed to keep the level of giving at the same rate.

It is particularly interesting to note that people express willingness to increase their contributions for the sake of keeping the parish school open—$100 on the average. This adds up to an aggregate gift of over 1.8 billion dollars—just about the same as the loss reported earlier.

Attendance at Catholic schools is a more important predic-

TABLE 8.9

CORRELATION COEFFICIENTS BETWEEN CONTRIBUTIONS TO THE CHURCH,
WILLINGNESS TO GIVE MORE TO THE SCHOOL AND
ASSORTED INDEPENDENT VARIABLES

Willingness to Give to School

Mass attendance	.17
Age	.00
Education	.00
Number of years of Catholic education	.07
Parental religiosity	.04
Approval of Changes	.01
Spouse's mass attendance	.16
Rigid sexual morality	-.16
Church's right to teach	.16
Anticlericalism	-.18
Satisfaction with the values taught in Catholic schools	-.03
Satisfaction with the quality of education in Catholic schools	.02
Number of Children	-.07
Tolerance toward black people	-.01

tor of contributions now than it was in 1963. Those who
have had more rather than less exposure to parochial schooling are better able to resist the downward trend in contributing.

The primary factor in this downward trend seems to be the
negative reaction of Catholics to the encyclical on the morality of family planning, *Humanae Vitae*. This negative reaction
cost the church slightly less than one billion dollars in 1974
alone.

This is all by way of saying that there is more money available for church contributions than many had previously

thought. This money would be especially available if it were made clear that it was to be spent on the parochial schools of the country. These funds have not been made available because people have not agreed with the church's teaching on sexual morality (and especially on birth control), because there has been a decline in respect for papal authority, and because the young people who have entered the Catholic population since 1963 are giving less money to the church (partly for the aforementioned reasons). The financial picture is not good, but it did not have to happen this way.

The long-range payoff for maintaining the parochial school system may be simply that it promotes higher levels of contributions. Changes that have occurred during the last decade indicate that this is so. Whether or not those from Catholic schools will continue their higher level of contribution is a question we cannot answer without monitoring these indicators over future time. We did not pose the question of our respondents, but it would be interesting to know specifically where people would like the church to put its resources—into building schools or perhaps into some other alternative. We suspect people would forego some of the "luxuries" in favor of having parochial schools more readily available.

The first step in answering such a policy-related question, however, would be to give the laity some kind of choice in the matter. The data presented in this chapter indicate that many of them would choose to keep their parish school open even at the cost of increasing their own financial burden. These data also indicate that decisions reached and implemented at the highest bureaucratic levels, as was the case with the encyclical *Humanae Vitae,* sometimes have pernicious and expensive effects among the faithful. People cannot be encouraged to believe that they are being consulted when in fact they are not without losing confidence and trust in their leadership.

9

Catholic Schooling and Attitudes toward Religious Leadership

Any human organization depends on its leadership for survival. The leaders are expected to have the organization's purpose and welfare on their minds to a much greater extent than the rank and file members. They are expected to devote more energy and effort to the organization's survival and progress. In most religious organizations the leadership is made up of full-time, professionally trained functionaries whose principal social role is to maintain and to promote the organization. If there is not a relatively stable replacement process by which the ranks of the religious functionaries are kept filled despite attrition caused by death and resignation, the organization will begin to have severe maintenance problems. Furthermore, if the credibility of the religious leadership suffers in the eyes of the rank and file members, then the credibility of the organization will suffer, because in spite of the theological arguments used to prove the contrary, the ordinary lay folk still consider the clergy to represent the church in a way in which the laity does not.

In 1955 there were 46,970 priests in the United States, and by 1965 this figure had increased dramatically to 58,432. However, during the past decade there has been virtually no increase in the total number of priests in the country, and at the same time there has been a general increase in the population and in the youthful age cohort in their twenties in particular. Even more alarming has been the decline in membership among the religious sisterhoods and brotherhoods. The following figures tell the story:[1]

	1955	1965	1975
Priests	46,970	58,432	58,909
Sisters	158,069	179,954	135,225
Brothers	8,752	12,271	8,625

Thus, since 1965, the priesthood has more or less held its own, while the sisterhood has suffered a 25 percent loss and the brotherhood has lost almost 30 percent. However, the statistics on seminarians predict a grim future for the priesthood as well. In 1965 there were 48,992 men enrolling in seminaries, while in 1975 the number had dropped 64 percent, to 17,802.

It is also known, from the NORC priesthood survey, that priests report themselves much less likely now to actively recruit young men for the priesthood than they were five years before the study (NORC 1971:303-304). (This represents a decline of from 64 percent to 33 percent among diocesan priests, and from 56 percent to 27 percent among religious priests.)

Finally, as we reported in previous chapters, two-thirds of the American Catholic population in 1963 said they would be very pleased if their son should choose to be a priest, and only 50 percent gave the same response in 1974. Catholic parents would be more likely to be very pleased if their son chose to become a business executive (66 percent) or a college professor (73 percent); they would be almost as pleased if their son chose a career as an author (47 percent) or stockbroker (48 percent).

In the present chapter we intend to examine the relationship between Catholic school attendance and a number of attitudes toward religious leadership. We shall ask, first, whether there is a relationship between attending parochial school and positive attitudes toward the clergy, and, second, whether this relationship has changed in the decade between the two NORC studies.

We must remember that the social change model used in the previous chapter accounted for all of the 16 percentage point change in attitudes toward the priesthood in the last decade. Only 13 percent of the decline (table 9.1) is due to cohort replacement, while 87 percent is due to value change. About half of the value change is the result of the decline in acceptance of papal leadership, and the other half results from a decline in acceptance of the church's sexual ethic. Within the cohort replacement component of the explanation, 7 percent is a direct result of cohort replacement, and 6 percent is an indirect effect through value change (3 percent relating to sexual orthodoxy and 3 percent relating to the pope). More than nine-tenths of the change in attitudes toward a son's entering the priesthood can be attributed directly or indirectly to a loss of respect for papal leadership and a decline in acceptance of the sexual ethic. If Catholics are less likely

TABLE 9.1

SOCIAL CHANGE MODEL AND DECLINE OF PER CENT
"VERY PLEASED" AT SON BEING A PRIEST

Cohort replacement		
Direct		7
Indirect through sex orthodoxy decline		3
Indirect through decline in acceptance of pope as successor to Peter		3
Total cohort change	13	
Change in sexual orthodoxy		47
Change in acceptance of pope as successor to Peter		40
Total change in values	87	
Unexplained by the model		0
Total	100	100

today to want their sons to become priests, and if they rank the priesthood lower than a career as a business executive or a college professor and equal to a future as an author or a stockbroker, it would appear that the principal reason is the negative reaction to the encyclical letter *Humanae Vitae.* The birth control stand of the church seems to have notably weakened respect for the priesthood as a vocation. Indeed, the direct path between time and support for the priesthood actually increases in our model. This suggests that support for the priesthood would have increased by 4 percentage points if it had not been for the lack of popular support for the birth control teachings and the decline in confidence in the papacy.

In this chapter we propose to try to sort out the influence Catholic schools may have in attitudes toward the clergy. It does not seem unreasonable to expect that value-oriented education would produce adults with higher levels of respect for those whose ex officio function it is to preach the values.

Fourteen questions were asked about religious leadership. The questions dealt with professional performance, political involvement, the desirability of a "religious vocation" for one's children, and the appropriateness of certain recommended changes in the regulations concerning religious leadership. Unfortunately, only the questions concerned with religious vocation were asked a decade ago, since most of the other issues concerning religious leadership have become salient only since the first NORC survey.

American Catholics give their clergy rather low marks on professional performance (table 9.2). Less than half considered them to be very understanding in dealing with the personal problems of adults or young people. Only 20 percent consider their sermons to be "excellent." As we noted earlier, the first and the third items were asked in both 1952 and 1965 in the *Catholic Digest* studies of American religious attitudes. There has been a steady deterioration in the Catholic evaluation of the professional performance of the clergy, a

TABLE 9.2

Attitudes of Catholics toward their Religious Leadership

A. Professional Competence   Percent

	Percent
Priests are "very understanding" of the practical problems of their parishoners. (Item 80)	48
Priests are "very understanding" of the problems of their teen-aged parishoners. (Item 81)	47
Priests' sermons are of "excellent" quality. (Item 82)	20

B. Anticlerical Attitudes (Percent agree strongly or somewhat)

Priests expect laity to be followers. (Item 94-B)	43
Priests are not as religious as they used to be. (Item 94-E)	47
Priests are unconcerned about people, only themselves. (Item 94-F)	17

C. Political Activism (Percent agree strongly or somewhat)

Priests should not use pulpit for social issues. (Item 94-A)	51
Priests may get involved in national and local politics. (Item 94-C)	48

D. Vocations

Unhappy if daughter became a nun. (Item 94-D) (Percent disagree strongly)	50
Very Pleased if son became a priest. (Item 70-B)	50

E. Changes in the Priesthood

Women should be ordained to priesthood. (Item 94-H) (Percent agree strongly or somewhat)	29
Sympathy for priests who have resigned. (Item 95) (Great Deal)	32
Accept married clergy	80
In favor of married clergy	63

deterioration not matched by similar deterioration in Protestant and Jewish evaluations in 1965. In 1952 Catholics rated their clergy higher than did Protestants or Jews in preaching performance and ability to handle problems; in 1965 they rated them lower than did Protestants and Jews (Marty, Rosenberg, Greeley 1968). We do not have any comparative data for Protestants and Jews in 1974.

Whether there has actually been a decline in professional competence among the clergy or an increase in expectations among the Catholic laity is very difficult to judge. It should be noted, though, that the decline in positive evaluation is not limited to the well educated; it has occurred at all educational levels.

While only a minority of the Catholic population give the clergy high professional ratings, a majority do reject charges against them of merely expecting the laity to be followers (down 5 percentage points from 1963) and of not being as religious as they used to be. Only 17 percent can be persuaded that "priests have lost interest in the problems of the people and are concerned only about themselves." Priests are still absolved from the charges of classical anticlericalism.

On the subject of political involvement, the Catholic population evenly divides, with half saying that a priest should not use the pulpit to discuss social issues and almost half saying that it is all right for the priest to get involved in national and local politics if he wishes. The picture that emerges, then, is of a vote against professional competence but also a vote against anticlericalism and a draw concerning political involvement.

As we have observed before, only half of the American Catholics would be very pleased if a son decided to become a priest. The same proportion reject strongly the idea that they would be unhappy if a child of theirs should choose to become a nun (a decline of 10 percentage points since 1963). The priesthood and the sisterhood, in other words, seem to have about the same level of approval among Catholics in 1974.

Finally, 29 percent are in favor of the ordination of women priests. Thirty-two percent express a great deal of sympathy with those who have left the priesthood (and 40 percent more express some sympathy). Eighty percent could accept a married clergy, and 63 percent are positively in favor of a married clergy.

In summary, support among Catholics for a religious vocation for their children has declined in the last ten years; there is a fair amount of sympathy with those who have left the priesthood; and strong support for a married clergy. Priests are rated relatively low on professional ability, but the overwhelming majority do not think they are selfish or unconcerned about the people. The population divides evenly on the controversial issue of the social and political involvement of priests.

Older people are more likely to approve the professional performance of priests (table 9.3), but they are also slightly more likely to think that priests expect laity to be followers and that priests are less religious than they used to be. Furthermore, as might be expected, the younger respondents are more likely to approve of changes than the older ones; and they are less likely to approve of religious vocations for their children. A positive evaluation of the professionalism of the clergy relates negatively with education, but so, too, do anticlerical judgments. The better educated are more in sympathy with change in the priesthood. But there is no significant relation between education and vocational support. Practically the same observation can be made about Catholic education. More years of Catholic schooling mean lower ratings for the professional competence of the clergy, but also the less likelihood of endorsing anticlerical statements. Catholic education correlates positively with sympathy for the resigned clergy and for women as priests, but there is no significant relationship between attending Catholic schools and support for a married clergy.

There is a modest .13 correlation between Catholic education and the vocation support index. However, as we have

TABLE 9.3

CORRELATIONS (R) WITH ATTITUDES TOWARD THE CLERGY

Attitudes toward the Clergy	Age	Education	Catholic Education
Professionalism			
Sermons	.26	-.20	-.12
Youth problems	.26	-.13	-.09
Practical problems	.26	-.07	-.03
Anticlerical			
Expect laity to be followers	.09	-.21	-.20
Less religious than they used to be	.11	-.26	-.22
Think only of self	---	-.23	-.21
Changes			
Favor women priests	-.15	.28	.08
Favor married priests	-.17	.21	----
Sympathy for resignees	-.23	-.11	.11
Vocations			
Priest	.15	---	----
Nun	.12	---	----
Vocation support index	.15	---	.13

seen in previous chapters, modest correlations are all that one can expect when studying educational impact.

We now propose to apply the religious behavior model developed in chapter 5 to Catholic attitudes toward the clergy to determine whether or not, when pertinent background factors are taken into account, there is any relationship at all between Catholic education and attitudes toward religious leadership. We will use five indices: the vocation support index, for which we have data in both 1963 and 1974; the priest as professional index; the anticlerical index; the change index; and the social involvement index.

While the correlation between Catholic education and vocation support in 1974 is a modest .13, it is still substantially higher than the correlation in 1963 (.03) (table 9.4). There was, in other words, no significant correlation between attend-

ing Catholic schools and enthusiasm for religious vocation in
one's family in 1963; there is one in 1974. Furthermore,
there is a moderate negative relationship between Catholic education and positive evaluation of the priest as professional,
and a rather strong negative relationship between attendance
at Catholic schools and anticlericalism. The more years one
has attended Catholic school, the lower one rates priests professionally; but the more likely one is to reject anticlerical
charges against them. There does not seem to be any significant relationship between Catholic education and support for
change in the ministry or social activism.

TABLE 9.4

CORRELATIONS (R) BETWEEN NUMBER OF YEARS
OF CATHOLIC EDUCATION AND ATTITUDES
TOWARD RELIGIOUS LEADERSHIP

Attitude Indices	1963	1974
Vocation index	.03	.13
Priest professionalism index		.11
Anticlericalism index		-.28
Change in priesthood index		.04
Social activism index		.01

The religious behavior model (table 9.5) does not appreciably diminish the relationship between Catholic education
and support for religious vocation. The beta in 1974 is .12, as
opposed to a beta of .02 in 1963. Spouse's religiousness and
age become stronger predictors in the second period of time,
with the result that the religious behavior model explains four
times as much variance (8 percent as opposed to 2 percent) in
1974 as it did in 1963. Support for religious vocations, in
other words, has declined less precipitously among those who
have had Catholic education, so that the net result is a
stronger relationship between Catholic education and support
for vocations than there was ten years ago.

TABLE 9.5

STANDARDIZED CORRELATIONS (BETAS) BETWEEN RELIGIOUS BEHAVIOR MODEL AND ATTITUDES TOWARD RELIGIOUS LEADERS

	Vocation Index		Priest Pro-fessionalism Index	Anticlerical Index	Change in Priesthood Index	Social Activism Index
	1963	1974				
Age	.07	.20	.24	.00	-.09	-.15
Sex	.06	.06	.05	.00	-.02	.09
Parents' religiousness	.07	.06	-.03	-.04	-.05	.03
Spouse's mass attendance	.06	.16	.21	.17	-.04	.03
Educational attainment	.09	.06	-.08	-.17	.28	.05
Years of Catholic education	.02	.12	.00	-.17	.00	.04
Variance explained	.02	.08	.15	.15	.11	.08

On the other hand, the relationship between Catholic education and a low rating of priests as professionals disappears entirely, we presume because the negative evaluation derives not so much from having more years of Catholic education as from simply having more years of education.

However, a moderately large relationship of -.17 does persist in the religious behavior model even after all the other variables are standardized between Catholic education and the anticlerical index. The number of years in Catholic school does have a net impact on one's propensity to reject anticlerical statements.

Finally, the principal predictor of support for change in the priesthood continues to be education (a beta of .28). There is no relationship at all between attending Catholic schools and support for such change. In summary, number of years in Catholic schools does affect sympathy for religious vocations and rejection of anticlericalism. In the former case, the relationship has grown stronger in the last decade because Catholic school Catholics have not withdrawn their support for priestly vocations quite as rapidly as have other Catholics. There is, however, no relationship between attendance at Catholic school and evaluation of priest as professional or sympathy for change in the style of the priestly ministry. Nor does Catholic education affect reaction to priests' political and social involvement. These variables respond only to the influence of age. The younger respondents, not surprisingly, are more likely to approve of the activist clergy.

If we look at those who come from highly religious backgrounds (table 9.6), we see that while a strong religious background does not affect the relationship between parochial schooling and support for vocations, it does have an interesting impact in the relationships between parochial schooling and three other variables. For the highly religious there is a negative relation of -.3 between number of years in parochial school and anticlerical attitudes. Also, there is a negative relationship of -.2 in the evaluation of priests' professionalism, and a positive correlation of .1 with support for priestly change. In other words, even though there is generally no relationship between an evaluation of professional performance and change in the ministry, on the one hand, and parochial schooling, on the other, among those from highly religious backgrounds there are such relationships with the number of years in parochial school. Catholic schooling does produce, in those from highly religious family backgrounds, a tendency to evaluate negatively the professionalism of priests and to support change in the forms of the ministry (such as the ordina-

TABLE 9.6

STANDARDIZED CORRELATIONS (BETAS) BETWEEN YEARS OF CATHOLIC
EDUCATION AND ATTITUDES TOWARD RELIGIOUS
LEADERSHIP FOR CERTAIN SUBGROUPS

A. By Parental Religiousness

	High	Low
Vocation index 1963	.05	.03
Vocation index 1974	.12	.12
Anticlerical index	−.30	−.10
Priest professionalism index	−.20	.04
Change in priesthood index	.11	−.02
Social activism index	.06	−.07

B. By Age (1974)

	Under Thirty	All Respondents
Vocation index	.28	.12
Anticlerical index	−.38	−.11
Priest professionalism index	.02	−.09
Change in priesthood index	.06	.00
Social activism	.18	.04

tion of married men and the admission of women to the priesthood).

Similarly, in the Vietnam cohort, the number of years of parochial school has a very strong effect (.28) on support for religious vocation, and a very strong negative effect (-.38) on anticlericalism. If one really wishes to find an impact of parochial schooling on attitudes toward religious leadership, then one will find it not in the general population but among those from highly religious family backgrounds (from whom those with priestly vocations are most likely to come) and among those under thirty. If the Vietnam cohort is to be typical of the future of American Catholicism, then at least as far as attitudes toward the clergy and support for vocations are concerned, parochial schools may be more important than ever.

Only 8 percent of the variance in the vocation index is explained by the religious behavior models we have been using in this study. Therefore it seems appropriate to ask whether we could improve our ability to predict support for religious vocations by adding to the model attitudes toward the clergy. In addition to demography, religious background, education, and parochial education, we might expect that attitudes toward vocations might be affected by attitudes toward the clergy and general attitudes toward the church. Are specific attitudes toward clerical performance more important or less important than one's general attitudes toward the church? How much would one improve support for religious vocation if one introduced such changes as a married clergy or the ordination of women, or if one improved the professional performance of priests?

The standardized coefficients in table 9.7 suggest that general attitudes toward the church—particularly sexual orthodoxy and Catholic activism—and educational achievement are more likely to influence support for religious vocation than are the specifically clerical issues of professionalism or change in the ministry. However, attitudes toward the clergy are reasonably important too. We must conclude that no single modification to the structure of the church or the behavior of the clergy would make a religious vocation for their children more desirable to today's Catholics. A case may be made for the ordination of women and married men, for permitting the clergy to marry, and for improving sermons; but these changes should not be justified on the grounds that they will lead to a complete turnaround in the declining support for religious vocations among the Catholic population. Changes of this sort will not affect in the slightest the sexual attitudes of American Catholics, for example; and it is this change which seems to be the principal cause for the decline in support of vocations. It would appear that only a broad restructuring of church policy and practice would stand much chance of reversing the deterioration.

TABLE 9.7

STANDARDIZED CORRELATIONS (BETAS) WITH VOCATIONAL ATTITUDES

	Priest	Nun	Vocation Index
Clergy Attitudes			
Priest change	-.12	-.09	-.12
Anticlergy	-.11	-.12	-.14
Hierarchy support	.10	.09	.11
Priest professionalism	.01	.09	.08
General Church Attitudes			
Sexual orthodoxy	.15	.13	.16
Activism	.23	.10	.17
Closeness to the Church	.10	.11	.13
Social Class			
Education	-.15	-.13	-.16
R^2	.18	.21	.25

However, it must still be emphasized that the deterioration is least rapid among those who have had Catholic education. The positive relationship between years of Catholic education and support for vocations has *increased* since 1963, and it is particularly strong among two critical groups—the Vietnam co-hort, which may represent the church of the future; and the highly religious families, where vocations are most likely to be found. It may well be that in the future religious leadership in the church will be drawn even more from Catholic school families than it has been in the past.

The increase in the relationship between number of years in Catholic schools and support for religious vocations in one's family seems to be limited to certain ethnic groups (table 9.8). At both time points, the Irish are the strongest sup-porters of religious vocations, and the other groups follow in their accustomed pattern—German, Polish, Italian, and Spanish-speaking. The range of difference between the Irish and the Spanish-speaking falls from a half of a standard devia-tion in 1963 to a quarter of one in 1974.

TABLE 9.8

Z SCORES FOR RELATIONSHIPS BETWEEN CATHOLIC EDUCATION AND
ATTITUDES TOWARD THE CLERGY FOR ETHNIC GROUPS

(Mean = 0, Standard Deviation = 100)

Ethnic Group	Vocation Index		Professional Competence 1974 Only	Anticlericalism 1974 Only
	1963	1974		
Irish	20	15	-15	-30
German	10	14	09	-16
Polish	04	06	-30	01
Italian	-15	-10	-18	06
Spanish-speaking	-31	-11	31	34

But the increase in the net relationship (in the religious be-havior model) is limited to two of the Eastern and Southern European groups—from a beta of .04 for the Poles in 1963 to .27 in 1974, and from .12 to .33 for the Italians. For the Irish, on the other hand, there now emerges a *negative* rela-tionship between number of years of Catholic education and support for vocations. The Irish, traditionally the source of large numbers of vocations (17 percent of the Catholic population and 34 percent of its priests), are still the leaders, but attendance at parochial school makes them *less* likely to support vocations. Nor can this be attributed to higher levels of educational achievement for the Irish, since the religious behavior model takes that into account. Furthermore, even though they are low on anticlericalism, the Irish are also low on the professional competence scale; and it is precisely among those who have gone to Catholic schools that there is the lowest rating of priests' professional competence and the highest propensity toward anticlericalism. One has the impression that the Irish are getting turned off by their clergy—in particular, those Irish who went to Catholic schools. However, for the other groups (with the exception of the Spanish-speaking, for clerical competence) there is a moderate to strong relationship between attendance at Catholic schools and positive attitudes towards the clergy (table 9.9).

TABLE 9.9

NET STANDARDIZED CORRELATIONS (BETAS) BETWEEN CATHOLIC EDUCATION
AND ATTITUDES TOWARD THE CLERGY

Ethnic Group	Vocation Index		Professional Competence 1974 Only	Anticlericalism 1974 Only
	1963	1974		
Irish	.01	-.10	-.12	.09
German	.14	.09	.08	-.20
Polish	.04	.27	.14	-.46
Italian	.12	.33	.18	-.25
Spanish-speaking	.15	.12	-.02	-.19

Given the historical Irish contribution to vocations, the data in tables 9.8 and 9.9 ought to provide grounds for serious worry to policy-makers in the church. Catholic schools are turning other groups toward the clergy, but they are turning the Irish against them. Since the decline in support for vocations seems to be a result of the birth control encyclical, one might conclude that the Catholic school Irish were more embittered than others by this encyclical.

One can test for this possibility by applying a simplified version of Social Change Model II to the Irish (Fig. 9.1). The pooled relationship between having more than ten years of Catholic education and being "very pleased" with a son's choosing a priestly vocation is .04—those who went to Catholic schools are at both times more likely by 4 percentage points to want their sons to be priests than those who did not. If the change in sexual ethics had an especially deleterious effect on those who had Catholic education, one would expect an interaction in which those who had Catholic education would in 1974 be significantly lower than the pooled average if they now were in the lower category in support for the sexual ethic. If this group was not significantly lower in its support for a priestly vocation in 1963, but had become so in 1974, it would be reasonable to conclude that it was precisely the addition of new recruits to the group that rejected the church's sexual teaching that brought the relationship down. Those Catholic-educated Irish who had turned against the church's sexual morality would in the process have turned more sharply against support for a priestly vocation than the typical Irish Catholic respondent.

Such a significant interaction was indeed found. The relationship between Catholic education and enthusiastic support for a priestly vocation for one's son among those who had more than ten years of Catholic education and who tended to reject the church's sexual teaching was -.19, or 23 percentage points below the pooled average for those who went to Catholic schools. In 1963, 83 percent of the parochial school Irish were ready to say they would be very pleased if their son chose the priesthood (17 percentage points above the national Catholic average). By 1974 this had fallen to 45 percent (5 percentage points below the national average). Since the average decline was only 16 percent nationally, one concludes

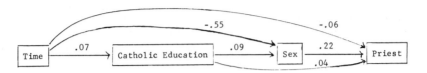

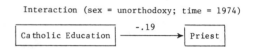

Interaction (sex = unorthodoxy; time = 1974)

Figure 9.1--Relationship of Irish to Social Change Model II

that almost all of the change was brought about by the change in sexual attitudes among the Catholic-educated Irish. The sexual shift, then, seems to have had a particularly harmful effect on attitudes towards the clergy among those who were once its strongest supporters—the Catholic-educated Irish.

The Catholic clergy once enjoyed an almost unparalleled respect among their laity. That respect seems to have been notably diminished in the last decade. Now the priest no longer enjoys the prestige of such high-status professionals as the business executive and the college professor, and barely matches such other professionals as the stockbroker or the writer. Most of this decline can be explained by the decline in acceptance of papal authority and of the church's sexual ethic without recourse to the changing social class of the Catholic population or the well-publicized resignations of many clergy in the last ten years. One of the paradoxical effects of this decline, however, is that the relationship between Catholic education and vocational support, virtually nonexistent a decade ago, has increased to such a degree that it has now become statistically significant. Furthermore, the relationship between the number of years of Catholic education and vocational support is quite strong among two important groups, those under thirty and those from highly religious families. Therefore, not merely despite the change in support for religious vocation, but apparently because of the change, Catholic schools are now more important in producing support for religious leadership than they were in 1963.[2]

10

Parochial Schools and Value Orientation

One of the primary purposes of any system of education which purports to be value-oriented is to instill in its students specific beliefs about how the world "really" operates on a fundamental level. Ordinary values and beliefs focus on the day-to-day occurrences of life and provide linkages between events. We may choose which candidate we will support, for example, by relying upon a set of political beliefs which link our idea of the way things ought to be done with what we think is possible under the circumstances. Or we may allow our values and beliefs to influence our judgments of groups who differ from us. These stereotyped generalizations are often based on relatively few experiences, and, frequently, bad ones at that.

Our conception of the "ultimate nature of reality," of how the world "really" operates is represented by a different kind of belief or value system. One of the most basic human questions is whether or not there is order in reality. Is there a purpose and meaning to life, or is it all a charade that will someday turn into chaos? In the ultimate sense of things, will it all work out for the good, or is there a malevolent ending hiding in wait to snare us? The way in which people answer these questions has a direct influence on what kind of guidelines they will use for living out their time. One's sense of the nature of ultimate reality provides a model or paradigm according to which more proximate decisions can be made.

The anthropologist Clifford Geertz speaks of these ultimate value systems as being general orientations toward reality.

They provide both a model *of* and a model *for* reality as it truly exists. For example, if we were to engage in building a dam across a river, we would first formulate a conception of just what such a structure should do. We might then try to devise a small-scale model of our conception. This would be the process of creating and using a model *of* a specific reality. When we actually build our dam, however, the scale model would not be of much use; we would need a set of precise instructions or blueprints, and this is analogous to having a model *for* a specific reality.

Systems of ultimate values perform both functions. They provide the conceptual framework within which we exist and they provide the rules by which we feel we ought to live. Professor Geertz has described the cultural system that is religion in just these terms. Religious values both shape and are shaped by reality. They tell us what the world is really like, and they tell us how to act in conformity with our conception of ultimate reality.

The Catholic religious tradition has long held to a specific set of ultimate values which might be subsumed under the descriptive title of "hopefulness." The revelations and doctrine concerning the salvation of humankind by the redemptive sacrifice of Jesus Christ can best be described as promulgating a hopeful world-view and a benevolent conception of ultimate reality. This tradition teaches that although there is a great deal of evil in the world and although it appears that evil must triumph in the end, in the final analysis good will prevail.

It is undoubtedly true that not everyone who calls himself or herself a Catholic espouses this hopeful world-view, but it is the ideal set forth by the teachings of the Roman Catholic church. Therefore we would expect that value-oriented education designed and maintained by that church would attempt to instill hopefulness and confidence in a benevolent God in those students who attend parochial schools. It is important to note that the school is by no means the only locus in which ultimate values are formed. Even more important in this regard is the family. However, the parochial schools have as one of their stated goals the formation of religious values and a religious perspective on living in their students. How well they accomplish this goal and the relationship between ultimate values and the more proximate social and religious attitudes is the focus of this chapter.

A Typology of Ultimate Values

In previous research (McCready and Greeley 1972), two of the present authors designed a set of survey items to measure hopefulness and other ultimate value orientations. The items were in the form of short vignettes or situations which presented people with sudden tragedies or crises of the sort that in fact do happen in real life (see Adult Questionnaire, 1974, questions 107-110, Appendix III). In one we asked people how they thought they would react if their doctor told them they had an incurable disease and would soon die. In another we asked them how they thought they would react if a retarded child were born to them. In still another we asked how they saw themselves reacting to the prolonged suffering of a dying parent.

These kinds of situations call upon us for some kind of interpretation because they challenge our supposition that there is meaning in the universe. They confront the evil in the world and force us to consider the possibility that perhaps everything is ultimately chaotic after all. If a person does have a meaning system or a set of ultimate values, items of this kind should draw them out.

Each item contained six possible responses plus several categories for those who could not or would not answer the questions. (These latter categories accounted for, on the average, no more than 6 or 7 percent of the responses.) The first answer represented a simplistic confidence that everything works out for the good somehow. The second category represented a fundamentalist turning toward God with no real recognition of the tragedy or the evil involved in the situation. The third response characterized an attitude of resignation to the inevitable. The fourth category represented an emotionally hostile reaction to the situation posed, and the fifth response depicted gratitude for whatever good could be found in the situation. The final response represented an understanding of the evil and the tragic nature of the situation, but included a belief that the final chapter has not yet been written and that ultimately things will turn out benevolently.

The vignettes were combined into a summary variable which was then converted into a five-category descriptive typology (see Appendix VII). The five types of ultimate values are "religious optimism," "secular optimism," "hopefulness," "pessimism," and "diffuseness."

Religious optimists achieve belief in an optimistic future by denying the present evil. Secular optimists similarly deny evil in the world, but they do not depend on God to support their contention. Pessimists are either hostile or resigned to the tragedies that befall us in life; there is no appeal to God, nor is there any expression of confidence in a positive outcome. The diffuse are basically a residual category of those who have no clear systematic reaction to the situations posed in the vignettes.

The "hopeful" respondents are those who display some understanding of the existence of evil, while at the same time holding to their belief that the situation will end in a way that is ultimately positive and influenced by a benevolent reality. This is a subtle and multifaceted world-view. It is a sophisticated cosmology which has doubtless been influenced by many different factors. Before we examine the causes and correlates of hope and the other value orientations, let us examine the performance of this measure of ultimate values in a previous survey to see if it has behaved consistently in two different research settings.

In table 10.1, we can see that the proportion of the Catholic population in each category is quite consistent in the two studies. None of the differences between Catholics in 1973 and 1974 is greater than 5 percent. The fact that these proportions are so similar is a good indication that the vignette items measure some consistent facet of the belief structure of the population. If the proportions had been very different in the two years, it might well have been that people were responding randomly to the vignette items. As it is, every indication points to the fact that these life situation vignettes do in fact tap some deep perspective concerning the way in which people order reality. When faced with tragedy people will call upon their deep-seated understanding of the nature of the universe in order to interpret and give meaning to the event before them. And this holds true, apparently, even in the hypothetical setting of an interview.

TABLE 10.1

COMPARISONS BETWEEN RESPONSE PATTERNS ON ULTIMATE VALUES
TYPOLOGY FOR VARIOUS POPULATIONS

(Percent)

Ultimate Value	1973 Total Population	1973 Catholic Populations	1974 Catholic Populations
Secular optimism	19	15	19
Pessimism	26	31	34
Religious fundamentalism	19	18	17
Hopefulness	17	17	16
Diffused	19	19	14
n	(1467)	(368)	(925)

In table 10.2 we can see that hopefulness tends to decline somewhat among the older age groups, while religious optimism tends to increase. Pessimism also tends to decline slightly. The remainder of the types are more or less invariant with age. With the exception of the religious optimists, most of the age differences are quite small. The religious optimists do tend to be older than the norm, but it is impossible to determine whether this is a life-cycle phenomenon or a generational one.[1] (A life-cycle phenomenon is a function of respondents' age; people tend to act a certain way because they are a certain age. An example would be the rebellion of the young against the rule of their parents—all young men and women go through this in one way or another; it is part of gaining an identity and growing up. A generational phenomenon is a characteristic of a particular age cohort and is the result of certain experiences that had a lifelong influence on the way the members of the cohort thought or behaved. The influence of the Great Depression on those who reached adulthood during the early 1930s certainly left a mark on those people for life. The fear that what seems secure will suddenly vanish does not go away just because the economy looks bright.)

The time comparison and the age analysis both indicate that the typology does in fact measure a set of values in a consistent manner, and that these values are not simply a function of the age distribution of the population.

Hopefulness and Catholic Education

As we have stated previously, the value system that most embodies the teachings of the Roman Catholic church's approach to life is hopefulness. In table 10.3, we can see that there is a substantial relationship between attending Catholic schools for ten years or more and being a hopeful person. However, it is possible that this is a spurious relationship, one in which some other variable is actually influencing both the amount of education and the high hopefulness score.

In order to test for this effect we have used a method for fitting categorical data to linear flow charts pioneered by James A. Davis (1972). In Fig. 10.1, the decimal coefficients represent the influence between the two linked variables, accounting for the influence of all the other variables in the

TABLE 10.2

COMPARISONS BETWEEN RESPONSE PATTERNS ON ULTIMATE VALUES
TYPOLOGY FOR VARIOUS AGE GROUPS

(Percent)

Ultimate Values	Less than 30	30-40	40-50	50 and over
Secular optimism	27	26	32	26
Pessimism	24	23	19	15
Religious fundamentalism	11	13	15	25
Hopefulness	19	18	16	12
Diffused	19	20	18	21
n	(268)	(177)	(156)	(305)

TABLE 10.3

COMPARISONS BETWEEN RESPONSE PATTERNS
OF ULTIMATE VALUES TYPOLOGY
BY YEARS OF CATHOLIC EDUCATION
(Percent)

	0	1-10	10+
Secular optimism	23	30	31
Pessimism	22	19	17
Religious fundamentalism	20	15	10
Hopefulness	15	12	24
Diffused	20	24	16
N	(419)	(303)	(172)

model. For example, level of education and number of years of Catholic education have a linking coefficient of .21, which is rather high. This means that the two variables are quite strongly associated with each other.

As we can see in Fig. 10.1, Catholic education is twice as powerful an influence on hope as is educational level. Therefore the relationship which we noticed in table 10.3 is certainly not spurious. Catholic education's influence on hopefulness is quite independent from that of educational level, and it is much stronger. he value-oriented thrust of the parochial schools is to some extent accomplishing just what the schools were designed to do: promulgate and nurture a specific world-view.

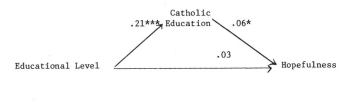

```
*** = .001
 ** = .01
  * = .05
```

Figure 10.1

However, educational level is not the only potentially inter-fering factor in the relationship between Catholic education and hopefulness. It could be that the people who are hopeful came from very religious families, and that that is why they espouse the world-view they do. In this case, they might be more likely than others to seek a religiously oriented educa-tional experience, thereby giving the appearance of association between Catholic education and hopefulness when in reality it is the home and parents that produced such an orientation.

In Fig. 10.2, we can see that Catholic education is still the stronger predictor of hopefulness. Parental religiosity does have some influence but not as much as the parochial school experience. In Fig. 10.3, we can see that the same holds true even when we control the effect of education by considering only those people who attended college. Catholic education is more important for producing hopeful people than is parental religiosity.

Figure 10.2

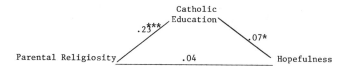

Figure 10.3:   For Those Who Attended College

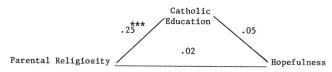

Another way of looking at this phenomenon is to explore the relative effects of family and parochial schooling on another religious value system. If the Catholic schools are supposed to foster hopefulness—and we have shown that they do—they should also have a negative influence on the shallow and naive set of religious values we have called religious optimism.

In Fig. 10.4, we can see that this is in fact the case. Parental religiosity has a small positive influence on religious optimism, but the number of years one has spent in a parochial school environment has a much higher negative impact. In Fig. 10.5, we can see that the separation between the family's influence and that of the Catholic schools is about the same as it was in Fig. 10.4 (.09 as opposed to .11, controlling for education).

Catholic education has been shown to be more important than either education or parental religiosity for fostering

Figure 10.4

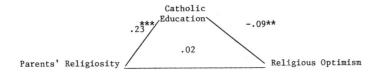

Figure 10.5:   For Those Who Attended College

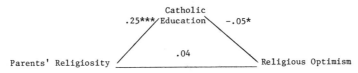

hopefulness and limiting its opposite in religious values, religious optimism. As an institution of secondary socialization,
the parochial schools have done quite well. They have fos-
tered the set of ultimate values espoused by the Catholic tradition more effectively than the religiosity of parents or the
secular educational establishment. The next question is
whether or not this ultimate value of hopefulness makes any
difference in the way in which Catholics live their daily lives?
Does it relate to other more proximate attitudes? Does it have
any effect on religious attitudes or behavior? Do hopefulness
and the parochial school experience together have an effect
on social attitudes?

Let us discuss the last question first by investigating the impact of hopefulness and parochial school attendance on one
very important social attitude, tolerance for those of a different race.

The Catholic religion has always stressed the common
humanity of men and their responsibilities toward each other.

The precept "Love thy neighbor" is one of the primary commandments of the church, and many of the teachings from the central authorities have been directed toward questions of social justice and the equality of all men in the eyes of God. Therefore we would expect that people who received a good deal of their education in parochial schools would be more accepting than others of racial and social diversity in the society. Since hopefulness is the appropriate orientation of the parochial schools, there ought to be a positive relationship between hopefulness and tolerance as well.

In Fig. 10.6, we can see that education and hopefulness have about the same influence on tolerance. Each is responsible for about a 20 point net percentage increase in tolerance of whites toward blacks. In other words, a person both well educated and hopeful would be almost 40 points higher on tolerance than someone who was neither well educated nor hopeful.

Figure 10.6

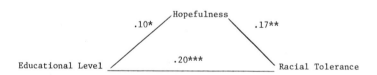

Figure 10.7: For Those Who Attended College

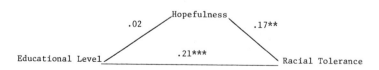

It is difficult to separate the influence of Catholic education from that of education per se, since the more Catholic
education one has, the more education one has. We focused
only on those people who attended college and constructed a
model for them. In Fig. 10.7, we can see that both Catholic
education and hopefulness have strong effects on tolerance,
holding education constant. In other words, even among the
well educated, a Catholic education and espousal of a hopeful
world-view markedly increase the level of racial tolerance.

Hopefulness and Religious Attitudes

In this section we will examine the relationship between
the ultimate values of our respondents and their attitudes
about various religious topics. If hopefulness is the dominant
value orientation of the Christian, then we would expect it to
be related to some other, more proximate, religious attitudes
in a consistent fashion. This is in fact the case, as we can see
in table 10.4. The hopeful people score highest on Catholic
activism, use of the sacraments, approval of various kinds of
changes stemming from the Second Vatican Council, and the
specific indicators of Catholic activity we asked about in
1974. They score lowest on anticlerical sentiment. On the
other hand, the religious optimists score highest on support
for vocations, rigid sexual views, and competency of priests.
The secular optimists are quite close to the mean on almost
all items; and the pessimists are generally well below the
mean, except on the index of anticlerical feeling, where they
are one-quarter of a standard deviation above the mean.

In general, the hopeful people score high on those measures
that relate to activity, and they tend to approve of those
changes in the church instituted by the Vatican Council. The
religious optimists tend to score high on those factors closely
related to the authority of the church, such as support for
priests and vocations and the upholding of the traditional sexual morality.

TABLE 10.4

STANDARD SCORES ON RELIGIOUS SCALES BY ULTIMATE VALUES

	Religious Optimism	Secular Optimism	Hopefulness	Pessimism	Diffusion
Catholic Activism	22	-05	58	-42	03
Support for Vocation	36	13	25	-38	-23
Sexual Orthodoxy	62	07	14	-31	-18
Doctrinal Orthodoxy	39	-04	38	-34	-15
Church's Right to Teach	25	-08	26	-19	-09
Sacramental Scale	43	-04	54	-39	-28
Anticlerical	-10	07	-48	28	-04
Priest Competence	36	-18	22	-22	-16
Vatican II	-25	04	16	01	15
Change Priest	-32	10	18	13	21
"New Ways"	-24	07	12	27	-03
Catholic Media Activism	17	-03	34	-27	-09
New Style Activism	22	-10	53	-40	10
Old Style Activism	12	05	39	-43	14

It is a well-known fact in the social sciences, however, that education influences many attitudes and values. Since the religious optimists are not as well educated as the hopefuls, we might speculate as to whether or not the differences noticed in table 10.4 are really the result of education and not of differing value perspectives.

TABLE 10.5

STANDARD SCORES ON RELIGIOUS SCALES BY ULTIMATE VALUES
ADJUSTED FOR EDUCATION

	Religious Optimism	Secular Optimism	Hopefulness	Pessimism	Diffusion
Catholic Activism	44	02	49	-43	-14
Support for Vocation	16	02	26	-18	-06
Sexual Orthodoxy	54	-12	27	-23	-19
Doctrinal Orthodoxy	41	-02	38	-29	-18
Church's Right to Teach	28	-04	26	-21	-06
Sacramental Scale	37	05	31	-30	-12
Anticlerical	-20	04	-43	26	03
Priest Competence	31	-18	26	-17	-13
Vatican II	-23	02	14	-01	10
Change Priest	-45	07	05	15	05
"New Ways"	17	05	00	-02	-26
Catholic Media Activism	10	-02	31	-16	-14
New Style Activism	26	07	33	-26	-02
Old Style Activism	25	06	32	-29	-09

In table 10.5, we have adjusted the standard scores on the various religious attitude measures for the effect of education and presented them for each of the ultimate value types. To the extent that the scores on table 10.5 are different from those in table 10.4, education is an important factor. To the extent that they are the same, education is not a factor, and ultimate values are shown to have an impact on religious attitudes. Controlling for education, the hopeful still score highest on the various indices of activism and lowest on anticlericalism. The religious optimists are still highest on rigid sexual morality and priestly competence. Some of the other relationships have changed, however. For example, the hopeful are no longer well ahead of the religious optimists in terms of their use of the sacraments, and the hopeful are more likely to support vocations. The secular optimists are still quite close to the mean on most of the measures, and the pessimists are still generally well below it.

The introduction of education into the relationship between ultimate values and proximate religious attitudes does not seem to have changed anything very much. The religious optimists, with their confined and constricted conception of the nature of ultimate reality, tend to be supportive of those religious attitudes approved by the authorities, while the hopeful, who seem to have a more balanced religious perspective, are more supportive of church activities and of individual priests. Since we have already shown a relationship between Catholic education and hopefulness, we would assume that some of the effects of a hopeful world-view would be transmitted through parochial education.

In the next section we will discuss several models for these religious attitudes and the relative influence of Catholic education and hopefulness on them. Using the model for fitting categorical data to linear flow charts that we introduced above, we will try to ascertain which of the two variables, Catholic education and hopefulness, influences each of the attitudes more.

Catholic Education, Hopefulness, and Religious Attitudes

The relative influence of Catholic education and hopefulness on the entire range of religious attitudes is measured by constructing a model for each specific attitude. Fig. 10.8 consists of one model for Catholic activism that is fully described. Below it is the list of net percentage differences for the remainder of the undrawn models. The model for sexual orthodoxy is the same as that for activism, for example, but with different numbers placed on the lines; and so it is for each of the other attitudes.

Figure 10.8

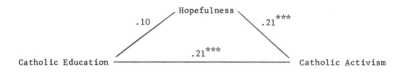

Catholic Education to:	Hopefulness to:	
.06	.09	Sexual Orthodoxy
.13***	.25***	Doctrinal Orthodoxy
.08	.11	Church's Right to Teach
.13***	.13***	Sacramental Index
-.22***	-.21***	Anticlerical
.01*	.19***	Priest Competence
.12**	.00	Priestly Change
-.05	.02*	"New Ways"
.08***	-.18***	Activism
.16***	.19***	Media Activism
.14***	.20***	Vatican II

*** = .001
** = .01
* = .05

Catholic education and hopefulness about the ultimate nature of reality have about the same influence on whether one is an "active" Catholic or not. They also have equal influence on one's use of the sacraments and on one's anticlerical sentiments.

Catholic education is more important than hopefulness for feelings that the priesthood should change and be expanded and for participation in the programmatic kinds of church activity, such as retreats, discussion groups, and other group activities. Being a hopeful person is more important than Catholic education for everything from sexual orthodoxy to feeling that priests are competent. In some of these instances the differences are slight and both factors are obviously important there; but in some the differences are considerably greater. For example, with regard to doctrinal orthodoxy, hopefulness is almost twice as important as Catholic education. People who are hopeful are 25 percent higher on the measure of orthodoxy, given the influence of Catholic education. People who are hopeful and who attended Catholic schools are 38 percent higher on doctrinal orthodoxy than those who neither are hopeful nor attended Catholic schools. People who are hopeful are more likely to approve both the church's right to teach in sensitive areas of human life and the new ways of teaching religion in the schools. Almost all of the influence on the feeling that priests are competent stems from hopefulness rather than from Catholic educational experiences. Use of the Catholic media and support for the changes instituted by the Second Vatican Council are also slightly more influenced by people's hopefulness than by their parochial schooling.

Having been to parochial schools, then, seems to have had special influence only on people's tolerance for changes within the priesthood and on their participation in what might be called Catholic "group" activities. In the first case, it may. be that people who receive more parochial education simply know more about the nature of the priesthood and therefore are not bothered so much by the idea of some changes they might consider nonessential, such as celibacy and the ordination of women priests. These things are not part of the core doctrine of the church, and they can be changed by the governing agencies rather easily. In the second case, it may be that people have been exposed to some of these Catholic groups in their educational experiences, and that this carries over into their adulthood. Retreats and discussion groups are common at many parochial school institutions.

Most of the religious attitudes seem to be influenced by hopefulness rather than by parochial schooling directly. There is no way of knowing, of course, but it seems likely that hopefulness starts long before a child first attends school and that it may be nurtured or smothered during the school experience. The way we are taught to look at the world around us has its beginnings in the earliest socialization experiences. These experiences are not available to us in these data, but the fact that this value, hopefulness, is related to many of our religious attitudes and behaviors indicates that there is a close connection between ultimate and proximate values on the religious level.

Our profile of the hopeful people is that they have a subtle understanding of the duality of good and evil. They purportedly believe that good is slightly stronger and will triumph in the end. This is a "religious" perspective on life in the broad sense of the term. It may be that for people with this kind of perspective the details of church policy and doctrines are not obstacles to belief. They support traditional church positions as well as post-conciliar innovations. They are not easily labeled "liberal" or "conservative"—tags seem inappropriate here. For a church in transition, these characteristics could be supportive. Hopefulness is a Christian perspective, and these data indicate that Catholic education has a part in producing it. Hopefulness, in turn, is more important than parochial schooling in fostering support for most religious attitudes and behavior.

Conclusion and Summary

In this chapter we have described a method of ascertaining the ultimate values of our respondents, and we have used this method to examine the relationship between parochial school education, hopefulness, and other religious attitudes. Parochial

schools were found to have had a positive effect on producing
a hopeful world-view in those respondents who attended Catholic schools for more than ten years (see table 10.3). In Fig.
10.1 we saw that Catholic education, not just educational
level, was the more important factor in producing a hopeful
perspective toward ultimate reality. The relationship between
Catholic education and hopefulness has been firmly established. Since hope is the embodiment of the Christian perspective on life, we can say that the parochial schools' effort to
inculcate a specific value system into their students has been
moderately successful.

An all-encompassing world-view is certainly not produced
simply by attending a specific kind of school. It begins much
earlier than that, of course. However, it is important to recognize that the parochial schools do nurture and support such a
positive world-view.

Parochial school education is also more important than
parental religiosity in terms of producing hopefulness in our
respondents. Parents who are very religious are more likely to
send their children to Catholic schools, of course, and in that
way there is an indirect influence on hopefulness, but the direct influence of the schools on hope is greater than the
direct influence of the parents.

Catholic education and hopefulness combine to have a
strong positive influence on racial tolerance for our respondents. Of the two variables, parochial education is a slightly
stronger influence than hopefulness.

Particular religious behavior patterns, such as activism and
acceptance of change in the church, are associated with hopefulness, but it is not very strongly associated with rigid sexual
mores, unlike its contrary attitude, religious optimism. To be
hopeful is to be less constrained and more open to change.
This world-view or ultimate value bespeaks a confidence in
the eventual triumph of the forces of good over those of evil,
clearly a welcome perspective for a church in transition.
Those people imbued with this orientation toward life are less

likely to become preoccupied with the narrow and insignificant details of religion. They support changes and innovations as experiments that ought to be tried, but they are loyal to tradition. They are not as likely as others to join movements and organize discussion groups, but they are aware of what is going on in their church, and they are active in many other ways. We have the sense that these people are sensible to the existence of both good and evil in the world and secure in their belief in the eventual dominance of good. Such security could be a valuable asset to a church that is in considerable disarray.

If the church wants to husband its hopeful people, it must recognize the magnified importance of the parochial school system. In terms of human resources, Catholic schools are a tremendous asset for the changing church. They tend to produce people who are change-oriented and flexible, but secure in both their world-view and their loyalty to past traditions and values. Parochial schools are also producing people who are more tolerant of others and better able to cope with our increasingly diverse society.

This is not a bad record for a value-oriented system of education. The parochial schools are having the kind of influence on students they say they want to have. And it appears that the more Catholic schooling a person has, the greater the effects. Hopefulness is an ultimate value system that is a subtle and complex perspective toward the world. No one factor can ever explain it all; however, the parochial schools have a considerable impact on forming just such a perspective in their students. In a day and age when schools are frequently criticized for being antithetical to human values and for being "conformity factories," data which indicate that some schools are able to encourage the formation of positive values in their students constitute a refreshing and hopeful sign.

11

Conclusion

This has been a study of value-oriented education under the stress of social change—change which concentrated on the values themselves and which the value-oriented education was supposed to reinforce. By way of capsule summary, we would state a paradox: The value-oriented schools have survived the forces of change rather well; they are, nevertheless, in serious trouble.

There have been tremendous demographic changes in the American Catholic population since the restricted-immigration laws were passed in the early 1920s. The children and the grandchildren of the last wave of immigrants to arrive from southern and eastern Europe between 1880 and 1920 have been acculturated into American society. In terms of income, education, and occupation, Catholics in general lag behind only the Episcopalians, the Presbyterians, and the Jews. Irish Catholics have been above the national average socially and economically since the turn of the century; and in the years since the Second World War, the younger generation of Poles and Italians has pulled even with the national norms. Indeed, in the Vietnam cohort, the income of Irish and Italian Catholics is higher than that of Jews, Presbyterians, and Episcopalians. In terms of economic success, occupational prestige, and educational attainment, then, it is safe to say that the acculturation process of the immigrants, their children, and their grandchildren has come to an end.

One of the major social questions of the era since the end of the Second World War (isolated by David Riesman twenty years ago) was what would happen religiously and politically to the Catholic ethnic groups as they moved into the upper middle class. In 1955 one would have guessed that they would remain loyal religiously but would change politically. In fact, the opposite seems to have occurred. Despite the improvement of their social condition and their movement to the suburbs, American Catholics are no less likely to be Democrats today than they were twenty years ago. And they continue to be just slightly left of center politically. (Indeed, the proportion of American Catholics on the "far left" sixth of the political spectrum has increased from 12 to 20 percent in the last twenty years.)

While there has been relatively little political change, there has been considerable religious change since the 1963 NORC study. Church attendance, prayer, Catholic activities, acceptance of key doctrinal items, and, above all, acceptance of the church's sexual teaching have declined dramatically in the wake of the Second Vatican Council. The apostasy rate has doubled, approaching almost 30 percent among the college-educated young. Only the weekly reception of communion has increased during the past ten years.

But these changes *cannot* be linked to the increased educational attainment of the younger cohort of American Catholics, who have come of age since 1963. Indeed, only about one-fifth of the decline of Catholic religious practice can be explained by lower levels of religious behavior among the Vietnam generation. Even among this group, it is their youthfulness and *not* their higher level of education that accounts for their different style of religious practice. Thus the change in the American Catholic church in the last decade is not the result of an influx of a new and different younger population nearly so much as it is the result of changes actually taking place in Catholic adults who were over twenty in the 1963 study and are over thirty in the 1974 study.

Nor is the change the result of a negative reaction to the Second Vatican Council. Quite the contrary, American Catholics overwhelmingly endorse the conciliar changes, with two-thirds of our respondents being in favor of the changes and only one-fifth against them. The supposedly highly controversial English liturgy gets an 87 percent approval; and about two-thirds of American Catholics are willing to endorse even more changes, such as the introduction into the Roman church of a married clergy. Nor does support for the changes introduced by the Second Vatican Council lead to lower levels of religious behavior. Again, quite the contrary. Those who supported conciliar changes show higher levels of religious behavior than those who opposed it. The decline in American Catholicism has indeed occurred since the Second Vatican Council, but the decline was not caused by the Council.

Our elaborate social change models show that the decline in Catholic religious practice can be accounted for almost entirely by a change in sexual attitudes and in attitudes toward the papacy among American Catholics. It would appear that the deterioration of American Catholicism is the result of a negative response to the birth control encyclical *Humanae Vitae*. It is clear from the research of Westoff and his colleagues that American Catholics began to use the birth control pill as a substitute for the rhythm method in the early 1960s. The belated papal decision disapproving this method of family limitation was ineffective both in preventing the use of the pill and in inhibiting any major change in the sexual attitudes of American Catholics. It also apparently seriously impaired the credibility and authority of the papacy, leading to a sharp decline in mass attendance and a sharp increase in apostasy in the years immediately after the encyclical.

It would then appear that there were two forces at work in the American Catholic church in the decade since 1963: a positive force linked to the Vatican Council and a negative force linked to the birth control encyclical. Left to itself, the Council would have produced an increase in Catholic religious behavior of about one-sixth. The birth control encyclical by itself would have produced a decline of perhaps as much as one-half. The two forces combined led to a decline in Catholic religious behavior of about one-third. The negative effects of the birth control encyclical masked the positive effects of the Council. But if it had not been for the Council, the deterioration of religious behavior within American Catholicism would have been much worse.

However, in the midst of all the other changes, support for the parochial schools continues to be strong. Eighty percent of the American Catholic population favors the continuation of such schools, and there is no variation of this support by age. Similarly, there is apparently substantial willingness to contribute funds toward keeping the local parish school open. While only about half of the American Catholics go to church every week, eighty percent would be willing to contribute more money to keep the parish school operating, and neither the willingness to contribute nor the amount one would contribute varies by age. If our respondents are to be believed, there may be as much as two billion dollars per year available to support Catholic schools—a potential resource which is not being utilized by the American church.

By an overwhelming majority American Catholics approve of new methods of religious education, sex education in schools, and the presence of lay teachers on the school faculties. As a decade ago, three-quarters of them support state aid for parochial schools. While part of the explanation for the decline in enrollment in Catholic schools may lie in their increased costs, in fact the principal reason seems to be exactly the same as it was a decade ago: nonavailability. Hence the decline in Catholic school enrollment since 1963 is almost entirely the result of the failure to build new schools—a failure that occurred in the face of overwhelming support for the schools and an apparent willingness to pay for them.

Do the schools merit such support?

One of our principal concerns in this research project was whether those who attended value-oriented schools would be more or less accepting than others of changes in the value system inculcated in those schools. The response to that question is clear: Even though support for the changes of the

Second Vatican Council is overwhelming, those who went to Catholic schools are even more likely to support them than those who did not. Neither has the change in Catholicism in the last ten years led to a diminution of the impact of parochial schools. The net correlations between years in Catholic school and sexual orthodoxy, doctrinal orthodoxy, and the church's right to teach, as well as with mass attendance and confession, have declined. But the net correlations between Catholic school attendance and participation in Catholic activities, support for religious vocations, and contributions to the church have increased. And among certain subpopulations, so has the correlation between Catholic school attendance and private prayer.

The scores of American Catholics on all these measures have declined—sometimes drastically—over the past ten years. The increased correlation between Catholic school attendance and such measures as religious behavior is the result of the fact that the decline has been much less precipitous among those Catholics who attended parochial schools.

When we use the Catholicity factor as a summary measure, we can assert that the plusses outweigh the minuses, and that despite the changes of the past decade, Catholic schools are more important now than they were a decade ago. Indeed, the .23 correlation between years of parochial school attendance and the Catholicity factor in 1974 is impressive by any of the current measures of educational impact now available to us. Catholic schools *do* have an impact which is net of education, parental religiousness, spouse's religiousness, age, sex, and educational attainment. With the decline of the importance of parental religiousness and educational level in 1974, Catholic education is second only to religiousness of spouse in predicting religious behavior. So not only absolutely but also relative to other factors, the importance of Catholic education has *increased* since 1963.

Nor has the impact of Catholic schools been limited just to religious behavior. The values and attitudes thought to be de-

sirable by the Catholic leadership (such as religious hopefulness and racial tolerance) also correlate with Catholic school
attendance in 1974. In 1963 this correlation between racial
attitudes and years of Catholic school attendance existed only
for those who had attended college. In 1974 it had increased
(to an impressive .22) for those who attended college and also
was to be found at a lower level in the whole Catholic population (.07).

Furthermore, the impact of Catholic education in 1974 was
especially strong for three groups that would be critical for
the institutional future of Catholicism—young people under
thirty, men from very religious backgrounds, and members of
those eastern and southern European ethnic groups whose
level of religious practice has traditionally been at or beneath
the average.

Finally, the increase in the relationship between years of
Catholic schooling and such institutional variables as financial
contribution to the church, participation in Catholic activities,
favorable attitudes toward the clergy, and vocation support, as
well as private prayer in the important subpopulations, would
suggest that it is not only among those groups important for
the future of the institution but also on those matters which
have considerable institutional import that the greatest effect
of Catholic schools is to be observed. At a time when the institution is in severe crisis because of the negative effect of
the change in sexual ethics, parochial schools would seem to
have an important role to play in training the people who will
eventually provide support for institutional rejuvenation and
resurgence.

The standardized correlations on which the assertions of
the previous paragraph have been made are not high in any
absolute sense, but they are "moderate" to "high" (as far as
most social research goes) and quite high compared to most
educational impact studies. One way to put the matter would
be to say that the standardized correlations which justified
school integration are substantially lower than the stan-

dardized correlations we used to justify parochial schools.

If we return to the two tables we presented in the introduction as criteria for the success and survival of alternative
education and fill in the blanks implicit there, we find a
mixed picture (tables 11.1 and 11.2).

TABLE 11.1

CRITERIA FOR SUCCESS OF VALUE-ORIENTED EDUCATION
AFTER DECADE OF PRESSURE ASSESSED

Criteria	Assessment
Organizational involvement	Limited success
Ethical values	Failure
Organizational knowledge	Maintained
World view	Apparent limited success
Racial attitudes	success
Organizational loyalty	A mixture of failure and success

TABLE 11.2

CRITERIA FOR SURVIVAL OF ALTERNATE EDUCATION
AFTER DECADE OF PRESSURE ASSESSED

Criteria	Assessment
1. Positive relation to elite groups	Ambiguous
2. Continued support of non-elites	Overwhelming
3. Persistence of motivations	Motivations unchanged
4. Emergence of new motivations	Uncertain but not necessary for non-elites in view of items 2 and 3

The Catholic schools were a complete failure in maintaining
the sexual ethic during the decade of crisis. They were a suc-

cess in strengthening the relationship between school attendance and positive racial attitudes and enjoyed a limited success in the areas of organizational involvement, doctrinal
knowledge, and organizational loyalty. They did not arrest
completely the deterioration of loyalty, but the deterioration
was less rapid among those who had been to Catholic schools,
so that, on balance, the relationship between number of years
of Catholic education and those variables has increased in the
last decade—especially among certain key groups, such as
those under thirty. Finally, while we have no measures from
1963 of basic world-view, there was a relationship in 1974 between Catholic school attendance and a "hopeful" view of the
cosmos.

There continues to be a relationship between social class
and support for Catholic schools, but the upper levels of the
elite (who were not included in the study) seem to have less
faith in the schools than they did a decade ago. On the other
hand, the support of the non-elites persists, and the motivations for this support are substantially unchanged since 1963.
The critical issue would seem to be whether the non-elites will
be able to force a change in elite attitudes.

Are the schools worth the resources of money and personnel that have been poured into them? That is a question
of value to which social scientists cannot provide an answer.
It is an organizational truism, however, that one should not
abandon an institution that produces a certain desirable effect
unless one is certain that there is available another institution
that will produce *at least* the same effect. In the words Max
Weber never used, "A bird in the hand is worth two in the
bush."

The claim of the religious education movement to have a
successful alternative in the form of "religious instruction" is
simply not supported by the data. In many areas of religious
behavior, such instruction has only slight impact; in other
areas, it has no impact at all. Religious instruction is in no
sense an adequate substitute for Catholic schools, and this is

true even when we look at those products of religious instruction under the age of thirty (holding educational level and parental religiousness constant), who presumably have benefited from the enthusiasm of the religious education movement. Since we have no information available (none exists) on the amount of money put into religious instruction, we cannot calculate a statistic of relative financial payoff. Still, it is not unreasonable to say that on the basis of our data there is no way religious instruction can return a greater payoff than Catholic schools, for the latter, however much they may cost, do accomplish something. Religious instruction aims to teach all and displays a symbolic interest in the children who do not attend Catholic schools, and in those terms it may justify whatever resources American Catholicism puts into it, but in terms of its impact on adult religious behavior, the religious education movement must be considered a waste of time, money, and personnel on the basis of the present data.

We can therefore summarize the findings of this volume by saying that despite the traumatic religious occurrences in the Catholic church in the United States during the last ten years:

1. Support for Catholic schools among the American Catholic population is as strong as ever, and there is available a substantial amount of unused resources (perhaps as much as two billion dollars a year) to sustain the schools in existence.

2. Far from declining in effectiveness in the past decade, Catholic schools seem to have increased their impact. In a time of general decline in religious behavior, the rate of decline for those who have gone to Catholic schools is much slower. The correlation between Catholic school attendance and religiousness is especially strong for those under thirty.

3. In terms of the future of the organization, Catholic schools seem more important for a church in time of traumatic transition than for one in a time of peaceful stability.

But despite these three favorable judgments, attendance at Catholic grammar schools continues to decline (though there has been a moderate increase in recent years in attendance at

Catholic high schools). We have suggested that the principal reason for this decline is unavailability of schools. And the principal reason for this unavailability is simply that schools have not been constructed. There is no reason in the world to think that this trend will be reversed. There is money, support, and rationale for the continuation of Catholic value-oriented education, but the prognosis for such continuation seems poor.

To understand this paradox, one must realize that the decision-making structure of the Catholic church in the United States is not responsive either to popular sentiment or to empirical evidence. The leadership of the American church has only very slight information on what the reality is outside of its own meeting rooms. It tends to project into that reality its own fears and discontents. When American Catholic bishops say—though off the record—that the laity do not want Catholic schools, they are not reflecting any systematically gathered information, but rather projecting into the laity their own fears and hopes. What they mean, of course, is that "We do not want to build any more Catholic schools, because we don't think we can continue to raise the money to support them." (It may also be that in order to raise the money they would have to give up more control over the schools than they are willing to allow.) Such attitudes do not yield to empirical evidence.

Thus one could expect a change in policy (real policy as opposed to verbal policy—bishops still verbalize enthusiastically about Catholic schools although they will not build them) only when the organizational structure of the American church has become much more open, sensitive, and responsive to the feelings of the rank and file membership—and, correspondingly, when the rank and file membership is no longer ready to play a passive role in decision-making. If the bishops presently feel the need and the responsibility to make decisions independently of data and of consultation with the laity, it must also be said that the Catholic laity passively accept, for the most part, such a division of labor. Since we see no evidence that either condition is likely to change in the future, we must report that although support for Catholic schools is one of the few things in the American church that has not changed in the last ten years, attendance at such schools is likely to continue to decline in the years ahead. "There are," as the senior coauthor of *The Education of Catholic Americans* has often remarked, "many ironies in the fire."

Afterword

At the suggestion of the publisher, I am doffing my sociologist's cap to don my social commentator's beret. The chapters in this volume are the result of a joint effort, and while I must bear the major burden of the blame for what is wrong with them, they represent the collective analysis of the entire research team. From this point on, I speak only for myself. The reader should be aware that my colleagues may or may not agree with what I set down here.

There was no such personal afterword at the end of *The Education of Catholic Americans*. On the contrary, that volume was launched into an unfriendly world with a sociological shrug of the shoulders which said, in effect, "See if you can figure out what it means, fellows and girls." People promptly set out to do so, for the most part following the example of the *New York Times* reporter who apparently thumbed through the book simply to find those things unfavorable to Catholic schools. There seem to have been four principal popular conclusions these people drew from "reading" *The Education of Catholic Americans*: (1) Rossi and I had proved that Catholic schools didn't work—and hurray and hallelujah!; (2) Rossi and I had proved that Catholic schools didn't work and we ought to be ashamed of ourselves; (3) Rossi and I had proved that Catholic schools did work—and hurray and hallelujah!; (4) Rossi and I had proved that Catholic schools did work and clearly we had sold out to the hierarchy.

The modest conclusion of *The Education of Catholic Americans*, that under some circumstances Catholic schools had some impact and that no other institution yet available had comparable impact, didn't seem to satisfy anyone. There were occasions when enthusiastic crusaders found data in the book that weren't even there. At one Catholic educational meeting, for example, a sociological nun with messianic proclivities proclaimed that we had found that Catholic education had no impact on racial attitudes. We had found rather the opposite: Catholic schools did have an impact on racial attitudes but only at the college level (an impact which in 1974 had increased at the college level and had spread throughout the entire system). Ill-tempered lout that I am, I arose for a point of order and said it wasn't so, thus angering the nun and her crusading supporters.

I don't propose to make the same mistake again. I intend to say what I think this research project demonstrates. Anyone who wants to read it carefully is perfectly free to come up with his own conclusions, but at least mine will be on public record.

Note well that these personal conclusions are not proven social science. They are merely the conclusions of the social scientist who is the principal investigator in this research enterprise. Other social scientists of solid capabilities and good will might draw different conclusions. It is their privilege. Lay people (in this case, non-social scientists) may also reach different conclusions. Conclusions one draws from empirical evidence are affected by one's antecedent values and by one's expectations for the future. People can agree on what a body of data says and disagree with its implications.

Before I continue, let me make clear what my own intellectual history is on the subject of Catholic schools. I began work on the 1963 project with a modest predisposition in favor of the schools, but with a willingness to yield in the face of evidence that they had little impact on people's adult behavior. Had I been a pastor before the time of the study, I would have been moderately but not passionately inclined to build a parochial school in my parish.

After the research was concluded, my predispositions became more favorable to Catholic schools on the basis of the dictum quoted in the final chapter of this report: "A bird in the hand is worth two in the bush." Catholic schools did accomplish something, and in the absence of any other institution that did better, it was wise to stick with what we had. Obviously the schools did not work miracles; they did not produce saints, they did not transform people's personalities completely, they did not undo the impact of home, family, peer group, ethnic background, social class, neighborhood, and society. They were not terribly powerful counteragents to the influence of the first six years of life or the nineteen hours a day a young person is not subject to school influence. But they did something, and in this imperfect world of ours, any institution that did something was not to be tossed away lightly.

My sympathy and predisposition toward Catholic schools became stronger in the ensuing decade. I was offended by the romantic irrationality of those who thought that religious instruction programs run by the Confraternity of Christian Doctrine would work a marvelous transformation in American Catholicism. Also I became convinced by the educational impact research that occurred during the last ten years that the coefficients of association Rossi and I reported in 1963 were not unimpressive.

I entered this project with two hunches. First, I thought that American Catholics would overwhelmingly approve of the Second Vatican Council, and, second, I felt that those who went to Catholic schools would be more likely to approve the changes than those who did not. But I had no inclination either way to judge whether the correlations between Catholic school attendance and adult behavior would go up or down in the wake of the Vatican Council. I suppose I inclined ever so slightly to think that they might have gone down. (Nor, as was mentioned in the body of the report, did any of us think that the explanation for the decline in American Catholicism would point to the birth control encyclical. The data forced us to that conclusion.)

At the end of this study, I find myself more strongly committed to Catholic schools than I have ever been. Paradoxically, my own pilgrimage seems to have run just opposite to that of the leadership of the American church.

On the subject of the birth control encyclical, my predispositions are a matter of public record. Shortly after it was issued, I wrote a column that raised the possibility that the 1968 encyclical could be a disaster for the American church. Nonetheless, I would have said before this project began that the deterioration in American Catholicism, which I suspected we would find, was the result of the confusion and uncertainty generated by the Second Vatican Council. I would not have thought beforehand that our evidence would so cleanly and sharply attribute the deterioration not to the Council but to the birth control encyclical. If I had thought beforehand that we might develop such a finding, I would certainly have written it into our initial proposal to the National Institute of Education, because I would have looked brilliant indeed when the data sustained my prediction. Much less did I expect to uncover evidence of the positive and negative dynamic at work in the church since 1963, the one clearly linked to the Council and the other clearly linked to *Humanae Vitae*. Again, to have called the shot on that one would have been a brilliant coup. In retrospect, I guess I am not surprised at the findings, but we did not anticipate them; rather they were forced upon us by the data.

I lay out these predispositions because I think the reader of this personal afterword has a right to know what they are. He will have to judge for himself whether I am a competent enough sociologist and an honest enough human being to prevent my predispositions from distorting the data or the analysis. They will certainly shape my concluding observations.

The reader who is interested in Catholic schools in the Catholic church but not interested in sociological methodology will have found this book hard to read. Our tools of analysis have grown more elaborate and complicated since *The Education of Catholic Americans* appeared, but they have enabled us to do far more than we were able to in 1964. Of course, the addition of the time dimension in the present analysis adds yet more complexity. The "lay" reader may resent having to plow through betas, z scores, and mathematical models. I can only respond that it is absolutely necessary to lay out in detail this formidable methodological apparatus. Many of our findings are surprising; no one should be expected to believe them without the evidence on which we based them. Consider, for example, the following assertions:

1. Only about one-sixth of American Catholics continue to support the church's birth control teaching.

2. There has been no change in support for Catholic schools.

3. The overwhelming majority of American Catholics endorse the changes of the Second Vatican Council.

4. The encyclical and not the Council is responsible for the deterioration of American Catholicism in the last decade. Had it not been for the Council, the deterioration would have been worse.

5. The correlation between Catholic school attendance and tolerant racial attitudes has increased in the last decade.

6. On the whole, the Catholic schools seem to be more important to a church in transition than to a stable church.

A year ago, one might have repeated the above assertions to a group of people interested in Catholic education with confidence that only a minority of those present would agree with any of them. (Indeed, if I myself had been presented with like assertions at that time, I might well have hesitated to accept some of them.)

Still, all the above propositions are true, supported by the data, I think, beyond any reasonable doubt. Even the reader who does not want to wrestle with the methodological complexities of this report will have to concede that the data and the analysis on which our conclusions are based are out in the public domain and available for professional criticism. The data tapes from which this volume emerged are available for anyone who would care to use them. The reader who does not like our findings and is either unwilling or unable to struggle through our methodology is welcome to hire his own social scientist to reanalyze the data.[1]

Now let me list the personal conclusions with which I come away as this project draws to an end:

1. The Vatican Council was one of the most successful religious phenomena in human history. A dramatic and sudden change occurred in aspects of Catholic life which had not been touched for a millennium and a half. Within a decade, these changes had been accepted by the overwhelming majority of American Catholics, by virtually all of the subpopulations within the American Catholic community. Furthermore, the Council unleashed in the church positive forces which, if given half a chance, would have made for growth not decline.

2. The blighting of the success of the Vatican Council can be attributed to a failure of leadership, in particular, failure in the area of sexuality. *Humanae Vitae* was as much a symptom as a cause. The concerns of the pope when he wrote the encyclical were surely valid—the importance of human life, the sanctity of marriage, the link between sexuality and procreation. There are undoubtedly life-hating forces in the world, and they may be even stronger now than they were ten years ago. But the mistake made by the encyclical, and still made by many Catholics, is summarized by the dictum that support for birth control inevitably leads to support for abortion. There is, however, no necessary logical or psychological link between the two. Our evidence would indicate that the overwhelming majority of American Catholics are quite capable of making the distinction between the two moral issues. Concern of Catholics about family limitation led to widespread use of the birth control pill as an alternative to rhythm before the issuance of *Humanae Vitae*. It was not

based on a rejection of the sanctity of marriage, the sacredness of sex, or the importance of human life. There were two other issues at work to which the pope alluded in the encyclical but whose importance he did not seem to fully grasp.

First, the rapid decline in infant mortality and the increase in life expectancy mean that the human race does not need a virtually unlimited number of pregnancies from each fertile woman to sustain itself in existence. On the contrary, unlimited fertility, at least at the present time, would produce a disaster for humankind (though if the Ice Age, which many climatologists see impending, does return, then we have a completely different situation). A woman can easily have seven live births before she is thirty, and each of these will most likely grow into a very lively child, demanding attention, concern, affection, clothes, food, chauffeuring, education, insurance. Those Catholic women who began to use the pill in the 1960s were not against children or marriage; they did not doubt the sanctity of human life. But they came to doubt seriously that the heavenly Father and the Lord Jesus expected each of them to have seven children before they were thirty and ten before they were forty.

Second, *Humanae Vitae* acknowledged but did not seem to grasp the importance of sexuality in the giving and receiving of love in the modern world. Personal development and self-fulfillment have become one of the principal goals of humankind, and sexual love is one of the principal means for achieving this goal. Surely the Catholic tradition, committed as it is to intimate relationship with a personal God and to the view that married love reflects the passion of the relationship between God and his people, must rejoice in principle at such a change.

One still encounters some Catholics (mostly clergy) who think that sustained self-denial in a marriage relationship over a long period of time is a good and healthy form of behavior. One can be prepared to concede that it may be so for some people, but that under ordinary circumstances, it is not. The underlying assumption that sexual abstinence is in principle better than sexual "indulgence" must be rejected as a Manichaean and a puritanical principle rather than a Catholic one.

There are many difficulties, physical and psychological, in the quest for self-fulfillment through sex (as is testified by the popularity of an apparently endless series of how-to-do-it books). The principal question that faces most married people is how to keep the excitement and challenge of their sexual life and the struggle for deeper and richer human intimacy alive amidst the frictions, distractions, tensions, and conflicts of their common life. If the church had been willing to devote its energies to speaking to that issue (and I believe that there are available substantial religious resources it could draw upon), the years after the Vatican Council might well have shown a tremendous surge in religious behavior instead of the decline we have seen. Instead it fixated on the narrow issue of the mechanics of reproduction, thus losing, I think, a magnificent opportunity.

Married people concluded that the largely celibate ecclesiastical authority simply did not understand the problems that married people had to face, and ought not, therefore, to be taken seriously when it addressed itself to marriage problems. I am forced to conclude that *Humanae Vitae* gave them no reason to change their minds.

Quite simply, the encyclical was a shattering blow to the ecclesiastical loyalty of many American Catholics. (Witness the decline in the support for priestly vocations among that formerly rich source of supply for the priesthood, the Catholic-educated Irish.) They have not left the church in great numbers because of it (though apostasy has increased), but they have considerably diminished enthusiasm for a wide variety of Catholic practices. They expected better from the church, particularly in the wake of the Council. Anyone who can remember the disbelief with which we read *Humanae Vitae* in 1968 can understand the widespread, inarticulate feeling of many American Catholics that the church had let them down. I have no doubt that historians of the future will judge *Humanae Vitae* to be one of the worst mistakes in the history of Catholic Christianity—and this particularly because it seems to have nipped in the bud the splendid prospects for growth and development set in motion by the Second Vatican Council.

We are now in a situation of theological impasse. *Humanae Vitae* is still the law of the Church; loyalty to it seems to be an absolute criterion for promotion to the hierarchy. But in the United States and in every other country where research has been done, the encyclical is ignored by the laity and most of the lower clergy. One has the impression that support for it is eroding even among the hierarchy. Many theologians promptly rejected it. I know very few respected theological commentators who are prepared to support it today. While no one has claimed that the encyclical is infallible, there is nonetheless a constitutional crisis for the church in its general unacceptance. It is a crisis which appears insoluble at the present time.

A number of theologians have suggested to me privately that *Humanae Vitae* will be non-handled, as was the condemnation of Galileo. Over the centuries it will be ignored, thus becoming a dead letter. Eventually—three, four hundred years from now—it will be repealed. This is the way non-acceptance has had its impact on official teachings in the past.

I'm sorry, but I don't think that will do. The Galileo controversy, as important as it was to intellectuals, had nothing to do with what goes on in the beds of married people two or three nights a week, every week of the year. *Humanae Vitae* will have to be repealed before the church can achieve any credibility as a sexual teacher. Repeal won't restore credibility; but the church will not even be listened to until the encyclical is modified. On the basis of the findings in this report, I am inclined to think that deterioration will continue, perhaps at a lower rate, until Catholicism is able to find in the rich resources of its tradition a new, deeper, more subtle, and broader approach to sexuality than the one it is presently offering to its laity. The sooner this task is begun the better, but it cannot even begin until the mistake made in *Humanae Vitae* is acknowledged and repudiated.

The failure of leadership is even more a structural failure than a sexual one. The response of the hierarchy to the world after *Humanae Vitae* was both mixed and ambiguous. There were a few statements of enthusiastic support at the one end of the spectrum and a few veiled rejections at the other. In between, there were a considerable number of very ambiguous documents of which the lower clergy and the laity could make whatever they wished. With one or two exceptions (like the Archdiocese of Washington, D.C.), no attempt was made in the United States or elsewhere to enforce the encyclical. Most American bishops are well aware now and were so at the time of what would happen in the confessional, and they took no effective measures to assure that priests would not continue to advise the laity, in effect, to make up their own minds. Nor, when the data of the NORC priest study became available, which revealed how many priests were doing this, did the bishops of the United States make any sustained effort to correct such obvious noncompliance with the teaching of the encyclical.

One important leader of the American church who learned beforehand of the encyclical called in a team of writers and marriage educators to prepare an extremely ambiguous document which, in effect, signaled his clergy and laity that it was their problem, not his. He then departed for Alaska so as to be out of the city on the day the encyclical was released. If he has ever seriously tried to enforce it in his diocese, it has escaped my notice.

Quite bluntly, the response of the American hierarchy to the encyclical was two-faced. On one side, they endorsed it publicly, and the majority of them accepted it privately; on the other, they signaled clearly and unmistakably to their laity that they had to make up their own minds, and to their clergy that they (the bishops) were not about to enforce the encyclical by revoking the confessional faculties of those who would not swear an oath to enforce it, for example. In short, the bishops knew from the beginning that the encyclical was unenforceable.

But if they knew the day after its publication that it was not enforceable, they also knew it the day before. They surely did not communicate to the pope their judgment of the encyclical before it was issued. They still have not done so. One very much doubts that the word got through to Rome loud and clear before *Humanae Vitae* that in the United States it simply wouldn't work. Indeed, one suspects that this judgment was made individually by bishops but never even spoken in a collective meeting. In public discussion certainly and in private discussion most probably, but the American hierarchy, as well as the other hierarchies in the world, communicated to the pope what they thought he wanted to hear and not what they thought was the truth. Doubtless, this is the way the structure of the Catholic church is presently constituted. One communicates upward only those things one thinks will receive a positive reception (much like the CIA investigator-researcher who was permitted to report only a fixed number of Viet Cong soldiers—no matter how many there actually were). Under such circumstances, however, the information flow in an organization becomes very problematic, and decisions are made either in the absence of any information or, worse still, in the presence of very bad and inaccurate information. The decision-making process which led to *Humanae Vitae* was flawed from top to bottom, and the Holy Father, who, after all, did not create the system, was forced to make a decision without having adequate or accurate information. The disaster of *Humanae Vitae* was a system failure.

I make this judgment not to excuse the personal responsibilities of those involved. The Vatican's theological politicians (like Monsignor Carlo Columbo) who worked behind the scenes in the Vatican to reverse the recommendation of the pope's birth control commission (why have the commission if political operators can reverse its almost unanimous findings?) must be severely judged by the court of history.

The second failure of leadership which I detect in the pages of this report is that of the American hierarchy and, to a lesser extent, that of the Catholic intelligentsia to understand or to appreciate Catholic schools. Timid, cautious administrators that they are (with such marvelous blunders on the record as the two million dollars invested in Penn Central paper shortly before that railroad went bankrupt), the American Catholic hierarchy has been appalled at the skyrocketing costs of parochial education. It is apparently unaware of the dramatic increase in the Catholic standard of living that has occurred in the last quarter of a century. (Real income between 1945 and 1975 has more than doubled for American Catholics.) Catholics have far more "disposable income" to spend on parochial schools now than they did in the 1930s, and there is every reason to think that they are ready to dispose of substantially more of that income in support of Catholic schools than they were in the past. Changes in the administration and financing of Catholic education would be absolutely imperative to making such funds available, but there is so much caution and fear and mediocrity in the leadership of the American church that it seems much easier to close schools down or to refuse to build new ones than to risk innovative techniques of administering and funding Catholic schools. While the hierarchy is not usually sensitive to the party line of the liberal-left Catholic intelligentsia, the opposition of this group to the schools has provided the hierarchy with a convenient rationale for phasing out Catholic education—all the while, of course, pretending to endorse it enthusiastically.

Quite bluntly, the hierarchy should get out of the Catholic education business and turn the funding and administration of the schools over to the laity. There is, of course, great fear expressed at such a suggestion. How could the laity handle such a task? (As though there was not a nation across our borders to the north where the laity have more than adequately demonstrated that they could.) If Catholic parents want parochial schools, then they should be responsible for the funding and administration of them. If they cannot raise the money for the schools within the Catholic population (and our data suggests that they can), then it is they and not the hierarchy who should organize a campaign to force the Supreme Court to reverse its bigoted decisions on the subject of Catholic schools. To proceed on such a path would involve a substantial surrender of power, of course, by the bishops and by the parish clergy. No one likes to surrender power; no one likes to think of money, especially "Catholic money," being spent without having much say about how it is spent. What is the point of being a bishop, after all, if you don't have the ultimate power of the purse strings? Why be a bishop at all if other people are responsible for spending *your* money?

Nor does it appear that the Catholic intelligentsia has ever really stopped to consider that Catholic schools are not an inkblot onto which one can project one's aggressions and frustrations toward the institutional church. It also seems not to have occurred to them that at a time when alternative education is becoming a very important issue among America's secular intelligentsia, the only large and functioning alternative to the moribund state educational monopoly is the Catholic schools. The hundreds and thousands of black parents who are sending their children to Catholic schools in the inner city know what is the available alternative to the monstrously inept public school bureaucratic monopoly. But the Catholic intelligentsia is so interested in outnativing the nativists that it has been thus far afraid to seriously explore the contribution and to defend the existence of an alternative religious education system. Indeed, all one has to do is to say something positive about Catholic schools in Official Liberal Catholic quarters and one is immediately deemed a conservative. At one time, one's badge of Official Liberalism was the proud announcement that one had pulled one's children out of the parochial schools. It is interesting to note that at least some people have had sense enough to change their minds and have since put their children back into the schools. When *Commonweal* carries an article entitled, "Why I Sent My Children Back to Catholic Schools," we will know that the Catholic intelligentsia has turned the corner.

Just as *Humanae Vitae* was more the result of a system failure than of individual malice, so the bizarre paradox of Catholic schools in the United States is a result of system failure. Attendance declines and construction comes to a halt because those in decision-making positions are unaware of the support for and the importance of Catholic schools for the overwhelming majority of American Catholics. American Catholicism is not structured in such a way that the attitudes of the laity are communicated upward or that periodic evaluation of institutional effectiveness can occur. The hierarchy and the intelligentsia may disagree on many things, but they agree on one thing: their minds are made up—they need not be bothered by evidence of what ordinary people think or of how effective the various institutional apostolates of the church might be. The ordinary lay person takes for granted that nobody cares much what he thinks. And most laity are inclined to accept passively decisions that are made by ecclesiastical leadership and to ignore the advice and conventional wisdom offered by the intelligentsia.

Catholic schools, an extraordinarily powerful asset of the American church, will go down the drain with hardly a voice raised in protest because the decision-making system of the American church has permitted a policy to evolve concerning the schools which virtually guarantees their continued decline. It is again not a question of malice but of systematic ignorance, that is to say, ignorance built into the decision-making system.

After fifteen years of doing research on things Catholic, I am not so naive as to expect that this report will make the slightest bit of difference. It will gain some transient publicity in the newspapers; it will be cited by partisans on one side or the other of the debate; it will be the subject of papers delivered at religious sociological meetings by unknown professors from small schools; it will creep into bibliographies and footnotes; and perhaps occasionally someone will speak favorably of its pioneering use of Professor Davis's social change models. The policy-makers and the self-proclaimed intellectual leaders of the American church couldn't care less.

It is worth noting that both the 1963 and 1974 NORC Catholic school studies were funded by non-Catholic agencies, the former by the Carnegie Corporation and the latter by the National Institute of Education. A multi-billion dollar enterprise such as Catholic education either cannot afford or does not need basic evaluation research of its own. And the Catholic church has neither the need of nor the desire for systematic research to evaluate the impact of the Vatican Council and the birth control encyclical on American Catholicism. Fifty million members, almost two hundred thousand religious professionals, hundreds of thousands of students—who needs data to make decisions?

This is a cynical and melancholy conclusion, but there is no other way to conclude this report. I see the great promise of the Vatican Council blighted; I see the strong institution blown apart by a monumental blunder made far away because of an incredibly bad information-processing system; I see a great resource wasted because of the timidity and fear bred by systematic ignorance. Those who are responsible for the protection and development of that resource allow it to waste away—all the while protesting a total commitment to it. I am enough of an Irishman to know that I should expect no better of church leadership; I am enough of an American to be angry about it.

Andrew M. Greeley

APPENDICES

Appendix I

SAMPLE DESIGN AND FIELD WORK

The listing of Catholic respondents for this study was composed of all those who gave Catholic as their religious preference on seven cycles of the Continuous National Survey (CNS) which was undertaken at NORC between April, 1973, and November, 1973.

The selection of households and individuals for the CNS was based on the NORC Master Probability Sample of Households—a multistage, stratified, full-probability sample of all persons, 18 years of age and older, living in households within the 48 contiguous United States. In the first stage of sampling, 101 Primary Sampling Units (counties or groups of counties) were selected. Within each of these selected PSU's, two additional stages of sampling were employed to select six ultimate segments.

Within each ultimate segment, a listing of all dwelling units was made by the NORC field staff. Specific sample addresses were selected by appropriately sampling from these ultimate segment listings. Within each selected dwelling unit, a single respondent was selected with equal probability from a listing of all eligible respondents.

Each respondent who was designated a Catholic on the selected CNS waves was listed to be re-interviewed for the Catholic School Study. Despite some prior apprehensions, conducting a second interview with the same respondents in the course of a year appears not to have influenced the refusal rate to any noticeable extent.

330

This procedure yielded an initial listing of 1,204 cases. Ninety-seven of these cases were lost, bringing the net listing to 1,147. Cases were lost for the following reasons: 8 deaths, 6 invalid CNS cases, 1 duplicate, and 42 individuals who, while saying their religious preference was Catholic in the CNS study, turned out not, in fact, to be of the Catholic faith. This last was a methodological finding of some note: asking a respondent for his or her religious preference produces results different from those obtained when a researcher asks a respondent for his or her present religion.[1]

Field Work

Field work for the study was conducted between March 1, 1974, and June 6, 1974. A team of forty interviewers conducted in-person interviews which averaged 84 minutes in length. Whether or not respondents should be informed before being interviewed that the study was one of Catholics only was a matter of some concern to the investigators. A decision was made to allow interviewers to use this information as a last resort if they felt it might be useful in convincing otherwise reluctant respondents to participate. A comparison of responses where this option was exercised with responses where it was not carried out was made and showed no apparent differences in the answers obtained.

The final number of completed cases was 927; this constitutes an 81 percent completion rate. The final sample was 57 percent female, 86 percent white, 81 percent between the ages of 20 and 59, 85 percent native born, and only 16 percent never married.

The refusal rate for the study was 12 percent. The remaining losses were due to reasons other than refusals. This completion rate compares favorably with the study of a decade ago, when the refusal rate was 18 percent and the completion rate 77 percent. Whatever other changes Catholics have experienced, they are becoming neither less cooperative nor less loquacious.

Appendix II

QUESTIONNAIRES
FROM 1963 NORC STUDY,
ADULT AND ADOLESCENT

I. 1963 Questionnaires

TIME INTER- VIEW BEGAN	:

NORC 476 CA
11/63

NATIONAL OPINION RESEARCH CENTER
University of Chicago _____(1-4)

Segment	
Case Number	

(5-9)

Mr.
Mrs. _____   _____
Miss   (first name)   (last name)

_____
(street address)

_____
(city and state)

Hello, I'm _____ from the National
Opinion Research Center. We're making a study
which deals mostly with the kinds of schools
people have attended, and also with other topics
of current interest. I believe you received a
letter a few weeks ago telling you I would be
stopping by.

1. Taken altogether, how would you say things are these days--would you say that you are very happy, pretty happy, or not too happy?

                                    Very happy . . . 7 15/6

                                    Pretty happy . . 8

                                    Not too happy . . 9

2. Has anyone talked to you about his personal problems in the last few months?

                            Yes . (ASK A AND B). X*16/y

                            No . (SKIP TO Q. 3) 0

   *IF YES:

A. Who was that?	
	17/
	NAP- 1
	NAN- 2
B. What was the problem?	
	18/
	NAP- 1
	NAN- 2

3. Have you spent any time in the past few months helping someone who needed help?

                            Yes . (ASK A AND B). X*19/y

                            No , (SKIP TO Q. 4) 0

   *IF YES:

A. Did you do that by yourself, or did others join in giving this help?	
By myself 3	20/
With others 4	NAP- 1
	NAN- 2
B. What did you do? Could you tell me a bit about it?	
	21/
	NAP- 1
	NAN- 2

4. We are interested in how Americans judge certain actions. Here is a card with some answers on it. Which answer comes closest to telling whether you agree or disagree with each statement?

(HAND RESPONDENT CARD A.)	Agree Strongly	Agree Somewhat	Disagree Somewhat	Disagree Strongly	Don't Know	
A. It is alright to ask an insurance company for more money than you deserve after an auto accident if you think they might cut your claim.	X	0	2	3	1	22/y
B. Even though you find some people unpleasant, it is wrong to try to avoid them.	5	6	8	9	7	23/4
C. A married couple who feel they have as many children as they want are really not doing anything wrong when they use artificial means to prevent conception.	X	0	2	3	1	24/y
D. A salesman has the right to exaggerate how good his product is when a customer is too suspicious.	5	6	8	9	7	25/4
E. Two people who are in love do not do anything wrong when they marry, even though one of them has been divorced.	X	0	2	3	1	26/y
F. There is an obligation to work for the end of racial segregation.	5	6	8	9	7	27/4
G. It is alright to refuse to talk to some member of the family after a disagreement, especially if the argument was the fault of the other.	X	0	2	3	1	28/y
H. If the government wastes tax money, people don't have to be too exact on their income tax returns.	5	6	8	9	7	29/4
I. It would be wrong to take considerable time off while working for a large company, even though the company would not be hurt by it at all.	X	0	2	3	1	30/y
J. It is not really wrong for an engaged couple to have some sexual relations before they are married.	5	6	8	9	7	31/4
K. Even though a person has a hard time making ends meet, he should still try to give some of his money to help the poor.	X	0	2	3	1	32/y

Now I would like to ask about your background.

5. First of all, where were you born?   (STATE OR COUNTRY)

_____ *   33-34/
                                                              yy

*IF OUTSIDE U.S.:

A. How old were you when you came to the U.S.?   35-36/
                                                              NAP- yy
                                                              NAN- XX

6. Were you brought up mostly on a farm, in open country but not on a farm,
    in a small town, in a small city, or in a large city or its suburbs?

                    Farm . . . . X 37/y
                    Open country (not farm) 0
                    Small town - 10,000 1
                    Small city - 10,000-500,000 2
                    Large city or suburb - 500,000+ . . . 3

7. Where were your father and mother born?

    A. First your father? _____   38-39/
                            (STATE OR COUNTRY)   NAP- yy
                                                              NAN- XX
                                                              DK - 99

    B. And your mother? _____   40-41/
                          (STATE OR COUNTRY)   NAP- yy
                                                              NAN- XX
                                                              DK - 99

(ASK ONLY IF BOTH PARENTS WERE BORN IN THIS COUNTRY.)

8. How many of your grandparents were born in this country?

                                        None 0 42/
                                        One . . . . 1 NAP- y
                                                        NAN- X
                                        Two 2
                                        Three . . . 3
                                        Four 4
                                        Don't know . 5

'9. A. What is your main national background--on your father's side? On your
        mother's side?

    IF CURRENTLY MARRIED, ASK B:

    B. What is your (husband's, wife's) main national background? First on
        (his) (her) father's side? On (his) (her) mother's side?

	A. Respondent's		B. Spouse's	
	Father	Mother	Father	Mother
English, Scotch, Welsh, English Canadian, Australian, New Zealand	00	00	00	00
Irish	01	01	01	01
German, Austrian, Swiss	02	02	02	02
Scandinavian	03	03	03	03
Italian	04	04	04	04
French, French Canadian, Belgian	05	05	05	05
Polish	06	06	06	06
Russian or other Eastern European	07	07	07	07
Lithuanian	08	08	08	08
Spanish, Portuguese, Latin American, including Puerto Rican	09	09	09	
Other (SPECIFY)_____	0X	0X	0X	
Don't know	3y	3y	3y	3y
Not currently married	—	—	1y	1y
	43-44/ 2y	45-46/ 2y	47-48/ 2y	49-50/ 2y

10. Did you always live together with both of your real parents up to the time
     you were 16 years old?

                                    Yes . . . . X 51/y

                                    No . (ASK A AND B) . 0*

     *IF NO:

     A. What happened?

                                                            52/
                                                            NAP- y
                                                            NAN- X

     B. How old were you when it happened?   53-54
                                                            NAP- yy
                                         Age   NAN- XX

11. We are also interested in what Americans think about religious matters.
I am going to read you a number of statements. Please tell me the statement that comes closest to your own personal opinion about each of the
statements.

(HAND RESPONDENT CARD B.) First... (READ)	Certainly True	Probably True	I am uncertain whether this is true or false	Probably False	Certainly False	
A. There is no definite proof that God exists.	X	0	1	2	3	55/y
B. God doesn't really care how He is worshipped, so long as He is worshipped.	5	6	7	8	9	56/4
C. God will punish the evil for all eternity.	X	0	1	2	3	57/y
D. Science proves that Christ's Resurrection was impossible.	5	6	7	8	9	58/4
E. Jesus directly handed over the leadership of His Church to Peter and the Popes.	X	0	1	2	3	59/y
F. A good man can earn heaven by his own efforts alone.	5	6·	7	8	9	60/4

12. Here is a sheet with a number of statements about which different people have different opinions. Please circle the letter of the answer which is closest to your own feeling. (HAND RESPONDENT GREEN SHEET.)

For example, if you agree strongly, you would circle "A"; if you disagree strongly, you would circle "D." You can choose any of the four answers on the sheet.

		Agree Strongly	Agree Somewhat	Disagree Somewhat	Disagree Strongly	Don't Know	
A.	In the long-run, war with the Communists is almost certain.	X	0	2	3	1	_8/y
B.	I would try to stop the planned parenthood association from having a meeting in my community.	5	6	8	9	7	_9/4
C.	Usually parents are just too busy to explain the reasons behind the orders they give their children.	X	0	2	3	1	10/y
D.	The Federal government should give religious schools money to help pay teachers' salaries and build new buildings.	5	6	8	9	7	11/4
E.	Negroes shouldn't push themselves where they are not wanted.	X	0	2	3	1	12/y
F.	A student should be free to make up his own mind on what he learns in school.	5	6	8	9	7	13/4
G.	Laws should change with the times.	X	0	2	3	1	14/y
H.	White people have a right to live in an all white neighborhood if they want to, and Negroes should respect that right.	5	6	8	9	7	15/4
I.	The United States should do more to help the poorer nations by building hospitals, schools, and homes in those places.	X	0	2	3	1	16/y
J.	Each country should be willing to give up some of its power so that the United Nations could do a better job.	5	6	8	9	7	17/4
K.	A family should have as many children as possible and God will provide for them.	X	0	2	3	1	18/y
L.	I would strongly disapprove if a Negro family moved next door to me.	5	6	8	9	7	19/4
M.	Working men have the right and duty to join unions.	X	0	2	3	1	20/y
N.	The government is responsible for preventing wide-spread unemployment.	5	6	8	9	7	21/4
.O.	The Federal government ought to provide aid for the local public schools.	X	0	2	3	1	22/y
P.	Jews have too much power in the United States.	5	6	8	9	7	23/4
Q.	When parents are wrong they should always be willing to admit it to their children.	X	0	2	3	1	24/y

Q. 12 continued on facing page.

12. Continued

	Agree Strongly	Agree Somewhat	Disagree Somewhat	Disagree Strongly	Don't Know	
R. It is as important for a child to think for himself as to be obedient to his parents.	5	6	8	9	7	25/4
S. Rules should never be relaxed, because children will take advantage of it.	X	0	2	3	1	26/y
T. Negroes would be satisfied, if it were not for a few people who stir up trouble.	5	6	8	9	7	27/4
U. Jewish businessmen are about as honest as other businessmen.	X	0	2	3	1	28/y
V. People who don't believe in God have as much right to freedom of speech as anyone else.	5	6	8	9	7	29/4
W. Complete abstention from liquor is the best thing.	X	0	2	3	1	30/y
X. Books written by Communists should not be permitted in public libraries.	5	6	8	9	7	31/4

13. What was the highest grade in school your father completed?

No schooling . . . . (SKIP TO Q. 14) 3   34/1
6th grade or less . . . . (ASK C) 4+
7th or 8th grade . . . . (ASK C) 5+
Some high school . . . . (ASK B & C) 6#+
High school graduate . . . . . (ASK B & C) 7#+
Some college . . . . . . (ASK A, B, & C) 8*#+
College graduate or more . (ASK A, B, & C) 9*#+
Don't know . . . . (SKIP TO Q. 14) 2

*IF FATHER ATTENDED COLLEGE:
A. What kind of college did he go to--Catholic, non-Catholic, or both? (CIRCLE CODE UNDER A BELOW)

#IF FATHER ATTENDED HIGH SCHOOL:
B. What kind of high school did he go to--Catholic, public, or both? (CIRCLE CODE UNDER B BELOW)

+IF FATHER ATTENDED ELEMENTARY SCHOOL:
C. What kind of elementary school did he go to--Catholic, public, or both? (CIRCLE CODE UNDER C BELOW)

*A. IF FATHER ATTENDED COLLEGE:	#B. IF FATHER ATTENDED HIGH SCHOOL:	+C. IF FATHER ATTENDED ELEMENTARY SCHOOL:
Catholic . . . 0 35/	Catholic . . . 6 36/	Catholic . . . 0 37/
Non-Catholic . 1 NAP- y	Public . . . . 7 NAP- 4	Public . . . . 1 NAP- y
Both . . . . . 2 NAN- X	Both . . . . . 8 NAN- 5	Both . . . . . 2 NAN- X
Don't know . . 3	Don't know . . 9	Don't know . . 3

14. What was the highest grade in school your mother completed?

                              No schooling . . . . . . (SKIP TO Q. 15) 3   <u>38</u>/1
                              6th grade or less . . . . (ASK C) 4+
                              7th or 8th grade . . . . (ASK C) 5+
                              Some high school . . . . . . (ASK B & C) 6#+
                              High school graduate . . . . (ASK B & C) 7#+
                              Some college . . . . . . (ASK A, B, & C) 8*#+
                              College graduate or more (ASK A, B, & C) 9*#+
                              Don't know . . . . . . (SKIP TO Q. 15) 2

*IF MOTHER ATTENDED COLLEGE:
A. What kind of college did she go to--Catholic, non-Catholic, or both?
    (CIRCLE CODE UNDER A BELOW)

#IF MOTHER ATTENDED HIGH SCHOOL:
B. What kind of high school did she go to--Catholic, public, or both?
    (CIRCLE CODE UNDER B BELOW)

+IF MOTHER ATTENDED ELEMENTARY SCHOOL:
C. What kind of elementary school did she go to--Catholic, public, or
    both? (CIRCLE CODE UNDER C BELOW)

*A. IF MOTHER ATTENDED COLLEGE:	#B. IF MOTHER ATTENDED HIGH SCHOOL:	+C. IF MOTHER ATTENDED ELEMENTARY SCHOOL:
Catholic . . 0 <u>39</u>/	Catholic . . 6 40/	Catholic . . 0 <u>41</u>/
Non-Catholic. 1 NAP- y	Public . . . 7 NAP- 4	Public . . . 1 NAP- y
Both . . . . 2 NAN- X	Both . . . . 8 NAN- 5	Both . . . . 2 NAN- X
Don't know . 3	Don't know . 9	Don't know . 3

15. What was your father's (or stepfather's) main occupation during the time you
    were growing up?   <u>42-43</u>/
    Occupation: _____ Industry:_____   NAP- yy
                                                                        NAN- XX

16. On the whole, how happy would you say your childhood was--<u>extremely happy</u>,
    <u>happier than average</u>, <u>average</u>, or <u>not too happy</u>?

                              Extremely happy . . . 5 <u>44</u>/4
                              Happier than average . 6
                              Average 7
                              Not too happy 8
                              Other (SPECIFY)_____
                              _____ 9

17. Everything considered, how happy would you say your parents' marriage was while you were growing up? Would you say <u>extremely happy</u>, <u>happier than average</u>, <u>average</u>, or <u>not too happy</u>?

Extremely happy . . . 0 <u>45</u>/
Happier than average . 1 NAP- y
NAN- X
Average 2
Not too happy 3
Other (SPECIFY) _____
_____ 4

---

18. A. When you were growing up, what was your <u>father's</u> (stepfather's) religious preference? (CIRCLE CODE UNDER <u>A</u> BELOW.)

B. When you were growing up, what was your mother's (stepmother's) religious preference? (CIRCLE CODE UNDER <u>B</u> BELOW.)

A. Father's (stepfather's) religious preference	B. Mother's (stepmother's) religious preference
Protestant . . . . . . 0 <u>46</u>/	Protestant . . . . . . 0 <u>47</u>/
Catholic . . . . 1 NAP- y NAN- X	Catholic . . . . 1 NAP- y NAN- X
Jewish 2	Jewish 2
Other (SPECIFY) _____	Other (SPECIFY) _____
_____ 3	_____ 3
None 4	None 4

19. A. What is your religious preference?

Protestant . (ASK B, THEN DISCONTINUE INTERVIEW) 5*<u>48</u>/4
Catholic . . . . (ASK B) 6*
Jewish . . . (ASK B, THEN DISCONTINUE INTERVIEW) 7*
Other . . . (ASK B, THEN DISCONTINUE INTERVIEW) 8*
None . . . . (DISCONTINUE INTERVIEW) 9

*UNLESS "NONE":

B. Were you raised a (Catholic) (Protestant) (Jew)?

Yes . . . . 2 <u>49</u>/
No . . . [ASK (1)] 3# NAP- 0
NAN- 1

#IF "NO" TO B AND RESPONDENT IS CATHOLIC:

(1) How old were you when you became a Catholic?

_____
age

<u>50-51</u>/
NAP- yy
NAN- XX

20. A. How religious would you say your father was while you were growing up-- very, somewhat, not too, or not religious at all?

    B. How religious was your mother?

	A. Father	B. Mother
Very religious	6	1
Somewhat religious	7	2
Not too religious	8	3
Not at all religious	9	4
Don't know	5	0
No (father) (mother) present	3	y
	52/4	53/X

---

21. When you were growing up--
(HAND RESPONDENT CARD C.)

ASK A AND B UNLESS NO FATHER PRESENT:

	More Than Weekly	Weekly	1-3 Times a Month	Couple Times a Year	Almost Never	Don't Know	
A. About how often did your father attend (Mass) (Church)?	5	6	7	8	9	4	54/NAP- 2 NAN- 3
B. About how often did your father receive Communion?	5	6	7	8	9	4	55/NAP- 2 NAN- 3

ASK C AND D UNLESS NO MOTHER PRESENT:

C. About how often did your mother attend (Mass) (Church)?	5	6	7	8	9	4	56/NAP- 2 NAN- 3
D. About how often did your mother receive Communion?	5	6	7	8	9	4	57/NAP- 2 NAN- 3

---

22. A. How religious would you say you are at the present time?

    IF CURRENTLY MARRIED:
    B. How religious would you say your (wife)(husband) is at the present time?

	A. Respondent	B. Spouse
Very religious	X	6
Somewhat religious . .	0	7
Not too religious . .	1	8
Not at all religious .	2	9
Not currently married.	-	4
	58/y	59/5

IF CURRENTLY MARRIED:

23. What is your (husband's) (wife's) religious preference?

Protestant 1 60/X
Catholic 2
Jewish 3
Other (SPECIFY)_____
_____ 4
None 0
Not currently married y

24. A. How many brothers do you have? (Includes any no longer living.)

_____   ┌──┬──┐   61-62/
number   └──┴──┘   NAN-yy

B. How many sisters do you have? (Includes any no longer living.)

_____   ┌──┬──┐   63-64/
number   └──┴──┘   NAN-yy

IF NO BROTHERS OR SISTERS, SKIP TO Q. 26.

25. How many brothers and sisters were raised Catholics?   ┌──┬──┐   65-66/
                                                               └──┴──┘   No Sib-yy
_____*   No Ans-XX
number

IF NONE, SKIP TO Q. 26.

*IF ANY, ASK A AND B:

A. (Of those raised as Catholics:) How many are not practicing Catholics
today?

_____   ┌──┬──┐   67-68/
number   └──┴──┘   No Sib-yy
                                 No Cth-XX
                                 No Ans-99

B. (Of those raised as Catholics:) How many married
Catholics?   ┌──┬──┐   69-70/
                                                   └──┴──┘   No Sib-yy
_____   No Cth-XX
number   No Ans-99

---

26. Think of the neighborhood in which you grew up.
How many of your neighbors were Catholics--more   BEGIN DECK 3
than half, about half, less than half, or none?

(HAND RESPONDENT CARD D.)   More than half . 1   8/0
                                             About half . . . 2
                                             Less than half . 3
                                             None 4

---

27. Here are some statements about the way in which families regard their
religion. Tell me whether each statement was true or not
true about your family when you were growing up.

		True	Not True	DK	
A.	We were religious but not very devout.	X	1	0	9/y
B.	There was a close relative who was a priest or a nun.	3	5	4	10/2
C.	Priests visited the house.	7	9	8	11/6
D.	We were Catholics, but we couldn't take some of the rules too seriously.	X	1	0	12/y
E.	We always had masses said for dead relatives.	3	5	4	13/2
F.	Mother was an active member of parish organizations.	7	9	8	14/6
G.	Father was an active member of parish organizations.	X	1	0	15/y
H.	Someone in the family attended novena services regularly.	3	5	4	16/2
I.	Catholic magazines and newspapers came into the house regularly.	7	9	8	17/6
J.	Someone in our family did charitable work for the church (like visiting hospitals and help- the poor).	X	1	0	18/y

28. Here are some experiences that people sometimes have when they are growing
up. Was each of these true for you? First.... (CIRCLE CODE FOR EACH
ACTIVITY WHICH WAS TRUE FOR RESPONDENT.)

I wanted to be a priest or nun 0	19/y
I made my Confirmation 1	

I stopped going to church as soon as I grew old enough
to be able to make my own decisions 2

I belonged to a parish club or played on an
athletic team 3

I dated a non-Catholic 4

I went steady with a non-Catholic 5

I played in the parish yard 6

I was known by name by a priest 7

I had a religious experience in which I really felt
close to God and the Saints 8

FOR MEN ONLY: I served as an altar boy 9

None of the above X

29. Thinking about the friends you had when you were about 13 or 14, how many
would you say were Catholic--more than half, about half, less than half,
or none?

> More than half X   20/y
> About half 0
> Less than half 1
> None 2
> Don't know--don't remember. 3

30. What about when you were 17 or so--how many of your friends were Catholic--
more than half, about half, less than half, or none?

> More than half 5   21/4
> About half 6
> Less than half 7
> None 8
> Don't know--don't remember. 9

31. A. How far did you go in school?

ASK IF CURRENTLY MARRIED:
B. How far did your spouse go in school?

	A. Self	B. Spouse
No schooling.	1	1
6th grade or less.	2	2
7th or 8th grade.	3	3
Some high school.	4	4
High school graduate.	5	5
Some college.	6	6
College graduate or more.	7	7
Don't know.	8	8
Not currently married.	-	9
	22/0	23/0

IF ATTENDED ELEMENTARY SCHOOL (Q. 31 A.):
32. When you were going to elementary school, about how many of the Catholic chil-
    dren in your neighborhood attended Catholic schools? Would you say more than
    half, about half, less than half, a few, or none?   OFFICE USE ONLY

                                        More than half 0   24/
                                        About half . . 1   No Sch-y
                                                             No Ans-X
                                        Less than half 2
                                        A few 3
                                        None 4

33. Thinking of the elementary schools you attended--did you go only to Catholic
    schools, only to public schools, or did you go to both kinds of elementary
    schools?
                                 Catholic only (SKIP TO Q. 34) 7   25/
                                 Public only . . . . . (ASK A) 8*   No Sch-5
                                                                    No Ans-6
                                 Both kinds . . . . . (ASK A) 9*

*IF ATTENDED ANY PUBLIC SCHOOLS:

A. While you were in public elementary school, was there ever a Catholic
    school your parents could have sent you to? As you recall, was there
    one most of the time, some of the time, or none of the time you were
    in public elementary school?
                                 Most of the time . [ASK (1)] 1+   26/
                                 Some of the time . [ASK (1)] 2+   No Sch-y
                                                                    No Pub-X
                                 None of the time . [ASK (2)] 3#   No Ans-0

    +IF CATHOLIC SCHOOL AVAILABLE:
    (1) Why do you think your parents sent you to public school(s)?
                                                    27/   28/
                                                    y- No Sch- y
                                                    X- No Pub- X
                                                    0- No Cth- 0
                                                    1- No Ans- 1

    #IF CATHOLIC SCHOOL NOT AVAILABLE:
    (2) Do you think your parents would have sent you to a Catholic ele-
         mentary school if there had been one you could have attended?
                                           Yes 8   29/
                                           No   (ASK a) 9** No Sch-4
                                                               No Pub-5
                                                               Cth Av-6
         **IF NO: No Ans-7
         ┌───
         │ a. Why would'nt your parents have sent you to a   30/
         │   Catholic school, do you think?   No Sch-y
         │   No Pub-X
         │   Cth Av-0
         │   If Yes-1
         │   No Ans-2

IF ATTENDED HIGH SCHOOL (SEE Q. 31 A.):

34. Now think back to your high school years. When you were going to high school, about how many of the Catholic students in your neighborhood attended a Catholic high school? Would you say more than half, about half, less than half, a few, or none?

OFFICE USE ONLY

More than half .	0	31/
About half . . .	1	No Sch-y
Less than half .	2	No Ans-X
A few	3	
None	4	

H I G H

35. Of the high schools you attended, did you go only to Catholic schools, only to public schools, or did you go to both kinds of high schools?

Only to Catholic schools. .(SKIP TO Q. 36 .	7	32/
Only to public schools . . . . . (ASK A).	8*	No Sch-5
Both kinds . . . . (ASK A).	9*	No Ans-6

S C H O O L

*IF ATTENDED ANY PUBLIC HIGH SCHOOLS:

A. While you were in public high school, was there ever a Catholic high school your parents could have sent you to? As you recall, was there one most of the time, some of the time, or none of the time you were in public high school?

Most of the time	[ASK (1)]. 1+	33/
Some of the time	[ASK (1)]. 2+	No Sch-y
None of the time	[ASK (2)]. 3#	No Pub-X
		No Ans-0

+IF CATHOLIC HIGH SCHOOL AVAILABLE:

(1) ·Why did you go to public high school?

34/	35/
y- No Sch- y
X- No Pub- X
0- No Cth- 0
1- No Ans- 1

#IF CATHOLIC HIGH SCHOOL NOT AVAILABLE:

(2) Do you think your parents would have sent you to a Catholic high school if there had been one you could have attended?

Yes	8	36/
No . . (ASK a)	9**	No Sch-4
		No Pub-5
		Cth Av-6
		No Ans-7

**IF NO:

a. Why wouldn't you go to a Catholic high school?

37/
No Sch-y
No Pub-X
Cth Av-0
If Yes-1
No Ans-2

ASK IF RESPONDENT ATTENDED ANY COLLEGE (SEE Q. 31 A.):
36. Did you attend only Catholic colleges, only non-Catholic colleges, or did
     you attend both kinds?

                                         Only Catholic . . . 7   38/
                                         Only non-Catholic . 8   NAP- 5
                                         Both kinds 9   NAN- 6

37. ASK IF RESPONDENT ATTENDED ANY PUBLIC ELEMENTARY SCHOOL:
     A. When you were attending public elementary school, did you receive
         religious instruction regularly from your church?

                                         Yes 2   39/
                                         No 3   NAP- 0
                                                                  NAN- 1
     ASK IF RESPONDENT ATTENDED ANY PUBLIC HIGH SCHOOL:
     B. When you were attending public high school, did you receive religious
         instruction regularly from your church or were you a member of a
         Catholic club?
                                         Instruction only . 6   40/
                                         Club only 7   NAP- 4
                                         Both 8   NAN- 5
                                         Neither 9

IF RESPONDENT IS SINGLE (NEVER MARRIED) SKIP TO Q. 49.
38. How many children have you and your (husband)   41-42/
     (wife) had?   _____   NR MAR-yy
                                         *   No Ans-XX
                            number
     *IF ANY, ASK A:
     A. How many have been baptized--all, some, or none of them?

                                   All . [ASK (1)]. 7** 43/
                                   Some   [ASK (1) . 8** NR MAR- 4
                                   None 9   No Cld- 5
                                                          No Ans- 6
         **IF ANY BAPTIZED:

             (Of those baptized) How many have been raised as Catholics--all, some,
             or none of them?
                                   All 2   44/
                                   Some 3   NR MAR- y
                                                          No Cld- X
                                   None 4   No Bpt- 0
                                                          No Ans- 1

39. Do you expect to have any (more) children?
                                   Yes . . . (ASK A) 7*   45/
                                   No 8   NR MAR- 5
                                   Don't know . . . 9   No Ans- 6
     *IF YES:
     A. How many?
                                                          46-47/
                     _____   NR MAR- yy
                     number   If No - XX
                                                          No Ans- 99

40. If you had your choice, what would be the ideal number of children you would like to have in your family?

48-49/
NR MAR-yy
No Ans-XX

_____
number

41. In what year were you and your (husband) (wife) married?

50-51/
NR MAR-yy
No Ans-XX

_____
year

42. Were you married by a priest?

Yes 8   52/
No (ASK A) 9* NR MAR- 6
No Ans- 7

*IF NO:

> A. What were your reasons for not being married by a priest?
>
> 53/
> NR MAR- y
> Priest- X
> No Ans- 0

IF ALL CHILDREN ARE PRE-SCHOOL AGE, SKIP TO Q. 48.

43. Did any of your children (Did your child) go to Catholic school(s)?

Yes . . . . . (ASK A) 7* 54/
No . . . . 8 No Cld- 5
No Ans- 6

*IF YES:

> A. Was that elementary school? High school? College?
>
> Elementary school . . . 2 55/
> High school . . . . . . 3 No Cld- X
> If No - 0
> College . . . . 4 No Ans- 1

44. Did any of your children (Did your child) go to any public or other non-Catholic schools?

Yes . . . . (ASK A) 8* 56/
No . . . . . (SKIP TO Q. 47) 9 No Cld- 6
No Ans- 7

*IF YES:

> A. Was that elementary school? High school? College?
>
> Elementary school [ASK (1)] 3# 57/
> High school . . . [ASK (2)] 4## No Cld- 0
> If No - 1
> College . . . . . [ASK (3)] 5+ No Ans- 2
>
> #IF ELEMENTARY SCHOOL:
>
> > (1) Why did your child (children) attend non-Catholic elementary school(s)?
> >
> > 58/
> > No Cld- y
> > If No - X
> > No Elm- 0
> > No Ans- 1
>
> ##IF HIGH SCHOOL:
>
> > (2) Why did your child (children) attend a non-Catholic high school?
> >
> > 59/
> > No Cld- y
> > If No - X
> > No HS - 0
> > No Ans- 1
>
> +IF COLLEGE:
>
> > (3) Why did your child (children) attend a non-Catholic college?
> >
> > 60/
> > No Cld- y
> > If No - X
> > No Col- 0
> > No Ans- 1

IF CHILD OR CHILDREN ATTENDS (OR ATTENDED) NON-CATHOLIC ELEMENTARY SCHOOL(S) ASK:
45. While in elementary school, (has your child) (have your children) received
    religious instruction regularly from your church?

Yes, all . 6	61/	
Yes, some . 7	No Cld- 2	
No 8	If No - 3	
DK 9	No Elm- 4	
	No Ans- 5	

IF CHILD OR CHILDREN ATTENDS (ATTENDED) NON-CATHOLIC HIGH SCHOOL(S) ASK:
46. While in high school did your child(ren) receive religious
    instruction regularly or (was) (were) your child(ren) a member
    (members) of a high school religious club?

Yes, all . 6	62/	
Yes, some . 7	No Cld- 2	
No 8	If No - 3	
DK 9	No HS - 4	
	No Ans- 5	

47. If you spent any money on Catholic school tuition for your
    children, on the average how much did you spend per year?

    Check if none /__/

    $_____

    63-66/
    No Cld-yyyy
    No Cth-yXXX
    None -Xyyy
    No Ans-XXXX

48. Did you ever speak to a child of yours about being a
    priest or a nun?

Yes . . 0	67/	
No . . . 1	No Cld- y	
	No Ans- X	

ASK EVERYONE:
49. As you see it, what, if any, are the advantages of sending a child
    to a Catholic school?

    68/
    y
    69/
    y

50. Where do you think improvements should be made in the Catholic schools?

    70/
    y
    71/
    y

51. Here is a list of things people generally like when they   BEGIN DECK 4
    see them in young children. Which two of the things on
    the list (do) (did) you find the nicest? (HAND RESPONDENT   _____
    CARD E.)   (CIRCLE TWO)
    A. When they listen to what you tell them to do 1   7/
    B. When they are neat and clean 2   0
    C. When they are polite and well-behaved with other people . 3
    D. When they hug and kiss you 4
    E. When they play nicely with other children 5
    F. When they learn to do something after they have tried
       for a long time 6
    G. When they play with you 7

52. I am going to read you a list of jobs. If a son of yours chose each job tell me whether you would feel very pleased, somewhat pleased, somewhat disappointed, or very disappointed. (CIRCLE CODES IN TABLE BELOW.)

		Very Pleased	Somewhat Pleased	Somewhat Dis- appointed	Very Dis- appointed	Don't Know	
A.	Business executive.	X	0	2	3	1	8/y
B.	High school teacher.	5	6	8	9	7	9/4
C.	Priest.	X	0	2	3	1	10/y
D.	Bank teller.	5	6	8	9	7	11/4
E.	Author.	X	0	2	3	1	12/y
F.	Carpenter.	5	6	8	9	7	13/4
G.	Stock broker.	X	0	2	3	1	14/y
H.	Furniture mover.	5	6	8	9	7	15/4

53. Would you prefer a job where you are part of a team, all working together, even if you don't get personal recognition for your work, or a job where you worked alone and others could see what you have done?

Part of a team 7   16/6

Work alone . . 9

Can't decide . 8

54. Which of these opinions comes closer to the way you feel? Some people feel that other persons can be counted on for important help in an emergency. Other people feel that these days one never knows whom he can count on.

Other persons can be counted on X   17/y

One never knows whom he can count on . . 1

Can't decide 0

55. Some people say that anyone who looks for meaning in life is just kidding himself. Other people say that you don't have to look too hard to find meaning in life. What do you think?

Anyone who looks for meaning is kidding himself . . . 3   18/2

Don't have to look too hard to find it 5

Can't decide 4

56. A. Some people say that for the average man things are getting worse. Other people say things are getting better. Which opinion comes closest to the way you feel? Would you say things are getting better or worse?

Better 7   19/6

Worse 9

Can't decide . . 8

B. Some people say that hard work is more important for getting ahead than having a nice personality and being well-liked. Other people say that having a nice personality and being well-liked are more important for getting ahead than hard work. Would you say hard work or a nice person- ality is more important?

Hard work X   20/y

Nice personality 1

Can't decide 0

5.7. Now we would like to ask about your religious practices.

	Every day	Several times a week	Every week	Several times a month	About once a month	Several times a year	About once a year	Practically never or not at all	
A. How often do you go to Mass?	1	2	3	4	5	6	7	8	21/0
B. About how often do you receive Holy Communion?	1	2	3	4	5	6	7	8	22/0
C. How often do you go to confession?	1	2	3	4	5	6	7	8	23/0
D. About how often do you stop in church to pray?	1	2	3	4	5	6	7	8	24/0
E. How often does your spouse go to church?	1	2	3	4	5	6	7	8	25/0

58. Here is a list of things that some Catholics do. During the last two years have you managed to--   (CIRCLE ANY WHICH APPLY.)

A. go on a retreat? 3   26/1

B. make a day of recollection? 4

C. read a spiritual book (or books)? 5

D. make a mission? 6

E. read Catholic magazines or newspapers regularly? 7

F. listen to a Catholic radio or TV program? 8

G. have a serious conversation with a priest about religious problems? 9

H. None of the above 2

59. Thinking of your three closest friends, what religion does each belong to? (ASK ABOUT FIRST, SECOND, THIRD CLOSE FRIEND AND ENTER BELOW.)

	First Friend	Second Friend	Third Friend
Protestant	1	1	1
Catholic	2	2	2
Jewish	3	3	3
No religion	4	4	4
Other (SPECIFY) _____	5	5	5
Don't know religion	0	0	0
No (1st)(2nd)(3rd) friend	y	y	y
	27/X	28/X	29/X

60. Of your <u>other</u> friends, how many would you say are Catholic--more than half, about half, less than half, or none?

```
                    More than half . . . . . . . . 6        30/4
                    About half . . . . . . . . . . 7
                    Less than half . . . . . . . . 8
                    None . . . . . . . . . . . . . 9
                    Don't know . . . . . . . . . . 5
                    Doesn't have any other friends . 3
```

61. Of your <u>Catholic</u> friends, about how many belong to the same parish as you do--more than half, about half, less than half, or none?

```
                    More than half . . . . . . . . 1        31/X
                    About half . . . . . . . . . . 2
                    Less than half . . . . . . . . 3
                    None . . . . . . . . . . . . . 4
                    Don't know . . . . . . . . . . 0
                    Don't have any Catholic friends. y
```

62. As a general rule, how important do you think it is for young people to marry a member of their own religion--<u>very important</u>, <u>fairly important</u>, or <u>not important at all</u>?

```
                    Very important . . . . . . . . 7        32/5
                    Fairly important . . . . . . . 8
                    Not important at all . . . . . 9
                    Don't know . . . . . . . . . . 6
```

63. If a child of yours wanted to marry someone who was not a Catholic, how do you think you would react?

```
                                                           33/y
```

64. How would you feel about a teen-ager of yours dating a non-Catholic? Would you oppose it strongly, oppose it but not strongly, or not oppose it at all?

```
                    Oppose strongly . . . . . . 7          34/5
                    Oppose but not strongly . . 8
                    Not oppose at all . . . . . 9
                    Don't know . . . . . . . . 6
```

65. How much money would you say your family contributes to the Church each year (not counting school tuition)?

```
    Check if none /__/       $_____
```

35-38/
No Ans-yyyy
None -XXXX

66. Would you say that you have neighbors in your home very often, often, not too often, or not at all?

Very often . . X		39/y
Often 0		
Not too often . 1		
Not at all . . 2		

67. Of the neighbors that visit you at home, what proportion of these is Catholic?

All or almost all 5	40/4
Most 6	
Some 7	
A few 8	
None or almost none 9	
Never have neighbors . . . 3	

68. How many of your neighbors are Catholic? Would you say almost all, more than half, about half, less than half, or almost none?

Almost all 0	41/y
More than half 1	
About half 2	
Less than half 3	
Almost none 4	
Don't know X	

69. How important do you feel it is for Catholics to choose other Catholics as their really close friends--very important, fairly important, or not important?

Very important 7	42/6
Fairly important 8	
Not important 9	

70. About how often do you pray privately?

Once a day . . . . . (ASK A AND B) 0*	43/y
Several times a week (ASK A AND B) 1*	
About once a week . (ASK A AND B) 2*	
Less than once a week(ASK A AND B) 3*	
Never. . . . . . (SKIP TO Q. 71) X	

*IF EVER:

A. As far as you're concerned, which two of the statements on this card are the most important reasons for praying? (HAND RESPONDENT CARD F.)

(CIRCLE TWO)

A) Prayer gives me peace of mind 0	44/
B) Prayer honors God 1	NEVER- y
C) Prayer makes up for past failings in some degree 2	No Ans-X
D) Prayer helps me adjust to life and its problems 3	
E) Prayer offers thanks to God 4	
F) Prayer helps me get something special when I want it . . . 5	

B. For what do you usually pray?

45/
NEVER- y
No Ans-X

71. Have there been times in your life when you felt especially religious?

Yes . . . . . (ASK A) X* 46/y

No 0

*IF YES:

A. When was that?

47/
NAP- 1
NAN- 2

72. What is the name of your parish church?

48/
Answered- y
No Ans- X
D.K. - 0
No Par- 1

_____

73. Are you a member of any religious organizations?

Yes (ASK A, B, AND C) 8* 49/7

No. . (SKIP TO Q.74) 9

*IF YES:

A. What are the names of these organizations?

B. Are you active in (NAME OF ORGANIZATION)?

C. Have you ever been an officer of (NAME OF ORGANIZATION)?

	A. Name	B. Active	C. Officer
1.	50/ NAP-y NAN-X	Yes . 4 51/ No . 5 NAP-2 NAN-3	Yes . 8 52/ No . 9 NAP-6 NAN-7
2.	53/ NAP-y NAN-X	Yes . 4 54/ No . 5 NAP-2 NAN-3	Yes . 8 55/ No . 9 NAP-6 NAN-7
3.	56/ NAP-y NAN-X	Yes . 4 57/ No . 5 NAP-2 NAN-3	Yes . 8 58/ No . 9 NAP-6 NAN-7
4.	59/ NAP-y NAN-X	Yes . 4 60/ No . 5 NAP-2 NAN-3	Yes . 8 61/ No . 9 NAP-6 NAN-7

74. Most parishes are so big nowadays that it is very difficult for the priests to know their parishioners by name. Do you think (your priest) (any of your priests) knows (know) you by name?

Yes . X 62/y

No . 0

75. What is the name of your pastor?

63/
Answer- 1
No Ans- 2
No Pst- 3
D.K. - 4

76. Have your parish priests or other priests ever visited your home?

Yes . (ASK A) 2* 64/1
No 3

*IF YES:

A. About how often do they visit?

About once a month or more . 6   65/
Several times a year . . . . 7 If No-4
Once a year . . . . 8 NAN -5
Once every few years 9

77. I am going to read to you a list of things about which many people disagree. Do you think that the Church has the right to teach what position Catholics should take on such issues?

		Yes	No	Don't Know	
A.	Government regulation of business and labor	X	1	0	66/y
B.	Racial integration	3	5	4	67/2
C.	Whether the U.S. should recognize Red China	7	9	8	68/6
D.	What are immoral books or movies	X	1	0	69/y
E.	Proper means for family limitation	3	5	4	70/2
F.	Federal aid to education	7	9	8	71/6
G.	Communist infiltration into government	X	1	0	72/y

78. Here is another sheet with a number of statements on it. Please circle the letter which indicates how much you personally agree or disagree with each statement.
(HAND RESPONDENT PINK SHEET.)

		Agree Strongly	Agree Somewhat	Disagree Somewhat	Disagree Strongly	D. K.	
A.	Love of neighbor is more important than avoiding meat on Friday.	X	0	2	3	1	_8/y
B.	It is always wrong to say something that might make a person question his faith, even if what one says is true.	5	6	8	9	7	_9/4
C.	The Catholic Church teaches that large families are more Christian than small families.	X	0	2	3	1	10/y
D.	Although Christ saved the spiritual world by his death and resurrection, the material world is under the control of the devil.	5	6	8	9	7	11/4
E.	Husband and wife may have sexual intercourse for pleasure alone.	X	0	2	3	1	12/y
F.	The world is basically a dangerous place where there is much evil and sin.	5	6	8	9	7	13/4
G.	The Catholic Church teaches that a good Christian ought to think about the next life and not worry about fighting against poverty and injustice in this life.	X	0	2	3	1	14/y
H.	The Catholic Church teaches that if there is ever a majority of Catholics in the country, Catholicism must become the official religion of the United States.	5	6	8	9	7	15/4
I.	Even people who won't work should be helped if they really need it.	X	0	2	3	1	16/y
J.	Parts of the Mass ought to be said out loud and in English.	5	6	8	9	7	17/4
K.	There is basic opposition between the discoveries of modern science and the teaching of the Church.	X	0	2	3	1	18/y
L.	Most Protestants are inclined to discriminate against Catholics.	5	6	8	9	7	19/4
M.	Most priests don't expect the laity to be leaders, just followers.	X	0	2	3	1	20/y
N.	Protestants don't really take their religion seriously as compared to Catholics.	5	6	8	9	7	21/4
O.	Catholics must support laws which outlaw the sale of birth control devices.	X	0	2	3	1	22/y
P.	Only people who believe in God can be good American citizens.	5	6	8	9	7	23/4
Q.	It would make me somewhat unhappy if a daughter of mine became a nun.	X	0	2	3	1	24/y
R.	Protestant ministers should not be permitted to publicly teach things which are opposed to Catholic doctrine.	5	6	8	9	7	25/4
S.	God's purpose is clear to me in all the events of my life.	X	0	2	3	1	26/y
T.	My religion provides me with answers to all the important problems in my life.	5	6	8	9	7	27/4

79. In national politics, do you consider yourself a Democrat or Republican?

Democrat 0	<u>28</u>/y
Republican 1	
Independent (ASK A) 2*	
Other . . (ASK A) 3*	
Don't know (ASK A) X*	

*IF INDEPENDENT, OTHER OR DON'T KNOW:

A. In general, would you say you are closer to the Democratic or Republican party in national politics?

Democratic 7	<u>29</u>/
Republican 8	NAP-4
Neither 9	NAN-5
Don't know 6	

80. How many organizations do you belong to besides religious ones--such as unions, professional organizations, clubs, neighborhood organizations, etc.?

None 0	<u>30</u>/X
One . . . . . (ASK A & B) 1*	
Two . . . . . (ASK A & B) 2*	
Three or four (ASK A & B) 3*	
Five or more. (ASK A & B) 5*	

*UNLESS "NONE":

A. In general, would you say you are <u>very active</u> in these organizations, <u>fairly active</u>, or <u>inactive</u>?

Very active 7	<u>31</u>/
Fairly active 8	None-5
Inactive 9	No Ans-6

B. How many of the members of these organizations you belong to are the same religion as you are? Would you say <u>more than half</u>, <u>about half</u>, <u>less than half</u>, or <u>almost none</u>?

More than half 1	<u>32</u>/
About half 2	None-y
Less than half 3	No Ans-X
Almost none 4	
Don't know 0	

81. Do you read any <u>non</u>-religious magazines regularly?

Yes 6	<u>33</u>/5
No 7	

82. How interested are you in what goes on in the world today? For instance, do you follow the international news <u>very closely</u>, <u>fairly closely</u>, or <u>not too closely</u>?

Very closely . . . 0	<u>34</u>/X
Fairly closely . . 1	
Not too closely . 2	

83. What about local news--the things that happen here in your (town) (area)?
Do you follow local news <u>very closely</u>, <u>fairly closely</u>, or <u>not too closely</u>?

Very closely 4   <u>35</u>/3
Fairly closely 5
Not too closely 6

---

84. Do you ever get as worked up by something that happens in the news as you
do by something that happens in your personal life?

Yes 8   <u>36</u>/7
No 9

---

85. Here is a list of ways we might know different people. Which kind of person
on that card is the <u>closest relationship</u> you have with each of the following
groups? (HAND RESPONDENT CARD G.)

First, an Irish-American--what is the closest association you have had with
an Irish-American?

(READ LIST OF ETHNIC GROUPS BELOW,
CODING ONE RESPONSE FOR EACH.)

	Relative	Best Friend	Close Friend	Friend	Neighbor	Co-worker	Knew in School	Acquaintance	Stranger or Never Met One	
A. Irish-American.	1	2	3	4	5	6	7	8	9	<u>37</u>/0
B. Protestant.	1	2	3	4	5	6	7	8	9	<u>38</u>/0
C. Italian-American.	1	2	3	4	5	6	7	8	9	<u>39</u>/0
D. German-American.	1	2	3	4	5	6	7	8	9	<u>40</u>/0
E. Jew.	1	2	3	4	5	6	7	8	9	<u>41</u>/0
F. Scandinavian.	1	2	3	4	5	6	7	8	9	<u>42</u>/0
G. Polish-American.	1	2	3	4	5	6	7	8	9	<u>43</u>/0
H. Negro.	1	2	3	4	5	6	7	8	9	<u>44</u>/0

---

86. Here is a short quiz which touches on practices and beliefs of the Catholic
Church. You are not expected to get them all correct--some you may find
rather difficult. (HAND RESPONDENT YELLOW SHEET.)

Please circle the number in front of the answer which comes closest to
being correct, in your opinion.

A. The word we use to describe the
fact that the Second Person of
the Trinity became man is--

Transfiguration 1   <u>45</u>/0
Incarnation 2
Transubstantiation 3
Immaculate Conception . . 4

Q. 86 continued on facing page.

86. Continued

B. Supernatural life is--   the life we receive from our parents 6   <u>46</u>/5
                                  sanctifying grace in our souls . . . 7
                                  our life after death 8
                                  the power to work miracles 9

C. The "mystical body" is--   Christ's body in heaven 1   <u>47</u>/0
                                  Christ in Holy Communion 2
                                  Christ united with His followers . . 3
                                  None of the above 4

D. Uncharitable talk is   the second commandment 6   <u>48</u>/5
    forbidden by--   the fourth commandment 7
                                  the eighth commandment 8
                                  the tenth commandment 9

E. A man is judged immedi-   general judgment 1   <u>49</u>/0
    ately after he dies. This   natural judgment 2
    judgment is called--   particular judgment 3
                                  final judgment 4

F. The Encyclicals "Rerum   Christian marriage 6   <u>50</u>/5
    Novarum" of Leo XIII and   Christian education 7
    "Quadragesimo anno" of   the condition of labor 8
    Pius XI both deal with--   Papal infallibility 9

87. Here are some questions which might be used on a radio or television quiz
     program. Some of them are fairly hard--let's see how many you can answer.

A. What ocean would one cross in going from the United States to   51/
    England?   NAN-y
                                        Don't know . . X   R -0
                                                            W -1

B. Could you tell me who Billy Graham is?   52/2
                                                                      NAN-2
                                        Don't know . . 3   R -4
                                                            W -5

C. What mineral or metal is important in the making of the atomic bomb?
                                                                      53/
                                                                      NAN-6
                                        Don't know . . 7   R -8
                                                            W -9

Q. 87 continued on next page.

87. Continued

    D. Will you tell me who Plato was?

<table>
<tr><td></td><td>54/
NAN-y</td></tr>
<tr><td>Don't know   X</td><td>R   -0
W   -1</td></tr>
</table>

    E. Will you tell me who Robert McNamara is?

<table>
<tr><td></td><td>55/
NAN-2</td></tr>
<tr><td>Don't know   3</td><td>R   -4
W   -5</td></tr>
</table>

    F. How about Charles Lindberg--can you tell me what he was famous for?

<table>
<tr><td></td><td>56/</td></tr>
<tr><td>Don't know   7</td><td>NAN-6
R   -8
W   -9</td></tr>
</table>

    G. Who wrote War and Peace?

<table>
<tr><td></td><td>57/
NAN-y</td></tr>
<tr><td>Don't know   X</td><td>R   -0
W   -1</td></tr>
</table>

    H. What is the name of the Pope?

<table>
<tr><td></td><td>58/
NAN-2</td></tr>
<tr><td>Don't know   3</td><td>R   -4
W   -5</td></tr>
</table>

88. What kind of work do you do?

    _____ * _____

        Occupation   Industry

<table>
<tr><td>59-60/
NAP- yy
NAN- XX</td></tr>
</table>

*IF EMPLOYED:

    A. What proportion of the people with whom you work are Catholic--more
        than half, about half, less than half, or almost none?

<table>
<tr><td>More than half . . . . . 6</td><td>61/</td></tr>
<tr><td>About half . . . . 7</td><td>NAP- 3
NAN- 4</td></tr>
<tr><td>Less than half . . . . . 8</td><td></td></tr>
<tr><td>None . . . . 9</td><td></td></tr>
<tr><td>Don't know . . . . . . 5</td><td></td></tr>
</table>

IF RESPONDENT IS A MARRIED FEMALE:

*89. What kind of work does your husband do?

<table>
<tr><td>_____</td><td>_____</td></tr>
<tr><td>Occupation</td><td>Industry</td></tr>
</table>

62-63/
NAP- yy
NAN- XX

90. (HAND RESPONDENT CARD H.) Adding up the income from all sources, what was (will be) your total family income in 1963?

A.	Under $2,000 0	64/y
B.	$2,000 to $2,999 1	
C.	$3,000 to $3,999 2	
D.	$4,000 to $4,999 3	
E.	$5,000 to $5,999 4	
F.	$6,000 to $6,999 5	
G.	$7,000 to $7,999 6	
H.	$8,000 to $9,999 7	
I.	$10,000 to $14,999 8	
J.	$15,000 and over 9	
	Don't know X	

91. One final question. There has been much talk lately about change in the Catholic Church. Do you think there ought to be any changes?

Yes . . . . (ASK A) X* 65/y

No 0

*IF YES:

A. What kind of changes would you like to see?

66/
NAP- 1
NAN- 2

92. At some date in the future, we may want to ask for brief interviews with the parents of the people who have granted interviews on this study so far. Could I have the name and address of each of your parents, if they are still living?

Father's Name _____   Mother's Name:_____

Street Address:_____   Street Address:_____

City and State:_____   City and State:_____

Father deceased: /__/   Mother deceased: /__/

TIME
INTER-
VIEW
ENDED
:

<u>INTERVIEWER'S REMARKS</u>

A. Length of interview:

    ____ hrs. _____ minutes

B. Sex of respondent:

    Male . . . . 1 <u>67</u>/0
    Female 2

C. We want to determine whether obtaining a number of personal interviews in a household affects the second, and subsequent respondents.

We shall compare all first interviews with all subsequent ones, to see if the responses are different.

Therefore, please circle the appropriate code below.

This was the <u>first personal interview</u> obtained in the household on this study . . 5 <u>68</u>/4

This was the <u>second or subsequent personal interview</u> obtained in this household on this study . . 6*

*IF SECOND OR SUBSEQUENT INTERVIEW:

(1) Do you have any evidence that this respondent and the first respondent talked over the interview before this interview was conducted?

          Yes . . . . . 8# <u>69</u>/7

          No 9

#IF YES:

a) What evidence do you have? What effect, if any, do you think this had on this respondent's answers?

                      <u>70</u>/y

D. Was anyone else present during all or part of the interview?

    No . . . . 1 <u>71</u>/0
    Yes, spouse 2
    Yes, parent 3
    Yes, child(ren) 4
    Yes, other relative . . 5

E. Did this respondent ask any questions about the study's "approval," or about its "clearance" with the Roman Catholic hierarchy in your area (the Diocese, parish priests, etc.)?

If anything like this occurred in this case, please describe the respondent's questions, your answers, and any action the respondent took or wanted to take before acquiescing to the interview.

                      <u>72</u>/y

Date of interview: _____

_____
          Interviewer's Signature

THE ADOLESCENT QUESTIONNAIRE

NORC 476 YG
11/63

NATIONAL OPINION RESEARCH CENTER
University of Chicago   (1-4)

STUDY OF YOUNG ADULT
ATTITUDES AND OPINIONS

Segment	
Case		(5-9)

Your household is one of about 3,000 in the United States in which young people are filling out this questionnaire.

The research is designed to give important data on people's past experiences and attitudes toward school, and opinions on current events of the day.

Feel free to answer exactly the way you feel, for no one you know will ever see the answers. Information obtained will be reported in terms of statistics; the report will read something like this: "Fifty per cent of the young men reported that they were members of elementary school clubs."

Almost all of the questions can be answered by circling one or more numbers or letters beneath the questions. For example:

I am a resident of .... (Circle one.)

Canada 1

United States .... ②

England............... 3

NOTE: After each question there is an instruction in parentheses.

1. If it says "(Circle one)," circle only the one number [or letter] which best describes your answer, even though some of the other answers might also seem true.

2. If it says "(Circle one number [or letter] on each line) please look to see that you have circled one and only one number [or letter] on each of the lines. For example:

	Agree	Disagree
A. There are 12 months in the year.	①	2
B. The sun rises in the North.	4	⑤
C. In the summer, grass is green.	⑦	8

25/X
Please ignore these numbers.

The numbers appearing in the right hand margin of the questionnaire are for office use only.

PLEASE BEGIN THE QUESTIONNAIRE WITH QUESTION 1 BELOW. THANK YOU!

1. What is your date of birth?

_____ _____ _____   17-18/y

(Month)   (Day)   (Year)

2. What is your sex? (Circle one.)   Male 1   20/

    Female 2

---

3. Here are some statements. How much do you agree or disagree with each one? (Circle one number on each line.)

	Agree Strongly	Agree Somewhat	Disagree Somewhat	Disagree Strongly	
A. Only people who believe in God can be good American citizens.	1	2	3	4	20/0
B. The teachings of my church are old-fashioned and superstitious.	6	7	8	9	21/5
C. A family should have as many children as possible and God will provide for them.	1	2	3	4	22/0
D. Negroes would be satisfied if it were not for a few people who stir up trouble.	6	7	8	9	23/5
E. A student should be free to make up his own mind on what he learns in school.	1	2	3	4	24/0
F. Love of neighbor is more important than avoiding meat on Friday.	6	7	8	9	25/5
G. Negroes shouldn't push themselves where they are not wanted.	1	2	3	4	26/0
H. The teachings of my church are too negative and not positive enough.	6	7	8	9	27/5
I. Books written by Communists should not be permitted in public libraries.	1	2	3	4	28/0
J. My religion teaches that a good Christian ought to think about the next life and not worry about fighting against poverty and injustice in this life.	6	7	8	9	29/5
K. Jewish businessmen are about as honest as other businessmen.	1	2	3	4	30/0
L. Working men have the right and duty to join unions.	6	7	8	9	31/5

---

4. Below are some statements about religion. Some people think they are true and some think they are false. (Circle the number on each line that comes closest to your own personal opinion about each statement.)

	Certainly True	Probably True	Probably False	Certainly False	
A. When you come right down to it, there is no definite proof that God exists.	6	7	8	9	32/5
B. God doesn't really care how He is worshiped, so long as He is worshiped.	1	2	3	4	33/0
C. There is a life after death.	6	7	8	9	34/5
D. God will punish the evil person for all eternity.	1	2	3	4	35/0

5. Below is a list of things some people feel are wrong and some people feel are right things to do. (Read each statement, starting with statement A, and circle one number on each line that comes closest to your own _personal_ feelings about each action.)

		Certainly right to do	Probably right to do	Neither right nor wrong	Probably wrong to do	Certainly wrong to do	Depends on why the person does it	
A.	Help another student during an exam.	1	2	3	4	5	6	36/0
B.	Heavy necking on a date.	1	2	3	4	5	6	37/0
C.	Having as little to do with Jews as possible.	1	2	3	4	5	6	38/0
D.	Handing in a school report that is not your own work.	1	2	3	4	5	6	39/0
E.	Joining a protest against a Negro who moved into an all-white neighborhood.	1	2	3	4	5	6	40/0
F.	Marrying someone with a different religion from your own.	1	2	3	4	5	6	41/0
G.	Sex relations with the person you intend to marry.	1	2	3	4	5	6	42/0

6. FOR BOYS: Below is a list of jobs. How would you feel if you had such a job?

   FOR GIRLS: Below is a list of jobs. How would you feel if your future husband had such a job?

   ALL: Circle one number on each line that best describes how you would feel —whether very pleased, somewhat pleased, somewhat disappointed, or very disappointed.

		Very Pleased	Somewhat Pleased	Somewhat Disappointed	Very Disappointed	
A.	Business executive.	0	1	2	3	43/y
B.	High school teacher.	6	7	8	9	44/4
C.	Priest.	0	1	2	3	45/y
D.	Bank teller.	6	7	8	9	46/4
E.	Author.	0	1	2	3	47/y
F.	Carpenter.	6	7	8	9	48/4
G.	Stock broker.	0	1	2	3	49/y
H.	Furniture mover.	6	7	8	9	50/4

7. Would you prefer a job where you are <u>part of a team</u>, all working together, even if you don't get personal recognition for your work, or a
job where you <u>worked alone</u> and others could see what you have
done? (Circle one choice.)

Part of a team with no personal recognition 7   <u>51</u>/6

Work alone with personal recognition 8

Can't decide 9

8. Some people say that hard work is more important for getting ahead
than having a nice personality and being well-liked. Other people
say that having a nice personality and being well-liked are more
important for getting ahead than hard work. Would you say <u>hard work</u>
or a <u>nice personality</u> is more important? (Circle one choice.)

Hard work X   <u>52</u>/y

Nice personality . . 1

Can't decide 0

9. Are you presently in high school?

Yes, I'm a freshman (1st year) 1   <u>53</u>/9

Yes, I'm a sophomore (2nd year) 2

Yes, I'm a junior (3rd year) 3

Yes, I'm a senior (4th year) 4

No, I have not yet begun 5

No, I left school without graduating 6

No, I have graduated 7

No, I have graduated and am in college 8

<u>IF YOU HAVE NOT YET BEEN TO HIGH SCHOOL: SKIP TO QUES-
TION 36 AND GO ON FROM THERE.</u>

<u>IF YOU ARE IN HIGH SCHOOL NOW: CONTINUE BELOW.</u>

<u>IF YOU HAVE BEEN TO HIGH SCHOOL: ANSWER QUESTIONS 10
THROUGH 35 AS YOU WOULD HAVE IN YOUR LAST YEAR OF HIGH
SCHOOL.</u>

10. A. <u>BOYS ONLY:</u>
If you could be remembered here at school for one of the following, which would you want it to be? (Circle one choice.)

An "A" student 6   <u>54</u>/R

Star athlete 7

Most popular 8

A leader in clubs and activities 9

B. <u>GIRLS ONLY:</u>
If you could be remembered here at school for one of the following, which would you want it to be? (Circle one choice.)

An "A" student 1   <u>55</u>/R

Cheer leader 2

Most popular 3

A leader in clubs and activities 4

11. How much time on the average do you spend doing homework outside of school? (Circle one choice.)

None or almost none	3	_56/2_
Less than one-half hour a day........	4	
About one-half hour a day	5	
About one hour a day	6	
About one and one-half hours a day ...	7	
About two hours a day	8	
Three or more hours a day	9	

12. If you feel that you were treated unfairly in some way by a teacher,
do you—(Circle one choice.)

feel free to talk to the teacher about it?	X	_57/y_
feel a bit uneasy about talking to the teacher?	0	
feel it would be better not to talk to the teacher? ...	1	

13. What if you disagree with something the teacher said. Do you—
(Circle one choice.)

feel free to disagree with the teacher in class?.....	7	_58/6_
feel uneasy about disagreeing in class?	8	
feel it would be better not to disagree in class?	9	

14. Do you ever remember disagreeing in class with what one of your
high school teachers said? (Circle one choice.)

Yes, often.............	1	59/0
Yes, occasionally	2	
Yes, once or twice	3	
Never.................	4	

15. Do your teachers treat everyone equally, or are some students
treated better than others in school? (Circle one choice.)

Some students receive much better treatment than others .	6	60/5
Some students receive somewhat better treatment than others	7	
Some students receive a little better treatment than others	8	
Everyone is always treated equally....................	9	

16. Thinking of all of the teachers you have this year, what words
below best describe most of them? (Circle as many numbers as
apply in each group.)

Interested in the subject 1	61/R	Interested in books...... 1	62/R
Stern 2		Narrow-minded.......... 2	
Devout............... 3		Intelligent 3	
Nervous.............. 4		Patient 4	
Fair 5		Unhappy 5	
Hard to please 6		Knows the score 6	
Self-controlled 7		Easy to talk to 7	
Interested in students.. 8		Quick-tempered 8	

17. Teachers sometimes like certain kinds of students. Here is a list
(Circle all the numbers which describe the kinds of <u>students</u> you
think your teachers like best.)

Quiet .... 1 <u>63</u>/R   Asks questions .... 1 <u>64</u>/R

Thinks for himself...... 2   Polite 2

Obedient 3   Interested in ideas 3

Quick to memorize...... 4   Voices his own opinions 4

Neatly dressed......... 5   Active on teams or clubs 5

Likes to work on his own 6   Interested in books 6

---

18. Is your high school co-educational or not? (Circle one choice.)

All male only .... 1 <u>65</u>/0

All female only 2

Co-educational, boys and girls attend the same classes 3

Co-educational, but boys and girls <u>rarely</u> or never
attend the same classes 4

---

19. Which of the items below fit most of the <u>boys</u> in your high school?
(Circle as many as apply.) (If you attend an all-girls' school, skip
this question.)

Friendly............... 0   Cheat on some exams ... 5 <u>66</u>/R

Girl-crazy 1   Sports-minded.......... 6

Studious 2   Active around the school 7

Out for a good time 3   Hard to get to know..... 8

Religious 4   Uninterested in school .. 9

---

20. Which of the items below fit most of the <u>girls</u> in your high school?
(Circle as many as apply.) (If you attend an all-boys' school, skip
this question.)

Think for themselves.... 0   Boy-crazy .... 5 <u>67</u>/R

Friendly............... 1   Studious 6

Hard to get to know..... 2   Out for a good time 7

Mad about clothes 3   Snobbish to girls outside their group 8

Active around school ... 4   Cheat on some exams ... 9

---

21. Suppose the circle below represented the life at your school. The
center of the circle represents the center of things in school. How
far out from the center of things are you? (Underline the number
which you think represents where you are.)

<u>68</u>/X

22. Which is more important to you—activities or friends associated with school, or activities and friends in the neighborhood, or somebody else not related to school? (Circle one.)

Groups, activities or friends related to school 3   10/2

Groups, activities or friends not related to school ... 4

23. How active would you say you have been in school activities? (Circle one.)

Very active 6   11/5

Pretty active 7

Not too active 8

Not active at all 9

24. Thinking of the teachers you now have in class, how good do you think they are in getting ideas across and gaining the students' interest? (Circle one choice.)

Very good X   12/y

Somewhat good 0

Good 1

Not too good 2

Not good at all 3

25. How often were you unprepared for class because you didn't study enough before it, or skipped doing your homework? (Circle one choice.)

Very often 5   13/4

Sometimes 6

Once or twice 7

Never 8

26. How often have you used crib notes, copied, or helped someone else out during an exam? (Circle one choice.)

On all or almost all exams.. X   14/y

Very often 0

Often 1

More than once or twice.... 2

Once or twice 3

Never 4

27. Which items below apply to your best friends who attend the same school as you do and are of your own sex? (Circle as many numbers as apply in each group.)

Quiet 1 15/R	Interested in ideas .....1·16/R
Out for a good time 2	Date a lot 2
Active around school ...3	Plan to go to college ...3
Religious 4	Interested in cars 4
Think for themselves ...5	Intellectual............5
Uninterested in school..6	Sports-minded..........6
Studious 7	BOYS ONLY: Girl-crazy. 7
Same religion as	GIRLS ONLY: Mad about
I am 8	clothes 8

28. What is the total number of students in the student body of your high school (or the one you graduated from)? (Circle one choice.)

Less than 200 ....1 17/0
200 to 500.............2
500 to 800.............3
800 to 1,500 4
1,500 to 3,000 5
3,000 or more 6

29. Different schools use different marking systems. Circle below the one number that indicates your general average through high school so far.

100 — 90% (Superior).......3   18/2
90 — 86% (Excellent)......4
85 — 81% (Good)..........5
80 — 76% (Fair) 6
75 — 71% (Average) 7
70 — 65% (Passing) 8
65 or less (Unsatisfactory) . 9

30. Did you ever attend any other high school besides the one you presently attend? (Circle one choice.)

No, this is the only high school I ever attended ....X 19/y
Yes, and I only attended public high schools..........0
Yes, and I attended church-related high schools.......1
Yes, and I attended both public and church-related
high schools 2

31. What is the name of the high school you presently attend?

20-21/

32. Is your high school a public, religious, or private high school? (Circle one choice.)

Public high school 0   22/X
Private (Catholic) high school 1
Private (other religious) high school .. 2
Private (non-religious) high school ... 3

33. Are you getting any formal religious training from your church while you are in high school (or were you a member of a high school religious club)? (Circle all the numbers which apply.)

Yes, I attend formal religious education classes....... 6   23/R

Yes, I am a member of a religious club in school 7

No, I am not a member of either a religious club or class 8

No, I am not a member of either a religious club or
class and neither is available 9

34. What proportion of the teachers in your high school are from the same religion as you are? (Circle one choice.)

All or almost all...... y   24/R

Over half X

About half 0

Less than half 1

Few or none 2

35. How well do you know the teachers at school who are from your own religious background? (Circle one choice.)

I know some very well 4   25/R

I know one or two very well... 5

I know them a little.......... 6

I don't know any very well.... 7

I don't know any at all 8

There are none............... 9

EVERYONE ANSWER THE FOLLOWING QUESTIONS:

36. Thinking of your last elementary school teacher, what items best describe him or her? (Circle all the choices that apply.)

Fair .... 1 26/R   Narrow-minded 1 27/R
Hard worker 2   Intelligent 2
Nervous 3   Patient 3
Treated me as an adult .. 4   Unrealistic 4
Devout 5   Let me do things on my own 5
Hard to please 6   Quick-tempered 6
Self-controlled 7   Easy to talk to 7
Stern 8   Unhappy 8

37. Teachers have different ways of keeping students in order. How often, if at all, did your elementary school teacher do the following things when displeased by a student?
(Circle one number on each line.)

	Often	Some-times	Once in a while	Never	
A. Waited until the student stopped what he was doing.	1	2	3	4	28/0
B. Lost his or her temper.	6	7	8	9	29/5
C. Ridiculed or made fun of the student.	1	2	3	4	30/0
D. Put him in a special place or gave him something silly to do or wear.	6	7	8	9	31/5
E. Gave him extra work to do.	1	2	3	4	32/0
F. Kept him after school.	6	7	8	9	33/5
G. Sent for the student's parent.	1	2	3	4	34/0

38. Teachers sometimes like certain kinds of students more than others. (Circle all the items that apply to the kinds of students your last elementary school teacher liked best.)

Quiet .... X 35/R   Likes to work on his own 5 36/R
Obedient 0   Polite 6
Quick to memorize 1   Thinks for himself 7
Interested in books 2   Active on teams or clubs 8
Neatly dressed 3   Voices his own opinions 9

39. What kind of elementary school did you attend? (Circle one choice.)

I only attended public school(s) 6 37/5
I only attended religious schools 7
I attended public and religious schools, but spent my 8th grade in public school 8
I attended public and religious schools but spent my 8th grade in a religious school 9

IF YOU ATTENDED PUBLIC ELEMENTARY SCHOOL AT ANY TIME: ANSWER QUESTION 40; IF NOT, SKIP QUESTION 40.

40. Did you regularly attend religious instruction classes?

Yes .... X 38/R

No, although some were available ... 0

No, none was available 1

---

41. About how many evenings a week do you spend at home? (Circle the total number.)

0   1   2   3   4   5   6   7   39/X

---

42. How much time do you spend outside of school with one or more members of the opposite sex, but not on a regular date?

None, or almost no time ... X 40/y

About an hour a day. 0

About two hours a day 1

About three hours a day ... 2

More than three hrs. a day . 3

---

43. Do you date?

No 3 41/3

Yes, very irregularly. 4

Yes, about once a month 5

Yes, once every two or three weeks 6

Yes, about once a week 7

Yes, about twice a week or more 8

---

44. Do you go steady or not?

Yes, I go steady. ...... X 42/y

No, I don't go steady... 0

---

45. Suppose you had a problem and you knew that however you solved it, someone would be disappointed in you. Which would be hardest for you to take? (Put a 1 next to the kind of disapproval you would find hardest to take, a 2 for the next hardest, a 3 for the third hardest, and a 4 for the least difficult one to take.)

A. Parents' disapproval __   43/0

B. Disapproval of a favorite priest or minister __   44/0

C. A closest friend's disapproval __   45/0

D. A favorite teacher's disapproval __   46/0

---

46. Below is a list of items on which some parents have rules for their teen-age children, while others do not. (Circle the number after each situation that your parents have definite rules for.)

Against use of the family car 0 48/X

Time for being in at night on weekends 1

Amount of dating 2

Against going steady 3

Time spent watching TV. 4

Time spent on home work..................... 5

Against going out with certain boys............. 6

Against going out with certain girls............. 7

Against dating someone of a different religion.... 8

No rules for any of the above items 9

47. Below is a list of items. (Circle the number next to the items which best describe what your father is like. Circle all that apply.)

Treats me as an adult.. 4 49/R   Knows the score 1 50/R

Fair 5   Hard to please 2

Patient 6   Self-controlled 3

Intelligent 7   Easy to talk to........ 4

                       Quick-tempered 5

Stern 8   Lets me work things

Head of the house 9   out myself 6

48. Below is a list of items. (Circle only those which are most true of you as a person. Most people choose three or four items, but you can choose more or fewer if you want to.)

Quiet .... 1 51/R   Ambitious 1 52/R

Out for a good time 2   Interested in ideas 2

Unhappy 3   Interested in cars 3

Active around school .. 4   Rebellious 4

Religious 5   Plan to go to college .. 5

Think for myself 6   Sports-minded......... 6

Uninterested in school . 7   Intellectual........... 7

49. What proportion of your friends are Protestant? Catholic? Jewish? (Circle one choice on each line.)

	All	Almost All	Most	About Half	Less Than Half	Very Few	None	
Protestant.	1	2	3	4	5	6	7	53/0
Catholic.	1	2	3	4	5	6	7	54/0
Jewish.	1	2	3	4	5	6	7	55/0

50. How close do you feel toward your church or religion—very close, pretty close, not too close, or not at all close? (Circle one.)

Very close 0 56/X

Pretty close 1

Not too close 2

Not at all close .. 3

51. What is your religious preference? (Circle one.)

Protestant (Denomination)_____ 5 57 4

Catholic 6

Jewish.................................... 7

Other (What?)_____ 8

None 9

IF YOU ARE CATHOLIC: ANSWER QUESTIONS 52 AND 53.

IF YOU ARE NON-CATHOLIC: SKIP TO QUESTION 54.

52. Below is a list of religious practices. (Circle one number on each line to indicate how often, if at all, you do these various things.)

	About once a year or less?	A few times a year?	About once a month?	2 or 3 times a month?	Every week?	More than once a week?	
A. Do you attend Mass ...	1	2	3	4	5	6	<u>58</u>/0
B. Do you receive Holy Communion ...	1	2	3	4	5	6	<u>59</u>/0
C. Do you go to Confession ...	1	2	3	4	5	6	<u>60</u>/0
D. Do you pray ...	1	2	3	4	5	6	<u>61</u>/0
E. Do you talk to a priest, brother or nun about things that bother you ...	1	2	3	4	5	6	<u>62</u>/0
F. Do you attend Church-(parish) sponsored meetings or activities (other than religious instruction) ...	1	2	3	4	5	6	<u>63</u>/0

53. Here is a short quiz which touches on practices and beliefs of the Catholic Church. You are not expected to get them all correct—some you may find rather difficult.

Please circle the number after the answer which comes closest to being correct, in your opinion.

A. The word we use to describe the fact that the Second Person of the Trinity became man is ..:
- Transfiguration .... 1 <u>64</u>/0
- Incarnation 2
- Transubstantiation 3
- Immaculate Conception. 4

B. Supernatural life is ...
- the life we receive from our parents. 6 <u>65</u>/5
- sanctifying grace in our souls...... 7
- our life after death 8
- the power to work miracles 9

C. The "mystical body" is ...
- Christ's body in heaven .... 1 <u>66</u>/0
- Christ in Holy Communion 2
- Christ united with His followers.... 3
- None of the above 4

D. Uncharitable talk is forbidden by ...
- the second commandment .... 6 <u>67</u>/5
- the fourth commandment 7
- the eighth commandment 8
- the tenth commandment........... 9

E. A man is judged immediately after he dies. This judgment is called ...
- general judgment .... 1 <u>68</u>/0
- natural judgment 2
- particular judgment 3
- final judgment 4

F. The Encyclicals "Rerum Novarum" of Leo XIII and "Quadragesimo anno" of Pius XI both deal with ...
- Christian marriage............... 6 69/5
- Christian education.............. 7
- the condition of labor 8
- Papal infallibility 9

IF YOU ARE NON-CATHOLIC, PLEASE ANSWER QUESTION 54.

54. Below is a list of religious practices. (Circle the number that indicates how often you do the various things listed.)

		About once a year or less	A few times a year	About once a month	2 or 3 times a month	Every week	More than once a week	
A.	Go to Church services.	1	2	3	4	5	6	70/0
B.	How often do you pray?	1	2	3	4	5	6	71/0
C.	How often do you say grace before meals, or morning or evening prayers?	1	2	3	4	5	6	72/0
D.	How often do you talk to your minister or rabbi about things that are bothering you?	1	2	3	4	5	6	73/0
E.	How often do you attend a Church sponsored group, meeting, or activity?	1	2	3	4	5	6	74/0

THANK YOU FOR YOUR COOPERATION!

Appendix III

QUESTIONNAIRES
FROM 1974 NORC STUDY,
ADULT AND ADOLESCENT

Appendix III

CONFIDENTIAL

Survey 4172
Feb., 1974

NATIONAL OPINION RESEARCH CENTER
University of Chicago

BEGIN DECK 01

EDUCATION AND VALUES IN AMERICA

CASE #: ☐☐☐☐☐   01-05/ | 0 | 06/

PSU #: ☐☐☐   07-09/   OFFICE USE

SEGMENT #: ☐☐☐   10-12/

PART: ☐   13/

LINE: ☐☐☐☐   14-17/

INTRODUCTORY STATEMENT:

My name is _____ from the National Opinion Research
Center. We're conducting a national survey of people's values
and their attitudes toward different kinds of schools. I'm
here to interview _____
                                     (NAME)
Is (he/she) at home?

| TIME | | AM |
| BEGAN | | PM |

DECK 01

First, we need to get some background information, so I will begin by asking you a little about yourself.

1. First of all, in what country were you born?

COUNTRY: _____   18-19/

   A. **ASK IF BORN OUTSIDE U.S.**: How old were you when you came to this country?

AGE: ⬚⬚   20-21/99

_____

2. In what year were you born?

YEAR: ⬚⬚⬚⬚   22-25/

_____

Now these are a few questions about your family background.

3. In what state or foreign country was your father born?

STATE OR FOREIGN COUNTRY: _____   26-27/99

Don't know 98

_____

4. In what state or foreign country was your mother born?

STATE OR FOREIGN COUNTRY: _____   28-29/99

Don't know 98

_____

5. How many of your grandparents were born in this country?

None 1   30/9

One 2

Two 3

Three 4

Four 5

Don't know 8

6. A. Think of your father's side of the family. Before settling in the United
   States, which <u>one</u> country did <u>most</u> of your father's family come from?
   <u>IF R NAMES MORE THAN ONE COUNTRY</u>: Which <u>one</u> of the countries that you
   just mentioned did <u>most</u> of his family come from?

   IF SINGLE COUNTRY IS NAMED, REFER TO NATIONAL
   CODES BELOW, AND ENTER CODE NUMBER IN BOXES.   } . . . [|]   31-32/99

   IF MORE THAN ONE COUNTRY IS NAMED, ENTER CODE 88.

   B. Now, think of your mother's side of the family. Before settling in the United
   States, which <u>one</u> country did most of your mother's family come from?
   <u>IF R NAMES MORE THAN ONE COUNTRY</u>: Which <u>one</u> of the countries that you
   just mentioned did <u>most</u> of her family come from?

   IF SINGLE COUNTRY IS NAMED, REFER TO NATIONAL
   CODES BELOW, AND ENTER CODE NUMBER IN BOXES.   } . . . [|]   33-34/99

   IF MORE THAN ONE COUNTRY IS NAMED, ENTER CODE 88.

   C. <u>ASK IF MOTHER'S AND FATHER'S FAMILIES COME FROM DIFFERENT COUNTRIES.</u>
   <u>OTHERWISE, GO TO Q. 7.</u>
   Which <u>one</u> of these nationalities do you feel closer to?

   REFER TO NATIONAL CODES BELOW, AND ENTER CODE
   NUMBER IN BOXES.   } . . . [|]   35-36/99

   IF R CAN'T DECIDE ON ONE COUNTRY, ENTER 88:

NATIONAL CODES

Africa	01	Italy	12
Austria	02	Lithuania	13
Canada (French)	03	Mexico	14
Canada (Other)	04	Philippines	15
Cuba	05	Poland	16
Czechoslovakia, Albania, Bulgaria, Roumania, Hungary, Yugoslavia	06	Puerto Rico	17
		Russia (USSR)	18
England, Wales, Scotland	07	Spain/Portugal	19
France	08	West Indies	20
Germany	09	Other (SPECIFY)	21
Greece	10		
Ireland	11	More than one country/ can't decide on one.	88
		Don't know	98

---

7. Are you currently married, widowed, divorced, separated, or have you never
    been married?

                                    Married 1   37/9
                                    Widowed . . . (SKIP TO Q. 10) . . 2
                                    Divorced . . . (SKIP TO Q. 10) . . 3
                                    Separated . . (SKIP TO Q. 10) . . 4
                                    Never married (SKIP TO Q. 10) . . 5

8. In what year were you and your (husband/wife) married?

                                                YEAR: [   ][   ]   38-39/99

                                        Don't know . . 98

9. A. Now think about your (husband/wife)'s side of the family. Before settling
        in the United States, which one country did most of (his/her) family come
        from, on (his/her) father's side?

        IF SINGLE COUNTRY IS NAMED, REFER TO NATIONAL
        CODES BELOW, AND ENTER CODE NUMBER IN BOXES.   } . . [   ][   ]   40-41/99
        IF MORE THAN ONE COUNTRY IS NAMED, ENTER CODE 88.

    B. Before settling in the United States, which one country did most of your
        (husband/wife)'s family come from on (his/her) mother's side?

        IF SINGLE COUNTRY IS NAMED, REFER TO NATIONAL
        CODES BELOW, AND ENTER CODE NUMBER IN BOXES.   } . . [   ][   ]   42-43/99
        IF MORE THAN ONE COUNTRY IS NAMED, ENTER CODE 88.

NATIONAL CODES

Africa	01	Italy	12
Austria	02	Lithuania	13
Canada (French)	03	Mexico	14
Canada (Other)	04	Philippines	15
Cuba	05	Poland	16
Czechoslovakia, Albania,		Puerto Rico	17
Bulgaria, Roumania,		Russia (USSR)	18
Hungary, Yugoslavia . .	06		
England, Wales, Scotland.	07	Spain/Portugal . . .	19
France	08	West Indies	20
Germany	09	Other (SPECIFY) . . .	21
Greece	10		
Ireland	11	More than one country/	
		can't decide on one.	88
		Don't know	98

10. For most of the years you were growing up, that is, up to the time you were
16 years old, did you live with <u>both</u> your own mother and your own father?

                                        Yes . . (GO TO Q. 11) . . 1   44/9

                                        No . . . . (ASK A) 2

    A. IF NO:

> HAND
> CARD
> 1

Which person or persons on this card best describes who you lived with
for most of your first 16 years?

                    Mother and stepfather 1   45/9

                    Father and stepmother 2

                    Mother only . . . . 3 ⎤

                    Father only . . . . 4 │ SKIP TO
                                                             │ INTERVIEWER
                    Other relative(s) (SPECIFY) _____ ⎬ INSTRUCTIONS
                                                             │ AFTER Q. 11.
                    _____ 5 │

                    Other person(s) (SPECIFY) _____

                    _____ 6 ⎦

11. Everything considered, how happy would you say your parents' marriage was while
you were growing up? Would you say it was extremely happy, happier than average, average, or not too happy?

                            Extremely happy 1   46/9

                            Happier than average . . . 2

                            Average 3

                            Not too happy 4

                            Don't know 8

INTERVIEWER INSTRUCTIONS:

> IF R DID NOT LIVE WITH OWN MOTHER AND OWN FATHER, ASK ALL SUBSEQUENT
> QUESTIONS REFERRING TO MOTHER AND FATHER ABOUT THE PERSON(S) NAMED IN
> Q. 10A.
>
> IF NO MOTHER OR MOTHER SUBSTITUTE, DO NOT ASK QUESTIONS REFERRING TO MOTHER.
>
> IF NO FATHER OR FATHER SUBSTITUTE, DO NOT ASK QUESTIONS REFERRING TO FATHER.

12. On the whole, how happy would you say your childhood was--extremely happy,
happier than average, average, or not too happy?

                            Extremely happy 1   47/9

                            Happier than average . . . 2

                            Average 3

                            Not too happy 4

                            Don't know 8

DECK 01

13. What is your present religion?

Catholic . . . . . (ASK A) 1   48/9

Protestant . . . . (ASK B) 2

Jewish . . . . . . (ASK B) 3

Other . . . (SPECIFY AND ASK B) . . 4

None . . . . . . (ASK B) 5

A. IF CATHOLIC:

Were you raised a Catholic?

Yes . . (GO TO Q. 14) . . 1   49/9

No . . (ASK [1] & [2]) . . 2

IF NO TO A:

[1] In what religion were you raised?

Protestant (SPECIFY DENOMINATION)   50/9

_____ 1

Jewish 2

Other (SPECIFY) _____ 3

No religion 4

[2] How old were you when you became a Catholic?

AGE: [   ] (GO TO Q. 14)   51-52/99

B. IF NOT CATHOLIC:

In what religion were you raised?

Catholic . . . . (ASK [1]) 1   53/9

Protestant . . . . 2 ⎤ READ SENTENCE

Jewish . . . . 3 ⎬ AT BOTTOM OF

Other . . . . 4 ⎰ PAGE TO R AND

None . . . . 5 ⎦ END INTERVIEW.

[1] IF RAISED CATHOLIC:

At what age did you leave the Church?

AGE: [   ] (GO TO Q. 14)   54-55/99

IF R NOT CATHOLIC NOW AND NOT RAISED CATHOLIC, END INTERVIEW AND READ:

"Since this interview deals primarily with Catholics' views on schools, we only need to interview people who are Catholic or who were raised Catholic. Thank you very much for your help."

IF R HAD NO FATHER OR FATHER SUBSTITUTE WHILE GROWING UP, SKIP TO Q. 21.

14. Now I'd like to ask you a few questions about your father. Thinking back to the
     time when you were growing up, that is, up to the time you were 16, what was
     your father's religion?

                              Catholic 1   56/9

                              Protestant . . . . 2 ⎤

                              Jewish . . . . 3 ⎥

                              Other (SPECIFY) _____   ⎥ SKIP TO
                                                                    ⎬ Q. 16
                              _____ 4 ⎥

                              None . . . . 5 ⎥

                              Don't know . . . . 8 ⎦

15. ASK IF FATHER CATHOLIC:

When you were growing up:	More than once a week	Once a week	2-3 times a month	Once a month	Couple times a year	Almost never	Don't know	
A. About how often did your father attend Mass? (READ CATEGORIES)	1	2	3	4	5	6	8	57/9
B. About how often did your father receive Communion? (READ CATEGORIES)	1	2	3	4	5	6	8	58/9

16. When you were growing up, how would you describe your father's personal
     approach to religion--was it very joyous, somewhat joyous, not at all joyous,
     or was he not religious?

                              Very joyous 1   59/9

                              Somewhat joyous 2

                              Not at all joyous . . . 3

                              Not religious   4

                              Don't know 8

17. What was the highest year or grade in school that your father completed?

No schooling . . . . (GO TO Q. 18) . . 01	60-61/99
6th grade or less . . . (ASK A) . . . 02	
7th or 8th grade . . . (ASK A) . . . 03	
Some high school . . .(ASK A & B) . . 04	
High school graduate .(ASK A & B) . . 05	
Some college . . . (ASK A, B & C) . . 06	
College graduate . (ASK A, B & C) . . 07	
Post-graduate . . . (ASK A, B & C) . . 08	
Don't know . . . . . (GO TO Q. 18) . . 09	

A. IF FATHER ATTENDED ELEMENTARY SCHOOL:

What kind of elementary school did he go to--Catholic, non-Catholic, or both?

Catholic 1	62/9
Non-Catholic 2	
Both 3	
Don't know 8	

B. IF FATHER ATTENDED HIGH SCHOOL:

What kind of high school did he go to--Catholic, non-Catholic, or both?

Catholic 1	63/9
Non-Catholic 2	
Both 3	
Don't know 8	

C. IF FATHER ATTENDED COLLEGE:

What kind of college did he go to--Catholic, non-Catholic, or both?

Catholic 1	64/9
Non-Catholic 2	
Both 3	
Don't know 8	

BEGIN DECK 02

18. A. What kind of work did your father usually do during the time you were
         growing up? That is, what was his job called?

               OCCUPATION: _____

                          Father did not work . (GO TO Q. 19) . 997   07-09/999
                          Don't know . . . . . (ASK B) 998

     B. What were some of his most important activities or duties?   10-11/99

---

19. When you were growing up, how close were you and your father? Would you say you
     were very close to each other, somewhat close, not very close, or not close at all?

                                 Very close 1   12/9
                                 Somewhat close 2
                                 Not very close 3
                                 Not close at all 4
                                 Don't know 8

---

20. Here is a list of characteristics that are sometimes used to describe people.
     I'd like you to select the three characteristics that come closest to describing
     what your father was like during the years you were growing up.

     HAND
     CARD
     2

     A. First, tell me the one characteristic on the card that comes closest
         to describing your father. CIRCLE ONE IN COLUMN A.

     B. Now, tell me the second closest characteristic. CIRCLE ONE IN COLUMN B.

     C. And now, the third closest. CIRCLE ONE IN COLUMN C.

	A. FIRST CHOICE	B. SECOND CHOICE	C. THIRD CHOICE
1) Competitive	01 13-14/99	01 15-16/99	01 17-18/99
2) Warm and loving	02	02	02
3) Dissatisfied	03	03	03
4) Decisive and firm	04	04	04
5) Sensitive to others' needs . .	05	05	05
6) Reserved	06	06	06
7) Personally ambitious	07	07	07
8) Satisfied	08	08	08
9) Don't know	09	09	09

IF R HAD NO MOTHER OR MOTHER SUBSTITUTE WHILE GROWING UP, SKIP TO Q. 28A.

21. Now I'd like to ask you a few questions about your mother. Again, thinking
     back to the time you were growing up, what was your mother's religion?

Catholic 1	19/9
Protestant 2	
Jewish 3	
Other (SPECIFY) _____	SKIP TO
_____ 4	Q. 23.
None 5	
Don't know 8	

22. ASK IF MOTHER CATHOLIC:

When you were growing up:

	More than once a week	Once a week	2-3 times a month	Once a month	Couple times a year	Almost never	Don't know	
A. About how often did your mother attend Mass? (READ CATEGORIES)	1	2	3	4	5	6	8	20/9
B. About how often did your mother receive Communion? (READ CATEGORIES)	1	2	3	4	5	6	8	21/9

23. When you were growing up, how would you describe your mother's personal
     approach to religion--was it very joyous, somewhat joyous, not at all joyous,
     or was she not religious?

Very joyous 1	22/9
Somewhat joyous 2	
Not at all joyous . . . 3	
Not religious 4	
Don't know 8	

24. What was the highest year or grade in school that your mother completed?

No schooling . . .	(GO TO Q. 25) . .	01	23-24/99
6th grade or less . . .	(ASK A) . . .	02	
7th or 8th grade . . .	(ASK A) . . .	03	
Some high school . . .	(ASK A & B) . .	04	
High school graduate .	(ASK A & B) . .	05	
Some college . . .	(ASK A, B & C) . .	06	
College graduate .	(ASK A, B & C) . .	07	
Post-graduate . . .	(ASK A, B & C) . .	08	
Don't know	(GO TO Q. 25) . .	09	

A. IF MOTHER ATTENDED ELEMENTARY SCHOOL:

What kind of elementary school did she go to--Catholic, non-Catholic,
or both?

Catholic	1	25/9
Non-Catholic	2	
Both	3	
Don't know	8	

B. IF MOTHER ATTENDED HIGH SCHOOL:

What kind of high school did she go to--Catholic, non-Catholic, or both?

Catholic	1	26/9
Non-Catholic	2	
Both	3	
Don't know	8	

C. IF MOTHER ATTENDED COLLEGE:

What kind of college did she go to--Catholic, non-Catholic, or both?

Catholic	1	27/9
Non-Catholic	2	
Both	3	
Don't know	8	

25. Did your mother ever work for pay for as long as a year during the following
periods of your life:

		Yes	No	Don't know	
A.	After you were born, but before you started first grade?	1	2	8	28/9
B.	When you were in grades 1 through 4?	1	2	8	29/9
C.	When you were in grades 5 through 8?	1	2	8	30/9
D.	When you were of high school age?	1	2	8	31/9

26. ASK IF YES TO ANY PART OF Q. 25.

A. What kind of work did your mother usually do while you were growing up?
That is, what was her job called?

OCCUPATION: _____

Don't know . (ASK B) . . 998   32-34/999

B. What were some of her most important activities and duties?

35-36/999

27. Now I'll give you again this list of characteristics that are sometimes used to
describe people. I'd like you to select the three characteristics that come
closest to describing what your mother was like during the years you were growing
up.

HAND
CARD
2

A. First, tell me the one characteristic on the card that comes closest
to describing your mother. CIRCLE ONE IN COLUMN A.

B. Now, tell me the second closest characteristic. CIRCLE ONE IN COLUMN B.

C. And now, the third closest. CIRCLE ONE IN COLUMN C.

	A. FIRST CHOICE	B. SECOND CHOICE	C. THIRD CHOICE
1) Competitive	01 37-38/99	01 39-40/99	01 41-42/99
2) Warm and loving	02	02	02
3) Dissatisfied	03	03	03
4) Decisive and firm	04	04	04
5) Sensitive to others' needs . .	05	05	05
6) Reserved	06	06	06
7) Personally ambitious	07	07	07
8) Satisfied	08	08	08
9) Don't know	09	09	09

28. When you were growing up, how close were you and your mother? Would you say you were very close to each other, somewhat close, not very close, or not close at all?

Very close	1	43/9
Somewhat close	2	
Not very close	3	
Not close at all	4	
Don't know	8	

28-A. <u>ASK IF R GREW UP WITH BOTH MOTHER AND FATHER.</u>

When you were growing up, how close were your mother and father to each other? Would you say they were very close to each other, somewhat close, not very close or not close at all?

Very close	1	44/9
Somewhat close	2	
Not very close	3	
Not close at all	4	
Don't know	8	

<u>ASK EVERYONE</u>:

29. Think of the neighborhood in which you lived longest while you were growing up. how many of your neighbors were Catholics--more than half, about half, less than half, or none?

More than half . . .	1	45/9
About half	2	
Less than half . . .	3	
None	4	
Don't know	8	

---

30. Are you still living in the neighborhood where you grew up, or close to it?

Yes, <u>in</u> the neighborhood	1	46/9
Yes, close to the neighborhood . .	2	
No . . . . . . (ASK A)	3	

A. <u>IF NO</u>: Are you still living in the city or town where you lived the longest when you were growing up?

Yes	1	47/9
No	2	

31. Think of the neighborhood in which you live now. Do you feel it is a very
     good neighborhood to live in, or about average, or not such a good neighborhood
     to live in?

                              Very good neighborhood 1   48/9

                              About average 2

                              Not such a good neighborhood . 3

                              Don't know 8

32. How many of your neighbors here in this neighborhood are Catholics--would you
     say almost all, more than half, about half, less than half, or almost none?

                              Almost all 1   49/9

                              More than half 2

                              About half . . . .'. 3

                              Less than half 4

                              Almost none 5

                              Don't know 8

33. How many of your neighbors here come from the same nationality background as
     you--more than half, about half, less than half, or none?

                              More than half 1   50/9

                              About half 2

                              Less than half 3

                              None 4

                              Don't know 8

IF R IS BLACK, SKIP TO Q. 35.

34. Are there any black people living in this neighborhood now?

                              Yes 1   51/9

                              No   2

                              Don't know 8

35. I am going to read some statements about which people have different opinions. I'd like you to tell me for each whether you agree strongly, agree somewhat, disagree somewhat, or disagree strongly.

		Agree strongly	Agree somewhat	Disagree somewhat	Disagree strongly	Don't know	
A.	Even people who won't work should be helped if they really need it.	1	2	3	4	8	52/9
B.	The world is basically a dangerous place where there is much evil and sin.	1	2	3	4	8	53/9
C.	Jewish businessmen are about as honest as other business-men.	1	2	3	4	8	54/9
D.	The Catholic Church teaches that a good Christian ought to think about the next life and not worry about fighting against poverty and injustice in this life.	1	2	3	4	8	55/9
E.	Husband and wife may have sexual intercourse for pleasure alone.	1	2	3	4	8	56/9
F.	There is basic opposition between the discoveries of modern science and the teach-ings of the Church.	1	2	3	4	8	57/9
G.	The government is responsible for preventing widespread unemployment.	1	2	3	4	8	58/9
H.	Jews have too much power in the United States.	1	2	3	4	8	59/9

IF R IS BLACK, SKIP TO Q. 36.

I.	Blacks shouldn't push them-selves where they're not wanted.	1	2	3	4	8	60/9
J.	White people have a right to live in an all-white neighbor-hood if they want to, and blacks should respect that right.	1	2	3	4	8	61/9

DECK 02

36. Now, a different question. Please tell me whether or not you it should be possible for a pregnant woman to obtain a <u>legal</u> abortion . . . READ EACH STATEMENT, AND CIRCLE ONE CODE FOR EACH.

	Yes	No	Don't know	
A. If there is a strong chance of serious defect in the baby?	1	2	8	62/9
B. If she is married and does not want any more children?	1	2	8	63/9

37. We are also interested in what Americans think about religious matters. Please select the answer from this card that comes closest to your own personal opinion about each of the following statements. First . . .

HAND CARD 3

	Certainly true	Probably true	I am uncertain whether this is true or false	Probably false	Certainly false	
A. There is no definite proof that God exists.	1	2	3	4	5	64/9
B. God will punish the evil for all eternity.	1	2	3	4	5	65/9
C. Jesus directly handed over the leadership of His Church to Peter and the Popes.	1	2	3	4	5	66/9
D. The Devil really exists.	1	2	3	4	5	67/9
E. God doesn't really care how He is worshipped, as long as He is worshipped.	1	2	3	4	5	68/9
F. It is a sin for a Catholic to miss weekly Mass obligation when he easily could have attended.	1	2	3	4	5	69/9
G. Under certain conditions, the Pope is infallible when he speaks on matters of faith and morals.	1	2	3	4	5	70/9

38. Here are a few questions about your education. ASK ALL PARTS OF QUESTION ABOUT
RESPONDENT BEFORE GOING ON TO ASK ABOUT R'S SPOUSE, IF R IS CURRENTLY MARRIED.

	RESPONDENT	R'S SPOUSE (IF CURRENTLY MARRIED)

A. What is the highest year or grade
in elementary school or high school
that (you/your [husband/wife])
finished and got credit for?
CODE EXACT GRADE.

	RESPONDENT		R'S SPOUSE	
No formal schooling	00	07-08/99	. . . 00	15-16/99
1st grade	01		. . . 01	
2nd grade	02		. . . 02	
3rd grade	03		. . . 03	
4th grade	04	GO	. . . 04	
5th grade	05	TO	. . . 05	GO
6th grade	06	Q'S	. . . 06	TO
7th grade	07	FOR	. . . 07	Q. 39
8th grade	08	SPOUSE	. . . 08	
9th grade	09		. . . 09	
10th grade	10		. . . 10	
11th grade	11	GO	. . . 11	GO
12th grade	12	TO	. . . 12	TO
Don't know	////	B	. . . 98	B

B. Did (you/he/she) ever
get a high school
diploma?

Yes (GO TO C) . 1   09/9   . . . 1   GO   17/9
No (GO TO C) . 0   . . . 0 >TO
                             DK . 8   C

C. Did (you/he/she) complete
one or more years of college
for credit--not including
schooling such as business
college, technical or
vocational school?

Yes (GO TO D).1   10/9   Yes (GO TO D) . 1   18/9
No . (GO TO   No . 0   GO
Q'S FOR   DK . 8   TO
SPOUSE) . 0   Q. 39

D. IF YES:
How many years did
(you/he/she) complete
--including any years
of graduate school?

	RESPONDENT		R'S SPOUSE	
1 year . . .	13	11-12/99	. . . 13	19-20/99
2 years . .	14		. . . 14	
3 years . .	15		. . . 15	
4 years . .	16	GO TO	. . . 16	GO TO
5 years . .	17	E	. . . 17	E
6 years . .	18		. . . 18	
7 years . .	19		. . . 19	
8+ years . .	20		. . . 20	
			DK . 98	

E. Do you (Does
[he/she]) have
any college degrees?

Yes . (GO TO F) . 1   13/9   Yes. (GO TO F).1   21/9
No . (GO TO Q'S   No (GO TO Q
   FOR SPOUSE) . 0   Q. 39) .0

F. IF YES:
What degree or
degrees?
CODE HIGHEST
DEGREE EARNED.

Junior college . . 2   14/9 2   22/9
Bachelor's (B.A.,
   B.S.) 3 3
Graduate 4 4

SEE Q. 38.   IF R HAS NO FORMAL SCHOOLING, SKIP TO Q. 47.

IF ANY SCHOOLING, ASK Q. 39:

39.   Think of the elementary schools you attended, that is, grades <u>one through eight</u>.
      Did you go only to Catholic schools, only to non-Catholic schools, or did you go
      to both kinds of elementary schools?

                                    Catholic only . (ASK A) . 1   23/9

                                    Non-Catholic only (ASK B). 2

                                    Both kinds (ASK A & B) . . 3

      A.   IF ATTENDED CATHOLIC OR BOTH:

      How many years did you complete in a Catholic elementary school?

                                    NUMBER OF YEARS: [ ][ ]   24-25/99

                                    Don't know 98

      B.   IF ATTENDED NON-CATHOLIC OR BOTH:

      When you were attending non-Catholic elementary school, did you receive
      religious instruction regularly from the Catholic Church?

                                    Yes . . . 1   26/9

                                    No . . . 2

40.   If you had it to do over again and you were able to choose between Catholic schools
      and non-Catholic schools, which kind would you have chosen for your <u>own elementary</u>
      education?

                                    Catholic schools 1   27/9

                                    Non-Catholic schools · · · · · 2

                                    Both kinds of schools 3

                                    Makes no difference 4

                                    Don't know 8

ASK Q'S 41 THROUGH 43 IF R HAD ANY HIGH SCHOOL EDUCATION

ASK Q'S 41 THROUGH 46 IF R HAD ANY COLLEGE EDUCATION

41. Think of the high schools you attended, that is grades 9 through 12. Did you go
    only to Catholic schools, only to non-Catholic schools, or did you go to both
    kinds of high schools?

    Catholic only . (ASK A) . 1   28/9

    Non-Catholic only
    (ASK B & C) 2

    Both kinds (ASK A, B, & C) 3

    A. IF ATTENDED CATHOLIC OR BOTH:

    How many years did you complete in a Catholic high school?

    NUMBER OF YEARS: [|]   29-30/99

    Don't know 98

    ASK B & C IF ATTENDED NON-CATHOLIC OR BOTH:

    B. When you were attending non-Catholic high school, did you receive religious
        instruction regularly from the Catholic Church?

    Yes 1   31/9

    No 2

    Don't know 8

    C. When you were attending non-Catholic high school, were you a member of a
        Catholic club, organization, or group?

    Yes 1   32/9

    No 2

    Don't know 8

---

42. If you had it to do over again and you were able to choose between Catholic schools
    and non-Catholic schools, which kind would you have chosen for your own high school
    education?

    Catholic schools 1   33/9

    Non-Catholic schools . . . 2

    Both kinds of schools . . . 3

    Makes no difference 4

    Don't know 8

43. When you were in high school, was there any particular teacher who encouraged you
     to go to college?

                                          Yes . . (ASK A) . . . 1   34/9

                                          No . (GO TO Q. 44) . 2

     A. IF YES: Was that teacher a man or a woman?

                                          A man [ASK (1)] . . . 1   35/9

                                          A woman [ASK (2)] . . 2

         (1) IF A MAN: Was he a priest?

                                          Yes 1   36/9

                                          No 2

         (2) IF A WOMAN: Was she a nun?

                                          Yes 1   37/9

                                          No 2

ASK Q'S 44 THROUGH 46 IF R HAD ANY COLLEGE EDUCATION.

OTHERWISE, SKIP TO Q. 47.

44. Did you attend only Catholic colleges, only non-Catholic colleges, or did you
     attend both kinds of college or university?

                                          Only Catholic (ASK A) 1   38/9

                                          Only non-Catholic . . 2

                                          Both . . (ASK A) . . 3

     A. IF CATHOLIC OR BOTH: How many years did you complete in a Catholic college or
         university?

                                          NUMBER OF YEARS: [|]   39-40/99

---

45. If you had it to do over again and you were able to choose between Catholic and
     non-Catholic schools, which kind would you have chosen for your own college educa-
     tion?

                                          Catholic college . . 1   41/9

                                          Non-Catholic college. 2

                                          Both kinds of college 3

                                          Makes no difference . 4

                                          Don't know 8

46. When you were in college and making decisions about your future, were you especially influenced by any particular teacher?

                                          Yes . . . (ASK A) . . 1   42/9

                                          No . (GO TO Q. 47) . 2

A.   IF YES: Was that teacher a man or a woman?

                                          A man . [ASK (1)] . . 1   43/9

                                          A woman [ASK (2)] . . 2

     (1) IF A MAN: Was he a priest?

                                          Yes 1   44/9

                                          No 2

     (2) IF A WOMAN: Was she a nun?

                                          Yes 1   45/9

                                          No 2

ASK Q'S 47-50 IF R IS MARRIED. OTHERWISE, SKIP TO Q. 51.

47. Taking all things into consideration, how satisfied are you with your marriage these
days? Would you say you are very satisfied, moderately satisfied, or not satisfied
at all?

                                          Very satisfied . . . 1   46/9

                                          Moderately satisfied. 2

                                          Not satisfied at all. 3

---

48. What is your (husband/wife)'s religion?

     _____ Protestant (SPECIFY DENOMINATION) . 1   47/9

                    Catholic 2

                    Jewish 3

     _____ Other (SPECIFY) _____ 4

                    None 5

                    Don't know 8

---

49. How religious would you say your (husband/wife) is at the present time? Would you
say (he/she) is very religious, somewhat religious, not too religious, or not at
all religious?

                    Very religious 1   48/9

                    Somewhat religious 2

                    Not too religious 3

                    Not at all religious 4

                    Don't know 8

---

50. Were you and your (husband/wife) married by a priest?

                                          Yes 1   49/9

                                          No 2

ASK EVERYONE:

51. How religious would you say you are at the present time--would you say you are very
     religious, somewhat religious, not too religious, or not at all religious?

                                    Very religious 1   50/9

                                    Somewhat religious 2

                                    Not too religious 3

                                    Not at all religious . . . 4

52. If you had your choice, what would be the ideal number of children you would like
     to have in your family?

                    NUMBER OF CHILDREN: [|]   51-52/99

                           Whatever God sends . . 97

                           Don't know 98

53. Do you have any children, including adopted children?

                           Yes . . . . (ASK A) . . . 1   53/9

                           No . . (GO TO Q. 62) . . . 2

     A. IF YES: How many children have you ever had, including adopted children?

                                    NUMBER: [|]   54-55/99

54. A. How many of your children have been baptized in the Catholic Church?

                                    NUMBER: [|]   56-57/99

                           None 00

     B. How many of your children have been or are being raised as Catholics?

                                    NUMBER: [|]   58-59/99

                           None 00

55. How many of your children are in elementary school or high school now--
     that is in grades 1 through 12?

                                    NUMBER: [|]   07-08/99

                           None (SKIP TO Q. 59). 00

56. ASK IF ANY CHILDREN IN ELEMENTARY OR HIGH SCHOOL NOW:
I'd like to ask you a little about each child you have in elementary or high school
now. First, tell me the first name of the oldest child you have in school now . . .

A.		B.		C.	
Name		Is (he/she) in elementary school or high school?		Is (he/she) in a Catholic or a non-Catholic school?	
ASK B & C FOR EACH CHILD		Elementary school (Grades 1-8)	High school (Grades 9-12)	Catholic	Non-Catholic
01.	09-10/99	1	2 11/9	1	2 12/9
02.	13-14/99	1	2 15/9	1	2 16/9
03.	17-18/99	1	2 19/9	1	2 20/9
04.	21-22/99	1	2 23/9	1	2 24/9
05.	25-26/99	1	2 27/9	1	2 28/9
06.	29-30/99	1	2 31/9	1	2 32/9
07.	33-34/99	1	2 35/9	1	2 36/9
08.	37-38/99	1	2 39/9	1	2 40/9
09.	41-42/99	1	2 43/9	1	2 44/9
10.	45-46/99	1	2 47/9	1	2 48/9

57. ASK IF ANY CHILD IN CATHOLIC SCHOOL [1 IN COLUMN C, Q. 56].
A. Why did you choose Catholic school(s) for your (child/children)? RECORD
VERBATIM. PROBE FOR REASONS.

                                                            49-50/99
                                                            51-52/99
                                                            53-54/99

B. How much tuition, if any, are you paying   55-58/9999
to Catholic schools this year, including $_____
elementary and high schools?   None 0000
                                               Don't know . . .9998

58. ASK IF ANY CHILD IN NON-CATHOLIC SCHOOL [2 IN COLUMN C, Q. 56].
A. Why did you choose non-Catholic schools for your (child/children)? RECORD
VERBATIM. PROBE FOR REASONS.

                                                            59-60/99
                                                            61-62/99
                                                            63-64/99

B. How many of your children in non-Catholic NUMBER:[   ]   65-66/99
school(s) are receiving religious instruc-
tion regularly from the Catholic Church? None 00

BEGIN DECK 05

59. How many of your children, if any, are attending a college or university now?

                                             NUMBER: ☐☐   07-08/99

                                 None (GO TO Q. 60) . 00

    A. IF ANY: How many of those in college now are in a Catholic college or
        university?

                                             NUMBER: ☐☐   09-10/99

                                 None 00

60. How many of your children have completed their education and are out of school now?

                                             NUMBER: ☐☐   11-12/99

                                 None (GO TO Q. 61) . 00

    A. IF ANY: How many of your children who are out of school now ever attended a
        Catholic school--including elementary, high school, or college?

                                             NUMBER: ☐☐   13-14/99

                                 None 00

61. Do you have any children of preschool age, that is, children who have not started
    first grade?

                                 Yes . . (ASK A) . . . 1   15/9
                                 No (GO TO Q. 62). . . 2

    A. IF YES: Do you intend to send your preschool (child/children) to Catholic
        or to non-Catholic school?

                                 Catholic 1   16/9
                                 Non-Catholic 2
                                 Don't know 8

62. IF R IS BLACK, SKIP TO Q. 64. OTHERWISE ASK EVERYONE.
    A. Would you yourself have any objection to sending your children to a school
        where a few of the children are black?

                                 Yes . (GO TO Q. 63) . 1   17/9
                                 No. . (ASK B) 2
                                 Don't know (ASK B). . 8

    B. IF NO OR DON'T KNOW TO A: Where half of the children are black?

                                 Yes . (GO TO Q. 63) . 1   18/9
                                 No. . (ASK C) 2
                                 Don't know (ASK C). . 8
        C. IF NO OR DON'T KNOW TO B: Where more than half of the children are
                    black?

                                 Yes 1   19/9
                                 No. 2
                                 Don't know. 8

63. <u>ASK IF R HAS CHILDREN NOW IN ELEMENTARY OR HIGH SCHOOL</u> [Q. 55].
Are there any Black children in your (child's/children's) school(s) now?

Yes 1	20/9
No. 2	
Don't know. . 8	

<u>IF RESPONDENT IS NOT CURRENTLY MARRIED, SKIP TO Q. 65.</u>
64. Do you expect to have any (more) children?

Yes . (ASK A) . . . 1	21/9
No. 2	
Don't know. 8	

   A. <u>IF YES</u>: How many (more) children do you expect to have?

                         NUMBER: [|]   22-23/99

                         Whatever God sends . 97
                         Don't know 98

65. Suppose you were in a parish that had an elementary school that had been in existence for as long as you could remember and had done a good job of educating children. The pastor announced one Sunday that the school would have to close because
of financial problems unless everyone in the parish gave some extra money to support it. Would you be willing to donate more money to keep the school going, that
is, more than you give now?

Yes . (ASK A) . . . 1	24/9
No. . (GO TO Q. 66). 2	
Don't know (ASK A) . 8	

   A. <u>IF YES OR DON'T KNOW</u>: Here is a list of possible contributions that could be
   made to keep the school going. Which one of these extra contributions would
   be the most you would be willing to give on a yearly basis? You can just tell
   me the letter.

   ```
   HAND
   CARD
    4
   ```

A. Under $5 1	25/9
B. $5 to $25. . . . 2	
C. $26 to $50 . . . 3	
D. $51 to $100. . . 4	
E. $101 to $200 . . 5	
F. $201 to $500 . . 6	
G. $501 or more . . 7	
Don't know . . . 8	

66. As you see it, what, if any, are the advantages of sending a child to a Catholic
     school? (<u>RECORD VERBATIM</u> AND THEN CODE ALL THAT APPLY.)

                    Religious instruction; learn about the
                       Catholic Church 01

                    Exposure to a religious atmosphere . . 02

                    Moral teachings; learn about right
                       and wrong 03

                    Better teachers; more dedicated   26-27/99
                       teachers 04   28-29/99
                                                                       30-31/99
                    Better program, instruction,   32-33/99
                       curriculum 05   34-35/99
                    More discipline; more demanded of
                       students 06

                    Children are physically safer 07

                    Children get to attend school with
                       classmates of their own race 08

                    Other(s) 09

                    No advantage 88

                    Don't know 98

_____

67. A. How satisfied, in general, are you with the <u>religious values</u> being taught in
         the Catholic schools? Look at this card and pick a number from 1 to 7, with
         1 indicating you are <u>most unsatisfied</u> and 7 indicating you are <u>most satisfied</u>.

HAND
CARD
  5   Unsatisfied   1   2   3   4   5   6   7   Satisfied

                                                           Don't know . 8   36 9

     B. How satisfied, in general, are you with the <u>education</u> children receive in the
         Catholic schools? Again, pick a number from 1 to 7, with 1 indicating you are
         <u>most unsatisfied</u> and 7 indicating you are <u>most satisfied</u>.

         Unsatisfied   1   2   3   4   5   6   7   Satisfied

                                                           Don't know . 8   37 9

68. Now I'd like to read some statements about Catholic schools. For each statement, would you tell me whether you agree strongly, agree somewhat, disagree somewhat, or disagree strongly?

		Agree strongly	Agree Somewhat	Disagree somewhat	Disagree strongly	Don't know	
A.	I am responsible for help-ing to financially support the school in my parish only if I have children in it.	1	2	3	4	8	38/9
B.	Lay teachers, regardless of ability, will never be able to do as good a job with Catholic students as is done by nuns.	1	2	3	4	8	39/9
C.	The Catholic school sys-tem has outlived its usefulness and is no longer needed in modern day life.	1	2	3	4	8	40/9
D.	Most parents who send their children to Catholic schools will settle for lower aca-demic standards as long as the school has a strong religion program.	1	2	3	4	8	41/9
E.	Sex education should be taught in Catholic schools.	1	2	3	4	8	42/9
F.	The Federal government should give religious schools money to help pay teachers' salaries and build new buildings.	1	2	3	4	8	43/9
G.	Parents who send their children to Catholic schools should get a refund on their local taxes.	1	2	3	4	8	44/9
H.	Catholic schools would get federal support if it were not for the anti-Catholic feelings in the government.	1	2	3	4	8	45/9
I.	The government should give tuition money directly to parents and let them decide for themselves which school they want their children to attend.	1	2	3	4	8	46/9

69. Now I'd like to get your opinion on something having to do with <u>public</u> schools. Suppose the local public schools said they needed more money. As you feel now, would you vote to raise taxes for this purpose, or would you vote against raising taxes for this purpose?

Favor tax increase . . 1	47/9
Against tax increase . 2	
Don't know 8	

70. I am going to read you a list of jobs. If a son of yours chose each job, tell me whether you would feel very pleased, somewhat pleased, somewhat disappointed, or very disappointed.

HAND CARD 6		Very pleased	Somewhat pleased	Somewhat disappointed	Very disappointed	Don't know	
A.	First, a business executive . . .	1	2	3	4	8	48/9
B.	A priest	1	2	3	4	8	49/9
C.	An author	1	2	3	4	8	50/9
D.	A stockbroker	1	2	3	4	8	51/9
E.	A college professor	1	2	3	4	8	52/9

IF R. HAS ANY CHILDREN, ASK Q. 71.   IF NOT, GO TO Q. 72.

71. When you speak to your children about religious beliefs and values, how sure of things do you feel? Do you feel very sure, pretty sure, not too sure, or not sure at all?

Very sure 1	53/9
Pretty sure 2	
Not too sure 3	
Not sure at all . . . 4	
Never speak to children about religion 5	
Don't know 8	

72. Now I would like to ask you about your own religious practices.

HAND CARD 7 — USE CATEGORIES AS PROBES IF NECESSARY.	Every day	Several times a week	Once a week	2 or 3 times a month	Once a month	Several times a year	About once a year	Practically never or not at all	
A. How often do you go to Mass?	1	2	3	4	5	6	7	8	07/9
B. About how often do you receive Holy Communion?	1	2	3	4	5	6	7	8	08/9
C. How often do you go to Confession?	1	2	3	4	5	6	7	8	09/9
D. About how often do you stop in church to pray?	1	2	3	4	5	6	7	8	10/9
ASK IF MARRIED: E. How often does your (husband/ wife) go to Mass?	1	2	3	4	5	6	7	8	1 '9
F. How often does your (husband/ wife) receive Holy Communion?	1	2	3	4	5	6	7	8	12/9

73. ASK IF R. GOES TO MASS ONCE A WEEK OR MORE OFTEN (1, 2, OR 3 IN 72-A). Why do you go to Mass as often as you do? RECORD VERBATIM.

13-14/99
15-16/99

74. ASK IF R. GOES TO MASS 2 OR 3 TIMES A MONTH OR LESS OFTEN (4, 5, 6, 7, 8 IN 72-A). Why do you not go to Mass more often? RECORD VERBATIM.

17-18/99
19-20/99

DECK 06

75. About how often do you pray privately?

Once a day 1	21/9
Several times a week . 2	
About once a week . . 3	
About once a month . . 4	
Less than once a month 5	
Never 6	

---

76. Of course religion plays a different role in the lives of different people. How
    important is religion in your life? Would you say it is very important, somewhat
    important, not too important, or not at all important?

Very important 1	22/9
Somewhat important . . 2	
Not too important . . 3	
Not at all important . 4	

---

77. Is your parish church always open during the day for people to stop in and pray?

Yes 1	23/9
No 2	
Don't belong to a parish (SKIP TO Q. 84) 3	
Don't know 8	

---

78. Some parishes provide a lot of activities for their parishoners. Others do not
    provide too many. How about your parish--would you say there are a lot of activ-
    ities, a few activities, or practically none at all?

A lot of activities . 1	24/9
A few activities . . . 2	
Practically none . . . 3	
Don't know 8	

---

79. Do you belong to any parish organizations?

Yes . (ASK A) 1	25/9
No 2	

A. IF YES: How many parish organizations do you belong to?

One 1	26/9
Two 2	
Three 3	
Four or more 4	

80. How would you rate the priests in your parish on their ability to understand
    your practical problems--would you say they are very understanding, fairly
    understanding, or not very understanding?

Very understanding . . 1   27/9

Fairly understanding . 2

Not very understanding 3

Don't know 8

81. How would you rate the priests in your parish on their ability to understand the
    problems of teen-aged boys and girls--do you think they are very understanding of
    the problems of teen-agers, fairly understanding, or not very understanding?

Very understanding . . 1   28/9

Fairly understanding . 2

Not very understanding 3

Don't know 8

82. Do you think the sermons of the priests in your parish, in general, are excellent,
    good, fair, or poor?

Excellent 1   29/9

Good 2

Fair 3

Poor 4

Don't know 8

83. In general, would you say you approve or disapprove of the way the priests in your
    parish are handling their job?

Approve 1   30/9

Disapprove 2

Don't know 8

ASK EVERYONE.

84. Do you belong to any Catholic groups or organizations other than parish groups?

Yes . . (ASK A) . . . 1   31/9

No 2

A. IF YES: How many Catholic groups do you belong to, not counting parish groups?

One 1   32/9

Two 2

Three 3

Four or more 4

85. Here is a list of things some Catholics do. During the last two years, which, if any, of these things have you done? Take your time and read through the entire list. I can read the list to you, if you prefer. CIRCLE ALL THAT RESPONDENT HAS DONE.

HAND LIST		

a.	Gone on a Retreat 01	33-34/99
b.	Made a Day of Recollection or Renewal . 02	35-36/99
c.	Read a spiritual book 03	37-38/99
d.	Made a Mission 04	39-40/99
e.	Read Catholic magazines or newspapers . 05	41-42/99
f.	Listened to a Catholic radio or TV program 06	43-44/99
g.	Had a serious conversation with a priest about religious problems . . . 07	45-46/99
h.	Attended a Cursillo 08	47-48/99
i.	Attended a pre-Cana or Cana Conference. 09	49-50/99
j.	Went to a Charismatic or Pentecostal Prayer Meeting 10	51-52/99
k.	Attended an informal Liturgy at your home or a friend's home 11	53-54/99
l.	Made a Marriage Encounter 12	55-56/99
m.	Attended a religious discussion group . 13	57-58/99
n.	None of these 14	59-60/99

86. How much money would you say your immediate family contributes to the Catholic Church each year, not counting school tuition?

$ _____   61-64/9999
       (AMOUNT OR RANGE)

None 0000
Refused 9997
Don't know 9998

87. How many organizations, if any, do you belong to besides religious ones--such as unions, professional organizations, clubs, neighborhood organizations, etc.?

None 0   65/9
One 1
Two 2
Three or four 3
Five or more 4

BEGIN DECK 07

88. Now think of your three closest friends. What religion, if any, does each belong to?	Friend A	Friend B	Friend C
	07/9	08/9	09/9
Protestant	1	1	1
Catholic	2	2	2
Jewish	3	3	3
Other (SPECIFY) _____			
_____	4	4	4
No religion	5	5	5
No (1st) (2nd) (3rd) friend . .	7	7	7
Don't know (his/her) religion .	8	8	8

89. Now I'd like to ask you about something very different. How often have you had an experience where you felt as though you were very close to a powerful, spiritual force that seemed to lift you out of yourself?

HAND CARD 8

Once or twice (ASK A-D) . . . 1   10/9
Several times (ASK A-D) . . . 2
Often . . . . (ASK A-D) . . . 3
Never in my life(GO TO Q.90) . 4
I cannot answer this
 question (GO TO Q. 90) . . . 5

ASK A-D IF R. HAS EVER HAD EXPERIENCE:

A. Many people who have had such experiences say that there are "triggers" or specific events or circumstances that set them off. Have any of the events or circumstances listed on this card ever started such an experience for you? Just give me the letters of the ones that have. CODE AS MANY AS APPLY.

HAND CARD 9

a) The beauties of nature such as a sunset . . 01   11-12/99

b) Watching little children 02   13-14/99

c) Child birth 03   15-16/99

d) Prayer 04   17-18/99

e) Reading the Bible 05   19-20/99

f) Listening to a sermon 06   21-22/99

g) Sexual lovemaking 07   23-24/99

h) Your own creative work 08   25-26/99

i) Looking at a painting 09   27-28/99

j) Being alone in Church 10   29-30/99

k) Listening to music 11   31-32/99

l) Reading a poem or a novel 12   33-34/99

m) Moments of quiet reflection 13   35-36/99

n) Attending a church service 14   37-38/99

o) Physical exercise 15   39-40/99

p) Something else (PLEASE DESCRIBE) _____

_____ 16   41-42/99

89. Continued

B. Those who have had these kinds of experiences have given various descriptions
    of what they were like. Here is a list of some of the things they say happen.
    Have any of them ever happened to you during any of your experiences? Just
    tell me the letters of the ones that have happened to you. CODE AS MANY AS
    APPLY.

HAND
CARD
10

a) A feeling of a new life or of living in a new world . . . 01   07-08/99

b) A sense of the unity of everything and my own part in it 02   09-10/99

c) An experience of great emotional intensity 03   11-12/99

d) A great increase in my understanding of knowledge 04   13-14/99

e) A feeling of deep and profound peace 05   15-16/99

f) Sense that all the universe is alive 06   17-18/99

g) Sense of joy and laughter 07   19-20/99

h) Sense of my own need to contribute to others 08   21-22/99

i) A feeling of desolation 09   23-24/99

j) A sensation of warmth or fire 10   25-26/99

k) A sense that I was being bathed in light 11   27-28/99

l) A loss of concern about worldly problems 12   29-30/99

m) A feeling that I couldn't possibly describe what was
   happening to me 13   31-32/99

n) The sensation that my personality has been taken over by
   something much more powerful than I am 14   33-34/99

o) A sense of being alone 15   35-36/99

p) A certainty that all things would work out for the good . 16   37-38/99

q) A confidence in my own personal survival 17   39-40/99

r) A sense of tremendous personal expansion, either psychological or physical 18   41-42/99

s) A conviction that love is at the center of everything . . 19   43-44/99

t) Something else (PLEASE DESCRIBE) _____

   _____ 20   45-46/99

C. Approximately how long did your   A few minutes or less . 1   47/9
    experience(s) last? (Average   Ten or fifteen minutes . 2
    time if more than one.)   Half an hour 3
                                         An hour 4
                                         Several hours 5
                                         A day or more 6

Appendix III

89. Continued

D. ..ow think of your experience or, if you have had more than one, think of the one that was most powerful. On a scale from 1 to 5, with 1 indicating moderate intensity and 5 indicating extremely strong intensity, where would you place that experience? CODE NUMBER.

|HAND|
|CARD|
|11|

48/9

Moderate   1   2   3   4   5   Extremely strong

Don't know. can't say . . . 8

90. ASK EVERYONE:

In general, do you approve or disapprove of the way Pope Paul is handling his job?

49/9

Approve . . . 1

Disapprove . 2

Don't know . 8

91. As you know, there have been a lot of changes in the Catholic Church over the last ten years or so. I'd like to get your opinion on whether you approve or disapprove of each of the following changes.

		Approve	Disapprove	Don't know	
A.	Saying the Mass in English instead of Latin	1	2	8	50/9
B.	Guitar music during Mass	1	2	8	51/9
C.	The "handshake of peace" at Mass	1	2	8	52/9
D.	Lay people distributing Communion at Mass	1	2	8	53/9
E.	Nuns wearing regular clothes instead of habits	1	2	8	54/9
F.	Reducing the number of liturgical activities, like rosary devotions, novenas, and benedictions	1	2	8	55/9
G.	New and progressive ways of teaching religion to school children	1	2	8	56/9

92. All in all, as far as you are personally concerned, do you think the changes in the Church have been for the better, for the worse, or don't they make much difference one way or the other?

57/9

For the better . . 1

For the worse . . . 2

Don't make much difference . . . 3

Don't know 8

DECK 08

93. In general, do you approve or disapprove of the way the American bishops are handling their job?

Approve 1   58/9

Disapprove 2

Don't know 8

94. As I read some statements about the clergy, please tell me for each whether you agree strongly, agree somewhat, disagree somewhat, or disagree strongly.

		Agree strongly	Agree somewhat	Disagree somewhat	Disagree strongly	Don't know	
A.	Priests should not use the pulpit to discuss social issues.	1	2	3	4	8	59/9
B.	Most priests don't expect the laity to be leaders, just followers.	1	2	3	4	8	60/9
C.	It's all right for a priest to get involved in national and local politics if he wants to.	1	2	3	4	8	61/9
D.	It would make me somewhat unhappy if a daughter of mine became a nun.	1	2	3	4	8	62/9
E.	Priests are not as religious as they used to be.	1	2	3	4	8	63/9
F.	Priests have lost interest in the problems of the people and are concerned only about themselves.	1	2	3	4	8	64/9
G.	Becoming a priest is not a good vocation for young people any more.	1	2	3	4	8	65/9
H.	It would be a good thing if women were allowed to be ordained as priests.	1	2	3	4	8	66/9

95. In recent years, many priests have decided to leave the priesthood and get married. Catholics have reacted to this in different ways--some feel the priesthood is a difficult and lonely life, while others feel that those men who leave the priesthood have backed down on their life-long commitments. How much sympathy do you have for the men who have left--a great deal, some, very little, or none at all?

67/9

A great deal . . 1

Some 2

Very little . . . 3

None at all . . . 4

Don't know . . . 8

96. If the Church were to change its laws and permit clergy to marry, would you be
able to accept this change?

Yes (ASK A) . . . 1	07/9
No 2	
Don't know . . . 8	

A. IF YES: Are you in favor of such a change?

Yes 1	08/9
No 2	
Don't know . . . 8	

97. I am going to read to you a list of things about which many people disagree. For
each, tell me if you think the church has the right to teach what position Catholics should take on that issue. First . . . REPEAT QUESTION AS NECESSARY.

	Yes	No	Don't know	
A. Racial integration	1	2	8	09/9
B. What are immoral books or movies	1	2	8	10/9
C. Proper means for family limitation	1	2	8	11/9
D. Abortion	1	2	8	12/9
E. Federal aid to education	1	2	8	13/9

98. Some Catholics no longer feel close to the Church. Others feel closer to the
Church than ever before. I'd like to know how you feel. Suppose this circle represents closeness to the Church. Where would you locate yourself on this circle,
with "1" representing the closest possible feelings, and "5" representing the most
distant feelings?

HAND
CARD
12

ENTER NUMBER: [ ]	14/9
Don't know . . 8	

A. How about 10 years ago--where would you locate
yourself for how you felt ten years ago?

ENTER NUMBER: [ ]	15/9
Don't know . . 8	

99. Have you yourself ever seriously thought about
leaving the Catholic Church?

Yes 1	16/9
No 2	
Don't know . . 8	

100. As a general rule, how important do you think
it is for young people to marry a member of
their own religion--very important, fairly
important, or not important at all?

Very important 1	17/9
Fairly impor- tant 2	
Not important at all . . . 3	
Don't know . . 8	

101. If a child of yours wanted to marry
someone who was not a Catholic, how
do you think you would react? Would
you oppose it strongly, oppose it
somewhat, or not oppose it at all?

Oppose strongly . . 1	18/9
Oppose somewhat . . 2	
Not oppose at all . 3	
Don't know 8	

102. We are interested in how Americans judge certain actions. I am going to read a list of statements. After I read each statement, tell me whether you **agree strongly**, **agree somewhat**, **disagree somewhat**, or **disagree strongly** with the statement.

		Agree strongly	Agree somewhat	Disagree somewhat	Disagree strongly	Don't know	
A.	Even though a person has a hard time making ends meet, he should still try to give some of his money to help the poor.	1	2	3	4	8	19/9
B.	Two people who are in love do not do anything wrong when they marry, even though one of them has been divorced.	1	2	3	4	8	20/9
C.	There is an obligation to work for the end of racial segregation.	1	2	3	4	8	21/9
D.	A married couple who feel they have as many children as they want are really not doing anything wrong when they use artificial means to prevent conception.	1	2	3	4	8	22/9
E.	A pre-school child is likely to suffer emotional damage if his mother works.	1	2	3	4	8	23/9
F.	It is not really wrong for an engaged couple to have some sexual relations before they are married.	1	2	3	4	8	24/9
G.	When a person has a disease that cannot be cured, doctors should be allowed to end the patient's life by some painless means if the patient and his family request it.	1	2	3	4	8	25/9
H.	A family should have as many children as possible and God will provide for them.	1	2	3	4	8	26/9

103. Now I'd like to ask you a few questions about Presidential elections. If your
     party nominated a woman for President, would you vote for her if she were quali-
     fied for the job?   27/9

                                      Yes 1
                                      No 2
                                      Don't know 8

---

104. If your party nominated a Jew for President, would you vote for him if he were
     qualified for the job?

                                      Yes 1   28/9
                                      No 2
                                      Don't know 8

IF R IS BLACK, SKIP TO Q. 106.

105. If your party nominated a Black for President, would you vote for him if he were
     qualified for the job?   29/9

                                      Yes 1
                                      No 2
                                      Don't know 8

---

106. There are many groups in America. We would like to get your feelings toward
     some of them. Here's a card on which there is something that looks like a ther-
     mometer. We call it a "feeling thermometer" because it measures your feelings
     toward these groups. Here's how it works. If you don't feel particularly warm
     or cold toward a group, then you should place it in the middle, at the 50 degree
     mark.

     If you have a warm feeling toward a group, or feel favorably toward it, you
     would place it somewhere between 50° and 100°, depending on how warm your feel-
     ing is toward the group.

     On the other hand, if you don't feel very favorably toward a group--that is, if
     you don't care for it too much--then you would place it somewhere between 0° and
     50°.

     INTERVIEWER: TAKE SOME TIME TO EXPLAIN HOW THE THERMOMETER WORKS, SHOWING R THE
                   WAY IN WHICH THE DEGREE LABELS CAN HELP HIM TO LOCATE THE GROUP.

     HAND
     CARD
     13
                                                              Ratings

          A. Our first group is Polish Americans.
              Where would you put them on the
              thermometer?   _____ A   30-32/999

          B. Protestants   _____ B   33-35/999

          C. Jews   _____ C   36-38/999

          D. Blacks.   _____ D   39-41/999

          E. Latinos (Mexicans, Puerto Ricans,
              Cubans)   _____ E   42-44/999

Now I am going to describe some situations to you. These are things that happen to people sometimes, and I want you to <u>imagine</u> that they are happening to you. Please tell me which response on the card comes closest to your own feelings. Be sure to read all the possible responses before giving me your answer.

107. You have just visited your doctor and he has told you that you have less than a year to live. He has also told you that your disease is incurable. Which of the following statements comes closest to expressing your reaction?

| HAND |
| CARD |
| 14 |

a) It will all work out for the best somehow 1   45/9

b) No one should question the goodness of God's decision
    about death 2

c) There is nothing I can do about it so I will continue
    as before 3

d) I am angry and bitter at this twist of fate 4

e) I have had a full life and am thankful for that 5

f) Death is painful, but it is not the end of me 6

g) I cannot answer this question 7

h) None of the above 8

108. Imagine that one of your parents is dying a slow and painful death and try to figure out for yourself if there is anything that will enable you to understand the meaning of such a tragedy. Which, if any, of the following statements best expresses your state of mind in this situation?

| HAND |
| CARD |
| 15 |

a) They are in pain now, but they will be peaceful soon . . . 1   46/9

b) Everything that happens is God's will and cannot be bad . 2

c) There is nothing to do but wait for the end 3

d) This waiting is inhuman for them; I hope it ends soon . . 4

e) We can at least be thankful for the good life we have
    had together 5

f) This is tragic, but death is not the ultimate end for us . 6

g) I cannot answer this question 7

h) None of the above 8

109. Imagine that you have just had a child anu tnat the doctor has informed you that it will be mentally retarded. Which of the following responses comes closest to your own feelings about this situation?

| HAND |
| CARD |
| 16 |

a) We will try to take care of this child, but it may have to be put in an institution; either way it will all work out 1   47/9

b) God had his own reasons for sending this child to us 2

c) We must learn to accept this situation 3

d) I love the baby, but why me? 4

e) I'm just plain glad to have the child here 5

f) God has sent us a heavy cross to bear and a special child to love 6

g) I cannot answer this question 7

h) None of the above 8

---

110. Almost every year hurricanes level homes, flood towns, destroy property, and take human lives. How can we make any sense out of such disasters which happen, apparently, by chance? Which of the following statements best describes your answer?

| HAND |
| CARD |
| 17 |

a) We can never really understand these things, but they usually have some unexpected good effect 1   48/9

b) We cannot know the reasons, but God knows them 2

c) We cannot know why these occur and we have to learn to live with that fact 3

d) The government is responsible for seeing that these disasters do as little harm as possible 4

e) I am grateful that I don't live in a hurricane area 5

f) I am not able to explain why these things happen, but I still believe in God's love 6

g) I cannot answer this question 7

h) None of the above 8

IF R IS FEMALE, ASK A AND HAND CARD 18-A.

IF R IS MALE, ASK B, AND HAND CARD 18-B.

---

111. A. FEMALES ONLY:

Now, imagine that you are married and you become pregnant, but you and your husband have serious reasons for not wanting to have another child. Which of the statements on this card best expresses what your reaction would be?

HAND CARD 18-A	

I definitely would
have an abortion . . . 1   49/9

I would consider
having an abortion . . 2

I definitely would not
have an abortion . . . 3

Don't know 8

B. MALES ONLY:

Now, imagine that you are married and your wife becomes pregnant, but you and your wife have serious reasons for not wanting to have another child. Which of the statements on this card best expresses what your reaction would be?

HAND CARD 18-B	

I would definitely want
my wife to have an
abortion 1   50/9

I would want my wife to
consider having an
abortion 2

I would definitely not
want my wife to have
an abortion 3

Don't know 8

112. Now, some final questions about yourself. Presently are you working full time,
      working part time, going to school, keeping house, or what? CIRCLE ONE CODE
      ONLY. IF MORE THAN ONE RESPONSE, GIVE PREFERENCE TO SMALLEST CODE NUMBER THAT
      APPLIES.

                                                                              51/9
                     Working full time (35 hours or more). . . . 1

                     Working part time (1 to 34 hours) 2

                     Unemployed, laid off, looking for work . . 3

                     Retired 4

                     In school . . . . (ASK A) 5

                     Keeping house . . . . . (ASK A) 6

                     Other (SPECIFY AND ASK A) _____

                     _____ 7

      A. ASK IF R IS IN SCHOOL, KEEPING HOUSE, OR OTHER: Did you ever work for as
          long as a year?
                                        Yes . (ASK Q. 113) . . . 1   52/9
                                        No . (SKIP TO Q. 114) . 2

113. A. What kind of work (do/did) you normally do? That is, what (is/was) your main
          job called?

                     OCCUPATION: _____

      B. What (do/did) you actually do in that job? What (are/were) some of your main
          duties?
                                                                        53-55/999

                                                                        56-57/999

      C. For whom (do/did) you work--that is, what kind of place or organization?

                     INDUSTRY: _____

114. Taken all together, how would you say things are these days--would you say that you
      are very happy, pretty happy, or not too happy?
                                        Very happy 1   58/9

                                        Pretty happy . . . 2

                                        Not too happy . . 3

IF R IS NOT MARRIED, SKIP TO Q. 117.

115. Is your (husband/wife) presently working full time, part time, going to school, keeping house, or what? CIRCLE ONE CODE ONLY. IF MORE THAN ONE RESPONSE, GIVE PREFERENCE TO SMALLEST CODE NUMBER THAT APPLIES.

Working full time (35 hours or more) 1   59/9

Working part time (1 to 34 hours) 2

Unemployed, laid off, looking for work . . . 3

Retired 4

In school . . . . . . (ASK A) 5

Keeping house . . . . . (ASK A) 6

Other (SPECIFY AND ASK A) _____

_____ 7

A. ASK IF R'S (HUSBAND/WIFE) IS IN SCHOOL, KEEPING HOUSE, OR OTHER: Did (he/she) ever work for as long as a year?

Yes . (ASK Q. 116) . . . 1   60/9

No (SKIP TO Q. 117) . . 2

Don't know (SKIP TO
Q. 117) 8

116. A. What kind of work (does/did) your (husband/wife) normally do? That is, what (is/was) (his/her) main job called?

OCCUPATION: _____

B. What (does/did) (he/she) actually do in that job? What (are/were) some of (his/her) main duties?

61-63/999

64-65/999

C. For whom (does/did) (he/she) work--that is, what kind of place or organization?

INDUSTRY: _____

117. If you had your choice, would you prefer a job where you are part of a team, all working together, even if you don't get personal recognition for your work, or would you rather have a job where you worked alone and others could see what you have done?

Part of a team . 1   66/9

Work alone . . . 2

Can't decide . . 8

BEGIN DECK 10

118. Here is a card showing amounts of yearly incomes. In which of these income groups
      did your total family income fall last year--1973--before taxes and other deduc-
      tions? This includes income from all sources. Just tell me the letter.
      PROBE FOR ESTIMATE IF R IS UNCERTAIN.

HAND CARD 19	A. Under $2,000 01	07-08/99
	B. $ 2,000 to $ 3,999 . . 02	
	C. $ 4,000 to $ 5,999 . . 03	
	D. $ 6,000 to $ 7,999 . . 04	
	E. $ 8,000 to $ 9,999 . . 05	
	F. $10,000 to $12,499 . . 06	
	G. $12,500 to $14,999 . . 07	
	H. $15,000 to $17,499 . . 08	
	I. $17,500 to $19,999 . . 09	
	J. $20,000 to $24,999 . . 10	
	K. $25,000 to $29,999 . . 11	
	L. $30,000 or over . . . 12	
	Refused 13	
	Don't know 98	

---

119. CODE RESPONDENT'S SEX: Male . . . 1   09/

                                                     Female . . 2

---

120. CODE RESPONDENT'S RACE   White 1   10/
      (BY OBSERVATION):   Black 2
                                       Latino (Mexican,
                                          Puerto Rican, Cuban) 3
                                       Other (SPECIFY) _____

                                       _____ 4

---

121. We've talked a lot about changes   Yes . . (ASK A) . . . 1   11/9
      in the Catholic Church. Do you   No 2
      think there ought to be any more   Don't know (ASK A) . . 8
      changes?

      A. ASK IF YES OR DON'T KNOW: What kind of additional changes would you like to
          see? (RECORD VERBATIM.)

                                                               12-13/99

                                                               14-15/99

                                                               16-17/99

Thank you very much for your time and help.

Now, I have one last question.
(RECORD TIME ENDED AND THEN ASK Q. 122)

TIME	AM
ENDED:	PM

DECK 10

ASK IF R HAS ANY CHILDREN (Q. 53):

122. One last question. Do you have any teen-aged children--that is, any boys or girls between the ages of 13 and 19 (including those 13 and 19 years of age)?

Yes . . . . . (ASK A) . . . 1   18/9

No . . (END OF INTERVIEW) . 2

     A.   IF YES: How many teen-aged children do you have, who are living in this household now?

ENTER NUMBER: ☐☐   19-20/99

EXPLAIN TO RESPONDENT: I would like to leave (this/these) short questionnaire(s) for your teenager(s) to fill out. The letter from our Director on the front page explains what our study is about and how the questionnaire should be filled out.

I will leave an envelope (for each one) to return the questionnaire to our Chicago office. No stamp is needed--just ask your teenager(s) to drop it in the mailbox as soon as possible. The numbers I put on the back will notify my office that the questionaire(s) (is/are) from the correct household. They will not be associated with your name.

ENTER NUMBER OF "MAIL-BACK" QUESTIONNAIRES YOU LEFT WITH THIS R:

NUMBER: ☐☐   21-22/99

IF NUMBER OF QUESTIONNAIRES LEFT WITH R IS LESS THAN THE NUMBER OF TEEN-AGERS ENTERED IN QUESTION 122A, CODE REASON FOR DIFFERENCE:

Refused to allow 1   23/9

Other (SPECIFY) _____ 2

THIS IS IMPORTANT:

> BE SURE TO ENTER THE NUMBERS (CASE, PSU, SEGMENT, PART AND LINE) FROM FACE SHEET OF THIS QUESTIONNAIRE INTO THE BOXES ON THE LAST PAGE OF EACH YOUTH QUESTIONNAIRE THAT YOU LEAVE.
> NEXT TO THE CASE NUMBER, THERE IS AN ADDITIONAL DETACHED BOX, FOR A ONE-DIGIT NUMBER, WHICH YOU MUST ALSO ENTER ON THE BACK OF EACH YOUTH QUESTIONNAIRE. THIS NUMBER REPRESENTS THE NUMBER OF SELF-ADMINISTERED QUESTIONNAIRES THAT WERE LEFT AT THE HOUSEHOLD. FOR EXAMPLE, IF ONLY ONE YOUTH QUESTIONNAIRE IS LEFT IN A HOUSEHOLD, ENTER '1' IN THE DETACHED BOX OF THAT QUESTIONNAIRE; IF TWO YOUTH QUESTIONNAIRES ARE LEFT, ENTER '1' IN THE BOX OF ONE QUESTIONNAIRE AND '2' IN THE OTHER; AND SO ON.

<u>INTERVIEWER REMARKS</u>
(TO BE FILLED OUT <u>IMMEDIATELY</u> AFTER LEAVING RESPONDENT)

A. LENGTH OF INTERVIEW: _____ Minutes   24-26/999

B. In general, what was the respondent's attitude toward the interview?
    CODE ONE.

                Friendly and interested 1   27/9
                Cooperative but not particularly
                    interested 2
                Impatient and restless 3
                Hostile 4

C. Was respondent's understanding of the questions ... CODE ONE:
                        Good 1   28/9
                        Fair 2
                        Poor 3

D. DATE OF INTERVIEW: ⬚⬚   ⬚⬚
                        Month   Day
                        29-30/99   31-32/99

E. INTERVIEWER'S SIGNATURE: _____

F. INTERVIEWER'S NUMBER: ⬚⬚⬚⬚⬚   33-37

G. Did you exercise the option to introduce this as a study of Catholics?

                    Yes . .(ANSWER A) . 1   38/9
                    No 2

    A. <u>IF YES</u>: Did you exercise the option <u>before</u> you began the interview
                    or at some time during the interview?

                    Before the interview began . . 1   39/9
                    During interview (ANSWER B) . 2

        B. <u>IF DURING INTERVIEW</u>: Please indicate at which question
            you stated that this is a study of Catholics.

                            Q. #:_____   40-42/999

THE ADOLESCENT QUESTIONNAIRE

1. First of all, we're interested in your opinions on various topics that are of concern to people today. Please read each of the statements below and indicate for each whether you agree strongly, agree somewhat, disagree somewhat, or disagree strongly, by circling the appropriate number. (CIRCLE ONE IN EACH ROW.)

		Agree strongly	Agree somewhat	Disagree somewhat	Disagree strongly	Can't answer/ Don't know	
A.	A pre-school child is likely to suffer emotional damage if his mother works.	1	2	3	4	8	7/9
B.	The Catholic school system has outlived its usefulness and is no longer needed in modern day life.	1	2	3	4	8	8/9
C.	The Catholic Church teaches that a good Christian ought to think about the next life and not worry about fighting against poverty and injustice in this life.	1	2	3	4	8	9/9
D.	Jewish businessmen are about as honest as other businessmen.	1	2	3	4	8	10/9
E.	A family should have as many children as possible and God will provide for them.	1	2	3	4	8	11/9
F.	Sex education should be taught in Catholic schools.	1	2	3	4	8	12/9
G.	White people have a right to live in an all-white neighborhood if they want to, and Blacks should respect that right.	1	2	3	4	8	13/9
H.	It is not really wrong for an engaged couple to have some sexual relations before they are married.	1	2	3	4	8	14/9
IF YOU ARE BLACK ANSWER THIS QUESTION:							
I.	Whites shouldn't push themselves where they're not wanted.	1	2	3	4	8	15/9
IF YOU ARE WHITE ANSWER THIS QUESTION:							
J.	Blacks shouldn't push themselves where they're not wanted.	1	2	3	4	8	16/9

2. We're also interested in what young people think about religious matters. Again, please read each of the following statements, and circle the answer that comes closest to your own personal opinion. (CIRCLE ONE IN EACH ROW.)

		Certainly true	Probably true	I am uncertain whether this is true or false	Probably false	Certainly false	
A.	There is no definite proof that God exists.	1	2	3	4	5	17/9
B.	God will punish the evil for all eternity.	1	2	3	4	5	18/9
C.	The devil really exists.	1	2	3	4	5	19/9
D.	God doesn't really care how He is worshipped, as long as He is worshipped.	1	2	3	4	5	20/9
E.	It is a sin for a Catholic to miss weekly Mass obligation when he easily could have attended.	1	2	3	4	5	21/9

3. Taken all together, how would you say things are these days--would you say that you are very happy, pretty happy, or not too happy? (CIRCLE ONE)

Very happy . . 1   22/9
Pretty happy . 2
Not too happy . 3

These next questions are about you and your family.
(IF YOU HAVE NOT BEEN RAISED BY YOUR PARENTS, ANSWER THESE WITH REGARD TO THE PEOPLE WHO RAISED YOU.)

			Very close	Somewhat close	Not at all close	
4.	A.	How close to each other would you say you and your mother are--are you very close, somewhat close, or not at all close? (CIRCLE ONE)	1	2	3	23/9
	B.	How about you and your father--are you very close to each other, somewhat close, or not at all close? (CIRCLE ONE)	1	2	3	24/9
	C.	How close to each other would you say your father and mother are--would you say that they are very close to each other, somewhat close, or not at all close? (CIRCLE ONE)	1	2	3	25/9

5. Below is a list of words that are sometimes used to describe people. Read through
the entire list carefully and . . .

A.	B.
Select the one word that comes closest to describing your FATHER. Circle the number next to this word in Column A-1.	Read through the list once again. Select the one word that comes closest to describing your MOTHER. Circle the number next to this word in Column B-1.
Now select the word that comes second closest to describing your father and circle the number next to this word in Column A-2.	Now select the word that comes second closest to describing your mother and circle the number next to it in Column B-2.
Finally, select the word that comes third closest to describing your father and circle the number next to this word in Column A-3.	Finally, select the word that comes third closest to describing your mother and circle the number next to it in Column B-3.

	A. Father				B. Mother		
	Column A-1	Column A-2	Column A-3		Column B-1	Column B-2	Column B-3
1) Competitive . . .	1	1	1	Competitive . . .	1	1	1
2) Warm and loving .	2	2	2	Warm and loving .	2	2	2
3) Dissatisfied . .	3	3	3	Dissatisfied . .	3	3	3
4) Decisive and firm	4	4	4	Decisive and firm	4	4	4
5) Sensitive to others' needs .	5	5	5	Sensitive to others' needs .	5	5	5
6) Reserved	6	6	6	Reserved	6	6	6
7) Personally ambitious . . .	7	7	7	Personally ambitious . . .	7	7	7
8) Satisfied	8	8	8	Satisfied	8	8	8
9) None of these . .	0	0	0	None of these . .	0	0	0
FOR OFFICE USE ONLY →	26/9	27/9	28/9	FOR OFFICE USE ONLY →	29/9	30/9	31/9

			Very sure	Pretty sure	Not too sure	Not sure at all	Doesn't speak to me about religion	FOR OFFICE USE ONLY
6.	A.	When your mother speaks to you about religious beliefs and values, how sure of things does she seem? (CIRCLE ONE)	1	2	3	4	8	32/9
	B.	When your father speaks to you about religious beliefs and values, how sure of things does he seem? (CIRCLE ONE)	1	2	3	4	8	33/9

FOR OFFICE
USE ONLY

7. A. How would you describe your father's personal approach to religion? (CIRCLE ONE)	Very joyous	Somewhat joyous	Not at all joyous	Not religious
	1	2	3	4

DECK 01

34/9

B. How about your mother's personal approach to religion, how would you describe it? (CIRCLE ONE)	1	2	?	4

35/9

These are some questions about your own religious behavior.

8. What is your present religion? (CIRCLE ONE)

Catholic 1

Protestant (SPECIFY DENOMINA-
  TION) _____ 2

Jewish 3

None 4

Other (SPECIFY) _____ 5

36/9

9. (CIRCLE ONE NUMBER IN EACH ROW.)	Every day	Several times a week	Once a week	2 or 3 times a month	Once a month	Several times a year	About once a year	Practically never or not at all
A. About how often do you pray privately?	1	2	3	4	5	6	7	8

37/9

ANSWER B, C, AND D
IF YOU ARE A CATHOLIC.

B. How often do you go to Mass?	1	2	3	4	5	6	7	8

38/9

C. About how often do you receive Holy Communion?	1	2	3 ·	4	5	6	7	8

39/9

D. How often do you go to Confession?	1	2	3	4	5	6	7	8

40/9

10. How important is religion in your life?

Very important 1

Somewhat important 2

Not too important 3

Not at all important . . . 4

41/9

FOR OFFICE
USE ONLY

DECK 01
42/9

11. How sure of your religious beliefs   Very sure 1
     and values are you? (CIRCLE ONE)
                                                      Pretty sure 2

                                                      Not too sure . . . 3

                                                      Not sure at all . . 4

ANSWER Q. 12 IF YOU ARE A CATHOLIC.

12. A. How would you rate the priests in   Very understanding . . . 1   43/9
         your parish on their ability to
         understand the problems of teen-   Fairly understanding . . 2
         aged boys and girls? (CIRCLE ONE)
                                                     Not very understanding . 3

     B. In general, how would you rate   Excellent 1   44/9
         the sermons of the priests in   Good 2
         your parish? (CIRCLE ONE)
                                                        Fair 3
                                                        Poor 4

     C. Some parishes provide a lot of   There are a lot of
         activities for their parishoners.   activities 1   45/9
         Others do not provide too many.   There are a few
         How about your parish? (CIRCLE ONE)   activities 2
                                                     There are practically
                                                       no activities 3

13. How much do you admire the kind of   Very much admire   . . . 1   46/9
     life nuns and priests lead? (CIRCLE   Somewhat admire 2
     ONE)   Do not admire much at all 3

     A. FOR BOYS: Have you ever seriously   Yes 1   47/9
         thought about becoming a priest?
         (CIRCLE ONE)   No 2

     B. FOR GIRLS: Have you ever seriously
         thought about becoming a nun?   Yes 1   48/9
         (CIRCLE ONE)
                                                     No 2

14. A. Is there any priest (or priests)   Yes 1   49/9
         that you feel especially close to?
         (CIRCLE ONE)   No 2

     B. Is there any nun (or nuns) that   Yes 1   50/9
         you feel especially close to?
         (CIRCLE ONE)   No 2

15. Do you think women should be allowed to be priests? (CIRCLE ONE)

                                                     Yes 1   51/9

                                                     No 2

Appendix III

The next four questions discuss things that happen to people sometimes.
Please try to __imagine__ that they are happening to you.

16. You have just visited your doctor and he has told you that you have less
than a year to live. He has also told you that your disease is incurable. Which of the following statements comes closest to expressing
your reaction? (CIRCLE ONE NUMBER)

    a) It will all work out for the best somehow 1

    b) No one should question the goodness of God's decision about
death 2

    c) There is nothing I can do about it so I will continue as before 3

    d) I am angry and bitter at this twist of fate 4

    e) I have had a full life and am thankful for that 5

    f) Death is painful, but it is not the end of me 6

    g) I cannot answer this question 7

    h) None of the above 8

17. Almost every year hurricanes level homes, flood towns, destroy property,
and take human lives. How can we make any sense out of such disasters
which happen, apparently, by chance? Which of the following statements
best describes your answer? (CIRCLE ONE NUMBER)

    a) We can never really understand these things, but they usually
have some unexpected good effect 1

    b) We cannot know the reasons, but God knows them 2

    c) We cannot know why these occur and we have to learn to live
with that fact 3

    d) The government is responsible for seeing that these disasters
do as little harm as possible 4

    e) I am grateful that I don't live in a hurricane area 5

    f) I am not able to explain why these things happen, but I still
believe in God's love 6

    g) I cannot answer this question 7

    h) None of the above 8

18. Imagine that one of your parents is dying a slow and painful death and
try to figure out for yourself if there is anything that will enable you
to understand the meaning of such a tragedy. Which, if any, of the following statements best expresses your state of mind in this situation?
(CIRCLE ONE NUMBER)

    a) They are in pain now, but they will be peaceful soon 1

    b) Everything that happens is God's will and cannot be bad 2

    c) There is nothing to do but wait for the end 3

    d) This waiting is inhuman for them; I hope it ends soon 4

    e) We can at least be thankful for the good life we have had
together 5

    f) This is tragic, but death is not the ultimate end for us . . . 6

    g) I cannot answer this question 7

    h) None of the above 8

19. Imagine that you have just had a child and that the doctor has informed
    you that it will be mentally retarded. Which of the following responses
    comes closest to your own feelings about this situation?   (CIRCLE ONE
    NUMBER)

    a) We will try to take care of this child, but it may have to be
        put in an institution; either way it will all work out 1   55/9

    b) God has His own reasons for sending this child to us 2

    c) We must learn to accept this situation 3

    d) I love the baby, but why me? 4

    e) I'm just plain glad to have the child here 5

    f) God has sent us a heavy cross to bear and a special child to
        love 6

    g) I cannot answer this question 7

    h) None of the above 8

20. What kind of elementary school   Catholic only 1   56/9
    (that is, for grades one   Non-Catholic only (ANSWER A) . 2
    through eight) did you (or do   Both Catholic and
    you) go to: non-Catholic (ANSWER A) . . 3

    A. IF YOU EVER WENT TO A NON-CATHOLIC ELEMENTARY SCHOOL: Did you
        receive religious instruction regularly from the Catholic Church
        while you were attending non-Catholic elementary school?

                                           Yes 1   57/9

                                           No 2

21. Are you presently in school?   Yes . . (ANSWER A & B). . . . 1   58/9
    (CIRCLE ONE AND FOLLOW
    INSTRUCTIONS)   No . (ANSWER C ON NEXT PAGE) . 2

    IF YOU ARE IN SCHOOL NOW:

    A. What grade or year are you in?

                        8th grade or less 0   59/9
                        Freshman in high school (9th grade) 1
                        Sophomore in high school (10th grade) 2
                        Junior in high school (11th grade) 3
                        Senior in high school (12th grade) 4
                        Freshman in college 5
                        Sophomore in college 6
                        Junior in college 7
                        Senior in college 8

    B. What kind of school are you in now?

                        Public school 1   60/9

                        Parochial or private Catholic school . . . 2

                        Private non-Catholic school 3

21. Continued

IF YOU ARE NOT IN SCHOOL NOW:

C. What is the last grade or year in school you completed and got
    credit for?

8th grade or less 0	61/9
Freshman year of high school . 1	
Sophomore year of high school . 2	
Junior year of high school . . 3	
Senior year of high school . . 4	
Freshman year of college . . . 5	
Sophomore year of college . . . 6	
Junior year of college 7	
Senior year of college 8	

22. ANSWER THIS QUESTION IF YOU ARE NOW ATTENDING A NON-CATHOLIC ELEMENTARY
     SCHOOL OR HIGH SCHOOL.

(CIRCLE ONE IN EACH ROW)

	Yes	No	
A. Is there a Catholic school in your neighborhood you could be going to if you wanted to?	1	2	62/9
B. Do you receive religious instruction regularly from the Catholic Church?	1	2	63/9
C. Do you belong to any Catholic clubs or groups?	1	2	64/9

23. When you have your own family, what would
     be the ideal number of children you would
     like to have? (CIRCLE ONE)

None 0	65/9
One 1	
Two 2	
Three 3	
Four 4	
Five 5	
Six 6	
Seven 7	
Eight or more . 8	

24. If you had your choice, would you prefer a job where you are part of a team, all working together, even if you don't get personal recognition for your work, or would you rather have a job where you worked alone and others could see what you have done? (CIRCLE ONE)

Part of a team . . . 1   66/9

Work alone 2

Can't decide 8

25. Please write the year in which you were born in the last two boxes below.

| 1 | 9 | | |

67-68/99

26. What race do you consider yourself? (CIRCLE ONE NUMBER)

White 1   69/9

Black 2

Other (SPECIFY) _____

_____ 3

27. Are you male or female? (CIRCLE ONE NUMBER)

Male 1   70/9

Female 2

Thank you very much for your help. Please put this survey into the envelope addressed to National Opinion Research Center and drop it into a mailbox. No postage is required.

Appendix IV

FREQUENCY DISTRIBUTIONS
FOR SOCIAL CHANGE
MODEL III

1. FREQUENCY DISTRIBUTIONS FOR CHANGE MODEL III - VOCATION SUPPORT

Time	Cohort	Sexual Orthodoxy	Accept Papal Authority	Holy Communion Reception	Vocation Support	
					Not "Very Pleased"	"Very Pleased"
		Low	No	Not weekly	158	115
				Weekly	0	3
			Yes	Not Weekly	153	242
	Not Viet-nam			Weekly	3	15
		High	No	Not weekly	65	99
				Weekly	2	15
1963			Yes	Not weekly	134	459
				Weekly	16	154
	Vietnam*					
		Low	No	Not weekly	119	56
				Weekly	21	16
			Yes	Not weekly	45	58
	Not Viet-nam			Weekly	22	33
		High	No	Not weekly	13	13
				Weekly	6	10
			Yes	Not weekly	4	23
				Weekly	3	39
1974		Low	No	Not weekly	94	40
				Weekly	5	11
			Yes	Not weekly	40	32
	Vietnam			Weekly	2	4
		High	No	Not weekly	2	4
				Weekly	1	2
			Yes	Not weekly	1	6
				Weekly	0	5

*The Vietnam cohort was not interviewed in 1963.

2. FREQUENCY DISTRIBUTIONS FOR CHANGE MODEL III - PRAYER

Time	Cohort	Sexual Orthodoxy	Accept Papal Authority	Holy Communion Reception	Prayer Less than Daily	Prayer Daily
		Low	No	Not weekly	132	149
				Weekly	0	3
	Not Viet-nam		Yes	Not Weekly	133	264
				Weekly	0	18
		High	No	Not weekly	53	115
				Weekly	2	15
1963			Yes	Not weekly	133	461
				Weekly	15	156
	Vietnam*					
		Low	No	Not weekly	92	83
				Weekly	4	34
	Not Viet-nam		Yes	Not weekly	36	67
				Weekly	12	43
		High	No	Not weekly	8	18
				Weekly	1	15
			Yes	Not weekly	6	21
				Weekly	4	36
1974		Low	No	Not weekly	73	60
				Weekly	3	13
	Vietnam		Yes	Not weekly	33	39
				Weekly	1	5
		High	No	Not weekly	2	4
				Weekly	1	2
			Yes	Not weekly	4	3
				Weekly	0	5

*The Vietnam cohort was not interviewed in 1963.

3.   FREQUENCY DISTRIBUTIONS FOR CHANGE MODEL III - CATHOLICITY FACTOR

Time	Cohort	Sexual Orthodoxy	Accept Papal Authority	Holy Communion Reception	Catholicity Factor	
					Under 1963 Mean	Over 1963 Mean
1963	Not Vietnam	Low	No	Not weekly	177	40
				Weekly	0	3
			Yes	Not Weekly	218	96
				Weekly	4	12
		High	No	Not weekly	71	60
				Weekly	2	12
			Yes	Not weekly	172	330
				Weekly	12	126
	Vietnam*					
1974	Not Vietnam	Low	No	Not weekly	121	18
				Weekly	19	14
			Yes	Not weekly	66	29
				Weekly	23	26
		High	No	Not weekly	13	7
				Weekly	4	9
			Yes	Not weekly	9	12
				Weekly	5	33
	Vietnam	Low	No	Not weekly	100	11
				Weekly	7	7
			Yes	Not weekly	56	8
				Weekly	2	3
		High	No	Not weekly	3	1
				Weekly	2	1
			Yes	Not weekly	1	0
				Weekly	1	4

*The Vietnam cohort was not interviewed in 1963.

4. FREQUENCY DISTRIBUTIONS FOR CHANGE MODEL III - CATHOLIC ACTIVITIES

Time	Cohort	Sexual Orthodoxy	Accept Papal Authority	Holy Communion Reception	Catholic Activities	
					Low	High
1963	Not Vietnam	Low	No	Not weekly	166	71
				Weekly	1	2
			Yes	Not Weekly	79	93
				Weekly	7	12
		High	No	Not weekly	192	58
				Weekly	5	15
			Yes	Not weekly	258	344
				Weekly	38	146
	Vietnam*					
1974	Not Vietnam	Low	No	Not weekly	153	39
				Weekly	21	20
			Yes	Not weekly	23	4
				Weekly	7	8
		High	No	Not weekly	77	31
				Weekly	33	27
			Yes	Not weekly	18	10
				Weekly	10	30
	Vietnam	Low	No	Not weekly	121	11
				Weekly	10	7
			Yes	Not weekly	3	2
				Weekly	1	2
		High	No	Not weekly	53	17
				Weekly	3	3
			Yes	Not weekly	2	2
				Weekly	0	5

*The Vietnam cohort was not interviewed in 1963.

5.   FREQUENCY DISTRIBUTIONS FOR CHANGE MODEL III--MASS ATTENDANCE

Time	Cohort	Sexual Orthodoxy	Accept Papal Authority	Mass Attendance Less than Weekly	Weekly
		Low	No	163	125
			Yes	129	248
	Not Vietnam		No	64	12⁄
		High	Yes	76	698
1963					
	Vietnam*				
		Low	No	122	91
			Yes	58	100
	Not Vietnam		No	13	29
		High	Yes	5	64
1974		Low		107	45
			Yes	50	29
	Vietnam		No	3	5
		High	Yes	0	13

*The Vietnam cohort was not interviewed in 1963.

Appendix V

DESCRIPTION OF SCALES

Name of Scale	Year	Mean	Standard Deviation	Range	Items
PARENTAL RELIGIOSITY	1963	1.30	1.00	0-3	1. Thinking back to the time when you were growing up, that is, up to the time you were 16, what was your father's religion?
	1974	1.49	1.14	0-3	2. When you were growing up, about how often did your father attend mass?
					3. When you were growing up, about how often did your father receive Holy Communion?
					4. Thinking back to the time when you were growing up, what was your mother's religion?
					5. When you were growing up, about how often did your mother attend mass?
					6. When you were growing up, about how often did your mother receive Communion?

A value of 1 was assigned if one parent was Catholic and attended mass weekly. If both parents were Catholic and both attended mass weekly, a value of 2 was given. A value of 3 was given if both parents were Catholic, both attended mass weekly, and at least one received Communion every week. The rest were all given a score of 0. If the data on any one of these items was missing, the case was excluded.

Name of Scale	Year	Mean	Standard Deviation	Range	Items
SEX MORES	1963	1.76	1.04	0-3	1. Two people who are in love do not do anything wrong when they marry, even though one of them has been divorced.
	1974	.74	.90	0-3	2. A married couple who feel they have as many children as they want are really not doing anything wrong when they use artificial means to prevent conception.
					3. It is not really wrong for an engaged couple to have some sexual relations before they are married.

Name of Scale	Year	Mean	Standard Deviation	Range	Items

SEX MORES
(Continued)

A "Disagree somewhat" or "disagree strongly" response on item 1 was given one point; a "disagree somewhat" or "disagree strongly" response on item 2 was given one point; and a "disagree strongly" response on item 3 was given one point. The scores on the three items were added together. A score of 3 is high on holding to rigid sex norms.

DOCTRINAL	1963	1.49	.88	0-3	1. There is no definite proof that God exists.
	1974	.88	.85	0-3	2. God will punish the evil for all eternity.
					3. God doesn't really care how He is worshipped, as long as He is worshipped.

A response of "certainly false" on item 1 was given one point; a response of "probably false" or "certainly true" on item 2 was given one point; and a response of "certainly true" on item 3 was given one point. The scores on the three items were added together. A score of 3 is high on doctrinal orthodoxy.

CHURCH AS TEACHER	1963	2.38	1.18	0-3	1. Do you think that the Church has the right to teach what position Catholics should take on:
	1974	1.78	1.39	0-3	a. racial integration.
					b. what are immoral books or movies.
					c. federal aid to education.

An affirmative answer on any of these items was given 1 point. The scores on the three items were added together to form a scale. A high score indicates agreement with the Church's right to teach on the topics listed.

SACRAMENTAL	1963	.95	.71	0-2	1. How often do you go to mass?
	1974	.84	.86	0-2	2. How often do you receive Holy Communion?

Respondents were given 1 point if they went to mass once a week or more and 1 point if they went to Communion several times a month or more.

Name of Scale	Year	Mean	Standard Deviation	Range	Items
ACTIVITIES (Continued)					2. How much money would you say your immediate family contributes to the Catholic Church each year, not counting school tuition?
					3. About how often do you receive Holy Communion?
					4. About how often do you pray privately?

Contribution to the Church was dichotomized at the mean for each year. The items were added together and the total was divided by 8.

Name of Scale	Year	Mean	Standard Deviation	Range	Items
PRIEST AS PROFESSIONAL	1974	0	100	-148.52- 308.67	1. How would you rate the priests in your parish on their ability to understand your practical problems--would you say they are very understanding, fairly understanding or not very under- standing?
					2. How would you rate the priests in your parish on their ability to understand the problems of teenaged boys and girls--do you think they are very understanding of the problems of teenagers, fairly understanding, or not very understanding?
					3. Do you think the sermons of the priests in your parish, in general, are excellent, good, fair, or poor?
					4. In general, would you say you approve or disapprove of the way the priests in your parish are handling their job?
					5. Some parishes provide a lot of activities for their parishioners. Others do not provide too many. How about your parish--would you say there are a lot of activities, a few activities, or practically none at all?

The items were individually converted to z-scores and added together to make a scale. The scale was then converted into a z-score.

Name of Scale	Year	Mean	Standard Deviation	Range	Items
PRIEST--SOCIAL INVOLVEMENT	1974	2.90	1.22	1-5	1. Priests should not use the pulpit to discuss social issues.
					2. It is all right for a priest to get involved in national and local politics if he wants to.

This is an additive scale. The two items were added together and the total was divided by two. A high score indicates approval of priests discussing social issues and getting involved in politics.

Name of Scale	Year	Mean	Standard Deviation	Range	Items
ANTI-CLERICAL	1974	0	100	-148.53-308.67	1. It would make me somewhat unhappy if a daughter of mine became a nun.
					2. Priests are not as religious as they used to be.
					3. Priests have lost interest in the problems of the people and are concerned only about themselves.
					4. Becoming a priest is not a good vocation for young people any more.
					5. Most priests don't expect the laity to be leaders, just followers.

The individual items were converted to z-scores and added together to make the scale. The scale was then converted to a z-score.

Items	Factor Loadings			Year
	Vatican II	Change Scale 2	Change Scale 3	1974
1. I'd like to get your opinion on whether you approve or disapprove of the following changes:				
a. saying the mass in English instead of Latin.	-.25315	.09549	-.09154	
b. guitar music during mass.	-.27133	-.00371	.07268	
c. the "handshake of peace" at mass.	-.40726	-.29441	.01459	
d. lay people distributing Communion at mass.	-.12094	-.02579	.33821	
e. nuns wearing regular clothes instead of habits.	-.02737	.35921	.06539	
f. reducing the number of liturgical activities, like rosary devotions, novenas, and benedictions.	.11188	.57713	-.02362	
g. new and progressive ways of teaching religion to school children.	-.13243	.32431	-.08198	
2. All in all, as far as you are personally concerned, do you think the changes in the Church have been for the better, for the worse, or don't they make much difference one way or the other?	-.31467	.10328	-.06333	
3. It would be a good thing if women were allowed to be ordained as priests.	.05138	-.14599	.58342	
4. If the Church were to change its laws and permit clergy to marry, would you be able to accept this change?	.07349	.12173	.445	
(a) Are you in favor of such a change?				

Items	Factor Loadings			Year 1974
	Liturgy	Media	Organizations	
1. Here is a list of things some Catholics do. During the last two years, which, if any, of these things have you done?				
a. made a day of recollection or renewal.	-.24744	-.05018	.14517	
b. read a spiritual book.	-.25593	.35087	-.17861	
c. read Catholic magazines or newspapers.	.04037	.40296	.1054	
d. listened to a Catholic radio or TV program.	.0646	.52743	-.09124	
e. had a serious conversation with a priest about religious problems.	-.36625	.0031	-.07892	
f. attended an informal liturgy at your home or a friend's home.	-.41984	-.10027	-.02095	
g. attended a religious discussion group.	-.38153	-.0155	.01392	
2. How much money would you say your immediate family contributes to the Catholic Church each year, not counting school tuition?	.03116	-.08354	.42703	
3. About how often do you receive Holy Communion?	.02713	.08479	.39173	
4. About how often do you pray privately?	.11414	.21626	.22149	
5. Do you belong to any Catholic groups or organizations other than parish groups?				
a. How many Catholic groups do you belong to, not counting parish groups?	-.03758	-.11249	.37555	

Items	Factor Loadings		Year
	Catholicity Factor 1	Catholicity Factor 2	1963-1974
1. Activities Scale	.28652	--	
2. Sex Mores Scale	.24587	--	
3. Sacramental Scale	.24892	--	
4. About how often do you pray privately?	.21399	.21315	
5. How much money would you say your immediate family contributes to the Catholic Church each year, not counting school tuition? (Converted into per cent of income)	.09663	.30164	
6. Doctrinal Scale	.20437	.12698	
7. Church as Teacher Scale	.17844	.28459	
8. Vocation Scale	--	-.13359	
9. How often do you go to mass?	--	.34414	
10. About how often do you go to confession?	--	.37095	
11. During the last two years, which, if any, of these things have you done?			
a. made a day of recollection or renewal.	--	-.05957	
b. read a spiritual book.	--	.1621	
c. read Catholic magazines or newspapers.	--	-.01008	
d. listened to a Catholic radio or TV program.	--	-.02177	
e. had a serious conversation with a priest about religious problems	--	-.15465	

Appendix VI

SOME SIMULATIONS
OF THE FUTURE OF
AMERICAN CATHOLICISM

It is important to observe that the simulations described here are something more than idle speculation.[1] They are based on five- and six-variable models resulting from observations at two points in time. In comparison with most attempts in sociology to anticipate future developments, and certainly as far as most exercises in futurology in the sociology of religion, the simulations are based on very hard and sophisticated data indeed—however naive they may be in comparison with econometric models.

Nor are the simulations predictions. They are rather scenarios based on a number of different systematic variations of assumptions about parameters in the models. If nothing unexpected happens in the world outside the model, then a reasonable man would wager that the shape of American Catholicism in 1989 would fall somewhere on the continuum created by our scenarios. But rarely does the world fail to provide the unexpected. The negative forces at work within American Catholicism are powerful. Even our "best case" scenario does not do much more than show a slight ascent on the right-hand side of a U curve.

The impact of the birth control encyclical seems almost irreversible. But our scenarios simply cannot take into account the possibility (some would think it to be likely) that the decision of the encyclical will be reversed. Nor can they allow for another ecumenical council or a new papacy very different from the present one. Indeed, scenarios can become self-defeating prophecies if those about whom they are written (or the leaders of the community about which they are written) take them with sufficient seriousness. Thus, at best, our scenarios should be considered tentative lines drawn into the future against which actual developments might be compared and with which the dynamics of such developments might be better understood.

Scenario I—Worst Case

In this possibility, the decline in acceptance of the church's sexual ethic and agreement with papal authority continues at the same rate as it has for the last ten years. In addition, those who become adults during the next decade are as much lower in their acceptance of sexual teaching and papal authority in comparison with the Vietnam cohort as it is in comparison with previous age groups now.

Under such circumstances, Catholicism in the year 1989 will look very little like the church of the early 1960s. Only one-third of the population will be attending weekly mass, only 29 percent will be "very pleased" at the prospect of a son's being a priest, a mere 1 percent will be above the 1963 mean for Catholic activities, and 12 percent will be giving more than $262 a year in inflation-free dollars. The Catholic church will appear anemic if not moribund. But private religious devotion, while not at the 1963 level, will continue to be quite strong, with 49 percent of the church membership praying at least once a day.

Scenario II—Continued Decline

The second scenario is less drastic. It assumes that the forces of deterioration set in motion by the birth control encyclical continue at the rate of the last ten years but that the new age cohort is like the Vietnam cohort in its attitudes toward sexual morality and papal leadership. The dynamics of deterioration are still at work, but the new generation of young people are not more unreligious than their immediate predecessors. One part of the deterioration, in other words, has been arrested.

Even in this less radical scenario the outlook for Catholicism in 1989 is bleak. Thirty-six percent will be attending mass regularly, 30 percent will be "greatly pleased" if a son should decide to be a priest, 6 percent will be high on Catholic activities, and 20 percent will be contributing more than $262 inflation-free dollars to the church. Fifty-one percent will be praying every day.

Thus, even if one makes a moderately hopeful assumption about those who will come of age in the next fifteen years, the situation of the Catholic church in the United States will still be very grim indeed by the end of the next decade if the deterioration set in motion by the birth control encyclical is not reversed.

Scenario III—One-Half Decline

In this and the following scenario, we assume that the negative effects of *Humanae Vitae* will lose their full force during the next fifteen years. In this third scenario we assume that there is no further deterioration among the young and that the rate of decline in acceptance of papal authority and sexual ethics slows to half of what it was between 1963 and 1974.

Even under such cautiously optimistic assumptions, losses will still be considerable. Church attendance will fall ten percentage points more (to 40 percent), support for a priestly vocation in one's family will decline 12 more percentage points (to 38 percent), the proportion high on the activities scale will be cut in half (from 28 to 13 percent), and only a quarter of Catholics will be contributing more than $262 inflation-free dollars to the church every year. Daily prayer will be seven percentage points lower than in 1963.

In other words, the blow struck in the 1960s is of such awesome severity to institutional Catholicism that even if its impact is cut in half during the next fifteen years, substantial deterioration will still take place.

Scenario IV—"Bottom Out"

This set of assumptions takes for granted that the worst is over for American Catholicism. The decline in acceptance of sexual teaching and papal authority is essentially finished. The new generation of young people will not be different in their religious behavior from the Vietnam generation. The trauma of the last ten years was sudden, sharp, and devastating—but its major force has been spent.

Still, decline will continue because less devout young people will become a greater part of the population, and more devout older people will become a smaller part. The cohorts over 30 were 69 percent of the population in 1974; they will be only 42 percent of the population in 1989 and will be over 45 besides. Mass attendance, support for priestly vocation, daily prayer, Catholic activities, and contributions will all slip a few percentage points in this scenario because of the gradual elimination by death of the more devout older generation and their replacement by the less devout younger generation. The worst will then be over, but gradual erosion will continue indefinitely until the last of those over 30 at the time of the 1974 survey will have departed the stage. Catholicism will be stumbling downward toward a new stability, which will still result in a church very different from what it was in 1963.

Scenario V—Rebound

As we noted before, there were in fact two forces at work within American Catholicism between the two NORC surveys. One was negative and associated with the *Humanae Vitae* encyclical, and the other was positive, associated with the Vatican Council. All previous scenarios (except IV) have assumed that this positive dynamic continues to work, and that in its absence the deterioration would be even worse. We now assume that the birth control dynamic has bottomed out but that the conciliar dynamic continues to work at the same rate it has for the last ten years. Thus, weekly reception of communion (our measure of conciliar influence) will have increased by 1989 to 54 percent of the Catholic population—a higher proportion than those attending mass in 1974 and the same proportion as will be attending mass in 1989, according to this scenario.

It must be stressed that this assumption is improbably optimistic. And at that the "rebound" is very slight. Mass attendance is up 4 percentage points; daily prayer, up 5 percentage points; Catholic activities, up 3 percentage points; and contributions of $262 real dollars, up 2 percentage points over the 1974 scores. The proportion "very pleased" over a son's decision to become a priest will remain unchanged. Thus in the rather unlikely event of the Vatican Council reforms' continuing to work at full force for the next fifteen years unimpeded by the trauma of the birth control encyclical, the turnaround will still be quite modest.

Scenario VI—Revival

The final scenario adds another element to the optimistic assumption listed in the previous one. It assumes that the Vietnam generation (though not yet its successors) begins to drift back into acceptance of the church's teaching on authority and sexuality—an event which will almost certainly require a change in both teachings. Thus half of the difference between the Vietnam generation and its predecessors, we assume, will be eliminated. Even under these most improbable circumstances, weekly church attendance will still be 16 percentage points lower than in 1963; support for a son's vocation, 14 percentage points lower; daily prayer, 5 percentage points lower; Catholic activities, 16 percentage points lower; and the proportion giving more than $262 in real dollars, 10 percentage points lower. Thus, within the parameters of our models, at any rate, the best that Catholicism can hope for is a very modest revival. (Although forces extraneous to our model, either within the church or outside of it—such as one of the periodic general religious revivals in the larger society— might have an effect which our models cannot anticipate.)

A. Mass

Year	Worst Case	Continued Decline	One-Half Decline	Bottom Out	Rebound	Revival
1963	72	72	72	72	72	72
1974	50	50	50	50	50	50
1979	44	45	49	51	51*	55
1984	34	37	44	50	53*	55
1989	33	36	40	49	54*	56

B. Priest

Year	Worst Case	Continued Decline	One-Half Decline	Bottom Out	Rebound	Revival
1963	66	66	66	66	66	66
1974	50	50	50	50	50	50
1979	42	42	46	49	49	51
1984	33	35	42	49	49	51
1989	29	30	38	48	50	52

C. Daily Prayer

Year	Worst Case	Continued Decline	One-Half Decline	Bottom Out	Rebound	Revival
1963	72	72	72	72	72	72
1974	60	60	60	60	60	60
1979	55	57	54	59	62	64
1984	51	53	54	59	63	65
1989	49	51	53	58	65	67

D. Catholic Activities

Year	Worst Case	Continued Decline	One-Half Decline	Bottom Out	Rebound	Revival
1963	50	50	50	50	50	50
1974	28	28	28	28	28	28
1979	15	19	23	26	28	29
1984	07	11	18	25	29	31
1989	01	06	13	24	31	34

*Interpolated

E. Contributions

Year	Worst Case	Continued Decline	One-Half Decline	Bottom Out	Rebound	Revival
1974	-13	-13	-13	-13	-13	-12
1979	-21	-19	-17	-16	-13	-12
1984	-28	-25	-19	-18	-12	-11
1989	-38	-30	-24	-20	-11	-10

Appendix VII

LIFE-SITUATION VIGNETTES

You have just visited your doctor and he has told you that you have less than a year to live. He has also told you that your disease is incurable. Which of the following statements comes closest to expressing your reaction?

A.	It will all work out for the best somehow.	9%
B.	No one should question the goodness of God's decision about death.	16
C.	There is nothing I can do about it so I will continue as before.	40
D.	I am angry and bitter at this twist of fate.	8
E.	I have had a full life and am thankful for that.	20
F.	Death is painful, but it is not the end of me.	7
	(Missing data	4%)

Imagine that one of your parents is dying a slow and painful death and try to figure out for yourself if there is anything that will enable you to understand the meaning of such a tragedy. Which, if any, of the following statements best expresses your state of mind in this situation?

A.	They are in pain now, but they will be peaceful soon.	17%
B.	Everything that happens is God's will and cannot be bad.	21
C.	There is nothing to do but wait for the end.	7

D. This waiting is inhuman for them; I hope it
    ends soon.   17
E. We can at least be thankful for the good life
    we have had together.   26
F. This is tragic, but death is not the ultimate end
    for us.   12
    (Missing data   4%)

Imagine that you have just had a child and that the doctor has informed you that it will be mentally retarded. Which of the following responses comes closest to your own feelings about this situation?

A. We will try to take care of this child, but it
    may have to be put in an institution; either
    way it will all work out.   19%
B. God had his own reasons for sending this
    child to us.   16
C. We must learn to accept this situation.   31
D. I love the baby, but why me?   5
E. I'm just plain glad to have the child here.   3
F. God has sent us a heavy cross to bear and a
    special child to love.   26
    (Missing data   4%)

Almost every year hurricanes level homes, flood towns, destroy property, and take human lives. How can we make any sense out of such disasters, which happen, apparently, by chance? Which of the following statements best describes your answer?

A. We can never really understand these things, but
    they usually have some unexpected good effects.   5%
B. We cannot know the reasons but God knows
    them.   19
C. We cannot know why these occur and we have
    to learn to live with that fact.   38
D. The government is responsible for seeing that
    these disasters do as little harm as possible.   4
E. I am grateful I don't live in a hurricane area.   12
F. I am not able to explain why these things

happen, but I still believe in God's love.   22
(Missing data   3%)

Each of the responses to the previous items reflects an orientation toward the nature of reality.

A = Optimism with no mention of God
B = Dependence on the will of God
C = Resignation to the event
D = Emotional response, usually negative
E = Gratitude for some perceived good
F = Awareness of the tragedy combined with confidence
    that there is still hope

These six responses were collapsed into four categories. C and D were combined into an indicator called "pessimism." A and E were combined into "secular optimism." B became "religious fundamentalism," and F is the indicator of "hopefulness."

The number of times a respondent answered in one of the above categories determined his place in the typology of ultimate values. If a person answered two or more of the four vignettes in the same way, he or she was classified as being "high" on that indicator. The indicators were then combined into a typology.

This was done by creating a four-digit number, each digit of which could be either a 1 or a 2. The digits represent, from left to right, hopefulness, religious fundamentalism, secular optimism, and pessimism. Thus the number 1112 would mean that the respondent was low on everything except pessimism; 2111 would mean he was high on hopefulness and low on everything else. The combinations of numbers were fitted into the typology in the following manner:

2111, 2112, 2121, 2211	Hopefulness
1211, 1221, 1212	Religious fundamentalism
1121	Secular optimism
1112	Pessimism
1111, 1122	Diffuse

9999   Missing data (respondents who did not answer any of the items)

Appendix VIII

CROSS TABULATIONS
WITH INDIVIDUAL
QUESTIONNAIRE ITEMS

CROSS TABULATIONS WITH INDIVIDUAL QUESTIONNAIRE ITEMS BY AGE,
EDUCATION, CATHOLIC EDUCATION, AND AGE AND EDUCATION

Question: "How would you rate the priests in your parish on their ability
            to understand the problems of teenaged boys and girls?" (Percent
            "very understanding")

Age in the twenties (n = 247)   34%

Educational Level

  High School(324)   45%

  College(237)   41%

High Catholic religious education (n = 114)   30%

Age and educational level combined

  Grammar school, age 30-40   46%(35)
  Grammar school, age 40+   62%(191)

  College, age under 30   38%(98)

Question: "How would you rate the priests in your parish on their ability
            to understand your practical problems?" (Percent "very under-
            standing")

Age in the twenties (n = 247)   34%

Educational level

  College(237)   41%

High Catholic religious education (n = 114)   37%

Age and educational level combined

  Grammar school, age 40+   58%(191)

  High school, age 40+   58%(41)

  College, age 40+   59%(83)

  College, under 30   34%(98)

Question: "Do you think the sermons in your parish in general are excellent,
            good, fair, or poor?" (Percent "excellent")

Age in the twenties (n = 247)   13%

Educational level
  College$_{(237)}$ 13%

High Catholic religious education (n = 114)   9%

Age and educational level combined
  College under 30   10%$_{(98)}$

  College, 30-40   11%$_{(53)}$

Question: "Some parishes provide a lot of activities for their parishioners.
            Others do not provide too many. How about your parish?" (Percent
            "a lot")

Educational level
  College$_{(237)}$ 53%

High Catholic religious education (n = 114)   63%

Age and educational level combined
  Grammar school, 40+   58%$_{(191)}$

  College, under 30   48%$_{(98)}$

Question: "Most priests don't expect the laity to be leaders, just followers."
            (Percent "disagree strongly")

Age
  20's$_{(247)}$ 21%
  30's$_{(158)}$ 21%
  40's$_{(133)}$ 26%

Educational level
  College$_{(237)}$ 29%

High Catholic religious education n = 114)   38%

Age and Educational level combined
  College, under 30   30%$_{(98)}$

Question: "Priests have lost interest in the problems of the people and are
           concerned only about themselves." (Percent "strongly disagree")

Educational level

   College(237)   63%

High Catholic religious education (n = 114)   66%

Age and Educational level combined

   High school, under 30   56%(112)
             30 - 40   53%(69)
             40+   63%(41)

   College, under 30   56%(98)
             30 - 40   63%(53)
             40+   60(83)

Question: "Priests are not as religious as they used to be." (Percent
           "disagree")

Age in the twenties (n = 247)   48%

Educational level

   College(237)   60%

High Catholic religious education   67%

Age and educational level combined

   College, under 30   54%(98)
             30 - 40   65%(53)
             40+   64%(83)

Question: "Priests should not use the pulpit to discuss social issues."
           (Percent "disagree")

Age in the twenties (n = 247)   58%

Educational level

   College (237)   59%

High Catholic religious education (n = 114)   46%

Age and educational level combined

    College, under 30   61%(98)

             30 - 40   63(53)

Question: "It's all right for a priest to get involved in national or local politics if he wants to." (Percent "agree")

Age in thirties (n = 158)   47%

Educational level

   College(237)   62%

High Catholic religious education (n = 114)   68%

Age and educational level combined

    High school, under 30   57%(112)

    College, under 30   63%(98)

            30 - 40   58%(53)

            40+   62%(83)

Question: "In recent years many priests have decided to leave the priesthood and get married. How much sympathy do you have for those who left?" (Percent "a great deal")

Age above sixty (n = 133)   19%

Educational level

   College(237)   44%

High Catholic religious education (n = 114)   45%

Low Catholic religious education (n = 95)   44%

Age and educational level combined

    Grammar school, under 30   18%(37)

            40+   19%(191)

    College, under 30   56%(98)

Question: "If the Church were to change its laws and permit clergy to marry,
           would you accept the change?" (Percent "yes")

Age in twenties (n = 247)   81%

Educational level

    College(237)   88%

High Catholic religious education (n = 114)   89%

High non-Catholic religious education (n = 156)   88%

Age and educational level combined

    College, under 30   88%(98)
                30 - 40   86%(53)
                40+   89%(83)

Question: "It would be a good thing if women were allowed to be ordained
           priests." (Percent "agree")

Age in twenties (n = 247)   39%

Educational level

    College(237)   46%

High Catholic religious education (n = 114)   29%

High non-Catholic religious education (n = 156)   30%

Age and educational level combined

    College, under 30   55%

Question: "If your son would choose to be a priest, how would you feel?"
           (Percent "very pleased")

Age in twenties (n = 247)   42%

Educational level

    College(237)   44%

Religious education

    Low non-Catholic(353)   50%
    Low Catholic(95)   34%
    High non-Catholic(156)   55%
    High Catholic(114)   53%

Question: "It would make me somewhat unhappy if a daughter of mine be-
           came a nun." (Percent "disagree strongly")

Age in twenties (n = 247)   47%

Educational level
  College(237)   48%

Religious education
  Low non-Catholic(353)   47%

  Low Catholic(95)   41%

  High non-Catholic(156)   65%

  High Catholic(114)   55%

HOUSEHOLD ENUMERATION

First, I have to ask for a little information about the members of your household.
How many people are living in this household? (BE SURE TO INCLUDE ALL CHILDREN
LIVING IN THE HOUSEHOLD, PEOPLE TEMPORARILY AWAY, ROOMERS, ETC.)

_____
number

Let's go from the oldest person in the household to the youngest.

    A. What is the name of the oldest person? The next oldest per-
        son? (ENTER NAME IN COLUMN A OF THE ENUMERATION TABLE.)

    B. How old was (he) (she) at (his) (her) last birthday? (ENTER
        AGE IN COLUMN B BELOW.)

    C. What is (his) (her) relation to the head of the household?
        (ENTER RELATION IN COLUMN C BELOW.)

    D. (ENTER M FOR MALE AND F FOR FEMALE IN COLUMN D.)

    E. What is (his) (her) marital status? (ENTER IN COLUMN E BELOW.)

	A	B	C	D	E	F
	Name	Age	Relation to Household Head	Sex	Marital Status	Indicate Respondent by √
1						
2						
3						
4						
5						
6						
7						
8						
9						
10						

NOTES

Chapter 1

1. See "Social Change and the General Social Survey: An Annotated Bibliography" (Chicago: NORC Social Change Project mimeo, 1974); James A. Davis, "A Survey-Metric Model of Social Change" (Chicago: NORC mimeo, July 1974); Abbott L. Ferris, *Indicators of Trends in the Status of Women* (New York: Russell Sage Foundation, 1971); and Greeley and Sheatsley (1971).

2. See James S. Coleman et. al., *Equality of Educational Opportunity* (Washington, D.C.: Government Printing Office, 1966).

3. Which is not to say that the effectiveness of the school was the same as the effectiveness of the family. Rather the findings were that the *greatest difference* between parochial school Catholics and non-parochial-school Catholics was to be found precisely among those who had devout parents. Parochial school graduates of devout families were themselves much more devout than public school Catholics from devout families.

4. McCready used retrospective data on grandparents, direct interview data from respondents who were also parents of teenage children, and interview data from teenagers in an adolescent sample. At the time of the 1963 Catholic school study, the statistical and computational tools did not exist for this sort of three-generational analysis. The model developed by McCready should be useful indeed in subsequent research of this sort.

5. All of the statistics should be treated with caution. The U.S. government (see *Current Population Reports*, February, 1975) reports private school enrollment (most of which are Catholic at the primary and

secondary levels). In 1965, Catholic school students (as reported by the *Directory*) were 98 percent of the private elementary students (as reported by the census). In 1975, they were 82 percent. We doubt that there has been that much of an increase in private non-Catholic schools. We suspect that at one time or the other the Catholic data were in error. At the secondary level the proportion at both time points was 78 percent.

6. A certain proportion of NORC interviewers informed respondents before or during the interview that the study was explicitly a study of American Catholics. There was no relationship between the responses of this subsample and those who were not so informed.

7. The model illustrated in Fig. 1.3 is completely mythical and does not represent any actual data on the relationship between age, education, and GRE scores.

8. In subsequent chapters the statistics on the paths will not be *r* but a beta, which is a "net standardized coefficient." Social-science readers will know the difference between a beta and an *r*; non-social-science readers can see the difference if they wish in some of the longer treatments of path analysis. See, in particular, Duncan (1966) or Spaeth and Greeley (1970:134-35).

Chapter 3

1. This chapter condenses and reports on the Catholic dimension of a larger and much more detailed analysis by Andrew M. Greeley, *The Demography of Denominational and Ethnic Groups* (Beverly Hills, Calif.: Sage Press, forthcoming).

2. I am indebted to Peter H. Rossi for the suggestion that ethnic groups might be studied in the same way.

3. By adding the two parochial school surveys, we have made the composite sample disproportionately Catholic. Due allowance has been made for that in the analysis reported in this chapter. The reader should not be surprised, however, if in inspecting the tables he discovers more Catholic respondents than the appropriate 25 percent.

4. Blacks are excluded from this analysis because it seems that the most relevant comparisons are between Catholics and other white Ameri-

cans, and that the racial factor would blur these comparisons. Similarly, black Catholics were excluded from most NORC surveys because they are so small a proportion of the American Catholic population that not enough of them would appear in the sample to warrant detailed analysis. A discussion of black Catholics, however, will be reported in *The Demography of Denominational and Ethnic Groups* (see note 1).

5. A score in which the various occupations in the country are ranked from 0 to 99.

6. For a discussion of these various techniques, see Robert P. Althauser and Michael Wigler, "Standardization and Component Analysis," *Sociological Methods and Research* 1, 1 (August 1972): 97-135.

7. Tables 3.13-3.16 are based only on the $NORC_2$ composite sample. They represent data collected after 1970. They also represent comparisons with the national average (including blacks), and are hence standardized on the national average and not on the Methodist mean. There will be some discrepancies between data reported in these tables and the previous tables.

8. The French Catholic data are reported here only for the sake of completeness. They should be treated with caution. Before 1970, NORC had a sampling point in Manchester, New Hampshire, and French respondents were concentrated in that area, for the most part. Since 1970 the Manchester sampling point has been eliminated. NORC's French-speaking respondents, in addition to some New Englanders, would also include a fair number of Louisiana Cajuns. Hence the small size of the French sample and the peculiar changes in its composition make it highly unreliable.

Chapter 4

1. A concise summary of the relationships between various religious groups and political parties appears in Seymour Martin Lipset, "Religion and Politics in the American Past and Present," in Lee and Marty, eds., *Religion and Social Conflict* (New York: Oxford University Press, 1964).

2. Beginning with Paul F. Lazarsfeld, Bernard Berelson, and Hazel Gaudet, *The People's Choice* (New York: Columbia University Press, 1944), most studies touching on religion and politics discuss the attraction of the religions to different parties. A representative sample are:

Bernard R. Berelson, Paul F. Lazarsfeld, and William N. McPhee, *Voting*
(Chicago: University of Chicago Press, 1954); Angus Campbell et. al.,
The American Voter (abridged edition) (New York: Wiley, 1964); Ger-
hardt Lenski, *The Religious Factor* (Garden City, New York: Doubleday, 1961).

3. See especially, Walter Dean Burnham, *Critical Elections and the
Mainsprings of American Politics* (New York: Norton, 1970), p. 91-174;
Philip E. Converse, "Possible Realignment in the South," in Angus
Campbell et. al., *Elections and the Political Order* (New York: Wiley,
1966), p. 212-44.

4. Tables A and B, taken from the SRC files, provide a sample of the
over-time changes in Catholic income and education. While, in table A,
the inner city and suburban Catholics begin in time 1 with an income
below that of white Protestants, by time 3 their incomes exceed the
white Protestant income. In all residence areas, the Catholic rate of
income growth exceeds that of white Protestants. Jews begin with an
income exceeding that of all other groups and maintain their lead. (In
this table income is not adjusted for inflation.)

TABLE A

MEDIAN INCOME AMONG THE THREE RELIGIOUS GROUPS (AS A PERCENTAGE
OF THE GRAND MEAN INCOME), TIME 1 VS. TIME 3,
BY RACE AND RESIDENCE PLACE

(Per Cent)

Group	Time 1 1952-1958	Time 3 1968-1972	Difference
Central City (White):			
Protestant	95	111	+16
Catholic	94	122	+28
Jew	111	143	+32
Suburb (White):			
Protestant	111	152	+41
Catholic	102	156	+54
Jew	151	213	+62
Other Areas (White):			
Protestant	83	112	+29
Catholic	87	121	+34
Jew	141	147	+ 6
Black and Spanish, All Areas:			
Protestant	45	73	+28
Catholic	73	98	+25

Table B, which notes means years of education, focuses on ethnic groups rather than on residence place. Again, in time 1, most Catholic ethnic groups (with the exception of the Irish Catholics) fall behind the white Protestant mean years of educational attainment. But the Catholics, on the average, gain faster than white Protestants, slightly exceeding their mean by time 3. Jews not only begin with the highest level of education (slightly higher than Irish Catholics), but they tie with Spanish-speaking Americans for the highest amount of education gained over the time period, putting the Jews farther ahead in educational attainment by time 3.

TABLE B

MEDIAN YEARS OF EDUCATION BY ETHNIC GROUP AT TIMES 1 AND 3

Group	Time 1 1952-1958	Time 3 1968-1972	Difference
English Protestant	10.1	11.3	1.2
Scandinavian Protestant	10.6	12.5	1.9
German Protestant	10.3	11.4	1.1
Other Protestant	10.5	10.8	.3
Irish Catholic	11.1	12.6	1.5
German Catholic	9.6	11.5	1.9
Polish Catholic	9.5	10.7	1.2
Slavic Catholic	9.7	11.4	1.7
Italian Catholic	9.6	11.2	1.6
Other Catholic	10.5	11.5	1.0
Jews	11.2	13.4	2.2
Blacks	8.6	10.2	1.6
Spanish	8.0	10.2	2.2
Other	10.9	12.4	1.5

For a more detailed analysis of the SES trends of the various ethnic and religious groups, see Andrew M. Greeley, "Making It: A Reconstruction of the Demographic History of Religio-Ethnic Groups in the 20th Century," an unpublished research note of the National Opinion Research Center, University of Chicago.

5. Samuel Lubell, *The Future of American Politics*, 2nd ed. rev. (New York: Harper, 1956), p. 41. Campbell et. al., *The American Voter*, op. cit., p. 92; also Lipset, op. cit.

6. Lipset, op. cit.; also Lawrence Fuchs, "Some Political Aspects of Immigration," in Fuchs, ed., *American Ethnic Politics* (New York: Harper and Row, 1968). Fuchs analyzes nativism in American politics, dealing more directly with nationality than with religion. Of course, nationality and religion are often bound together.

7. V. O. Key, Jr., "A Theory of Critical Elections," *Journal of Politics* 27 (1955), p. 3-18. Duncan Macrae and James A. Meldrum note in "Critical Elections in Illinois, 1888-1958," *The American Political Science Review* 54 (1960), p. 669-85, the same tendency of Smith's candidacy to wed Catholics to the Democrats and to drive Protestants into Republican ranks but emphasize that in this state "the more lasting effects of that change seem more closely related to urban-foreign background than to religion as such."

8. Harry A. Bailey, Jr., and Ellis Katz, eds., *Ethnic Group Politics* (Columbus: Merrill, 1969). This is one of the best readers on religion, nationality, and politics.

9. Ibid.

10. Key and Munger document this tendency among Indiana voters. In essentially similar counties they find continuing *contrasting* partisan attachments over time "at least to some extent independent of other social groupings." V. O. Key and Frank Munger, "Social Determinism and Electoral Decision: The Case of Indiana," in Burdick and Brodbeck, eds., *American Voting Behavior* (Glencoe, Illinois: Free Press, 1959), p. 281-99. Wolfinger's finding that New Haven Italians maintain their support for the Republican party because of early salient Italian candidacies lend further weight to the theory. Raymond E. Wolfinger, "The Development and Persistence of Ethnic Voting," *The American Political Science Review* 59 (1965), p. 896-908.

11. H. H. Remmers shows that high school students assume to a great degree the party identification of their parents. H. H. Remmers, "Early Socialization of Attitudes," in Burdick and Brodbeck, eds., *American Voting Behavior*, p. 55-67. Also, M. Kent Jennings and Richard G. Niemi, "The Transmission of Political Values from Parent to Child," *American Political Science Review* 62 (1968), p. 169-84.

12. The strength of adherence to the group standard depends on the salience of the political issue. Campbell et. al., op. cit., p. 92, study the Catholic voting patterns in regard to Catholic congressional candidates. For analysis of the 1960 election, see Philip E. Converse, "Religion and Politics: 1960 Election," in Angus Campbell et. al., *Elections and the Political Order* (New York: Wiley, 1966), p. 96-124. Berelson and Lenski find a tendency to conform to the group standard of party preference even when the group standard differs from parental party affiliation. Berelson, op. cit.; Lenski, op. cit.

13. When socioeconomic status rises over generations, these "cross pressures" lessen a Catholic's attraction to the Democratic party. Berelson, op. cit.

14. Peter H. Odegard in "Catholicism and Elections in the United States," in Odegard, ed., *Religion and Politics* (Englewood, New Jersey), p. 120-21, observes "under Democratic presidents Franklin Roosevelt and Harry Truman, one out of every four judicial appointments went to a Catholic as against one out of every 25 under Harding, Coolidge, and Hoover."

15. Jae-On Kim and Corwin E. Schmidt, "The Changing Bases of Political Identification in the United States: 1952-1972," University of Iowa, Department of Sociology, Sociology Working Paper Series, 74:3. The authors define canonical regression as a "method of analysis which uses (1) the canonical correlation with dummy variables as a means of quantifying categorical variables, (2) some features of discriminant function analysis as a means of measuring distances between groups, and (3) dummy regression (and MCA) as a means of displaying multivariate relationships."

16. Michael Parenti, "Ethnic Politics and the Persistence of Ethnic Identification," in Bailey and Katz, eds., *Ethnic Group Politics* (Columbus, Ohio: Merrill, 1969), p. 272.

17. Scott Greer, "Catholic Voters and the Democratic Party," *Public Opinion Quarterly* 25 (1961), p. 611-25.

18. Using the social characteristics of sex, age, region, religion, education, occupation, and income, Kim and Schmidt achieved correlations several points higher on Dimension I in the presidential elections they studied and averaging about ten points higher on Dimension II.

19. Describing the technique for deriving mean social background scores for each partisan group, Kim and Schmidt point out, "Because canonical correlation is a simple correlation between respective canonical variates and because these canonical variates are standardized to have a mean equal to zero, the expected canonical scores can be given by the following simple regression equations:

$$s_1 = r_1 p_1 \quad (1)$$

$$s_2 = r_2 p_2 \quad (2)$$

where s_1 and s_2 represent the canonical variates for partisan identification and r_1 and r_2 represent the canonical correlations."

20. The intricacies of construction of the scale will be described in full in Nie et. al., *The Changing American Voter*, funded by the 20th Century Fund, and tentatively to be published later this year.

A sample question from each issue area follows:

(1)*Black Welfare:* If Negroes are not getting fair treatment in jobs and housing, the government should see to it that they do.
Agree strongly; Agree but not very strongly; Not sure, it depends; Disagree but not very strongly; Don't know.

(2)*School Integration:* The government in Washington should stay out of the question of whether white and colored children go to the same school.
Agree strongly; Agree but not very strongly; Not sure, it depends; Disagree but not very strongly; Don't know.

(3)*Economic Welfare:* The government in Washington ought to see to it that everyone who wants to work can find a job.
Agree strongly; Agree but not very strongly; Not sure, it depends; Disagree but not very strongly; Don't know.

(4)*Size of Government:* Some people are afraid that the government in Washington is getting too powerful for the good of the country and the individual person. Others feel that the government has not gotten too strong for the good of the country.
Have you been interested enough in this to favor one side or the other? If yes: What is your feeling, do you think . . .
    a. Yes, the government is getting too powerful.
    b. Yes, the government has not gotten too strong.
    c. Other, depends. (Category not read to respondent.)

(5)*Foreign Policy:* The United States should keep soldiers overseas where they can help countries that are against Communism.
Agree strongly; Agree but not very strongly; Not sure, it depends; Disagree but not very strongly; Don't know.

21. The effects of education were removed by determining mean party identification scores through a dummy regression of religion, residence place, and education on party identification, and then by sub-

tracting that contribution made by the education beta. The technique of using dummy regression to obtain mean scores is outlined clearly in Jae-On Kim and Frank J. Kohout, "Special Topics in General Linear Models," in Nie et. al., *SPSS*, 2nd ed (New York: McGraw-Hill, 1975), p. 373-83.

22. John R. Petrocik, *Changing Party Coalitions and the Attitudinal Basis of Alignment, 1952-1972,* Ph.D. diss., Department of Political Science, University of Chicago.

Chapter 5

1. Interestingly enough, Wills was once a "conservative" and Hitchcock a "liberal."

2. As Crane Brinton has pointed out (*The Anatomy of Revolution*, rev. ed., New York: Random House, 1957), revolutions occur not so much during times when there is no change but rather during times when changes are occurring and institutional modifications are not keeping up with expanding expectations.

3. When the Catfit program pools coefficients showing relationships in time 1 with the same relationships in time 2, it ignores differences that are not statistically significant. As a result, there is some variation in the percentage point changes in the actual data (as presented in table 5.5) and the model data. The difference of weekly mass attendance, for example, is 21 percentage points in the actual data and 23 percentage points in the model data.

4. An analysis was also attempted using the doctrinal orthodoxy scale as the intervening variable. Since there was little difference between the impact of this scale on our model and the right to teach-racial integration variable, we discuss here only the models using the latter indicator.

5. Interestingly enough, the increases in communion reception would have also been much larger were it not for the factors linked to the encyclical. Communion reception would have gone up 22 percentage points instead of only 11, which would have been a tripling rather than a doubling of the weekly reception of communion.

6. If we consider the increase in weekly reception of communion to be the result of the Vatican Council and further assume that it measures

the positive impact of the Council, then the increase which would have occurred in the absence of the countervailing forces would have been 4 percentage points in the proportion being very happy with a son being a priest (to 69 percent), 5 percentage points in the proportion praying daily (to 77 percent), and 5 percentage points in the proportion above the 1963 median on the summary Catholicity factor, which we will discuss in the next chapter. The positive forces released by the Council were considerable.

7. Interestingly enough, Jennings notes a net gain for Catholics who did not attend college. This was due to a substantial number of non-college-educated respondents who had become Catholic since 1965. His net apostasy rate, then, is substantially less than calculated from the NORC sample.

8. The Gallup organization's question is slightly different from that asked by NORC. Gallup asked, "Did you attend church last week?" NORC asked, "How often do you go to church?" Hence in recent years the Gallup percentages have been somewhat higher than the NORC percentages. One could have gone to church last week and still not attend church every week.

Chapter 6

1. The materials in this section correspond to chap. 3 of *The Education of Catholic Americans*, "Religious Consequences of Catholic Education," pp. 53-76 of the Aldine Press edition.

2. An analysis of this variable will be postponed for a later chapter. It should be noted, however, that the raw differences presented in table 6.1 can be deceptive. In fact, as we shall see subsequently, one of the interesting changes over the last decade is that there is a stronger net correlation between Catholic education and support for religious vocation than there was a decade ago.

3. The analysis of the anticlerical, priest competence, and change in the priesthood scales will be deferred to chap. 8, which will discuss explicitly the relationship between Catholic education and attitudes toward religious leadership.

4. Chap. 4 of *The Education of Catholic Americans*, "The Search for an Explanation."

5. In fact they remarked that in terms of the effectiveness of Catholic education, it appeared that only those who came from such a background should be expected to show any impact from having attended Catholic schools.

6. See page 107 of *The Education of Catholic Americans*, Aldine edition.

7. The inclusion of spouse's church attendance is based on the reanalysis of the 1963 data performed by William McCready in "Faith of Our Fathers: A Study of the Process of Religious Socialization" (1972). Obviously there is a question as to whether self influences spouse or spouse influences self. In the model used in this chapter, we assume that spouse influences self. In fact, McCready's research suggests that the husband influences children and the wives influence husbands and not vice versa.

8. We shall also see an increase in the standardized relationship between vocation support and Catholic education (from .02 to .12).

9. Daniel Patrick Moynihan has noted on two occasions that *The Education of Catholic Americans* was the first of a series of research enterprises which showed how small the impact of schooling was on human behavior. (See the introduction to his own book, *Coping*, and the introduction to Andrew M. Greeley, *That Most Distressful Nation: The Taming of the American Irish*).

10. See, for example, Gerhard Lenski, *The Religious Factor* (Garden City, New York: Doubleday, 1961); R. W. Mack, R. J. Murphy, and S. Ellin White, "The Protestant Ethic, Level of Aspiration and Social Mobility," *American Sociological Review* 21 (June 1956):295-300; J. Veroff, S. Feld, and G. Gurin, "Achievement, Motivation, and Religious Background," *American Sociological Review* 27 (April 1962):205-217; B. C. Rosen, "Race, Ethnicity, and the Achievement Syndrome," *American Sociological Review* 24 (February 1959):47-60; Thomas O'Dea, *American Catholic Dilemma* (New York: Sheed & Ward, 1958); Andrew M. Greeley, *Religion and Career* (New York: Sheed & Ward, 1963); Marvin Bressler and Charles Westoff, "Catholic Education, American Values, and Achievement," *American Journal of Sociology* 49 (November 1963):225-233.

11. This did not prevent the prestigious journal, *Science*, from publishing an article in the summer of 1974 that reasserted the existence of

a negative correlation between Catholicism and achievement. Its conclusions were based on data at least fifteen years old without any reference to the literature that has accumulated in the last ten years.

Chapter 7

1. *1975 Official Catholic Directory* (New York: P. J. Kenedy and Sons, 1975).

2. Ibid.

3. Andrew M. Greeley and Peter H. Rossi, *The Education of Catholic Americans* (New York: Anchor Books, 1968), Appendix 4, "Correlates of Catholic School Attendance," pp. 288-311.

4. Koob and Shaw, "The Pressures on Catholic Education" in Shaw and Hurley, *Trends and Issues in Catholic Education* (New York: Citation Press, 1969), pp. 15-26.

Chapter 8

1. 1963 question: "If you spent any money on Catholic school tuition for your children, on the average, how much did you spend per year?" 1974 question: "How much tuition, if any, are you paying to Catholic schools this year, including elementary and high schools?" (Asked only of those respondents having children in elementary or high schools in 1974).

2. From time to time in this chapter we will shift from individual data to aggregate data. We do this so that we may estimate the financial picture for the church writ large. These changes will be highlighted when they occur.

3. "Inflation-free" means that all dollars are converted into their 1974 equivalents, using the Consumer Price Index. 1963 dollars are multiplied by 1.61 to convert them to 1974 dollars. (*Monthly Labor Review*, June 1975, p. 97, U.S. Dept. of Labor, Bureau of Labor Statistics.)

4. The 1963 data are not comparable due to the difference in the questions.

5. These proportions are based on the number of people having school-aged children.

Chapter 9

1. Data from press release accompanying 1975 issue of *The Official Catholic Directory*.

2. Cross tabulations with the individual items analyzed in this chapter by age, education, Catholic education, and age and education combined are presented in the appendix.

Chapter 10

1. It seems a little more plausible that this is a generational phenomenon, since it is probably the case that the older people in our sample were religious optimists when they were younger, as well.

Afterword

1. The present book is a research report, a year in preparation. It is still a very preliminary summary. There are many, many questions that have occurred to us, as we were pushing toward the preparation deadline, that bear further investigation. I hope that members of our team or other researchers continue the analysis in the years ahead. No research report can investigate every interesting piece of data accumulated. What routes are followed and what are set aside for future investigation is a matter of taste. It would surely be true that this report is incomplete, but it is also true that five times more pages and five years more analysis would still result in an incomplete report.

Notes to Appendices

Appendix I

1. For a further discussion of this point, see the forthcoming *Public Opinion Quarterly* article by Kathleen McCourt and Garth Taylor, "Determining Religious Affiliation Through Survey Research: A Methodological Note."

Appendix VI

1. Andrew Greeley and Garth Taylor of NORC are preparing a technical article on the use of the two NORC parochial school studies to simulate further developments within the American Catholic Church. As this report goes to press the article is still in preparation. This brief appendix presents some of the simulation material. Readers interested in the full technical details should write to the two authors at NORC for a copy of the paper.

Bibliography

Althauser, Robert P. and Michael Wigler. "Standardization and Component Analysis," *Sociological Methods and Research* 1,1(August 1972):97-135.

Barbour, Ian. 1974. *Myths, Models, and Paradigms: A Comparative Study in Science and Religion*. New York: Harper & Row.

Bogue, Donald J. *The Population of the United States*. New York: Free Press, 1959.

Davis, James A. 1974. "Communism, Conformity, Cohorts, and Categories: American Tolerance in 1954 and 1972-73." To be published in the *American Journal of Sociology*.

_____. 1972a. "Survey Replications, Log Linear Models, and Theories of Social Change." Chicago: National Opinion Research Center, lithographed.

_____. 1972b. "The Goodman Log Linear System for Assessing Effects in Multivariate Contingency Tables." Chicago: National Opinion Research Center, lithographed.

Duncan, Otis Dudley. 1966. "Path Analysis: Sociological Examples." *American Journal of Sociology* 72(July):1-16.

Gaffin, Ben. 1952. *Catholic Digest* Study was reported in John L. Thomas, S.J., *Religion and the American People*. Westminster, Maryland: The Newman Press, 1963.

Gallup. 1969. *Gallup Poll Reports, 1936-1968*. Princeton, New Jersey: American Institute for Public Opinion.

Geertz, Clifford. *The Interpretation of Cultures: Selected Essays*. New York: Basic Books, Inc., 1973.

Greeley, Andrew M. 1975. "Ethnicity and Inequality, or Max Weber Eat Your Heart Out." Paper presented at the meet-

ing of the American Association for the Advancement of
Science, New York, January 27.

_____. 1974. *Ethnicity in the United States.* New York:
Wiley Interscience.

_____. 1973. "The Religious Factor and Academic Careers:
Another Commentary." *American Journal of Sociology*
78(March):1247-55.

_____. 1969. "Continuities in Research on 'The Religious
Factor'—A Research Note." *American Journal of Sociology*
75(November):355-359.

_____ and Paul B. Sheatsley. 1974. "Attitudes Toward Racial
Integration: The South 'Catches·Up.'" In Justice Lee Rain-
water, ed., *Social Problems and Public Policy: I. Inequality.*
Chicago: Aldine Press, pp. 241-250.

_____ and Paul B. Sheatsley. 1971. "Attitudes Toward
Desegregation." *Scientific American*, December, pp. 13-19.

_____ and Peter H. Rossi. 1966. *The Education of Catholic
Americans.* Chicago: Aldine Press.

Hitchcock, James. 1971. *The Decline and Fall of Radical
Catholicism.* New York: Herder & Herder.

Jencks, Christopher, et al. *Inequality. A Reassessment of the
Effect of Family and Schooling in America.* New York:
Basic Books, Inc., 1972.

Juster, F. Thomas, ed. 1974. *Education, Income, and Human
Behavior.* New York: McGraw-Hill.

Light, Donald W., Jr. 1966. "Social Participation in Public
and Catholic Schools." *Review of Religious Research* 8, pp.
3-11.

McCready, William C. 1972. "Faith of Our Fathers: A Study
of the Process of Religious Socialization." Ph.D. diss., University of Illinois Circle Campus.

_____. 1966. "The Education of an American Catholic
Elite." M.A. thesis, University of Chicago.

_____ and Andrew M. Greeley. 1972. "The End of American
Catholicism." *America* October 28, pp. 334-338.

Marty, Martin E., Stuart E. Rosenberg, and Andrew M.
Greeley. 1968. *What Do We Believe?* New York: Meredith
Press.

Mosteller, Frederick and Daniel Patrick Moynihan. 1972. *On
Equality of Educational Opportunity.* New York: Random
House.

Nie, Norman H., John Petrocik, and Sidney Verba. 1975 (manuscript). *The Changing American Voter.*

NORC. *American Priests.* A report prepared for the United States Catholic Conference by the National Opinion Research Center, March 1971.

Rosenberg, Morris. 1964. "The Dissonant Religious Context and Emotional Disturbance." In L. Schneider, ed., *Religion, Culture, and Society.* New York: Wiley & Sons, pp. 549-559.

Rossi, Peter H. and Alice S. Rossi. 1961. "Some Effects of Parochial School Education in America." *Daedalus* 90 (Spring):300-28.

Ryan, Mary Perkins. 1964. *Are Parochial Schools the Answer?* New York: Harper & Row.

Sewell, Ellen. 1975. "The Growth of Black Political Participation 1952-1970." Ph.D. diss. in progress, University of Chicago.

Shaw, Russell and Richard J. Hurley, eds. *Trends and Issues in Catholic Education.* New York: Citation Press, 1969.

Westoff, C. F. and Larry Bumpass. 1973. "Revolution in Birth Control Practices of United States Roman Catholics." *Science* 179(January 5):41-44.

Wills, Garry. 1974. *Bare Ruined Choirs.* New York: Dell Publishing Co., paperback.

Andrew M. Greeley, a sociologist and Roman Catholic priest in the archdiocese of Chicago, is the author of over forty books, a syndicated newspaper columnist, the program director for the National Opinion Research Center at the University of Chicago, and presently the director of its Center for the Study of American Pluralism. *Time* magazine recently called Greeley "an informational machine gun who can fire off an article on Jesus to the *New York Times*, on ethnic groups to the *Antioch Review*, or on war to *Dissent*."

William C. McCready, assistant professor of sociology at Loyola University of Chicago, is the associate program director for the Center for the Study of American Pluralism at the National Opinion Research Center. His main areas of study include religion and ethnicity and the processes of family socialization. He is presently the managing editor of the journal *Ethnicity*. He has published articles in various journals including *America* and the *New York Times Magazine*. He is a coauthor of the book *Ethnicity in the United States* and another forthcoming work *The Diverse Society*. McCready received his Ph.D. in sociology from the University of Illinois—Chicago Circle.

Kathleen McCourt is the senior study director of the National Opinion Research Center at the University of Chicago, where she received her Ph.D. in sociology. She is the author of another book on working-class women and grassroots politics, soon to be published by the Indiana University Press. As a result of the research she did on her forthcoming book, she has spent the last two years at NORC conducting a survey of women in politics, interviewing 1,200 women and their husbands in the Chicago area.